Classic Tarot Spreads

Other books by Sandor Konraad:

Numerology: Key to the Tarot

Classic Tarot Spreads

Sandor Konraad

A Division of Schiffer Publishing
4880 Lower Valley Rd.
Atglen, PA 19310 USA

To Goethe
whose valedictory for a suffering humanity was
''More light!''

Classic Tarot Spreads
by Sandor Konraad

Library of Congress Catalog Card Number: 84-62282
International Standard Book Number: 0-914918-64-8

Edited by Marah Ren
Cover design by Ralph Poness and Robert Killam
Illustrations by Todd Sweet
Graphics by Robert Killam
Typeset by Patrice LeBlanc

Manufactured in the United States of America.

Published by Whitford Press
A Division of Schiffer Publishing, Ltd.
4880 Lower Valley Road
Atglen, PA 19310 USA
Phone: (610) 593-1777 Fax: (610) 593-2002
E-mail: schifferbk@aol.com
Please visit our web site catalog at
www.schifferbooks.com
or write for a free catalog.
This book may be purchased from the publisher.
Please include $3.95 postage.
Try your bookstore first.

In Europe, Schiffer books are distributed by
Bushwood Books
6 Marksbury Avenue
Kew Gardens
Surrey TW9 4JF England
Phone: 44 (0)181 392-8585;
Fax: 44 (0)181 392-9876
E-mail: Bushwd@aol.com

Please try your bookstore first.
We are interested in hearing from authors
with book ideas on related subjects.

Contents

Preface

It is not difficult to find books on the Tarot. Most of them, however, dwell upon the history, symbology, mythological associations, archetypal imagery, and metaphysical meanings of the cards. What is generally glossed over—or in many cases, omitted entirely—is the simple fact that the 78-card Tarot pack is a magical tool that will provide answers to any questions, help solve problems, or clear the way for difficult decision-making that an individual may be facing at a given moment in time. Before one can receive this help, it is only necessary to know how to spread the cards and read and interpret them in divination.

This book deals with this "hands on" aspect of the Tarot. Tarot texts often confuse the beginning student by offering multiple meanings of each card, which places a weighty burden on memory. In this book, the potential reader will find only the essential meanings needed for doing a reading. Additional meanings will be perceived by the reader through experience.

Some intelligent and skillful readers know only one or two ways of spreading the cards, which makes it difficult for them to answer certain types of questions or to do in-depth readings. It is important to have a variety of spreads at one's command because each spread is designed for answering certain types of questions.

The transcripts of client readings in the final section of this book offer examples of card and spread synthesis.

For the individual who wishes to apply the mighty and mysterious powers of the Tarot for living a saner and wiser life—or helping others to do so—the important thing is to handle the cards, practice the spreads, and begin to do readings.

By de-mystifying the meanings and providing a schematic, simplified, and readable set of guidelines, this book will help you to do that in no time at all.

Confessions of a
Reluctant Tarot Reader

A dry cleaning shop seems an unlikely place to be hit by lightning but that is where it all began. I had presented my garment claim-check to the young woman behind the counter and upon glancing at the name on the ticket her features lit up and she exclaimed, "Mr. Konraad— oh, you're the man who is into the Tarot!"

One did not have to be Sherlock Holmes to figure out how she had made the connection between the Tarot and me, for her accent indicated that she hailed from the South. Since the chamber maid at the New England guest home where I was staying for the summer was also from that region, it was possible that the two women were friends or roommates and had compared notes. My room at the guest home was brimming over with occult works—including one dealing with the Tarot, along with a Tarot pack.

But what this young woman did not know was that I was hardly "into" the Tarot but rather a total neophyte. A few weeks earlier I had gained permission from the headmaster of the school where I teach to set up a course in parapsychology and was summering at this salt-air village on Cape Cod for the purpose of preparing the curriculum. It was to be a survey course and the Tarot was only something I added at the last minute because the day before I left New York City for the Cape I had stopped off at an occult book shop to pick up some research materials and a book on Tarot found its way into my purchases. I selected a Tarot pack as well so as to familiarize myself with the imagery on the cards.

So, when the woman behind the counter in the dry cleaners said, "Oh, you're the man who is into the Tarot!," I was quick to correct her misconception by telling her the truth of the matter. "So you see,'' I ended my explanation lamely, ''I know next to nothing about the Tarot.''

The woman, however, desparately wanted a reading and was not going to take no for an answer.

Somehow the words I intended were not what came out of my mouth for I found myself saying, ''I have never done a reading in my life but I guess there has to be a first time for everything.''

While waiting for my first consultant to arrive I was having second thoughts. For one thing, I was somewhat shaky on the meanings of the cards in divination so I would have to keep thumbing through the Tarot book during the reading, which would be awkward at best.

Then too, my involvement with Tarot stemmed from its probable inclusion in the survey course on the occult that I was preparing. If I were to take up the Tarot at all in the course it would be in a scholarly vein: I planned to approach it historically and trace its origins and evolution over the centuries. Probably too, I would get into the symbolism of the beautiful and mysterious cards and discuss how the images related to ancient mythology and medieval history.

But to spread the cards and peer into the future—that was something else. Connected as it was in my mind with sleazy gypsy store-fronts and all one's questions on love, marriage, and career, there seemed to be something disreputable about it.

But more than anything else I was not convinced that the cards actually worked. I mean, how could they? It went against all rules of logic to think that a few cards selected at random could possibly relate to a person's life and foretell the future with any degree of accuracy—it did not make sense. I was about to make my way to the phone and beg off from what was clearly a ludicrous project when a knock at the door indicated that the young woman had arrived and with great reluctance I would have to go through with the charade.

I smiled grimly in an attempt to put a good face on the enterprise, drew up a table and chairs, and asked the woman to sit down. In what was probably a vain attempt to hide my skepticism, I asked her if she had a question concerning the future for which she sought an answer. She looked thoughtful for a moment and then said, ''Yes, a'mm wonderin' how a'mm goin' to do in graduate school next year.''

After handing her the pack to shuffle, I then threw my first spread according to the method given in Rolla Nordic's *The Tarot Shows the Path* (Samuel Weiser, Inc.: New York, 1979).

When I had turned over all the cards in the spread my worst fears were realized for none of the cards that came up seemed to have any bearing on the young woman's question. It was at this point that I realized that if the Tarot worked at all it had little or nothing to do with the cutting or shuffling or the pattern in which the cards were arranged but everything to do with ESP (extra sensory perception). It was all coming together now: A reader probably employed a Tarot pack in much the manner a psychic used a crystal ball. This was an interesting insight but I had the feeling that the young person seated across from me at the table was more concerned with an answer to her question than an explanation of how it was achieved. As I had never been accused of being psychic, I feared I would have no answer to give her.

I managed to mumble something and then replaced the cards in the pack and we repeated the process of shuffling and spreading the cards. Once again the cards were turned over and I gazed at them with quiet horror for it was now becoming increasingly clear that this was turning into a fiasco of the first magnitude. I understood enough of the Tarot deck at this point to know that the suit of Wands and the suit of Coins both had to do with career-related questions and there was not a single Wand or Coin card in the spread! I was tempted to tell my first—and probably last—consultant that the Tarot was obviously some kind of hoax that had been perpetuated over the centuries and as intelligent human beings we should realize that attempting to divine the future with pieces of colored cardboard had to be an exercise in futility and the last word in silliness.

But for some reason I did not.

For one thing, I noticed that some of the same cards that had been in the first spread had reappeared in the second one. Considering that the Tarot pack contains seventy-eight cards and that there were fewer than ten cards in the spreads I had thrown, the reappearance of several seemed a remarkable coincidence even though the cards did not seem to relate to the question. I made some perfunctory remarks and then once again we repeated the shuffling and spreading ritual—only this time I shuffled the pack with special thoroughness before handing it to the consultant to shuffle.

On this occasion, when the cards in the spread were turned over, I was amazed to see some of the same cards that had appeared in the other two spreads! Perhaps even more amazing, they were in roughly the same positions! Clearly the Tarot had absolutely no respect for the Law of Averages.

"Elaine, I am going to be honest with you," I said, upon regaining some semblance of my composure. "There is absolutely nothing here about graduate school."

"Nothing?"

"Nothing! But let me ask you this: Are you interested right now in a certain young man?," and I then proceeded to describe the young man as signified by the Page of Cups.

She replied in the affirmative.

"Okay, now we're getting somewhere," I said, "and since the Queen of Swords appears to be an obstacle, I am going to ask you, is there an older woman in the picture—someone rather opinionated and domineering,—quite possibly the young man's mother?"

"Why yes, that is absolutely correct," Elaine replied.

"Well, let's look at the matter straight," I said. "I can't answer your question about graduate school for the Tarot is not talking about graduate school. What the Tarot is talking about is your relationship with this young man and the problem concerning his mother, so why don't we pursue that question for the rest of the reading?"

Elaine was only too happy to comply, and by the end of the reading I was able to tell her that there would be hurdles to overcome, particularly the man's mother, but that by exercising patience, understanding, and tact with this woman, she would be successful.

After Elaine had left I went over the reading in my mind and it became increasingly clear that something was happening during the course of the reading although I was not quite sure what. For one thing, each spread was coherent and all of a piece. The information in regard to past and present aspects of a question was verified by the consultant. In an hour-long reading the Tarot was consistent; if it said something was likely to occur in the future it always said substantially the same thing when returning to the same question—it never contradicted itself. Against all laws of chance, some of the same cards kept reappearing in successive spreads. I also realized that the Tarot was not fortune-telling in the sense of telling you what is going to happen *to* you, but rather that it identified the responsibility of the individual by pointing out what the likely outcome would be if *you* were to choose a particular course of action. The outcome predicted by the Tarot might be positive or negative but the individual clearly had the option of exercising free will in the matter. So more than anything the Tarot appeared to act as a non-directive counselor.

But to me the single most incredible aspect of the reading was the fact that the Tarot did not bother with the question articulated by the consultant but rather selected the unspoken question of her psyche, acting as not only a wise counselor but as a highly perceptive psychologist as well!

The reading had actually answered two sets of questions: The consultant wanted to know what course of action to pursue concerning her young man and the Tarot had told her. But the hidden agenda of the reading had to do with my own reservations about the Tarot and it was brought home to me that the Tarot worked and was a force for good.

It is one thing to accept something and quite another to become truly involved with it and I doubt that I would have gone any further with the Tarot had it not been for another "coincidence" that occurred upon my return to New York at the end of the summer. I do not have my mail forwarded when I leave town for an extended period and so my tendency upon returning is to wade through the accummulated printed matter in a rather cavalier fashion and toss most of it into the circular file.

My wastebasket was soon screaming for mercy and I prided myself on having made a clean sweep. One letter, however, managed to tumble on to the floor, and I decided that this act of *chutzpah* on the part of a seemingly inanimate object had earned the letter a respectful reading. Wonder of wonders: It was an invitation to sign up for a course on Tarot by Rolla Nordic. I knew she was considered a leading authority on Tarot and I had brought her book with me to the Cape that summer. In thinking about how she got my name, there was a perfectly logical explanation for she had been a guest lecturer at a course on the occult that I had taken at the New School during the spring and she had most likely obtained the list of student names and addresses from the instructor.

So it all made sense. Perfectly logical. Easily explained. But still— there was something about the whole thing I couldn't quite put my finger on. Coincidence is what they call it but it was around this time that I was beginning to realize that calling something "coincidence" may well be the last refuge of the superstitious. Without further ado I signed up for the course and the Tarot has been my friend and counselor ever since.

Well, not entirely. If the truth be told, that last statement needs to be amended somewhat. For almost immediately I tried the Tarot on friends and kin who all commented on the accuracy of the readings and how they had been helped by them. Weeks or months later I would run into somebody I had read and the person would tell me that a future trend had turned out exactly as predicted and when they followed a course of action prescribed by the Tarot, the results had been everything the Tarot said they would be.

But while I was quick to consult the Tarot for others, I was hesitant to read my own cards and I realized much later that in the back of my mind I was still harboring some small measure of reluctance. In a sense, the Tarot was a prophet without honor in its own country for while I was generous in dispensing its prescriptions for others, I was slow to accept them for myself. But the events of the following summer were to change that rather radically.

With the cheerful sounds of Pomp and Circumstance at my school's commencement exercises I began to give serious thought to what I would do over the summer. Somebody has said that there are three reasons for going into teaching: June, July, and August. For many, there is a fourth reason, plugged into the first three, which is "getting away."

In regard to destination this particular summer, there was absolutely no question at all in my mind as to where I wanted to go for I hungered to return to that ocean Eden on the Cape that I had discovered the previous summer in setting up my parapsychology course. The only question was how I was going to fund it. I decided I was getting too old to be a waiter or a bellman and so I sifted other possibilities but failed to come up with anything concrete. Then the thought struck me, "Why not work as a Tarot reader?" But the more I thought about it the less viable it seemed as an option. Logic certainly dictated against it for there was the question of what I could use as a base of operations, how people would find out about me, and of course, the minor detail of earning enough through readings to pay my summer expenses. Logically, pragmatically, and realistically it was indeed a cuckoo idea.

About a week passed and I had just about reached the point where sanity was beginning to prevail and I was talking sense to myself and preparing to abandon what was obviously a harebrained enterprise when the Great Light Bulb in the sky lit up with the subliminal message flashing: "Ask the Tarot!"

It was with some trepidation that I removed my Tarot pack from the wooden box in which it resides and put the question to the cards. Nervously, I threw a spread, turned the cards over and found it hard to believe the sight that greeted my eyes. For there in the same spread were the Four of Coins (monetary attainment), the Four of Wands (more monetary attainment), The Empress and The Emperor (success), The Chariot (victory), the Ten of Coins or "Wall Street Card," (hitting the jackpot) and The Sun (happiness) and The World (joy) tossed in for good measure.

"Tarot," I said, "this is no time for horseplay. I am asking a serious question and I want a serious answer." I shuffled and threw a different spread. Again, there was an embarrassment of riches. Could it be? Was it possible? But after an hour's worth of spreads my last shred of reluctance had vanished. The Tarot was deadly serious and it was telling me that the life of a Tarot reader—at least, for the summer on Cape Cod—would give me both monetary and spiritual fulfillment. At this point I knew that there were times when the Tarot was shouting and this was clearly one of them.

Tossing abandon to the winds I packed my gear and set out for the Cape.

Admittedly, I was a bit apprehensive about the undertaking. I mean, I knew only that it was going to work—the Tarot had assured me of that—but I had no idea as to *how* it was going to work and not a single thought of where to start. And it had to work if I was not to return home in a barrel as my funds unaided by supplementary income would only see me through about half the summer.

Things were off to a good start, however, as I had been fortunate in securing a room at the last minute in the same charming guest home I had spent the previous summer. This proved to be a happy circumstance in several ways as the house itself—or rather, its owner—was to play a central role in the unfolding drama.

Upon my arrival I told the woman who ran the guest home what I had in mind. She merely looked thoughtful.

After unpacking I set out for a walk but just as I was going out the door this kind soul came up to me and said, "Mr. Konraad, would you have any objections to a story appearing in the local paper about what you are planning to do this summer?"

I gulped and allowed that I would have no particular objections. "Mrs. Kindsoul" informed me that she had a granddaughter, Karen, who was a reporter on the local paper. She then called Karen and an interview was set up for later in the week.

In the interim I wondered whether a newspaper story was going to do me more harm than good. For I had picked up the local weekly and saw that it was a fairly conservative paper in a fairly conservative community. And my impression of newspaper people was that they tended to be rather hard nosed about anything to do with the occult and I was fearful that possibly this Cape Cod reporter might turn out to be one of those "fearless" crusaders against anything and everything to do with the occult.

During the course of the interview it was impossible to perceive Karen's inner responses to the answers I was giving to her questions. At the conclusion of the interview I read Karen's cards and throughout the reading she remained inscrutable. So it was with some trepidation a few days later I picked up the paper and turned to the story. After looking over the lead I realized that my fears had been groundless, for the reading of Karen's cards had been in her words, "very much on the money," and the overall article was a ringing acclamation.

A day or so after the story appeared I received a phone call from a woman who had read the story and wanted a reading but in the interest of discretion she asked me if I could come out to her place. I didn't tell her that I had no place of my own—I didn't think Mrs. Kindsoul would have been particularly wild about my doing readings in the front parlor of her guest home—and merely replied that I would be happy to oblige. The reading proved to be an awesome experience for the woman held court in a sumptuous villa overlooking the sea where she played hostess to the Beautiful People who happened to be passing through. As it turned out, this woman had a single question: Would she get the million dollars she was asking from her ex-husband? The culminating cards of the first spread I threw for her were the Ten of Coins in the "immediate future" slot and The World as the "outcome." So without hesitation (I had learned to trust the Tarot fully by this time) I told her, "Not only will you get the million dollars you are asking for, but you will get it soon."

The precision of the Tarot in this instance was striking for I later learned that this woman's attorney had called her *the following day* to tell her that the offer had come through. Another consultant might have regarded this as coincidence but this woman definitely did not and she called everybody she knew—and she knew everybody—and told them about the reading and from that point on, the telephone at Mrs. Kindsoul's guest home started to ring for Mr. Konraad—and it simply didn't stop.

The summer proved to be everything (and more) that the Tarot said it would be. And it happened in a way that no amount of logic, common sense, or practical thinking could have foreseen. It came about through the individual efforts of an unlikely trinity—the owner of a guest home, a journalist, and a divorcee!

Toward the end of that summer I was strolling down the local Main Street when I happened upon Elaine, my first consultant, who it turned out was in town only for the day. She looked wonderful and there was a glow about her.

"How was graduate school?," I asked.

Elaine broke into a radiant grin. "Absolutely marvelous," she answered, "it couldn't have been better."

She punctuated her statement by giving me her hand and I noticed there was a sparkling addition on her third finger.

"Congratulations!," I said. "Tell me, was it the Page of Cups?"

"The Page of Cups it was—and is," she answered. "I really want to thank you for what you told me. It all happened just as you said."

"Oh, don't thank me, thank the Tarot; I was merely the middle man. But in any event, it is I who should be thanking you."

"Good heavens, why?," she exclaimed.

"Because if you hadn't asked for the reading, I don't know that I would have ever learned the secret of the Tarot. I mean, I might have just gone along for years treating it as an abstraction—you know, sort of an interesting curiosity. In all likelihood, I would have gone the road of so many others and simply placed it on a shelf and forgotten about it. But you forced me to put it to the test and it passed with flying colors. And that realization has literally changed my life.

"So, Elaine, thank *you* so much!"

Part One

Exploring Inner Space: Reading and Interpreting the Cards in Divination

A Tarot reading could be likened to a journey into space: The craft in this case is an unlikely transport vehicle for it is the seventy-eight-card pack of the Tarot. The pilot is the consultant, that is, the individual being read. Or, more specifically, it is the unconscious mind of that person. So this space journey differs from other space flights in that it could be seen as a journey into *inner* space. Quite literally, a journey into the mind.

For many people this is unexplored terrain and so this inner space journey can be quite revealing. Often the Tarot will pick up the question consciously posed but it always goes beyond the superficial and reveals the root of a problem or question.

To the uninitiated, a Tarot reading is fortune-telling. Every once in a while you will hear someone say, "I am going to a Tarot reader to have my fortune told." Nothing could be further from the truth.

But if a Tarot reading is not fortune-telling, what exactly is it? Quite possibly, it is not *exactly* anything but it could be likened to weather forecasting in that a certain pattern can be foreseen with certain probable results.

Most people tune in to a weather report before they leave for work in the morning not so much to find out what the weather is going to *do* to them, but rather, what *they* can do about the weather and that involves preparation. In short, they prepare to cope with *probable* conditions.

It is the same with a Tarot reading. The reader does not say what is going to happen to you but rather, what trends will be developing and what will be the probable outcome if a certain course of action is followed.

The major difference between a weather forecast and a Tarot reading is that the Tarot forecast is generally more accurate. The reason for this is that there are usually more variables in a weather forecast than in a Tarot reading. In a Tarot reading, most people have questions that have to do with their own decisions concerning a particular course of action.

Weather forecasting is aided by arrow-chasing area maps that reveal that the drop in the mercury expected the following day is not something that just simply happens but rather is connected to other atmospheric events that can be clearly seen on the map.

Now it is just possible that the pattern of our lives could also be "mapped" in some similar way. It is significant that most Tarot spreads deal not only with future time but also past and present. There is a reason for that as what we do or become in the future is the culminating point of a pattern of thoughts and actions rooted in the past and evolving in the present.

On another level the card of the past in a spread can aid the reader in counseling. Let us say that a young man comes for a reading. You learn that he is going with a girl but is not sure he wants to marry her. Now if the other cards in the spread indicate that his fears are groundless and that she is right for him, look very carefully at that card of the past. If, for example, that card is the Three of Swords—which usually means separation or divorce—it would indicate that he came from a broken home and fears making the same kind of marriage his parents did. You can then tell him that either he or his parents probably had a karmic debt to pay but there is absolutely no reason for him to fear that the same thing will happen to him for the Three of Swords—the "bad marriage" card—is not in the future, it is in the past, and therefore he has no cause for worry for there is only one Three of Swords in the Tarot pack and as far as he is concerned it is in the past and will remain in the past.

We have at this point perhaps a somewhat clearer view of the mechanics involved in a reading. But there is one question we have not taken up. And that is the real question. It might be phrased piecemeal: *Who* or *what* is the Tarot? *How* does it know what it knows? And finally, how does it deliver the goods in a reading? Important questions, all of them, but no one seems to know the answers. Let us attempt a supposition: Let us take as our starting point the belief that there is a Force or Being that is *omniscient*. And the Tarot is "the hot line" to this Cosmic Mind. In the ritual of cutting and shuffling the cards the consultant is, in effect, "dialing" the answer. And if we go one step further and make the assumption that this force is not only omniscient but also *omnipotent,* it would be the simplest of cosmic tasks to program a Tarot reading while the consultant is shuffling the pack.

This explanation is admittedly difficult to accept rationally but anyone who has ever witnessed or participated in a Tarot reading knows that something is happening that defies normal explanations. If a theory offers a reasonable description of something that would be otherwise unexplainable, it seems prudent to use it. The Tarot is a thing of beauty and a thing of truth but most mysterious. As Albert Einstein said, "The most beautiful experience we can have is the mysterious."

Let us now get into the preliminaries of doing a reading. The logical first step is to acquire a Tarot pack. It might be pointed out that while there are a number of different Tarot packs on the market, there are basically two types—the illustrated and non-illustrated. That is to say that in an illustrated deck, the fifty-six cards of the Minor Arcana depict scenes of people doing things; in a non-illustrated pack, these Minor Arcana cards bear only the symbols of the suit they represent such as Swords or Cups. If you are coming as a novice to the Tarot it would be best to start with a *non-illustrated* deck such as the Richard Gardner pack, the Oswald Wirth deck, or the Tarot de Marseilles. The vocabulary of the Tarot is limited to seventy-eight images and while a given card might mean one thing in one reading, in another reading, the same card might take on a somewhat different shade of meaning. If you start with an illustrated pack you are really beginning with a handicap for the inclination will be to confine your interpretation to the scene depicted on the card rather than to exercise your imagination and subconscious. In fact, in some cases the scene depicted is actually at variance with the traditional meaning of the card, which is confusing at best and can certainly help to distort a reading.

Another reason is that the Tarot is a magickal tool (This spelling is used to signify authentic magick as opposed to the illusory variety.) and the symbols are considered to be more effective when unadorned.

Illustrated packs do have their place in certain types of readings, but are really not the best with which to learn. Some illustrated decks such as the Rider pack and the Morgan-Greer pack are really quite beautiful and most suitable for meditation or certain types of spreads, particularly ones done in a life reading (see Part Three).

After acquiring your Tarot pack it would be good to become acquainted with it by holding each card face up in your hand and experiencing the impressions you receive. You might even try this before you read the meanings and later learn that some of your first impressions were pretty close to the mark. This would work best for the twenty-two cards of the Major Arcana for in all packs these cards have human figures on them and it is quite easy to relate to them. Try the Minor Arcana cards also and record your impressions. For instance, you could be looking at the Ten of Coins and feel that those ten large gold pieces represent a lot of money and you would be right for that card is known as the "Wall Street Card."

When you have finished examining the cards return them to the container in which they came. Always complete the ritual of a reading by putting away the cards. Before you do so it would be well to go through the pack and make sure that all cards are in the upright position in preparation for the next reading. An extra touch is to "seal" the pack in a positive way by placing benevolent cards—such as the card of The Sun and the card of The World—at the top and bottom of the deck.

You can also procure a cloth, preferably purple, and preferably silk or velvet, to wrap your cards in and perhaps a wooden box to contain them. You first return them to the cardboard box in which they came, then wrap the purple cloth around them, and the final step is to place them in the wooden box. The reason for all this is that Tarot packs are considered to be highly sensitive to all vibrations and so when not in use it is best to protect them in the manner just described. It is difficult to say exactly how important the above is regarding the effectiveness of the pack in a reading but what is of considerable importance is the reader's *attitude*. Compliance to Tarot traditions is an indication of her or his seriousness and respect for the Tarot.

One other thing: Never lend your pack to anyone else. It is yours and yours alone.

SUMMARY OF PRELIMINARY STEPS

Acquire Tarot pack.
Familiarize yourself with the cards.
Shuffle deck thoroughly.
Make sure all cards are upright.
"Seal" the pack by placing benevolent cards
at the top and bottom.
Return pack to original cardboard box.
Wrap purple cloth around it.
Place it in a wooden box which has a cover or lid.

The next step is the all-important one of learning the meanings of the cards. There are seventy-eight cards each with a meaning of its own. Tips will be given shortly in regard to looking for patterns that will considerably facilitate the learning process. Best not to try to digest it all at once but rather do it slowly. If you are willing to devote half an hour to an hour a day to learning the Tarot for one month you will find that by the end of the month you will be able to do reliable readings for yourself and others without the need to refer to this or any other book. In fact, it is best that you do not let yourself get into the habit of doing "open book readings." First of all, you are not going to inspire much confidence in the people you read if you have to keep thumbing through a book. Second, and more important, stopping to refer to a book hampers the imagination and serves to disrupt the rhythm and chemistry of a Tarot reading.

Here is a suggested schedule for learning the Tarot in a thirty-day period. This program will allow you to do readings with competence and in time you will be an accomplished reader.

Schedule for Learning the Tarot in Thirty Days

Day 1: Learn the basic patterns (see below) of the Major Arcana, the Minor Arcana, and the numerical correspondences of the first ten cards of both the Major and Minor Arcana.

Day 2: Learn the correspondences and meanings of the #1 cards in both the Major and Minor Arcana—The Magician and the four Aces. Take the cards out of the pack and meditate upon them. After you do so, associate each card with the meaning attributed to it.

Day 3: Review the meanings of the #1 cards. Learn the meanings of all #2 cards. Study and meditate upon the #2 cards. Take all #1 and #2 cards out of the deck and using those ten cards only, throw a spread (see Part Two) that uses less than ten cards such as the Horseshoe or Eastern Cross. Read and interpret the cards, referring to the book only after you have done the best you can without it. From here on, only the new cards to be learned for each day will be given but the method (described above) of review, studying and meditating upon the new cards, selecting all cards learned and using them in a reading, is the plan to follow each day.

Day 4: Learn the meanings of all #3 cards and repeat process given for Day 3.

Days 5–15: Concentrating on one number a day, continue to learn the meanings of all cards #4 through #15, repeating the process given for Day 3.

Day 16: Review everything to date.

Day 17: If you have been following the schedule, you have learned all fifty-six cards of the Minor Arcana; there are only eight more cards in the Major Arcana to learn! The emphasis from this point on will be review. Review all #1 cards. Learn card #15, The Devil, and repeat process given for Day 3.

Day 18: Review all #2 cards. Learn card #16, The Lightning-Struck Tower, and repeat process given for Day 3.

Day 19: Review all #3 cards. Learn card #17, The Star, and repeat process given for Day 3.

Day 20: Review all #4 cards. Learn card #18, The Moon, and repeat process given for Day 3.

Day 21: Review all #5 cards. Learn card #19, The Sun, and repeat process given for Day 3.

Day 22: Review all #6 cards. Learn card #20, Day of Judgment, and repeat process given for Day 3.

Day 23: Review all #7 cards. Learn card #21, The World, and repeat process given for Day 3.

Day 24: Review all #8 cards. Learn The Unnumbered Card (The Fool) and repeat process given for Day 3.

Day 25: Review all #9 and #10 cards and repeat process given for Day 3.

Day 26: Review all #11 and #12 cards and repeat process given for Day 3.

Day 27: Review all #13 and #14 cards and repeat process given for Day 3.

Day 28: Review Major Arcana cards #15, 16, 17 and 18 and repeat process given for Day 3.

Day 29: Review Major Arcana cards #19, 20, 21 and the card of The Fool and repeat process given for Day 3.

Day 30: Take a break—you have earned it!

Basic Patterns

Knowing how to recognize patterns can be a tremendous boon to the beginning student for with this knowledge under your belt you can do a general reading almost immediately and certainly long before you have mastered the individual meanings of each card in the seventy-eight-card Tarot deck. Some students of the Tarot may not have the time or inclination to commit seventy-eight cards to memory but might be interested in a short-cut method that would enable them to do readings of a general nature. If that is the case, this section on patterns can be both the starting and stopping point for you. Once you have mastered the few simple steps outlined here, you can do a coherent and intelligible reading. If you plan to do in-depth readings, you can work with pattern analysis while you are learning the ropes.

So whatever your desires or intentions, this section is the place to start.

The first thing to note is that the seventy-eight-card Tarot pack has a division into twenty-two cards of the Major Arcana and fifty-six cards of the Minor Arcana. There is also the subdivision of the Court Cards within the Minor Arcana of the kings, queens, knights, and pages. Now, let us get into the actual patterns:

Major Arcana

For the most part, the twenty-two cards in this category represent psychological states of mind or people. If there is a predominance of Major Arcana cards in a spread and the cards are basically positive, this would indicate a psychologically healthy person and one who could master events. These are the easiest cards to interpret in the Tarot for the figures depicted on the cards are usually a strong indication of whether the card is positive or negative in divination. The card of The Empress is clearly positive for an empress is a leader and the woman on the card is smiling and happy. The card of The Devil, as the name alone would suggest, is extremely negative and is further reinforced by the depiction of a frightening creature and two captives bound in chains.

Minor Arcana

Whereas the cards of the Major Arcana largely depict psychological states or people, the cards of the Minor Arcana have to do with material events. There are four suits in the Minor Arcana—Coins, Wands, Cups, and Swords—and each represents a different type of condition. Following are the primary guidelines:

Coins—questions having to do with money or business.

Wands—questions having to do with school, career, or creative ventures.

Cups—questions having to do with relationships, love, romance, marriage, and family.

Swords—questions having to do with problems, sorrows, afflictions.

Court Cards

As mentioned above, these cards are the kings, queens, knights, and pages and technically are part of the Minor Arcana but are really in a class by themselves. Although there are only sixteen of these cards in a seventy-eight-card deck, it is a rare spread that does not contain one or more of them and the reason for that is that they represent people and most people's questions have to do with other people.

If a king appears the question has to do with a man; a queen, a woman; and a page, a child or young man or woman. The one exception in the Court Cards is the knight, or horseman, which does not represent a person (usually) but rather, a person's thoughts. What type of thoughts would be indicated by the suit? The Knight of Coins would be thoughts about money or business; the Knight of Wands, thoughts about school or career; the Knight of Cups, romantic or loving thoughts; and the Knight of Swords, unhappy or bitter thoughts.

Numerical Correspondences

A truly major pattern has to do with the numbers on the cards. Cards bearing the same number will share some qualities in common. For example, since 1 is the first of the numbers and stands alone, anything under a 1-vibration will have qualities of independence and leadership. Since 1 is the starting point of the root numbers, the vibration is associated with beginnings, often of a powerful nature. All of these traits are exemplified by the Number One card of the Major Arcana, The Magician, and the four aces of the Minor Arcana.

These numerical correspondences are most clearly discerned by the cards bearing the root numbers one to nine. If you will memorize the root number pattern along with the pattern of the four suits of the Minor Arcana—Coins, Wands, Cups, and Swords—you will be amazed at the results when you sit down to do a reading *based on these patterns alone.*

Here is a table of root numbers with the meaning of each number as it applies in divination along with the corresponding cards from both the Major and Minor Arcana.

Table of Root Number Associations in the Major and Minor Arcana

1

Major Arcana: The Magician
Minor Arcana: Ace of Coins, Wands, Cups, and Swords
Divinatory Meaning: Beginnings

2

Major Arcana: The High Priestess
Minor Arcana: Two of Coins, Wands, Cups, and Swords
Divinatory Meaning: Conflict

3

Major Arcana: The Empress
Minor Arcana: Three of Coins, Wands, Cups, and Swords
Divinatory Meaning: Career

4

Major Arcana: The Emperor
Minor Arcana: Four of Coins, Wands, Cups, and Swords
Divinatory Meaning: Attainment

5

Major Arcana: The Hierophant
Minor Arcana: Five of Coins, Wands, Cups, and Swords
Divinatory Meaning: Fulfillment

6

Major Arcana: The Lovers
Minor Arcana: Six of Coins, Wands, Cups, and Swords
Divinatory Meaning: Decision

7

Major Arcana: The Chariot
Minor Arcana: Seven of Coins, Wands, Cups, and Swords
Divinatory Meaning: Change

8

Major Arcana: Justice (The card of Justice can represent
imbalance or balance. This is determined by the
surrounding cards in the spread.)
Minor Arcana: Eight of Coins, Wands, Cups, and Swords
Divinatory Meaning: Imbalance

9

Major Arcana: The Hermit
Minor Arcana: Nine of Coins, Wands, Cups, and Swords
Divinatory Meaning: A New Path

Minor Arcana

There are fifty-six cards in the Minor Arcana consisting of four suits of fourteen cards each. In each suit cards numbered 11 to 14 are known as the Court Cards and comprise the kings, queens, knights, and pages.

Instead of presenting each suit separately, the scheme here is to approach the cards numerically beginning with the four aces and ending with the four pages. The reason for this is so you can better see the numerical correspondences and start by learning the general meaning for a given number before tackling the four variations.

The Minor Arcana are said to deal with material conditions and events which are depicted by the following four suits:

Coins (or Pentacles)—finances, business
Wands (or Rods)—career, creative ventures
Cups (or Chalices)—matters of the heart
Swords (or Blades)—sorrows, afflictions

As with the Major Arcana, divinatory meanings will be given for both upright and reversed positions. But it is not essential to memorize the reversed meanings as in most cases it is simply *less* good or *less* bad. In practice, if you are using a non-illustrated deck it is often difficult to tell when a Minor Arcana card has been reversed. More than anything else, reversed cards in the Minor Arcana spell delays.

1

General Meaning: Beginnings

Ace of Coins: New financial venture.
Reversed: Financial setback or delay.

Ace of Wands: Start of program of study, job, career, or news of same.
Reversed: Problems or delays in starting something.

Ace of Cups: Beginning of romance. Letter from loved one.
Reversed: Difficulties in starting a relationship.

Ace of Swords: Failure of something to materialize. Bad news.
Reversed: Meaning is much the same, only slightly less so.

Combinations (in the same spread):
Three aces: Success assured.
Four aces: Powerful forces at work. Virtually a total new beginning to the life.

2

General Meaning: Conflict

2 of Coins: Conflict in money matters.
Reversed: Failure to read "the bottom line."

2 of Wands: Conflict over career or with business associates.
Reversed: Failure to do one's homework.

2 of Cups: The "Love Conquers All" card. Conflict has been resolved by patience and affectionate cooperation
Reversed: Problem not entirely solved.

2 of Swords: Conflict on several levels. Inability to resolve conflict.
Reversed: Hidden enemies at work.

Combinations:
   Three 2s: Need to reorganize.
   Four 2s: Traumatic period in the life.

3

General Meaning: Career

   3 of Coins: Contract. Business partnership. Marriage
               involving money.
   Reversed: Financial reversals in business or marriage.

   3 of Wands: Letter of acceptance. Position in education or
               the arts. Marriage based upon mutual interests.
   Reversed: Delay in acquiring desired post.

   3 of Cups: A marriage based upon deep affection.
   Reversed: Broken marriage.

   3 of Swords: Separation or divorce.
   Reversed: Domestic strife.

Combinations:
   Three 3s: Highly eventful period.
   Four 3s: Milestone in the life.

4

General Meaning: Attainment

   4 of Coins: Success in career through one's own efforts.
   Reversed: Job or career frustration.

   4 of Wands: Promotion or advancement. Financial windfall.
   Reversed: Delays or problems regarding career or legacy.

   4 of Cups: A lover, friend, or baby comes into one's life in
              a sudden or unexpected fashion.
   Reversed: Sexual or love problems.

4 of Swords: Loss. Illness requiring hospitalization.
Reversed: Personal, business, or health problems not as serious as expected.

Combinations:
Three 4s: Work is heavy and demanding.
Four 4s: Desire to get away from it all.

5

General Meaning: Fulfillment

5 of Coins: Financial fulfillment.
Reversed: Delay in receiving financial benefits.

5 of Wands: Fulfillment in career.
Reversed: Delays or reverses regarding career.

5 of Cups: Fulfillment in love. Emotional fulfillment.
Reversed: Lover untrue or neglectful.

5 of Swords: There will be problems but the spirit guides are in control.
Reversed: Difficulties will not be entirely cleared up.

Combinations:
Three 5s: A general good feeling about oneself and the world and everybody in it.
Four 5s: Everything is coming up roses.

6

General Meaning: Time of Decision

6 of Coins: Decision concerning an organization or group of people. A wedding.
Reversed: Problems or delays making or carrying out a decision.

6 of Wands: Decision concerning the theatre, art, music, or the occult.
Reversed: Difficulties in realizing one's creative potential.

6 of Cups: Decision involving love or marriage. Emotional decision.
Reversed: Disappointment concerning lover, mate, or family member.

6 of Swords: Warning card. Person is unable to make a decision and this card mandates that a decision be made if individual is ever to have peace of mind.
Reversed: Tension beginning to abate.

Combinations:
Three 6s: Much confusion.
Four 6s: Get life sorted out without further delay as this combination is an invitation to disaster.

7

General Meaning: Change

7 of Coins: A change in business or career. Business trip.
Reversed: Business change or trip does not work as planned.

7 of Wands: The card of The Writer. Also the card of The Student and The Teacher—but in regard to some type of change relating to career.
Reversed: Change in career due to frustration.

7 of Cups: Change regarding family or residence. Visit to or from relatives. A live-in relationship.
Reversed: Difficulties with home or family situation.

7 of Swords: Warning card. This is a more serious warning card than the 6 of Swords for it indicates that the person may be on the edge of a breakdown. Also a warning against accident—particularly with the 3 or 9 of Swords or The Lightning-

Struck Tower. Both the 6 and 7 of Swords in the same spread would indicate severe depression and possible suicidal tendencies.

Reversed: The problem of accident increases due to individual's extreme self-destructive tendencies at the present time.

Combinations:

Three 7s: Help may be expected from friends.

Four 7s: Probable neurosis if the individual does not slow down and learn to live one day at a time.

8

General Meaning: Imbalance

8 of Coins: Reckless spending. Imbalance in financial or business affairs.

Reversed: Financial losses can be trimmed.

8 of Wands: Imbalance in creative or career ventures. Card of The Politician—but usually with regard to some problem or impropriety.

Reversed: Problems with professional associates lessened through tact or diplomacy.

8 of Cups: Imbalance in love life or family matters.

Reversed: Positive action helps to heal situation regarding a relationship.

8 of Swords: General imbalance in personal affairs.

Reversed: Problems lessened by facing them openly and honestly.

Combinations:

Three 8s: Time to slow down as the psychological speed limit is being exceeded.

Four 8s: Professional counseling is clearly called for.

9

General Meaning: A New Path

9 of Coins: Unexpected costs in the way of money or emotions.
Reversed: Indicates a need to guard against unwise personal loans or investments.

9 of Wands: New friends or environment.
Reversed: A visit or communication with someone from the past.

9 of Cups: The Wish Card. A dream comes true.
Reversed: Delay in seeing a wish realized.

9 of Swords: Deep personal loss. Time of danger and/or endings.
Reversed: Need to soften one's nature or there can be much unhappiness.

Combinations:
Three 9s: Much going on in the way of correspondence and communications.
Four 9s: Be prepared to take on a number of added responsibilities.

10

General Meaning: Wins and Losses

10 of Coins: The Wall Street Card. It is the business or financial break for which one has been waiting.
Reversed: Profits less than anticipated.

10 of Wands: Major career gains. Potential is there for rising to the top of one's chosen field.
Reversed: Potential needs to be tapped and developed before it can bear fruit.

10 of Cups: Heavy emotional costs regarding someone else.
Reversed: Eccentric behavior can cause severance of a relationship.

10 of Swords: Emotional or psychological bankruptcy. The edge of the abyss of despair.

Reversed: Person beginning to learn to cope.

Combinations:

Three 10s: Much buying and selling.

Four 10s: Age of anxiety.

11

Kings
General Meaning: Men, Usually Over Thirty-Five

King of Coins: Business type. Rigid outlook. Well organized. Conservative.

Reversed: Presently ill or suffering from some affliction involving the physical body.

King of Wands: A counselor. Fair, honest, and just. Understanding person—one in whom you can confide.

Reversed: Somewhat puritanical. Tends to do everything "by the book." Something upside down in the life of this man.

King of Cups: A man of keen sensibilities. Artistically inclined. A good lover but somewhat manipulative.

Reversed: Not entirely honest with himself and others. The Great American Compromiser. May have identity problem.

King of Swords: A blunt, hardnosed forceful type. Often an executive, lawyer, or doctor.

Reversed: Highly insecure. May be suffering from mental illness or some type of psychosomatic complaint.

Combinations:

Three Kings: A prize, honor, or award in the offing.

Four Kings: Top-level meeting with VIPs.

12

Queens
General Meaning: Women,
Usually Over Thirty-Five

Queen of Coins: Highly organized female. Often a business
woman or executive.
Reversed: Difficult person to deal with as she is lacking in
basic human understanding. Woman presently
ill or bedridden.

Queen of Wands: Motherly type. Woman of keen insight and
understanding.
Reversed: Restless individual who tends to scatter her
energies.

Queen of Cups: Compassionate woman. Very warm and
affectionate. Devoted wife and mother.
Reversed: Love life is somewhat chaotic.

Queen of Swords: Strong-minded woman. Highly independent.
Widow, divorcee, or single woman.
Reversed: Domineering woman. Insecure person. May
have deep-seated sexual problems—particularly
if the reversed Queen of Swords appears in the
same spread with The Enchantress, The Devil,
or The Moon.

Combinations:
Three Queens: Discretion is called for at the present moment.
Four Queens: Words—uttered or published by consultant—can
be an explosive force.

13

Knights (or Horsemen)
General Meaning: Thoughts

Knight of Coins: Thoughts about money or business.
Reversed: Misunderstanding or poor judgment regarding
a business deal or investment.

Knight of Wands: Thoughts about career or what one does creatively.
Reversed: Inability to see clearly the road to take regarding career.

Knight of Cups: Loving and happy thoughts.
Reversed: Confusion regarding an affair of the heart.

Knight of Swords: Unhappy or bitter thoughts.
Reversed: Highly destructive thoughts. If reversed Knight of Swords appears in the same spread as the 2 or 7 of Swords, The Devil, or The Lightning-Struck Tower, individual is prone to violence—and violence of a most negative order.

Combinations:
Three Knights: It would be best at this time to shelve all decisions and go off on vacation.
Four Knights: A crisis of the worst kind is brewing.

14

Pages
General Meaning: Young People (Men or Women) Under Thirty-Five, Children, Infants, or Pets

Page of Coins: A serious young person. Quiet or withdrawn. Good head for studies or business.
Reversed: Tends to be stubborn. Somewhat careless with money.

Page of Wands: Fair-minded and straightforward youth. Loyal and faithful friend.
Reversed: Overly serious. Inclined to be a loner.

Page of Cups: Warm and affectionate youngster or young adult.
Reversed: Lacking in self-confidence. Spoiled brat.

Page of Swords: Independent and adventuresome youth. Willful and obstinate child.

Reversed: Obstreperous individual. Early rule of the rod is called for as this child has all the makings of a maverick and rebel.

Combinations:
Three Pages: Good news is on the way.
Four Pages: News pertaining to school or camp.

SUMMARY OF MEANINGS IN DIVINATION FOR MAJOR AND MINOR ARCANA

1

Major Arcana—The Magician: Self-mastery. Powerful will. Inspirational teacher.
Minor Arcana—Beginnings.

2

Major Arcana—The High Priestess: Duality. Moody or critical woman.
Minor Arcana—Conflict.

3

Major Arcana—The Empress: The launching of a creative enterprise. Marriage.
Minor Arcana—Career.

4

Major Arcana—The Emperor: Material attainment. Marriage.
Minor Arcana—Attainment.

5

Major Arcana—The Hierophant: A wise counselor. Spiritual fulfillment. Introspective man.
Minor Arcana—Fulfillment.

6

Major Arcana—The Lovers: A time of decision.
Minor Arcana—A time of decision.

7

Major Arcana—The Chariot: Victory.
Minor Arcana—Change.

8

Major Arcana—Justice: Balance or imbalance depending upon
      surrounding cards.
Minor Arcana—Imbalance.

9

Major Arcana—The Hermit: A searching. Spiritual renewal.
      Highly cautious individual.
Minor Arcana—A new path.

10

Major Arcana—The Wheel of Fortune: A turn in one's fortunes for
      the better.
Minor Arcana—Wins and losses.

11

Major Arcana—The Enchantress: Inner strength. Difficult period
      in the life. Aggressive woman.
Minor Arcana—Kings are men, usually over thirty-five.

12

Major Arcana—The Hanged Man: Sacrifice. Reverses. Total
      change of values.
Minor Arcana—Queens are women, usually over thirty-five.

13

Major Arcana—The Reaper: Change. Reaping what one has sown.
Minor Arcana—Knights are thoughts.

14

Major Arcana—The Angel of Time: Regeneration. Renewed inner
harmony and a more loving and understanding
acceptance of others.

Minor Arcana—Pages are young people (men or women) under
thirty-five, children, infants, or pets.

15

Major Arcana—The Devil: Fear. Division within the self.
Evil influences at work.

16

Major Arcana—The Lightning-Struck Tower: Psychological crisis.
Accident or disaster.

17

Major Arcana—The Star: Hope. New lease on life.

18

Major Arcana—The Moon: Deception. Delays. Illusion.

19

Major Arcana—The Sun: Paradise found. The love of the life.
Filling up with happiness.

20

Major Arcana—Day of Judgment: Decision of the utmost
importance is in the making.

21

Major Arcana—The World: Joy.

The Unnumbered Card

Major Arcana—The Fool: At or near the beginning of a spread
The Fool indicates confusion, simple-mindedness,
or ill-fated undertaking. At or near the end of a
spread the indication is that he is a magus, or wise
fool, who has had more than his share of challenges and hurts but who has grown in wisdom
and humanity.

Major Arcana

First to be taken up will be the twenty-two cards of the Major Arcana. In general, the Tarot Trumps, as they are known, refer to psychological states of mind or people. Following a brief description of the cards in regard to symbolism, mythology, and psychological meanings, will be the meaning in divination. Please note that the cards have one meaning upright and another when they are reversed.

   NOTE: Tarot packs differ somewhat in the way symbols are used and also in the artistic rendering of the figures depicted. The descriptions that follow pertain to the Oswald Wirth Deck.

le fou

The Unnumbered Card
The Fool

The single card that wears no number in the Tarot is the card of The Fool. Because of this, he is considered to be the most profound card of the Tarot for he can be seen as both the beginning and ending card of the Major Arcana. Garbed as he is in a suit of motley and wearing a cap and bells, he is reminiscent of the court jester of another age. Fools were considered to be essentially cases of arrested development or even demented. However, these very qualities of madness or simplicity endeared them to members of the court for they were considered to have a sacred quality about them and in their babblings the voice of God might be heard.

In modern playing card packs, The Fool is the one card from the Major Arcana that has survived. As The Joker he is not at all unlike his ancestor for he holds no rank or station but as a "wild" man he can pretty much go as he pleases and at times his power is equal to and even greater than that of a king. In a Tarot reading, The Fool has the same trick as his medieval counterpart of popping up like a jack-in-the-box when you least expect him. Often he will appear as the very first card in a spread and at other times as the very last. The meanings in divination differ and for that reason The Fool will be listed as both the beginning and ending card of the Major Arcana. When The Fool appears at or near the beginning of a spread, he is truly a fool for he is about to embark upon an enterprise for which he has not properly prepared himself.

Divinatory Meaning: Confusion. Simple-mindedness. Ill-fated undertaking.

Reversed: Inability to begin something due to conflicting drives.

le Bateleur

Arcanum I
The Magician

The Number I card of the Major Arcana, The Magician, is probably the card that more people identify with than any other, which is interesting considering the duality of the card. In some decks—the Rider Pack particularly—he appears as almost a Christ-like figure talking in parables to the multitudes. In most traditional packs, however, he seems more the carnival trickster, the confidence man, manipulating others with his sleight-of-hand techniques. It is perhaps this very duality that appeals to us for he speaks to both the dark and light sides of each of us. He appears to be performing before an unseen audience and he clearly relishes what he is doing. The Magician stands behind a table out in the open and in most Tarot packs the table contains a pentacle, a sword, a chalice, and a wand. Since these are the symbols for the four suits of the Minor Arcana and represent material conditions, The Magician is a forceful personality indeed for he is in control of both himself and his destiny.

Divinatory Meaning: Self-mastery. Powerful will. Inspirational teacher.

Reversed: An individual lacking in willpower or one who uses his or her will to exploit others. The clue as to which meaning pertains may be found in the surrounding cards: Exploitation would be suggested by the Eight of Swords or particularly the card of The Devil (another name for this card is The Black Magician). Surrounded by The High Priestess, The Emperor, or a King or Queen, the indication is that s/he is a weak person who has been dominated by an authority figure.

Arcanum II
The High Priestess

The first female figure, The High Priestess, is also considered to be a magician for she is said to represent Isis, the horned moon goddess of ancient Egypt. The central myth of the mystery religion of Isis was the story of how her husband, Osiris, was slain by his evil brother, Seth. Isis searched everywhere for his body and when she found it, she used her magick to bring Osiris back to life and by him conceived Horus, who became the Sun God. The resurrected Osiris also became a god and the myth of his death and resurrection was believed to have provided a pattern that human beings could follow. Those who became initiated into the Egyptian mysteries believed that they would gain eternal life.

In one hand The High Priestess holds a manuscript, in the other, a golden key. On the cover of the scroll appears the white and black symbol of yin and yang—the Law of Opposites. This Law is reinforced by the two poles she is seated between—a red one and a blue one, and also the floor beneath her throne, which is made up of contrasting white and black marble squares. This Law then will provide the golden key to the mystery of her own personality and once she learns it she will be able to integrate the differing forces within her psyche. She needs to work on herself, and until then to deal with her may be somewhat "difficult."

Divinatory Meaning: Duality. Moody or critical woman.

Reversed: A confused or neurotic person.

Arcanum III
The Empress

In many ancient religions the godhead was considered to be three-fold— a sacred trinity. Since Arcanum III is The Empress she may be seen as the woman who is here on earth to demonstrate the workings of heaven in the things of earth. This is suggested on the card by the scepter she holds, which is topped by the cross of spirit. Beside the Empress's throne a lily is growing and one is reminded of the Biblical parable about the lillies of the field and "even Solomon in all his glory was not arrayed like one of these." The ascending eagle on The Empress's shield further illustrates the connection between heaven and earth.

The Empress is said to be a depiction of Venus, who mothered humankind and thus is the goddess of love, creation, art, and beauty. The psychologist Carl Jung spoke of archetypes—figures or images with which people of all times could identify. He believed that the mother archetype was primary for the young child's first formative experience is with the mother. The Empress could be seen as the mother archetype for she is Venus, the heavenly mother—the great earth mother—the mother of us all.

Divinatory Meaning: The launching of a creative enterprise. Marriage.

Reversed: Setback in career. Divorce. Should the reversed Empress appear in the same spread with the Three of Swords (which indicates divorce) it could refer to an on-again, off-again marriage.

Arcanum IV
The Emperor

The eagle crest on The Emperor's throne establishes that he is the consort of The Empress. They complement each other well for as Arcanum III, The Empress is self-expressive, creative, and intuitive. Four, however, the number of The Emperor, is the number of earth, practicality, discipline, and reason. In Jungian terms, he is the authority figure father archetype, the *animus,* or male principle, as contrasted with the *anima* or female principle represented by The Empress. Since The Empress is associated with Venus, The Emperor could be seen as Mars, the god of war and destruction. In mythology, Mars was the lover of Venus and their child was Harmony, the ordered and regular arrangement of things.

The Emperor is considered quite positive when it appears in a spread. Not always as positive as The Empress, for The Emperor lacks her flexibility, openness, creativity, and spiritual values. When The Emperor appears in a spread, look at the surrounding cards. Flanked by Coins and Wands, the individual may be overly self-seeking and materialistic. But when The Emperor appears with The Hierophant, The Star, or The Empress, the consultant has built on a firm foundation.

Divinatory Meaning: Material attainment. Marriage.

Reversed: Failure to recognize one's potential or to attain material success. Divorce.

Arcanum V
The Hierophant

Arcanum V, The Hierophant, depicts another archetypal figure, and since the card is also known as The Pope, which means ''papa'' or ''father'' he is the spiritual father to his flock. ''Pontiff'' is an appellation for a pope, and the word stems from the Etruscans, meaning ''bridge builder.'' The spiritual father serves as the bridge between heaven and earth.

But the word, ''hierophant,'' by which this card is generally known, has a somewhat different meaning for in antiquity he was the chief priest of the Eleusinian Mysteries of ancient Egypt and was known as the Revealer of Sacred Things. This reminds us of the myth of Isis, the moon goddess hovering above the dead Osiris, the Sun God, to revive him. In the Eleusinian Mysteries, the hierophant made himself impotent by drinking hemlock, which was equivalent to Osiris lying dead. The rite of a ''sacred marriage'' performed between the hierophant and a priestess represented the union of Isis and Osiris. Later would be proclaimed the birth of Horus, who was to become the Sun God. The myth teaches that Osiris was born a man and became a god, thereby setting an example others could follow.

In his red robe and white beard, The Hierophant of the Tarot looks a little like St. Nicholas. The novices with their backs to us might be perceived as children telling Santa what they want for Christmas. But what they want is a far cry from what ''pop'' can afford so The Hierophant is counseling them and attempting to raise their spiritual quotient.

Divinatory Meaning: A wise counselor. Spiritual fulfillment. Introspective man.

Reversed: Identity crisis. Loss of faith. Should the reversed Hierophant appear in the same spread with the King or Queen of Wands it would indicate that the person had been seeing a psychiatrist or some other type of counselor.

Arcanum VI
The Lovers

Some Tarot decks depict only a man and a woman but in most packs Arcanum VI depicts a youth and two women. The older woman is said to be the youth's mother, the younger one, his lover. The youth has reached a crossroad in his life and must choose between them. It is not an easy choice for the young man to make for the road his mother is standing on represents security and the known; the path of his lover, adventure and the unknown. A difficult choice, yes, but a necessary one and in this case there will be help from the gods for Eros—or Cupid, as he is more commonly known —is about to release his Freudian shaft in the youth's direction. Cupid's role in this scenario is indeed interesting for the youth and two women may be seen as human types whereas he is a god. As allegory the message of the card seems to be that when we reach a crossroad of the life and wonder which road to take we can get help from the world of Spirit if we will open ourselves to it.

This card in divination may or may not depict actual lovers.

Divinatory Meaning: A time of decision.

Reversed: Inability to make a choice or face a decision.

Arcanum VII
The Chariot

As Arcanum VII, The Chariot could be seen mythologically as the product of Arcanum II, The High Priestess or Isis, and Arcanum V, The Hierophant, who (as Osiris) in the Eleusinian rite copulated with The High Priestess. The Charioteer then could be taken as Horus, the Sun God, driving the chariot of the sun. This may prove a difficult task for him as The Chariot is being pulled by two sleepy sphinx-like creatures and a sphinx is not usually noted for speed and mobility. The two creatures are clearly quite different and may be seen as conflicting inner forces. If The Chariot is taken to be the vehicle of personality for the driver, this can be seen as a critical time in the life for he has to reconcile these opposing forces before he can drive down life's road. He seems to be on the right track for the three stars on his crown suggest an integration of the forces that comprise personality—Id, Ego, and Superego. The fact that they appear on his crown indicates that basically he is comfortable with himself but total integration only comes through work. That he is ultimately successful is clear from the card's meaning.

Divinatory Meaning: Victory.

Reversed: Dark victory. Defeat.

Arcanum VIII
Justice

The figure in Arcanum VIII is rather formidable for in addition to the scales she holds in her left hand, in her right hand she wields the "terrible swift sword" of Divine Justice. Unlike human justice which is blind, this deity can take your measure with unerring accuracy. Actually, the whole idea of Divine Justice stems from the Egyptian belief that every soul—regardless of the class, rank, or station it occupied in life—was to be judged by Osiris. After death the soul was weighed in the balance against the feather of Maat, Goddess of Truth. To pass the test the dead person's conscience had to weigh exactly the same as the feather, so that the scales were in perfect equilibrium. Someone has said that it is not injustice we fear, but justice. We need not fear Divine Justice, however, for she helps us to find the proper balance for maintaining equilibrium and harmony in our lives.

Divinatory Meaning: Balance or imbalance depending upon the surrounding cards.

Reversed: The meaning is much the same, only slightly less so.

Arcanum IX
The Hermit

Having learned the balance of Justice, The Hermit teaches caution. He is afraid of the condemnation of others—criticism from those who do not understand—so he hides his light under his cloak. Essentially, he is in search of truth and since this is usually not a group activity, he appears solitary and withdrawn, treading the lonely path of his pilgrimage although he is at the same time a light and beacon to others. Jung talked about four basic stages of life: Childhood, Youth and Young Adulthood, Middle Age, and Old Age. He felt that the first major transformation of the individual occurs around puberty when the individual undergoes a "psychic revolution" and the psyche takes on a new shape and the individual emerges as a new person. Jung referred to this as a "psychic birth" and he felt that it was the single most important stage in a person's life. He pointed out that this occurs again during middle age and the man or woman over thirty-five must then meet the challenge of reordering the life around a new set of values—and Jung felt that they must be spiritual values. The Lovers' card could be seen as the "psychic birth" of the adolescent, and The Hermit as the psychic revolution of middle age. This might be thought of as the "Wilderness Card."

Divinatory Meaning: A searching. Spiritual renewal. Highly cautious individual.

Reversed: Rashness. Someone indiscreet or out of control.

la Roue de Fortune

Arcanum X
The Wheel of Fortune

The golden creature ascending on the right is thought to be Anubis, the dog-faced god of Egypt who weighed the souls of the dead. The bizarre figure descending on the left is said to be Typhon, the god of destruction and disintegration. Anubis is considered a positive force whereas Typhon is a negative force. It is the old story of good versus evil. The sphinx guarding the wheel reminds us of Arcanum VII, The Chariot, and the two sphinx types pulling the chariot of personality. Those sphinxes, remember, represented opposing forces within the personality that needed to be reconciled. Here again in Arcanum X is a depiction of the yin and yang principle and the need to integrate. What is interesting is that the opposing forces on the card are on the wheel, which is a mandala and a symbol of psychic wholeness, an indication that the super-structure for harmony is there.

Divinatory Meaning: A turn in one's fortunes for the better.

Reversed: The beginning of an unhappy or unlucky period.

Arcanum XI
The Enchantress

This card is known by several names including Fortitude and Strength. The Enchantress, however, suggests an allusion to Circe, the great enchantress in *The Odyssey* who turned men into animals. The card is numbered 11 which in numerology is considered a Master Number. People born under this vibration often have great difficulties to contend against. If, however, they live at the highest level of their being and rise above petty things and petty people they become "messengers of light." The Enchantress, although she appears to be in great danger, seems quite relaxed as she proceeds to close the jaws of the lion. She does not have to use brute strength for she has learned the lesson of The Wheel; she knows who she is; and in any situation she is able to remain calm and poised for she can now rely on her inner *strength*.

Divinatory Meaning: Inner strength. Difficult period in the life. Aggressive woman.

Reversed: Difficulty coping. Sexual perversion. If the reversed Enchantress appears with The Empress, The Emperor, or the Three of Cups, it would indicate sexual difficulties in the marriage.

Arcanum XII
The Hanged Man

In Arcanum XI, The Enchantress, although having an encounter with "the king of beasts," remained cool and collected. In Arcanum XII, The Hanged Man does not appear to be in a particularly comfortable position, suspended as he is by one foot from a gibbet. But like The Enchantress, The Hanged Man appears cool and relaxed. The position of The Hanged Man may indicate that the conventional values of society are topsy-turvy and that truth is the reverse of what most people think it is. In this position, the eyes of The Hanged Man are on the heavens, which suggests that the seeker after truth must concern her- or himself with the laws of the universe rather than the laws of society and, in a reversal of values, spiritually and psychologically stand on his or her head. This is not easy to do.

Divinatory Meaning: Sacrifice. Reverses. Total change of values.

Reversed: A grim omen for it would indicate that the individual was unable or unwilling to drop old habits and ways or make a needed sacrifice.

Arcanum XIII
The Reaper

When Arcanum XIII comes up in a spread it is usually greeted with a grimace for it is known to be "the death card" and in some packs it is labeled "Death." In most packs the imagery is rather vivid for The Grim Reaper appears as a skeleton wielding a scythe while engaging in the dance of death. If the truth be told, there are certain cards in the Minor Arcana that are closer to being "death cards"—at least, in the sense of physical death. In general, this is a positive card in divination for the type of death depicted is the ending of things in the life that need to leave the life so that other things can take their place. In actuality, The Reaper is not so much an outside force as he is the individual who reaps what s/he has sown. Since The Reaper is doing his dance of death in a green and fertile field, the card is really an image of the continuity of life in nature in which death is part of a cycle of life, death and life renewed.

Divinatory Meaning: Change. Reaping what one has sown.

Reversed: Inability to accept or make necessary changes.

Arcanum XIV
The Angel of Time

Temperance is the name some students of the Tarot give to this card but The Angel of Time seems more descriptive for according to Jung, "An angel personifies the coming into consciousness of something new arising from the deep unconscious." That "something new" may be suggested by the card's association with Aquarius, who in ancient Egypt was called Hapi, the god of the Nile, who ruled over both the agricultural waters that gave life to the soil and the spiritual waters that nourished the soul. Since The Angel of Time is pouring waters from a blue urn into a red one. This card could be seen as another depiction of the fusion of opposites. In this case, it is the unity of conscious and unconscious forces, which manifest as a pure liquid, suggesting free-flowing energy.

Divinatory Meaning: Regeneration. Renewed inner harmony and a more loving and understanding acceptance of others.

Reversed: Disenchantment with a change. Failure to accept or to understand others.

Arcanum XV
The Devil

According to Baudelaire, "The Devil's cleverest wile is to convince us that he doesn't exist." The Devil is only too real as a sleepy glance at the front page of any newspaper any day anywhere will tell you. Throughout all recorded history, a major problem in capturing and destroying him has been that he is a master of disguise. But there is a surefire method for penetrating his disguise: Throw a Tarot spread for yourself and if the card of The Devil comes up, simply go over to the mirror and take a long hard look at yourself and you will see him. Jung talked about the "Shadow," meaning a secret part of ourself which we need to confront if we are to become fully integrated human beings. In her fascinating work, *Jung and Tarot,* Sallie Nichols states that The Devil does have one redeeming feature and that is the golden antlers that he wears as "Horns are an ancient symbol for new life and spiritual regeneration, and golden antlers are specifically symbolic of divine fire." Rehabilitation in this case has to be an "inside job." If you are successful you can restore him to his original calling which was "Lucifer, the Messenger of Light."

Divinatory Meaning: Fear. Division within the self. Evil influences at work.

Reversed: Much the same, only slightly less so.

la Maison Dieu y

Arcanum XVI
The Lightning-Struck Tower

When someone comes up with a bright idea we often refer to the inspiration as "being hit by lightning." Arcanum XVI could be read as "the eureka card"— an instance of divine inspiration. Not everyone can reverse values with the calm and serenity of The Hanged Man and for some the only method for change is to get hit by lightning, which supposedly is why Martin Luther left the law and became a priest. The two figures on the card are head-downward like The Hanged Man. It is a reversal of their life. The ground has been cut out from under them so as to force them into building a new foundation with a broader base.

As on the card of The Reaper, one figure is humble, the other wears a crown. Material position counts for nought when spiritual progression is at stake.

Divinatory Meaning: Psychological crisis. Accident or disaster. The possibility of accident is greatly increased if The Tower appears in the same spread with the Three, Seven, or Nine of Swords.

Reversed: Still a crisis but slightly less so.

Arcanum XVII
The Star

The large shining star of Arcanum XVII is said to be Sirius, the star of Isis, which was connected with the Nile flood which brought new life to the land. We are reminded of Arcanum XIV, The Angel of Time, associated with Hapi, god of the Nile and the two waters, agricultural and spiritual. As was the case with The Angel of Time, the figure on this card holds two urns. But instead of pouring one into the other, she is pouring one into a pool of water and the other onto earth, suggesting that she has succeeded in finding the correct balance between things material and things spiritual. In addition to the large star at the top of the card, there are seven lesser stars. In works on alchemy, similar configurations are depicted, the smaller stars representing the seven stages of the alchemical process culminating in the "philosopher's gold"—the great star representing self-enlightenment. This is a positive card in divination.

Divinatory Meaning: Hope. New lease on life.

Reversed: Death of a dream.

Arcanum XVIII
The Moon

Arcanum XVIII might be considered the "Dark Night of the Soul." At the top of the card shines the waning moon of illusion. She sheds her light upon a winding path which leads between two towers to the Eternal City. But to reach that destination will not be easy for there is a moat to cross in which resides a gigantic beetle said to be Kheperer, the Egyptian scarab. Guarding the tower are two jackals, most likely in the employ of the evil goddess Hecate, who can tear an individual limb from limb. Hecate's cousin is the demure moon goddess, Artemis, who as Luna can drive men to lunacy. The pilgrim is at a critical stage of life's journey for if s/he allows him-/herself to be caught up in the spell and glamour of The Moon, s/he will never find the true insight and will end his/her days in illusion.

Divinatory Meaning: Deception. Delays. Illusion.

Reversed: Individual has been led astray but is "beginning to see the light."

Arcanum XIX
The Sun

The moon country of the preceding Arcanum was dark, mysterious and fraught with hidden dangers. But here in Arcanum XIX, two children, a boy and a girl, are playing under a radiant smiling sun. Their costumes are brief for they have nothing to hide and are at ease with themselves and each other. Significantly, the boy's outfit is red, the girl's is blue, suggesting once again the yin and yang principle. But where opposites appeared on other cards they were in the guise of sphinxes or monsters—and always apart. Here the boy and girl are touching and interacting in a very human way. The fence bordering their garden—which could be seen as a lost Eden—is constructed of both blue and red stones, further reinforcing the concept of opposing forces that have been reconciled. The fact that the figures on the card are children suggests that if one is to "be together" and find happiness in this world it is necessary to restore contact with what Jung called the "eternal child" in oneself. It is a very good sign when The Sun comes out in a spread.

Divinatory Meaning: Paradise found. The love of the life. Filling up with happiness.

Reversed: Paradise lost.

Arcanum XX
Day of Judgment

According to the ancient teachings, when the last trump shall sound, in a moment, in the twinkling of an eye, the dead would rise from their graves to be judged and then sent to heaven or hell. It has been said that heaven and hell most surely do exist but they are not somewhere "above" or "below," rather, they are what we build each day of our lives by the thought forms we create and the way we treat ourselves and others. We cannot give heaven to others if we are in our own personal hell. The fact that the three human figures on the card are rising from coffins suggests that life was death for them because they were blind to the heaven around them. Their eyes, however, have been opened and so have their ears for they are heeding the call of Michael, the angel of the last trump. And the music they hear is truly "heavenly" for they have become spiritually attuned. The three component parts of the personality which need to function as a unit if the person is to be psychologically whole, may be represented by these human figures of a man, a woman, and a child. The indication is that the opposites within have been reconciled and all systems integrated.

Divinatory Meaning: Decision of the utmost importance is in the making.

Reversed: Failure to rise to a challenge.

Arcanum XXI
The World

Someone has suggested that The World card stands for cosmic consciousness, or what Freud called "the oceanic feeling." Unlike The Reaper who was carrying out his mechanical dance of death, the beauteous maiden of The World is engaged in a spontaneous, free-flowing dance of life. This stands for joy, harmony, and the orderly course of the universe and time. The World's number is 21, the reverse of 12, which is the number of The Hanged Man. If you turn the card of The Hanged Man around, he appears to be dancing a jig. The dancing woman's legs form a cross, as the legs of The Hanged Man also do, but where he is upside down, she is right side up. The implication is that she represents The Hanged Man's original starting point and his ultimate goal. In her hands she holds both the solar and lunar wands, indicating that now the two are one. She dances, lives, and has her being within a laurel wreath which forms a mandala. By tapping the "eternal child" within, responding to the trumpet call from on high, the pilgrim hears the music of the morning stars and dances for joy.

Divinatory Meaning: Joy.

Reversed: A karmic bill falls due. It will be a trying period but one necessary for inner growth.

le fou 𝔴

The Unnumbered Card
The Fool

When The Fool comes up at the end of a spread the interpretive meaning is rather different than if he comes up at the beginning for he has stumbled and faltered and had his falls but each time he has jumped up, dusted himself off, and kept going on his journey. He has learned from his experiences and has grown outwardly and inwardly. At the beginning of the Tarot sequence he was nothing—a cipher—but now he is Arcanum XXII and 22 in numerology is the ultimate Master Number and often the number of the master. In the eyes of everyday mortals a fool is considered to be a child. And The Fool of the Tarot is more a child than most fools but that is the secret of his power. He is unfettered, moves spontaneously, and sees everything afresh with a childlike sense of awe and wonder. He is a fool only in the eyes of the world, within himself he is sublime. When he appears at or near the end of a spread it is significant.

Divinatory Meaning: The magus, or wise fool, has had more than his share of challenges and hurts but has grown in wisdom and humanity.

Reversed: In the approximate center of a spread, confusion or conflict. At or near the end of a spread, consultant has made an attempt to sort out his or her experiences but still has a way to go.

Part Two

Tarot Spreads: Questions of Concern

This section provides spreads which address any questions the consultant might have with regard to love, marriage, finances, travel, health, career, or any other immediate concern. Prior to consultant's arrival, the reader should check the Tarot pack to make sure that it is complete and that all cards are in an upright position.

Opening a Reading

A reading may vary from a few minutes to several hours. The average reading, however, takes between a half hour to an hour. Some readers prefer to do only one spread and go into each card in depth. Most readers, however, employ a variety of spreads and will throw four to eight spreads during the course of a reading. The particular spreads used in a given reading will depend on several factors but particularly the type of questions the consultant brings to the reading.

No two readers will use exactly the same method; what is important is that once you discover what feels right for you, it is a good idea to follow that same procedure in all the readings you do. Remember, a Tarot pack is a magickal tool and one of the cardinal rules of magick is that the best results are obtained by repeating a ritual as closely as possible to the way it was done before.

The exact method that you employ will only come through experience but here is a good one to start with: Ask consultant to concentrate on a question and while this is being done, shuffle the pack thoroughly. (In a Tarot reading the person being read is called the "consultant" or "querent"; the individual conducting the reading is called the "reader.") Then hand the pack to consultant and ask her or him to reverse three cards—that is, the individual will fan through the pack, turn a card around and do that with two other cards, but will leave the cards in the pack facing the same way as the rest of the pack. If after the cutting and shuffling, one of these three cards comes up, it will be significant.

The next step is to ask, "Are you right-handed or left-handed?" If the consultant replies, "Right-handed," you then say, "With your *left* hand, separate the pack into three piles and shuffle each. If the response is "Left-handed," you then ask the person to cut with the right hand. In other words, the consultant cuts with the *unconscious* hand rather than the *calculating* hand. The consultant does not have to use the unconscious hand to shuffle the cards but you should demonstrate the shuffling process so that it will be accomplished in a manner that does not reverse cards, i.e., overhand as opposed to dove-tailing.

When the shuffling has been completed, ask consultant to put the pack back together, again using the unconscious hand. You then pick up the deck and are ready to throw your first spread. You may use any spread you wish to open a reading but you will probably find that some work better than others. Most readers have their favorite openers and the two described below have been found to be particularly effective for different reasons. In Three Faces of Time, consultant personally selects each card in the spread whereas The Horseshoe Spread almost invariably focuses on the central issue or problem with the very first card the reader turns over. Here are the directions for both spreads:

Three Faces of Time

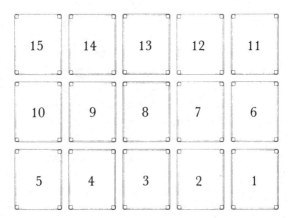

Following the cutting and shuffling ritual, fan the cards face down on the table forming a semi-circle. Ask consultant to concentrate on the question and while doing this to select cards. You might say something like this: "Pick up cards one at a time and then hand each one to me face down. Do not worry about how many; I will tell you when to stop." You, of course, know that there are fifteen cards you are going to use in this spread but you do not tell consultant that for then the tendency would be to concentrate on the number of cards rather than the question.

When you have fifteen cards that you have received from consultant, say, "Fine, that is enough," and put the rest of the pack aside. Hand the selected cards to consultant for shuffling (no cutting is necessary this time). Consultant then hands the cards back to you and you throw the spread according to the diagram. Notice that there are three horizontal rows indicating Past, Present and Future, and that you begin with the bottom row of the Past and lay the cards face down from right to left. Unless otherwise specified, in all spreads, always start with the top card of the deck, then the one below that, and so on.

You may begin the actual reading by turning over the center card of the Present row. That is the key card of the Present as are the other center cards the keys to the Past and Future. So first read and interpret the center card of the Present and then do the same with the center cards of the Past and Future rows.

When these three cards have been read and interpreted, go to the row of the Past and turn over and read each card individually in the sequence they were thrown. Then do the same with the Present and Future rows. When you have turned over and read all cards individually, look at the total configuration of all three time lines. Is there a particular emphasis on the Major Arcana? Court cards? Any one suit of the Minor Arcana that is heavily weighted? In the first instance, the question would have largely to do with consultant's state of mind; in the second, other people would be the dominating factor; in the third, the primary indicator would be the area ascribed to the suit of the Minor Arcana emphasized, so that Wands, for example, would suggest that the question had to do with work or career. Overall, what patterns are significant? Is the spread basically positive or negative? If it is about half and half, are the negative cards largely in the past and the positive cards in the future? If so, that is definitely something to focus on.

NOTE: It is important to be honest about what you see but it is even more important to be constructive. Remember, the consultant has come to you for help, not bad news. You cannot always tell the person what he or she wants to hear but you can present what you see in a manner that will be helpful.

The Horseshoe Spread

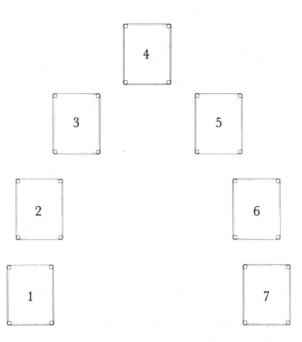

There are seven cards in this spread and after the consultant has cut and shuffled, throw the spread according to the diagram. Starting with card # 1, turn over each card separately, read and interpret it, and following in sequence, do the same with each card until all have been read. The meanings of each card are as follows:

Card #1—**Past:** This may be the immediate past, or it may go further back in time.

Card #2—**Present:** Immediate present.

Card #3—**Immediate Future.**

Card #4—**Card of Consultant:** Something on consultant's mind.

Card #5—**Attitude of Another:** This will usually be a person known to consultant and somehow connected with the question.

Card #6—**Obstacle:** If a favorable card comes up in this slot it would indicate that there is no real obstacle to overcome; if unfavorable, it would describe the type of obstacle consultant has to face.

Card #7—**Outcome:** This will be the logical culmination of the other cards in the spread.

NOTE: If this is to be the opening spread of the reading, it can be quite dramatic to begin by turning over the Card of the Consultant—Card #4.What is on consultant's mind is often the key to a reading.

Using a Significator

A significator is a card selected to represent the consultant. There are any number of methods for choosing a significator. In the following spread, the Eastern Cross, The Empress is always used for a woman, The Emperor for a man. In the second spread, the Celtic Cross, an astrological method may be used. The reader may also select a card that seems to be sympathetic with the consultant, or to allow the consultant to choose a card with which he or she can identify.

A spread employing a significator can be used at any point in the reading, but the time to do so particularly is when the reading appears to be somewhat out of focus or incoherent. A significator acts much in the manner of a television antenna and attracts focused energy to the spread.

Eastern Cross

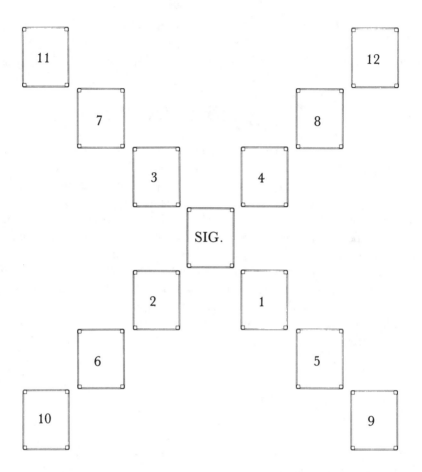

Begin by taking the significator out of the pack, The Empress for a female, The Emperor for a male. Most likely, the historical reason for this is that the shape of the spread forms the type of cross used in the Eastern Orthodox Church, and it was the emperor and empress of the Byzantine Empire who became the dominant Christian rulers when Constantinople became "the second Rome" and the world headquarters for Christianity.

After the significator has been removed from the deck, place it face up in the center of the table. Then hand the pack to the consultant and ask that the deck be cut into six piles. Next ask the consultant to shuffle each pile separately. Then take each pile, remove the top and bottom cards and discard the rest. When you have done this, hand the twelve remaining cards to consultant and request that this pile be shuffled. When this has been done throw the spread according to the diagram.

Once the cross has been formed, you then dismantle it with the exception of the pillars of the cross—cards numbered 9, 10, 11, and 12. Lay the other cards aside and arrange the four cards that will actually be read on both sides of the significator in this fashion:

The sequence and meanings for the reading are as follows:

Card #11—Past

Card #10—Card of Consultant

Card #9—Immediate Future

Card #12—Outcome

Celtic Cross

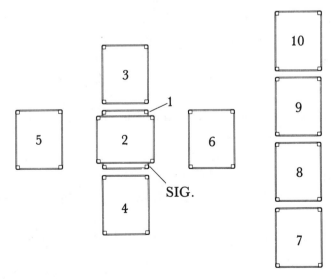

This is quite possibly the most popular Tarot spread for it packs a great deal of information into a few cards and is usually right on target. It is an excellent first spread. It is also a good concluding spread. And if you are only going to do one spread for the consultant, this one is ideal.

If you wish to choose a significator based on astrological association, first find out the consultant's Sun sign and age. You need at least a rough idea of consultant's age so that you can choose a Court Card from one of the four suits of the Minor Arcana to represent the consultant. Use a page for a man or woman under thirty-five, a king for a man over thirty-five, and a queen for a woman over thirty-five. Each astrological sign is associated with a suit of the Minor Arcana as follows:

Fire Signs—Aries, Leo, Sagittarius: Wands

Earth Signs—Taurus, Virgo, Capricorn: Swords

Air Signs—Gemini, Libra, Aquarius: Coins

Water Signs—Cancer, Scorpio, Pisces: Cups

So, if for example, you are doing a reading for a fortyish man who is a native of Sagittarius, you would use the King of Wands as the consultant's correct significator card.

After the significator has been removed from the pack, place it face up in the center of the table. When consultant has cut and shuffled and returned the pack to you, throw a spread according to the diagram. As you lay each card down, think or say aloud the following litany:

Card   #1— "This covers him." (Covering influence in the life at the moment)

Card   #2— "This crosses him." (Obstacle)

Card   #3— "This is above him." (The best that can be expected under the circumstances)

Card   #4— "This is below him." (Foundation of the question)

Card   #5— "This is behind him." (Past)

Card   #6— "This is before him." (Immediate future)

Card   #7— "This *is* him at this moment in time." (Card of consultant)

Card   #8— "This is for his house and home." (Immediate family)

Card   #9— "This is for his hopes and fears." (How expectations will be met)

Card #10— "And this is everything and all." (Card of Culmination)

Getting the Big Picture

Any of the following three spreads are informative when you are planning to do only one spread for a reading. They are also good when consultant has a number of things operating in the life for these spreads have a way of answering several questions at once.

The Pyramid Spread

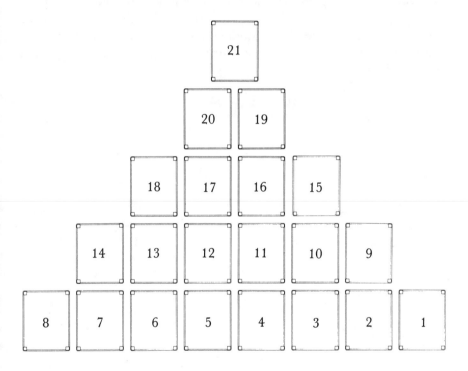

This is a particularly good spread for a question that goes well back or well ahead in time—or both. Follow the plan of the diagram by starting in the lower right hand corner of the table and lay eight cards face down going from right to left. Continue with this procedure in the ascending rows of respectively six, four, and two cards, and then the final card becomes the top of the pyramid. Starting at the lower right hand corner, count five cards and turn over the fifth card. Counting that card as one, repeat this procedure four more times until you have turned over the cards numbered 9, 13, 17, and 21. In each case, the card turned over represents the key to a particular time period. The time lines are as follows:

Cards #1–5—Distant Past

Cards #6–9—Past

Cards #10–13—Present

Cards #14–17—Immediate Future

Cards #18–20—Future

Card #21—Outcome

The method to follow is to start by reading card #5, the key to the Distant Past, then turn over cards #1–4 and interpret them in light of card # 5. Do the same with each successive time line. The card at the top of the pyramid should be studied and interpreted with particular care for it not only represents the outcome but it ties everything in the spread together.

Wheel of Fortune

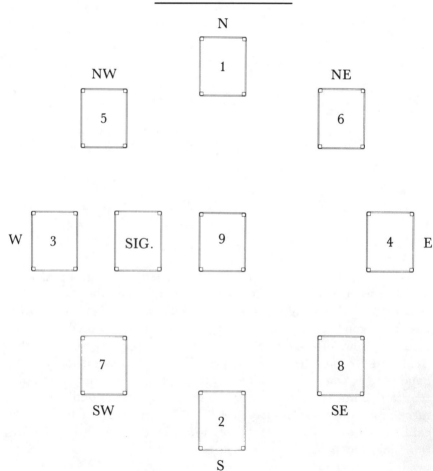

Choose a significator, using any of the methods suggested earlier and place it face up in the center of the table. This spread is in the shape of a compass, hence, the name. It is called the Wheel of Fortune and should that card appear in the spread it would be of special significance.

After consultant has cut and shuffled, take the top three cards from the pack and place them in the form of a fan face down in the pile designated #1 according to the diagram, which would correspond to the North on a compass. Continue this procedure of laying three cards at a time at the various compass points until you have eight piles on the rim of the wheel. The ninth pile you then place in the center of the compass to the right of the significator.

As you throw this spread think or say aloud the following:

Pile #1—"Three above you." (Covering influence)

Pile #2—"Three below you." (Matters in control of consultant)

Pile #3—"Three behind you." (Past)

Pile #4—"Three before you." (Immediate Future)

Pile #5—"Three for your house and home."

Pile #6—"Three for your hopes and fears."

Pile #7—"Three for what you *do* expect."

Pile #8—"Three for what you do *not* expect."

Pile #9—"And three for what is sure to come."

The Gypsy Spread

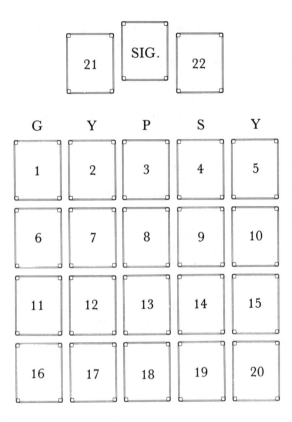

In this spread The Magician is used as a significator so he should be removed from the pack and placed face up at the top of the table before handing the deck to consultant for cutting and shuffling.

When pack has been returned to you, fan the cards on the table, forming a semi-circle, and ask consultant to choose twenty-two at random, one at a time, face down. After this has been done ask consultant to shuffle just those twenty-two cards and put the rest of the pack aside. Next throw the spread according to diagram the noting that you start with the top row and lay the cards from left to right. Card #20 completes the fourth horizontal row, and cards #21 and 22 go, respectively, to the left and right of significator.

You may, if you wish, as a memory aid, imagine the word "Gypsy" over the five vertical rows, so that cards #1, 6, 11, and 16 would be under the "G", cards #2, 7, 12, and 17 would be under the first "Y", and so on. Note that the cards are read in *vertical rows* starting with the "G" in "Gypsy" and ending with the final "Y" in that word. Following are the meanings for each row:

G (Cards #1,6,11,16)—**Gateway:** Questions under contemplation

Y (Cards #2,7,12,17)—**Yin:** Issues to meditate upon before taking action

P (Cards #3,8,13,18)—**Partnership:** Home and Career

S (Cards #4,9,14,19)—**Self:** Present psychic state of consultant

Y (Cards #5,10,15,20)—**Yang:** Issues to give the name of action

The final cards to be read are the ones on either side of the significator:

Card #21—Expectations of consultant

Card #22—To what extent consultant's expectations will be realized

Answering Questions Concerning Health

If consultant has a health problem, is contemplating an operation, or is simply concerned about his or her health, the following spreads are just what the doctor did not order but maybe should have. The first spread—Dr. Zodiac—is extremely accurate and if the health picture it presents is generally favorable, you can reassure the consultant and then turn to some other type of question. If, however, there does appear to be a serious health problem or if there is a decision to be made about having an operation, the thing to do is to proceed further and do the Planetary Mansions spread.

Dr. Zodiac

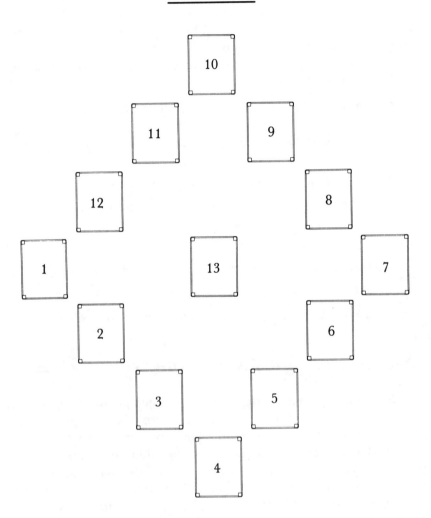

This spread deals with the signs of the zodiac and the parts of the body they rule, which are as follows:

Pile #1—Aries: Head and shoulders

Pile #2—Taurus: Throat

Pile #3—Gemini: Bronchial tubes, collarbone, fingers, arms, nervous system

Pile #4—Cancer: Breast, stomach

Pile #5—Leo: Heart, side, upper back

Pile #6—Virgo: Bowels, solar plexus

Pile   #7—Libra: Kidneys, lower back

Pile   #8—Scorpio: Sex organs, pelvis, bladder

Pile   #9—Sagittarius: Hips, thighs, liver

Pile #10—Capricorn: Knees, bony structure

Pile #11—Aquarius: Calves, ankles, bodily fluids

Pile #12—Pisces: Feet, psychic faculties

Pile #13—Overall Health

Begin the reading by turning over the cards in the first pile for Aries, and after reading and interpreting those, continue around the zodiac. Do not look for literal meanings of the cards in this spread but rather do the reading intuitively. Negative cards such as the suit of Swords would indicate the problem areas; mainly positive cards in a pile would suggest consultant is free and clear with regard to that portion of the body. A pattern of Sword cards combined with negative Major Arcana cards in a pile would indicate a given affliction was psychosomatic in nature. The final four cards in the center offer an overall picture of the health throughout life. The whole spread really hinges on these four cards and if they are positive, consultant essentially has nothing to worry about. This may appear a contradiction if a number of negative cards are scattered through the signs but in practice you will find it is not. Remember, this spread deals with the entire life and many people, who enjoy sound health in their mature years, had more than the usual number of childhood sicknesses. One pattern to look for: If Sword cards appear and are generally accompanied by one or more Tarot Trumps, the mental state of consultant is all-important as to whether or not a particular affliction manifests.

Planetary Mansions

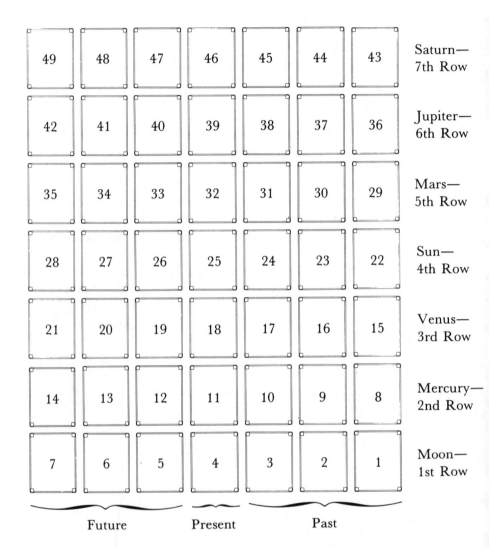

49	48	47	46	45	44	43	Saturn—7th Row
42	41	40	39	38	37	36	Jupiter—6th Row
35	34	33	32	31	30	29	Mars—5th Row
28	27	26	25	24	23	22	Sun—4th Row
21	20	19	18	17	16	15	Venus—3rd Row
14	13	12	11	10	9	8	Mercury—2nd Row
7	6	5	4	3	2	1	Moon—1st Row

Future   Present   Past

This spread is reminiscent of the "Chaldean order" of antiquity, which was concerned with the seven original planets and the afffairs of life they governed. If done thoroughly, the Planetary Mansions spread could easily constitute an entire reading. It is the logical follow-up to the preceding spread, for Dr. Zodiac *diagnoses* and pinpoints the health problem but this spread gets to the root of the matter and *prescribes* what needs to be done. You may wish to do only a superficial reading of the Mansions that are not of immediate concern to consultant and give a careful interpretation of the ones that are concerned with health. But do not be too hasty for more often than not, a health condition is related to something such as family or career and that could only be ascertained by a closer reading of all Mansions. The affairs ruled by each of the seven planets of antiquity are as follows:

Moon—1st Mansion: The home, women in general, the public, and if consultant is a man, his wife.

Mercury—2nd Mansion: Writing, intellectual activities, travel, brothers and sisters.

Venus—3rd Mansion: Love, partnerships, life style, friends.

Sun—4th Mansion: Health and vitality, honor, superiors, men in general, and if consultant is a woman, her husband.

Mars—5th Mansion: Creative energies, sexuality, accidents, strife, afflictions, and enemies.

Jupiter—6th Mansion: Religion, professional people, business, employment, speculation and gambling.

Saturn—7th Mansion: Sickness, old age, real estate, losses, disappointments, secret enemies.

Throw the spread according to the diagram. If you are going to interpret all the cards in the spread, start with the first Mansion of the Moon and read from right to left. In each Mansion the first three cards deal with the past, the middle card deals with the present, and the final three cards deal with the future.

Seven Tarot Trumps have planetary associations. Should a corresponding card come up in the Mansion it is linked with, it would be significant as an indication that the affairs of that Mansion are essentially benevolent. The correspondences follow:

Moon—The Chariot

Mercury—The Magician

Venus—The Empress

Sun—The Sun

Mars—The Emperor

Jupiter—The Angel of Time

Saturn—The World

Finding Answers to Difficult Questions

Most readings proceed on course, and before an hour has passed the consultant's questions have largely been picked up by the Tarot and answered with a reasonable degree of satisfaction. On occasion, however, this does not happen. Sometimes the cards seem to be elusive or vague and do not suggest a clear direction or interpretation. There are a number of reasons for this. For example, in a given question there may be so many variables operating that it is simply not possible to answer the question at the time of the reading. This, in fact, is often the case. But what you need to know at that point in the reading is whether or not the question *can* be answered at that time. The first of the following spreads, Opening the Key, will provide an immediate yes or no, and if the answer is yes, will answer the question in a rather interesting and elaborate way.

The second, The Churchyard Spread, is somewhat different in nature, for in addition to saying yes or no, it will indicate whether the question is the real question or only a *cul de sac*. If the question is not worth pursuing or if there is a deeper or more significant question, The Churchyard Spread will bring it to light.

NOTE: It is best in a given reading to throw only one of these two spreads if you get a "No" answer the first time around. For if the Tarot tells you, "No, that question cannot be answered at the present time," it would be pointless to ask it a second time.

Opening the Key

First, decide upon a significator but leave it in the pack. After consultant has shuffled, request that the pack be placed upon the table and then he or she should cut the deck *to the left* into two piles, and following, each of these two piles should be cut to the left again. From right to left (instructions are always from reader's point of view) these piles correspond to the four suits of the Minor Arcana, which cover the following:

Coins—Money, possessions

Wands—Matters of work and business

Cups—Love, marriage, pleasure

Swords—Troubles, afflictions, sorrow, losses

Now look through the pile corresponding to the type of question asked but be careful not to disturb the order of the cards should you receive a "Yes" answer. The significator should be in this pile. If it is not, abandon the question for at least twelve hours.

But if the significator does appear in the correct pile—and it will, surprisingly often—you must now fan the cards in a circle face up with the significator at the top, taking care to preserve the order of the cards. You must now isolate certain cards in the circle by counting from the significator in the direction he or she is looking. (If the significator is full face, count to the left of it.) Here is the numerical procedure to follow:

For kings, queens, and knights, count 4

For pages, count 7

For aces, count 11

For a small card of the Minor Arcana, count its own number

For The Fool, The Hanged Man, and Day of Judgment, count 3

For the other Trumps, count 12

Let us say that the circle has been formed with the significator at the top, which is the Queen of Cups. We know that queens count 4 so we start by counting her as the first card and moving to the left (counterclockwise). We stop at the fourth card and move it slightly out of the circle so we will know it has been counted. If that card is the Nine of Wands, we start our count with it, continue moving counterclockwise until we have counted nine cards, and the ninth card we nudge slightly so we know it has been counted. Continue the process until you reach a card you have stopped on before. Now, starting with the first counted card to the right of the significator and moving *clockwise,* read only those cards on which you landed. If the answer is clear, well and good. If not, you can pursue the question further in the following spread.

The Churchyard Spread

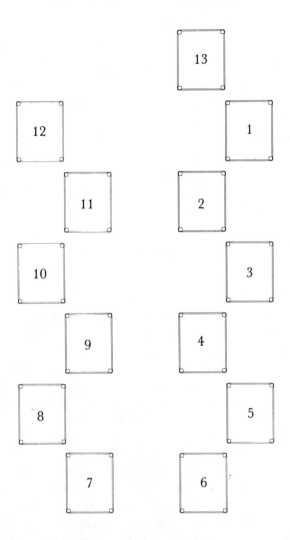

Earlier it was suggested that the reader start with Opening the Key and possibly continuing with this spread in the event of a ''Yes'' answer. But this spread would actually be the better one to start with if you feel there is a hidden agenda in the reading and that the consultant is not being entirely honest with you—and, more likely, with him- or herself— by concentrating on what you perceive as a relatively unimportant question. Sometimes the consultant is afraid to ask it; sometimes s/he just does not know it. This is certainly not unusual as it is quite difficult to unravel the component parts of major problems or questions. It is part of the human condition to lock some things away in the unconscious and not be aware one has done so.

Essentially, this spread will do one of two things: It will either say, "Yes, your question *is* important and this is what can be said about it at the present time." The information given may be abundant or scanty, depending upon other factors but if the latter, consultant will at least know that the question is worth pursuing further.

Or it will say, "Look, this is not the question you need to be asking: Here is the real one. . . . " Actually, in practice, it does not always work out quite that neatly and another possibility is that consultant will discover that his or her question is not trivial, but only that it is part of something larger that had not been taken into account.

In this spread The Fool is used as a significator so begin by removing him from the pack. After consultant has cut and shuffled, take the top twelve cards for the spread and place the rest of the deck aside. Then put The Fool face down in the approximate center of the twelve-card pile and hand it to consultant for further shuffling.

Next, lay the spread according to the diagram. Turn all the cards over and note the position of The Fool. If he appears at or near the end of the spread, the indication is that the question is indeed primary and the other cards will speak to that question. If, however, The Fool appears at or near the beginning of the spread, the indicator is that the question is not worth pursuing—at least, at this time—and the real question starts with the first card following The Fool. Once you have interpreted the question, read only those cards that follow The Fool in the sequence that the spread was thrown.

Looking at the Year Ahead

The following are mainly future time spreads and are most helpful in providing the consultant with the type of information needed to prepare for the year ahead.

The Horoscope Spread

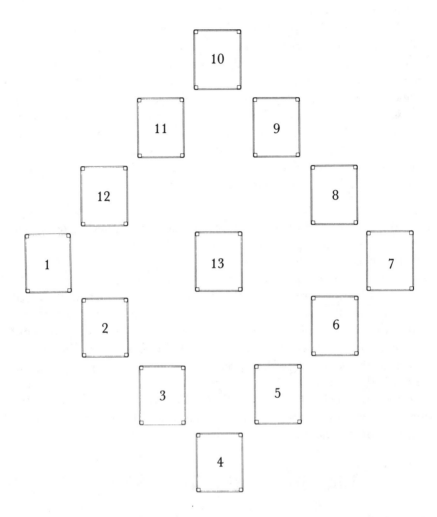

This spread is a good one to do if consultant is near a birthday and it works in much the same way that a solar return chart does in astrology. If consultant has celebrated a birthday in the recent past, you could set it up for the time of the last birthday and the spread would encompass past, present, and future. It is important, however, that you, the reader, decide *before* the cards are shuffled what twelve-month period you wish to look at. If more than six months have gone by since the consultant's last birthday, it is usually best to project it ahead to the next one. In other words, what this spread will do is to describe influences starting around the time of a natal day and extending from birthday to birthday in a twelve-month period.

This is also a good spread for answering questions as it deals with the Twelve Houses of the Zodiac, which comprise all conditions of humankind. In laying down the spread, the first card is placed on what astrologers call "the eastern horizon" (see diagram) and the rest of the cards are laid counterclockwise with the thirteenth card going in the center. Card #1 relates to the First House of Personality; card #2 to the Second House of Material Resources, and so on for the first twelve cards. The thirteenth card is read last and serves as a major indicator for the year. Before interpreting the spread it will be necessary to know the meanings of the Twelve Houses and they are as follows:

Twelve Houses of the Zodiac

First House of Personality: Covering influence for the year

Second House of Material Resources: Money, real estate

Third House of Communications: Communications, immediate environment, brothers and sisters, short trips

Fourth House of the Home: Home environment, the mother, ending cycles

Fifth House of Creativity: Self-expression, children, love affairs, speculation

Sixth House of Health, Work and Service: Physical and mental well-being, job, community endeavors, pets, and domestic workers

Seventh House of Partners: Partnerships both marital and business

Eighth House of Death and Regeneration: Death of something or somebody in the life, regenerating influences, legacies

Ninth House of Philosophy: State of mind, long journeys

Tenth House of Career: Occupation, place in life, the father

Eleventh House of Friends, Hopes and Wishes: Favorable influences and trends

Twelfth House of Secret Enemies: Limiting influences

Start the reading by turning over and interpreting the card in the First House and continue in sequence until all twelve Houses have been read and interpreted. The thirteenth card in the center is read last and provides the major overtone for the year.

The Calendar Spread

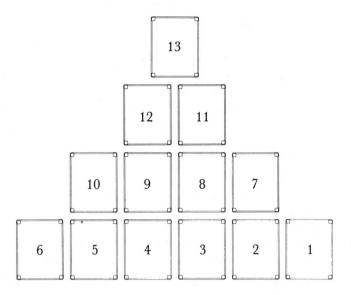

This also is primarily a future time spread and is helpful when consultant has some expectations for the year to come and wishes to zero in on the time period when certain things will begin to manifest. The first twelve cards in the spread deal with the twelve months following and the summit card of the pyramid is the indicator for the year. Traditionally, card #1 represents the month in which the reading is being conducted—or the following month if it is the closing part of the month— and the next eleven cards, the succeeding months.

Ending a Reading

There is no scientific formula for picking the optimum ending spread for a reading but the two following spreads do tie certain things together. The best time to end a reading is when all questions have been answered and the reader feels that a given spread provides the right psychological moment to bring down the curtain on a reading. Sometimes a spread will be thrown that is so definitive and so up-beat it would be almost a sin to go on. It is something that has to be played by ear. Each reading has its own individual flavor and rhythm and when the right final chord is struck, that is the time to call a halt. One problem, however, is that while a reader may feel that the reading is over, the consultant almost never does, so one has to build up to it gently. One technique is to say, "Well, I think your questions have been answered. Is there anything else that you wanted to ask?"

If the consultant says "No," then you can reply, "All right, then, for our final spread, would you like to take a look at the coming year?" Consultant will invariably answer in the affirmative and you can then exit with either the Horoscope or Calendar Spreads. If, however, consultant says, "Yes, there is...," your cue is to say, "If anything can shed light on that question, it is this final spread we are going to do which interestingly enough is called Light of a Star."

Light of a Star

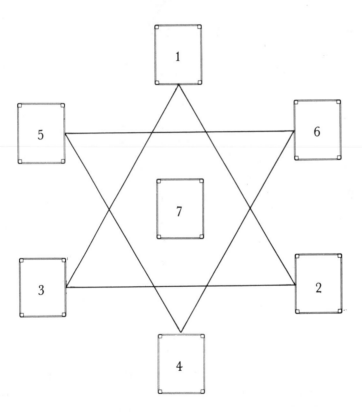

This spread takes its name from an imaginary six-pointed star, the points of which form stations for the past, present, and future of the question. The seventh station in the center of the star is the card of culmination. Following are the card meanings for each station:

First Station: Foundation of the question or problem

Second Station: The present as influenced by the past

Third Station: The immediate future seen as part of the web of past and present

Fourth Station: Type of action or lack of action that consultant must bring about for a harmonious result

Fifth Station: Others involved whose help may prove beneficial

Sixth Station: Opposing forces

Seventh Station: Outcome indicated by attitude and action of consultant as depicted in the preceding cards

Mystic Seven

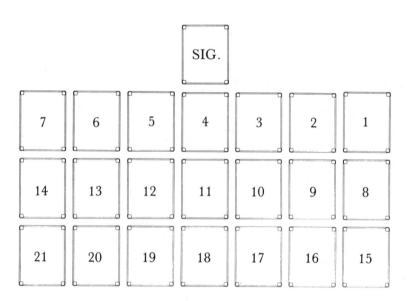

This is a particularly good spread to end with as most of the major cards that have appeared in previous spreads will reappear in the manner of a theatre cast taking a curtain call. But what makes this spread so interesting is that a pairing technique is employed so that these same cards which may have appeared over and over again in previous spreads take on a somewhat new meaning. It is almost like fitting together the pieces of a puzzle.

Begin by choosing a significator and then remove it from the pack and place it face up in the top center of the table. After consultant has cut and shuffled, take the pack and count down to the seventh card from the top. Remove it from the deck and place it face down on the far right of the top row beneath the significator (see diagram). From where you removed the last card count down seven cards again and place this one to the left of card #1. Continue this process until you have a top row of seven cards, a middle row of seven cards, and a bottom row of seven cards. During the counting take care not to disturb the order of the pack for when you reach the bottom, you simply return to the top and go through the pack again removing every seventh card. For example, if the bottom card is third in your count, the top card then becomes card #4, and so on.

When all the cards are in place, turn them over and comment briefly on the highlights and the meaning of the overall configuration. But the main part of the reading is the pairing process: Remove the first and last cards—cards #1 and 21—and place them next to each other off to the side of the spread. Now comment on the meaning of the paired cards as they relate to each other. Then remove card #2 and card #20 and do the same. Next will be card #3 and card #19, and you continue in this fashion until the pairs have been exhausted.

As this spread contains twenty-one cards that are actually read, there will be one card remaining that will not have a mate. If you are doing this as the ending spread then read and interpret this card with special care as it will have much to say about a particular question and quite possibly will be the key to the entire reading.

Part Three

Tarot Spreads: Life Readings

A life reading differs from an ordinary reading in that the consultant is less concerned with immediate questions and more questioning with regard to ultimate concerns. A life reading projects a picture of the entire life, its reason for being and its cardinal purpose. It can also take into account past lives of the consultant and it becomes possible to see that what we consider a lifetime is but a scene in an ongoing drama. A life reading can bring home to the consultant as nothing else can the answer to the question, "Who am I?"

A full life reading could be done on any of the seven spreads that follow, and two or three would be sufficient to digest at a single sitting. One technique that has proven satisfactory is to begin with standard spreads having to do with immediate questions and then move on to one or more of the life reading spreads.

As far as interpretation is concerned, life spreads are really the advanced course for the reader and should not be attempted by the beginner until he or she has achieved thorough mastery of the cards.

NOTE: Earlier it was suggested that a non-illustrated deck, such as the Oswald Wirth Pack depicted in this book, was best to learn on and to use in a standard reading. But life readings call for a shift in gears and for the type of spreads that follow, an illustrated deck, such as the Rider-Waite or the Morgan-Greer, might prove more evocative. Also, while the stated meanings of the cards still apply to some extent, the most profound results are usually obtained in a life reading by interpreting the cards intuitively. Just say the first thing that comes to mind; trust your instincts and do not hold back what intuitively comes to you.

The Twelve Houses

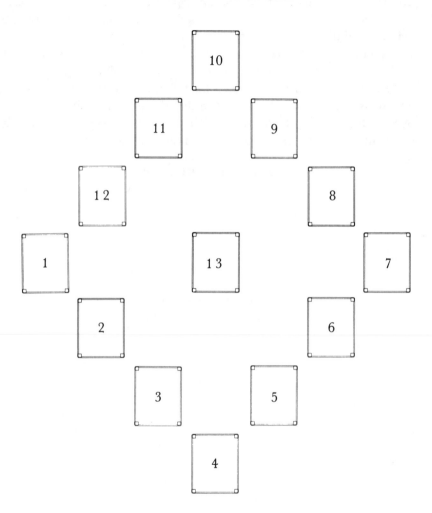

This is an excellent example of how a spread can be employed in different ways. For this spread appears in Part Two as The Horoscope Spread (see page 96) and the layout and meanings of the Houses are exactly the same. But the Twelve Houses differs from The Horoscope Spread in much the manner than an astrological solar return chart differs from a natal chart. In the first instance the emphasis is entirely on what may be expected in the year ahead. The natal chart, however, gets into a total picture of the life and personality. But the "wheel" and Houses are the same for both.

As far as the mechanics of the spread are concerned, the beginning process is the same as The Horoscope Spread and you lay the cards in exactly the same manner. Each of the twelve cards in the circle represents a House and the meanings for the Houses also remain the same. What is different is that before cutting or shuffling is done, you simply ask the Tarot for a picture of the natal chart of the consultant as represented by the twelve Houses of the zodiac. Each House card then will represent a major issue, individual or event in the life, and of affairs pertaining to that House. The thirteenth card in the center becomes extremely important for it represents the main indicator for the life.

The Tree of Life

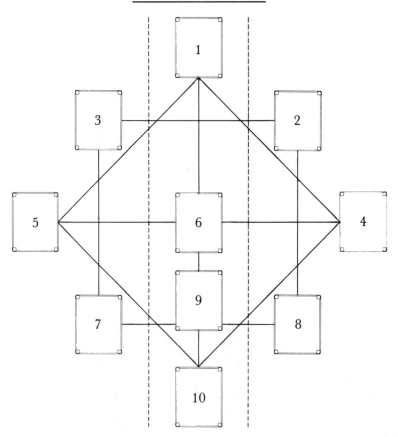

As is often the case, this spread can be employed in a life reading or for immediate questions. Begin by choosing a significator but leave it in the pack to fall where it may. After the pack has been cut and shuffled, lay out ten cards in the pattern of the cabalistic Tree of Life as shown by the diagram. Continue this procedure until each pile contains seven cards. Place the remaining cards aside. The meanings for the piles are as follows:

First Branch: Spiritual matters
Second Branch: Initiative, responsibilities
Third Branch: Sorrows and limitations
Fourth Branch: Money matters
Fifth Branch: Opposition, destructive factors
Sixth Branch: Achievement, the conscious mind
Seventh Branch: Love
Eighth Branch: Business, the arts, communication
Ninth Branch: Health, the unconscious
Tenth Branch: Home and family

The Cross of Destiny

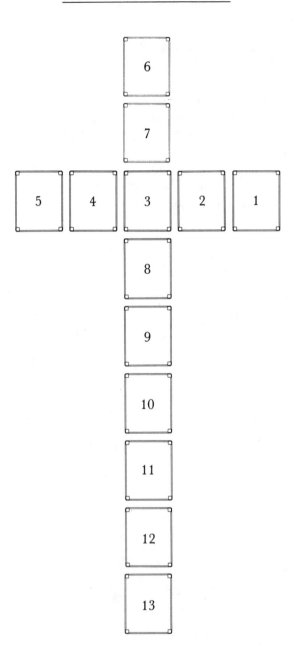

Upon cutting and shuffling, throw the spread according to the diagram. The sequence in which the cards are to be read and the meaning for each is as follows:

Card #4—Id: Physical you
Card #5—Ego: Mental you
Card #6—Superego: Moral you
Card #7-13—Highlights in the life
Card #2—Karma: Main lesson to be learned
Card #1—Central Purpose of the life
Card #3—Culmination

Squaring the Circle

15	16	17	18	19	20	21	22

(diagram with numbers 14, 13, 12, 11, 10 descending on the left; 23, 24, 25, 26, 27 descending on the right; triangle containing 37, 36, 38, 35, 39, 34, 40; inner circle containing 45, 46, 44, 47, 50, 43, 48, 42, 49, 41; bottom row 9, 33, 32, 31, 30, 29, 28; and 8, 7, 6, 5, 4, 3, 2, 1)

Following the diagram from right to left, form a horizontal row of seven cards, then moving up, a vertical row of seven cards, heading east a parallel horizontal row of seven cards, and a descending vertical row of seven cards, thus forming a square.

Within the square form a triangle with the base line of five cards, laying them from right to left, and then going up to form the left side of four cards, and the third side of three cards. Within the triangle, from right to left, form a circle of nine cards as depicted in the diagram. Finally, place one card in the center of the circle.

The square represents the physical plane—the body and its material attainments—past, present, and future; the triangle represents the psychological plane and has to do with mental activities; and the circle represents the spiritual plain and the higher level of being. The cards for all three planes should be read in sequence as they will show the type of development made by the individual, beginning with physical development, continuing with psychological changes, and culminating with spiritual growth.

The key card is the one in the center of the circle, which is read last as a final revelation for it will tie all three planes together and indicate the dominant influence in the life.

The Jungian Spread

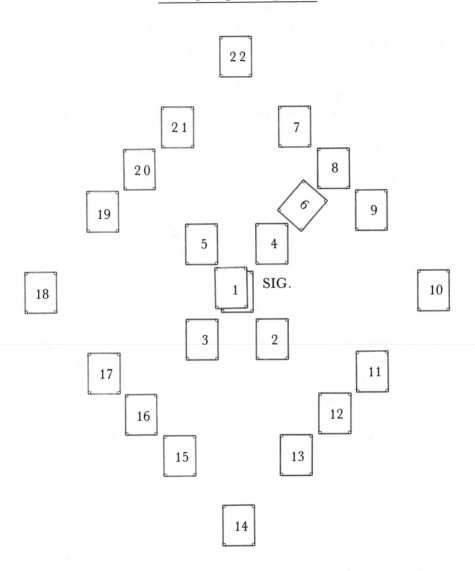

In view of the fact that a number of the descriptions of the Major Arcana cards in this book are laced with insights drawn from Jungian psychology, it is only appropriate that the life spread bearing the name of this pioneering psychologist be incorporated. In *A Dictionary of Symbols*, J. E. Cirlot speaks of the relationship of Tarot to Jungian concepts of integration noting that "Tarot cards comprise an image (comparable to that encountered in dreams) of the path of initiation. At the same time Jung's view...recognized the portrayal of two different but complementary struggles in the life of man: (a) the struggle against others (the solar way) which he pursues through his social position and calling; and (b) against himself (the lunar way) involving the process of individuation.''

The Tarot figures clearly correspond to Jung's theory of archetypes and it is these archetypal images in our unconscious that we must recognize and understand if we are to achieve self-realization. And to Jung, Self is "a God image, or at least cannot be distinguished from one." Selfhood is in fact the goal of the individuation process for it represents a totality of being.

To begin this reading, choose a significator and place it face up in the center of the table. After the consultant has cut and shuffled, lay the cards according to the diagram, noting that card #1 goes face down underneath the significator. This spread consists of an inner circle and an outer circle and they correspond to the inner life and the outer life of the individual having the reading. Following are the meanings for the inner circle:

Card #1—Shadow: This represents a hidden facet of the self that needs to be recognized and accepted before total integration is possible. Card is turned over and read last and then only if consultant wishes and the twenty-second card in the midnight position on the wheel appears favorable.

Card #2—Anima: Archetype embodying the feminine principle.

Card #3—Animus: Archetype embodying the masculine principle.

Card #4—Mother: Consultant's unconscious perceptions of motherhood.

Card #5—Father: Consultant's unconscious perceptions of fatherhood.

Card #6—Psyche: The animating life force based upon determining factors in early childhood and the unconscious.

Cards #7 to 22 of the outer circle represent key individuals, conditions and events in the life from youth to maturity.

NOTE: In a given reading, it is not possible to say in advance just how far in the life this spread will go. Occasionally it will draw a picture of the entire life up to old age and at other times it will go scarcely beyond the present. Clearly, the future is "not written in indelible ink" and the individual has the power to chart his or her own course.

Past Lives Spread

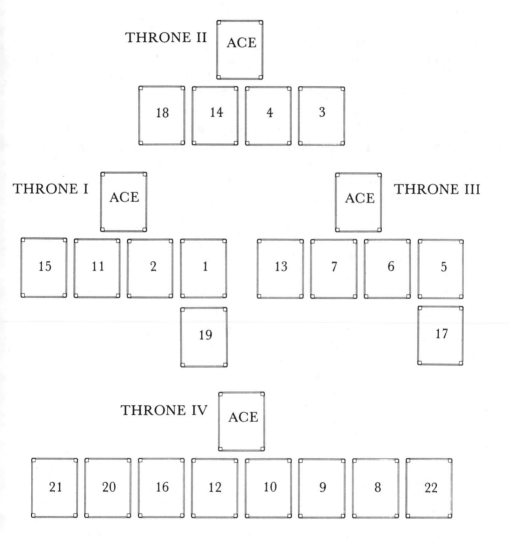

This spread is generally the *pièce de résistance* of any life reading for those who wish to mount Pegasus, the winged horse, and go riding off to the far country of time for a glimpse of another age and another life. Often as the story unfolds there is a gasp of recognition from the consultant—a feeling of *déja vu* as it were. But this spread does more than merely titilate by offering pictorial hints of past incarnations for it helps to depict the web of relationships between this life and those gone by. In actuality, the greater portion of this spread deals with the present life but when the past lives are revealed, the karmic influence is highly suggestive. If you will look at the diagram you will see that Throne IV, the one dealing with past lives is labeled "Psyche." There is a reason for this: In classical mythology, Psyche was the maiden who united with Eros, the god of love, and later became the personification of the soul. So the body is transient and is something we trade in when it becomes superannuated but the soul lives on. And this soul is fashioned by every thought we think, every word we utter, every deed we do in every second of every minute in every life we have ever lived. That is why Throne IV is the foundation of the physical square representing the individual through all time for it is our psyche or soul that determines the quality of present and future lives. Fate is not something that "happens to us," rather a series of "future reactions to past actions." It would seem that our character is our fate.

Familiarize yourself thoroughly with the cards of the Major Arcana before attempting this spread. In regard to Throne IV particularly, use your intuitive mind as you interpret the cards. If, for example, the card of The Sun comes up, you might see that as a life in a "sun-burned" land such as Egypt or Kenya. The card of The Chariot could suggest a gladiator in ancient Rome, The Magician, a traveling salesman during the Middle Ages. Imagination and intuition are the twin searchlights to beam on this throne of the far past.

For this spread, only the four aces and the twenty-two cards of the Major Arcana are used, so remove them from the pack but place the Trumps in one pile and the aces in another. Then hand the pile of aces to the consultant for shuffling and lay them down according to the diagram, starting with Throne I and ending with Throne IV. Next, have the consultant shuffle the Major Arcana pile and then place these cards in the following manner: The first two go in Throne I, the next two in Throne II, then *three* in Throne III, three in Throne IV, and one in Throne I as shown in the diagram. At this point you reverse direction and go counterclockwise and lay one card in each of the Thrones, continuing until you have laid down card #20 in Throne IV, after which you take the next-to-last card and place it at the beginning of Throne IV and the last card at the end.

This is admittedly a somewhat tricky spread to throw and the first few times you do it you may wish to consult the diagram as you lay the cards out. It is important to keep strictly to the stated arrangement for while Throne IV deals with past lives, the first three Thrones have to do with the present life. Also, each Throne is read in sequence going from left to right.

Begin the actual reading by turning over the ace in Throne I and comment on the meaning (see Table of Thrones below). Then read and interpret the Trumps in that Throne both individually and collectively. Continue this procedure until you have completed all four Thrones. On the following page is the meanings of the Thrones and the aces in each Throne:

Table of Thrones

Throne I—Destiny and Early Childhood

Ace of Coins: Strength and vitality
Ace of Wands: Work and responsibility
Ace of Cups: Love of pleasure, depletion
Ace of Swords: Poor health

Throne II—Career

Ace of Coins: Highly favorable
Ace of Wands: Great power
Ace of Cups: Insufficient effort
Ace of Swords: Delays and frustrations

Throne III—Love and Marriage

Ace of Coins: Powerful
Ace of Wands: Conflicts and difficulties
Ace of Cups: Joy
Ace of Swords: Quarrels

Throne IV—Psyche (Past Lives)

Ace of Coins: Unhappy or unlucky
Ace of Wands: Struggles
Ace of Cups: True beauty
Ace of Swords: Great power

Karmic Closeup

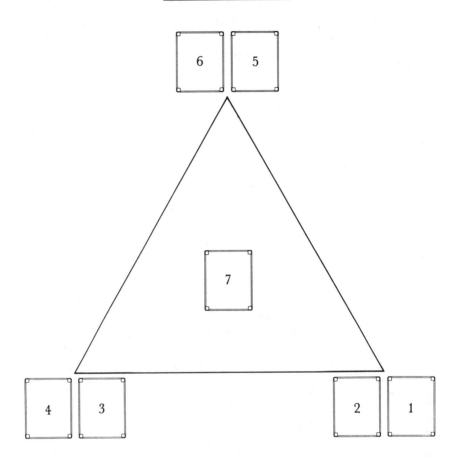

This spread may be imagined as taking the form of a triangle with a pair of cards at each angle and the card of karma in the center of the triangle and of the life.

This is a logical spread to do as a follow-up to Past Lives, for where that spread presented a kaleidoscope of several lives, this one allows for an intimate view of a single one—presumably, the most recent in time. Or, of course, the consultant can request a specific time period such as the medieval or the age of the renaissance. But if you ask for anything but the most recent life you have to be careful how you word the request. For instance, if you believe you were a historical figure during the Napoleonic era—maybe even Napoleon himself—you ask the Tarot for a picture of that life when the Karmic Closeup spread is thrown. But suppose you were not Napoleon. Suppose further that you were not even "in the body" on planet earth at that time, which is an entirely reasonable supposition for reincarnation theory holds that years and sometimes centuries go by between bodily incarnations. If a spread is thrown for a life that has not been lived, cards are obviously going to have to come up but what can they possibly tell you? It would only be an exercise in fantasy and most likely, the spread itself would not be coherent.

Now, should you have reason to feel that you lived in another age, the thing to do *before* throwing the Karmic Closeup spread would be to establish that by throwing another spread first to get an answer to the question, "Was I so-and-so?" There are various ways of doing this but a suggested method would be to do the Opening the Key Spread (see page 92). You would decide on a significator beforehand and for Napoleon, the card of The Emperor would fit nicely as would any of the four Horsemen, particularly the Knight of Swords. You would also have to determine which pile would be appropriate for your Napoleon significator to be in and you might decide that the Swords pile would be apt as any.

Should you do Opening the Key and the significator for what you believe to be a past incarnation does come up in the designated pile, and the story line in that pile also seems to be on target, you can then throw the Karmic Closeup with some measure of confidence.

But not so fast. You can take one more safety measure. Ask the Tarot for a natal chart of that life (see The Twelve Houses spread, page 107) and see if that life reading is reasonably descriptive of the life as you know it. Now for the acid test: If after throwing the two spreads just named you are still convinced that you were Napoleon (or whomever), ask the Tarot to cast a transit chart for a decisive year in the life (see The Horoscope Spread, page 96). Such a year for Napoleon would have been 1815, which was when he lost his empire in the Battle of Waterloo. If a Horseman comes up reversed along with other suggestive cards such as the reversed Emperor, the Lightning-Struck Tower, The Hermit, The Fool, and a bouquet of Sword cards it could indicate the past life connection you sought.

Throwing spreads such as Past Lives and Karmic Closeup are fascinating in and of themselves but they can also be used in an instructive manner. It would be a good idea to preserve the Past Lives and Karmic Closeup spreads that you throw for yourself and spend some time meditating over them. Also, you might find it helpful to ask yourself questions such as, "What was positive about that life?" "What was negative?" "What might I have done differently?" And particularly, you might ask yourself, "What should I be doing right *now* in this life to nourish my soul growth?'' And if you have trouble coming up with answers, simply ask the Tarot for it is on this plane that its teachings are most illuminating.

Any of the spreads in this book can be used for that purpose but you will probably find that Karmic Closeup is the most provocative. In throwing this spread, the first six cards are placed according to the diagram. But since the seventh is essentially the card of karma, and karma is the sum total of our thoughts and actions, the card is determined by the six others that represent the life. After the cards have been turned over and read, the reader finds the seventh card of the Karmic Balance Sheet by adding up the numbers of the six cards in the spread and then counting down in the pack until that number has been reached. This card will indicate what was left undone—or possibly, overdone—in a previous life, and what needs to be corrected in the present life if the Balance Sheet is to come out "in the black." Should the card of The Sun, The World, or The Fool appear in this position, it would suggest an old soul who has attained a high degree of involution and evolution.

Meanings for the cards are as follows:

Card #1—Destiny: Outer manifestation of the life
Card #2—Self: Inner purpose of the life
Cards #3 & 4—Major Influences: Shaping forces of the life
Card #5—Involution: Direction of the soul's journey in the life
Card #6—Evolution: Destination the soul reached in the life
Card #7—Karmic Balance Sheet: Main lesson to be learned
          in the present life

Part Four

Transcriptions
of Tarot Readings

Robin's Reading

Three Faces of Time (see page 76)   Eastern Cross (see page 80)
Wheel of Fortune (see page 84)   Light of a Star (see page 99)

The consultant is a young married woman with a career as a fabric designer. At the time of the reading she and her husband were planning to relocate.

Three Faces of Time

Past

1—5 of Cups
2—Ace of Wands
3—Knight of Coins
4—10 of Wands
5—Ace of Cups

Present

6—Queen of Swords
7—King of Wands
8—The Hermit
9—The Hanged Man
10—7 of Wands

Future

11—9 of Coins
12—4 of Swords
13—Justice
14—7 of Coins
15—The Emperor

SK: Robin, I know you have all kinds of questions at the moment so perhaps we should start by taking the one that is uppermost in your mind. I am going to fan the deck out on the table and what I would like you to do is pick cards one at a time and hand them to me. But while you are doing that I would ask that you concentrate on a particular question.

R: Okay.

SK: (Following the selection, shuffling, and throwing of the spread) Now that the spread is down, let me explain how it works: The bottom row has to do with the past, the center row with the present, and the top row with the future. I am going to begin by turning over the center cards of the Present row as that is the center of the present; it is the center of the spread; and in some ways it is the center of your life at the moment. It is the card of The Hermit and that is relevant for, like you, he is going on a journey and because he is setting out in darkness he is not quite sure of his way or just what he is going to find when he gets there.

R: Yes, that is my question.

SK: Now we turn over the center card of the past, which is the Knight of Coins. I interpret that to be a rather young person with thoughts of establishing herself in what she does creatively in the big city.

R: Career was all I could think of when I came to New York City.

SK: And now, looking at the center card of the future, we see the card of Justice. This is your card, Robin, for you can see that Justice is holding a pair of scales in one hand, which is the symbol for your sign, Libra. Your whole life is in effect a balancing act. And this is going to be particularly true in the immediate future for you are going to have to balance between what you do creatively and raising a family.

R: It is a lesson I am starting to learn.

SK: Okay, let's look at the line of the Past and see what else was important that bears on your question. The beginning card of the spread is the Five of Cups. Five is the number of fulfillment, in this case, emotional fulfillment and since it is followed by the Ace of Wands, the Knight of Coins, and the Ten of Wands, fulfillment for you—in the past—has centered around your artwork and designing fabrics.

R: I went through some pretty rough periods and my creative life is what kept me in one piece.

SK: The final card of the Past appears to be about three years ago for it is the Ace of Cups. This is the second ace that has come up, and aces are powerful cards for they have to do with important beginnings in the life. The first ace we turned over was the Ace of Wands, which has to do with a creative venture or career beginning, but the Ace of Cups means the beginning of something new and beautiful and that seems to be when love walked in.

R: For the first time in my life I realized that career is not necessarily everything.

SK: All right, let's look at the line of the Present. The first card is the Queen of Swords. Is there a woman executive with whom you deal right now who might also be helpful in the future?

R: Yes, there is. She has been very influential in introducing me to some of the top people in New York and she is going to continue to be a contact after I leave.

SK: The second card of the Past was the Ace of Wands, which was the beginning of your career. The second card of the Present is the King of Wands. Kings refer to men and this particular man is one who is very much on the same wavelength as you, so he most likely has to do with your second career—which is marriage.

R: That has been true for the past several months.

SK: It looks like the next few weeks are going to be a little tricky for The Hermit is in the dark and The Hanged Man is upside down. But take heart for you get help from the man next to The Hermit, the King of Wands—namely your spouse. And the line of the Present ends on an upbeat note with the Seven of Wands, which marks an important career change and that of course will be the time you and the King of Wands make your move.

R: These cards of The Hermit and The Hanged Man don't exactly look like happy cards.

SK: They are not but when one is embarking on a flight into the unknown there is usually a tense period after the countdown has started;

that is the message of The Hermit and The Hanged Man. The Hermit will be okay once he sees the light and so will The Hanged Man once he gets on his feet.

R: That is nice to hear but what do the cards say about the future?

SK: The first card of the Future line is the Nine of Coins. Nine is the number that has to do with endings and beginnings and is symbolized by the card of The Hermit, who is number 9 in the Tarot sequence. The Nine of Coins is saying only that this new beginning is going to require a cash outlay, which hardly comes as news to you.

R: True enough, but it is still not easy.

SK: The next card, the Four of Swords, indicates that there is probably going to be a waiting period for you after the move. I think that too is to be expected in view of the fact that you are expecting. When is the baby due?

R: Some time in June.

SK: So, you are not going to be able to do too much career-wise until after that. But you will notice that Justice—the woman who has told you to keep things in balance—is followed by the Seven of Coins.

R: Didn't you say that seven was the number of change?

SK: Absolutely. You remember, the Seven of Wands was the card that ended the line of the Present and had to do with a change in career.

R: And does the Seven of Coins mean a change in my financial situation?

SK: Yes, but the card specifically has to do with a business trip so travel of one kind or another is probably going to be included in this change.

R. But is it a change for the better or worse?

SK: There is positively no question about it, Robin, for the last card is The Emperor. And The Emperor is someone who makes it big. But it is all of a piece. For in the Past you have the Ten of Wands, indicating someone who has the potential to rise to the top of her profession. Be patient, keep things in balance, and have faith in the future for coronation day is coming!

Wheel of Fortune

Significator: The Empress

Pile #1—"Three above you"—The High Priestess, 3 of Wands, 5 of Cups

Pile #2—"Three below you"—Ace of Cups, 7 of Wands, 10 of Cups

Pile #3—"Three behind you"—The Moon, 6 of Coins, The Reaper

Pile #4—"Three before you"—The Magician, 10 of Wands, Ace of Wands

Pile #5—"Three for your house and home"—Knight of Coins, 5 of Wands, 8 of Wands

Pile #6—"Three for your hopes and fears"—3 of Swords reversed, Page of Wands, 8 of Swords

Pile #7—"Three for what you *do* expect"—6 of Cups, King of Wands, 7 of Cups

Pile #8—"Three for what you *do not* expect"—2 of Wands, The Angel of Time, The Hanged Man

Pile #9—"And three for what is sure to come"—The Devil, Justice, Strength

SK: The spread we are going to do next, Robin, is called the Wheel of Fortune. I think that it is an appropriate spread to do at this time as I always think of the Wheel of Fortune as a traveling card. Now, we are going to use a significator card. Is there any particular one you would like to use?

R: Yes, I think, The Empress.

SK: An excellent choice! Like you, she is a radiant and highly creative woman. And like you, she appears to be pregnant.

R: Well, having a child is a creative act.

SK: Agreed—and one that is second to none! Now if you will cut and shuffle I will do the rest.

R: Okay.

SK: You will notice that there are three cards at each of the rim points of the wheel. We are going to start with the "Three above you" pile, which has to do with covering influences in the life at the present time. In your case, the card of The High Priestess in this position strikes me as being similar to the card of Justice as this woman is between two poles—career and marriage—and it is not easy to find the proper balance.

R: But she is working at it.

SK: And succeeding to a large extent. For the Five of Cups—the card that started the last spread—reappears, and we know that it means emotional fulfillment. But before it was in the past next to the Ace of Wands, having to do with fulfillment in a professional career. Now, however, it flanks the Three of Wands, which has to do with marriage—and a marriage of true minds.

The "Three below you" pile represents current influences in the life. Hello, here is the Ace of Cups again, which came up in the Past in the last spread and was seen to be "the beginning of something new and beautiful," namely your marriage. But the Seven of Wands, which also came up in the last spread has to do with career change—and in your case, moving—makes for a somewhat emotionally trying period and so the Ten of Cups appears and Robin, I think you need to try and relax more and just live one day at a time.

R: It's just that there are so many things that have to be done before we leave; I mean it is an awesome task.

SK: I know exactly what you mean. The last time I moved, I said, "Never again!" This "Three behind you" pile has to do with the Past, and I see you have had a problem or two there as indicated by The Moon. Did you have a marriage that did not work out?

R: No, but I was engaged to someone for three years and it was very much an up-and-down affair.

SK: But the Death card indicates that you finally did end it, which is all to the good for in the Tarot, The Moon is always bad news. The death of that relationship allowed for the birth of a new and happier one culminating in marriage, which is indicated by the Six of Coins.

Now, we turn over the "Three before you" pile, which has to do with the immediate future. We see that the Ace of Wands and the Ten of Wands—both of which came up in the last spread—are back again, only this time in relation to the future. I associate the Ace of Wands with someone who builds on a firm foundation. The Ten of Wands, which comes up for you just about every time we do a reading, is associated with someone capable of professional success. With that card anywhere in a spread, there really are no worries career-wise; it is simply a matter of capitalizing on one's resources, particularly when the Ten of Wands is flanked by the Ace of Wands on one side and The Magician on the other. The Magician is associated with versatility and successful accomplishment.

R: Well, that is certainly nice to hear.

SK: Now, this pile is "Three for your house and home." There is the Knight of Coins again, the fellow who was the center of the Past in the last spread. We saw him as someone riding off to carve out a career and there is no question but that you will continue to do that. What is rather nice is that he is adjacent to the Five of Wands, which is fulfillment in what one does creatively. Because it is where you always work, it is logical that these cards should appear in the "House and Home" pile.

R: But, Sandor, doesn't that Eight of Wands kind of throw a monkey wrench into things? Every time you do a reading for me, eights come up all over the place. And you have said that eight is the number of imbalance, no?

SK: Well Robin, you are getting to be something of an expert on that particular number. Maintaining that not-so-delicate balance is going to be very much in the fore during the coming year in view of the fact that you are moving and expecting a child. "Eight" cards have to be read in terms of context. So the fact that the Eight of Wands is next to the Five of Wands, which is fulfillment in career, indicates that you are going to continue to create and get much satisfaction; it is just not going to be easy. Raising a baby is a full time job and so what you will be doing in effect will be holding down two full time jobs at once.

R: I guess it might be prudent if I put the fabrics on the shelf for a while and concentrate on the baby.

SK: I certainly would not argue with you there. In fact, looking at this next pile, "Three for your hopes and fears," I would say that if you were to attempt business as usual you would really run into problems. Because here is another eight—this time, the Eight of Swords—which indicates an imbalance in one's affairs and the Three of Swords reversed, which has to do with domestic strife.

R: That doesn't look good at all.

SK: True enough. But keep in mind, Robin, that a Tarot reading is not fortune telling in the usual sense of the word. You remember Dickens's *Christmas Carol,* don't you?

R: At this time of the year it is pretty hard to avoid it.

SK: Well, when the Ghost of Christmas Future shows Ebeneezer Scrooge the sad fate of Tiny Tim, Scrooge asks if this is what *will* be or *might* be and the ghost tells him that this is what will be *if* nothing is done to change the picture. And then Scrooge works to change things and change things he does. Tarot reading is a kind of Christmas Future experience: This will be the picture unless *you* work to change it.

R: It is good to know that we do have the power to change the future by altering our attitude and behavior.

SK: Exactly! The center of this pile is the Page of Wands, indicating the child. Surrounding the Page are two Sword cards. But if you make the child the center of your home and your heart, you will turn those swords into ploughshares.

R: You put that very well.

SK: Well, the Tarot can have a Biblical orientation. All right, now we come to the "Three for what you *do* expect" pile. Here we have the Six and Seven of Cups and the King of Wands. That seems fairly explicit. Six is the number of decision involving the domestic scene and that would be both the baby and the move, and seven is the number of change, which of course is the result of the decision. And the King of Wands, as we know, is your other half, and in your spread it is only natural that he would be in the center of any important decision and change involving the home.

R: It is amazing how the key cards have a way of coming up in the center.

SK: Yes, the Tarot does have a knack for placing the emphasis where it belongs. Now we come to the "surprise pile"—"Three for what you *do not* expect." In your case, it is not exactly a total surprise for the Two of Wands has to do with conflict regarding career and that of course would be motherhood vs. fabric designing. The Hanged Man is telling you that things are going to be upside down for a while but if you are patient, the result will be The Angel of Time. And as you can see, this woman—who incidentally looks very much like you—has two separate things and she is not only managing, she is joining them together and creating a new unity in her life.

R: What does that card actually mean in a reading?

SK: It is quite positive. Literally, the card means somebody who has made a major change in the life and learned to accept it and has also grown both inwardly and outwardly.

We are now ready for the final pile in the center—"Three for what is sure to come." Here is our old friend Justice again and she is right smack in the center of your future just as she was in the last spread.

R: Ouuugh, what is that card on the left? I don't like him at all!

SK: That is the card of The Devil: a most unpopular card. We have noted before that as a Libra the particular cross you have to bear in this life is in the shape of scales and learning how to find the correct balance. Now, you will notice that on the other side of Justice is the card of Strength. This woman is subduing a lion and she is able to do it because she has found the proper balance and developed inner strength. Anyone who can tame a lion certainly has the strength also to tell The Devil to go back where he came from.

And you can do that, Robin, for the card of Strength is on the *right* side of Justice and if you draw upon your own inner strength you will have Justice on *your* side.

Eastern Cross

> Card #11—Past: Queen of Swords
> Card #10—Consultant: 5 of Cups
> Card #9—Immediate Future: Knight of Swords
> Card #12—Outcome: 4 of Coins

SK: Now, Robin, do you have a question that has not come up yet that can be answered fairly simply—a yes-or-no question?

R: Yes, as a matter of fact I do.

SK: Okay, let's do the Eastern Cross; that is a most concise spread. The first card has to do with the past and it is the Queen of Swords. Let's see, she was in the line of the present in the first spread we did and we decided that she was the woman with whom you deal who is an important contact for you in your business ventures.

R: That's right.

SK: So the question then has to do with her in some way?

R: Yes, we talked on the phone the other day and I am going to see her Monday about a proposal that she has in mind.

SK: This card represents the attitude of the consultant and it is the Five of Cups. Remember that one?

R: Wasn't that the first card that came up when we started the reading?

SK: That's right. And I tend to look at first cards in a reading as having some special significance. The Five of Cups denotes emotional fulfillment and the fact that it was next to the Ace of Wands indicates that the Number One thing in your life has been the satisfaction you derive from what you do creatively. That has been true in the past and it is still true to some extent.

R: For quite a while, it was the only thing in my life that gave me fulfillment.

SK: Life cannot be changed overnight. The card of the Immediate Future is the Knight of Swords. This does not look very encouraging for the proposal. One way or another, I do not think you are going to be happy with it.

R: From just the few things she said on the phone, I had that feeling.

SK: In the first spread we did, the culminating card of the line of the Future was The Emperor and that means material attainment in the not-too-distant future. And the card for the Outcome of this spread is the Four of Coins, which is saying the same thing. It is not going to happen the moment you move, but in a few months it will come your way. It is unlikely that it will be connected with the woman in question.

R: Well, the important thing is that it is going to happen.

SK: Oh, it is going to happen all right; with the Four of Coins there I don't see how you could miss.

Light of a Star

First Station—Foundation of the question or problem: 10 of Wands
Second Station—The present as influenced by the past: The Wheel of Fortune
Third Station—Immediate Future: 9 of Coins
Fourth Station—Type of action or lack of action that the consultant must bring about for a harmonius result: Justice
Fifth Station—Others involved whose help may prove beneficial: King of Wands
Sixth Station—Opposing forces: The Devil
Seventh Station—Outcome as indicated by attitude and actions of consultant: Queen of Cups reversed

SK: Okay, Robin, let's close the reading with a spread called Light of a Star.

R: How poetic!

SK: Actually, it is quite descriptive as it really does shed light. It will sum up other things that have appeared in the reading but put them in a somewhat different light.

R: I'm ready.

SK: I throw this spread by imagining a six-pointed star and then place a card at each point of light and the last one in the center. The card at the First Station is considered to be the foundation of the question or problem. The card is the Ten of Wands and that, as you know, represents potential for rising to the top in whatever you do.

R: That card does seem to be following me.

SK: It may just be that the Tarot is trying to tell you something. Now the Second Station represents the present and it is The Wheel of Fortune. It looks like things are really starting to go your way.

R: Let's hope so.

SK: Also, I usually see this as a traveling card—after all it is a wheel—but the Tarot is telling you that all your systems are really Go.

R: Nice to hear.

SK: The Third Station is the Immediate Future and that is the Nine of Coins. That of course is a money card but it is money going out.

R: We know we are going to have to make some sacrifices.

SK: The Fourth Station is a most important one for it is going to indicate what it is that you will need to do in order to bring about harmony. This is a card you know very well indeed—Justice!

R: That means I must clean up my act, right?

SK: Right! But you won't have to struggle alone for the card I have just turned over, the King of Wands, indicates another whose help will prove beneficial. I think this year is going to be something of a challenge for you but at least it is comforting to know that you have a means of moral support—your husband—who is going to be there when you need him.

R: I am most thankful for that.

SK: We are going to look at the next card with special care for that represents opposing forces. Do you recognize this fellow?

R: Oh dear, that is The Devil again!

SK: One positive thing about this is that there has to be some kind of opposing force. And what the Tarot is telling you is that it is not an outside force but rather, the enemy within. You can say with Pogo, "We have seen the enemy and it is me!"

When The Devil comes up on that opposing forces station, that final card in the center of the star usually has some kind of problem connected with it. Yes, the tale is running true to form for the card is the Queen of Cups, usually a positive card; unfortunately, in this reading she is upside down.

The question is how to get this woman right side up. If we think of the King of Wands as your husband and the reversed Queen of Cups as you, we can see that they were very close to each other when we threw this spread. The only thing that came between them was The Devil. And The Devil is fear and fear alone.

R: I guess I have some work to do on myself.

SK: When The Devil came up before in that Wheel of Fortune spread, there were two other cards next to it. Do you remember what they were?

R: Oh, let's see. One was the card of the balance.

SK: Justice, right. The other was the card of Strength, the woman subduing the lion. Now, Robin, I would like you to do something for me.

R: What's that?

SK: I would like you to imagine, no, I want you *to be* the woman of Strength and then do something for yourself.

R: Which is?

SK: The Devil is fear, right? The way to get rid of fear is by confronting it directly. So, Robin, I would like you to take that card of The Devil and turn it around.

R: You mean, turn the card face down?

SK: That is precisely what I mean. (Robin turns over the card.) Can you still see him?

R: No, he has disappeared.

SK: You literally put him where he belongs. To make sure that he stays put, all you have to remember, Robin, is that you can always call on your own inner reserves to banish fear. Since The Devil was the only thing that came between you and the King of Wands, by casting him out, you will find something mysterious and wonderful is going to happen: the Queen of Cups, who was upside down, is going to be right side up and in perfect balance with herself and the world—and it will be in no small measure due to her own inner strength.

Patrick's Reading

The Horseshoe Spread (see page 78)
Celtic Cross (see page 81)
The Churchyard Spread (see page 94)
The Gypsy Spread (see page 86)

The consultant is a young Frenchman, who after living abroad for several years, at the time of the reading was planning to return to his homeland with his wife to start a new career.

The Horseshoe Spread

Card #1—Past: 9 of Coins
Card #2—Present: 10 of Swords
Card #3—Immediate Future: 9 of Wands
Card #4—Card of the Consultant: 6 of Swords
Card #5—Attitude of Another: Strength
Card #6—Obstacle: Queen of Coins
Card #7—Outcome: Ace of Coins

SK: Patrick, I'm going to start with this card, which is known as the card of the Consultant because it will give us some idea as to how you feel about the undertaking you have planned. It is the Six of Swords, which is a warning card. What it is warning you about is worry.

P: We are wondering if we are doing the right thing.

SK: That is why I am here, to see what the Tarot says about it. We will now look at the card of the Past, which is the Nine of Coins. I would say that it is the fairly recent past for that card means money going out and I imagine you have had any number of expenses in getting ready for your return to France.

I can see that this is not a particularly easy period for you. In addition to that Nine of Coins in the past, you have the Ten of Swords in the present. But this is to be expected for it is basically sadness at leaving friends behind—people you have grown to know and love.

P: It is also that we do not know whether we will ever see them again.

SK: Yes, I know just how you feel.

The card of the Immediate Future indicates that you should proceed with your plans. It is the Nine of Wands, which has to do with new friends and a new place.

This next card indicates how someone close to you feels about this change—perhaps your wife. The card of Strength in this position suggests this is difficult for her. The woman on the card is struggling with a lion but I think she can handle it; in fact, I *know* she can.

P: She does not speak French so she is concerned that she will have to begin at the beginning in learning the language.

SK: That would give one pause but it need not be a major thing. This card represents an obstacle and it is the Queen of Coins. The Queen of Coins often runs her own business so I think the obstacle—at least, as far as your wife is concerned—is having to abandon her business. But she can probably set herself up in France, don't you think?

P: That is what she hopes to do eventually and I have friends over there who may be able to help.

SK: It looks like it is going to work out, Patrick, as the outcome card is the Ace of Coins! Aces are very potent cards for they depict important beginnings in the life and the Ace of Coins has to do with money and career. This really tells us what we wanted to know as the card of the Immediate Future said you were going to a new environment but this card is the bottom line for it says that you are eventually going to be able to set yourself up in a new career.

Celtic Cross

Significator: The Sun

Card #1—"This covers you": 8 of Swords
Card #2—"This crosses you": 5 of Swords
Card #3—"This is above you": The Reaper
Card #4—"This is beneath you": 3 of Coins
Card #5—"This is behind you": 3 of Swords
Card #6—"This is before you": 9 of Coins
Card #7—"This *is* you": Page of Cups
Card #8—"This is for your house and home": Day of Judgment
Card #9—"This is for your hopes and fears": 7 of Cups
Card #10—"And this is what you can most definitely expect":
            5 of Wands

SK: You have chosen The Sun as a significator so we will place that over here on the table. I must say that it is truly appropriate as the sun is the ruler of Leo, which is your sign. It is also a beautiful card to identify with as it shows a boy and a girl who are playing together in what could be the Garden of Eden. We place the first card on top of the significator and say, "This covers you," for it represents the covering influence in the life at the moment. It is the Eight of Swords, which is an indication that things are a bit on the frenzied side at the moment.

P: As you know, Sandor, we are both rather nervous about going to France. At this point we have nothing solid at all to count on; we are just going over there and hoping that something will materialize.

SK: Well, I admire your bravado. The closing card of the first spread was the Ace of Coins and that is a pretty clear signal that you will find what you are looking for. With this card we say, "This crosses you," as it has to do with an obstacle. It is the Five of Swords which indicates help from sources that are not immediately apparent. Once you arrive in France, you may not have immediate results but there will be no real obstacle.

P: That I am happy to hear!

SK: "This is above you," tells what can be attained. This card usually means a major change in the life. One name for it is The Reaper and in this case I read it to mean that you will reap what you have sown. We will get a clearer picture of that when we come to the final card, which is the card of culmination.

"This is beneath you," is really the card that suggests the foundation of the issue. It is the Three of Coins so it appears that you are building on a firm foundation. I know that you are considering the restaurant business and I would say that you have had some pretty good training for that.

P: Yes, Sandor, I have gone to cooking school in France and have worked under some very fine people.

SK: "This is behind you," has to do with the past. The Three of Swords is a card of separation and I think it is going back to that time when you separated yourself from your homeland.

"This is before you," has to do with the immediate future and it is the Nine of Coins, which came up in the last spread and is concerned with expenditures. Perhaps not only monetary currency but emotional currency as well. What do you think, Patrick?

P: You know it is not easy to leave a place you have become friendly with.

SK: That is so true. Now this is an important card for we say, "This *is* you," and in some ways it is more you than any other card in this spread. It is the Page of Cups. The Page of Cups is a most loving warm-hearted young person and I would say it is a rather apt description of your wife. It is not a bad description of you either.

"This is your house and home," and here we find the Day of Judgment. This card has to do with a major decision in the life and in your case it has to do with the house and home. The man and woman on the card are husband and wife and they have done what they have talked about doing and they are absolutely jubilant.

P: Who is the third person on the card with his back to us?

SK: Well, Patrick, I don't know how to break this to you but that is the newest member of your family—so new that he hasn't arrived yet. But it won't be long. And, ah, don't be too sure that it's a "he."

"This is for your hopes and fears," is the Seven of Cups, which has to do with a change in the residence or a change in the family. In your case, both are very soon going to be true, and in this hopes-and-fears slot, you should not have any real worries about either.

Okay, now we come to the card of culmination, and so, "This is what you may definitely expect," and it is the Five of Wands.

P: Didn't you say, Sandor, that Wands have to do with job and career?

SK: Yes, Patrick, and in some ways this card is similar to the one that ended the last spread. Do you remember what card that was?

P: Wasn't that the Ace of Coins?

SK: Yes, indeed!

P: And you told me it had to do with starting a new career.

SK: And so it does. But this card goes a step further. For while the Ace of Coins has you starting a new and powerful career, with the Five of Wands you find fulfillment in that career!

The Churchyard Spread

> Card #1—The Lovers
> Card #2—10 of Coins
> Card #3—Queen of Swords
> Card #4—5 of Cups
> Card #5—Queen of Coins
> Card #6—The Fool
> Card #7—2 of Cups
> Card #8—9 of Coins

Card #9—King of Coins
Card #10—6 of Swords
Card #11—4 of Swords
Card #12—The Chariot
Card #13—9 of Cups

SK: Now, Patrick, what I would like you to do at this time is to concentrate on the most important question in your mind at the moment and I will throw a spread that may help to give us some fairly specific information on it.

P: Good! That is what I would like to know.

SK: First, I am going to take The Fool out of the pack as we are using him for a significator. Then after you have cut and shuffled, I am going to take the twelve cards off the top, insert The Fool and ask you to shuffle just those thirteen cards.

All right, now that the spread is down, I am going to turn all the cards over and look for The Fool. Much depends on where he appears in this spread: If he is at the beginning, there are going to be some real problems. If he is at the end, things should work out fairly well in regard to your question. If he is in the middle, there are going to be some obstacles but the cards following The Fool should give us some insight as to what they are and also tell us how things will work out eventually.

P: It looks like he is in the middle.

SK: Yes, I would say so. Your question has to do with the career you will be following in France?

P: Yes, that is the question I had. How did the cards tell you that?

SK: To be frank, I just assumed that was your question; I could not think of any other question that would be more on your mind at this moment. But it does appear in the cards. You will notice that the King and Queen of Coins are both in this spread?

P: Yes, I see that.

SK: You may remember that the Queen of Coins came up in the first spread we did. But it came up as an obstacle. We decided that since the Queen of Coins is usually a person who runs her own business, that it was your wife. But the card came up as an obstacle because she would have to give up her profession at least temporarily until you both get settled in France and until after the baby arrives. Your wife comes up again in this spread and again as the Queen of Coins. On one side of her is the Five of Cups so we see that giving up being the Queen of Coins will not be easy for her as she gets emotional fulfillment from her profession.

The first card after The Fool is the Two of Cups—the "Heart's Desire" card. So it looks like France is going to agree with both of you.

P: But there is that Nine of Coins again and when that came up in another spread didn't you say that it had something to do with financial difficulties?

SK: My friend, that has come up in *every* spread so far this evening so be prepared for a few lean days. But the point is that you do something about it for the card is followed by the King of Coins, which is you. I say that because the King of Coins is the husband of the Queen of Coins and so the indication here is that you are going to be the sole breadwinner in the family for a time. But I don't think that what you start with in France is what you are going to stay with. I know you have only tentative plans, Patrick, but what are they?

P: We plan to go first to the home of my parents in Paris and stay there for a while. While there I thought I would try to get back into the restaurant business as either a chef or a partner. But something else we have been talking about is buying a villa in the south of France and then turning it into a rather fancy bed and breakfast place.

SK: Okay, I think we are getting a fairly specific answer. The King of Coins comes up shortly after The Fool's arrival in Paris so we can read him as doing something in Paris—possibly a restaurateur, or a chef at one of the better places. Whatever it is, it is not working out as the King of Coins is surrounded by financial problems and worries. That is indicated by the Nine of Coins and the Six of Swords. It is further reinforced by the Four of Swords, which also suggests some problems living at the home of your parents.

With the closing cards of this spread we see an entirely different trend as depicted by The Chariot, which is victory, and the Nine of Cups, which is known as the "Wish Card." The Chariot is a card of movement. Your wish is granted but only *after* you climb into your chariot and drive to another destination. That is where you will find the victory!

The Gypsy Spread

21—Strength   Significator   22—Wheel of Fortune

G	Y	P	S	Y
1-6 of Swords	2-9 of Coins	3-The World	4-Ace of Coins	5-4 of Cups
6-5 of Swords	7-Page of Swords	8-The Lovers	9-9 of Cups	10-The Fool
11-King of Coins	12-8 of Wands	13-The Empress	14-2 of Swords	15-The Chariot
16-The Reaper	17-Queen of Coins	18-Page of Wands	19-The Hermit	20-9 of Wands

SK: The last spread we did, Patrick, gave us a fairly clear answer to your question. The final spread we are doing, which incidentally is called The Gypsy Spread, should bring everything into sharper focus and sum things up.

Each of these five vertical piles represents a letter in the word "gypsy." We will begin with "G," which stands for "Gateway" and has to do with questions you are contemplating.

The first card, the Six of Swords, is a warning card and it came up in the very first spread we did. But now we get more information. The Death card tells us that there is some anxiety on your part but specifically, it has to do with the major change of pulling up stakes in New York and returning to France. And the King of Coins tells us that you are concerned with just how you are going to set yourself up in business and bring in those coins once you hit France. But the card that gives us the answer is the Five of Swords because that tells us that while you may not immediately be able to control events, things will be working under the surface in your favor. It is going to take a little time before you experience your success.

P: I think, Sandor, that is well indeed as it has been some years that I have spent any time at home and so while we are living under the roof of my parents there will be time to think and talk and look around.

SK: There are two "Ys" in "gypsy." The first "Y" has to do with "yin," the second with "yang." As I'm sure you know, yin and yang are the dark and light components of the T'ai Chi symbol, which represents the Law of Opposites. The yin represents the dark, passive principle and the yang, the bright, active principle.

P: So these cards will tell me what I should *not* be doing?

SK: Yes. At least, not right away. The first card is the Nine of Coins. No spread for you, Patrick, would be complete without it, but since it falls in the yin row, the Tarot is telling you not to worry about money. There is a time for it to come in and a time for it to go out and this is the going out time.

P: The going out time is nothing new for me. The coming in time will be.

SK: The Eight of Wands is saying much the same thing, and the Queen of Coins is telling your wife to put her paint brushes away for the moment, and be tranquil and have her baby.

P: And, Sandor, the Page of Swords is the baby, no?

SK: Yes and no. I think it is more *your* baby than *the* baby. That is to say, what one does creatively is one's brain child. It could be a book. It could be a painting. It could be a bed and breakfast place. But you need to think it through before you bring it into the world.

P: Suppose that card had been in the yang pile. What would it have meant then?

SK: Just the opposite. Yang is action and had the Page of Swords come up there, the Tarot would have been saying, "This Mediterranean inn is your baby but if you want it to materialize, you are going to have to do something about it *toute suite.*"

P: But as long as it is yin, I just think about it.

SK: It does not have to stop there. You can write letters, make phone calls, look around, see people, talk it over, and get it all worked out on paper.

P: I see.

SK: The "P" row stands for "Partnership" and with The World, The Lovers, The Empress, and the Page of Wands, I would say that you have made a rather good marriage.

P: That I am happy to hear!

SK: If the truth be told, Patrick, I don't really think you needed either me or the Tarot to tell you that. But there are times when the Tarot gets up and dances a jig and it is doing that now. The card of The World is happiness personified and that happiness is with The Empress, a scintillating, charming, and creative person. And what she is creating right now will be manifesting in a few months—and that is the Page of Wands, a child who will really speak your language. And let's not forget the card of The Lovers. If any card says it, that one does. By the by, that card came up as the foundation card of the last spread. And since it was next to the Ten of Coins, which is often referred to as the Wall Street Card, this is a very solid marriage indeed!

P: I am glad I did something right!

SK: The ''S'' pile has to do with the Self and indicates your state of mind. I think, Patrick, you are doing more things right than you realize but maybe you don't always accept this.

P: Why do you say that?

SK: Because you have your own little built-in yin and yang. With the Ace of Coins and the Nine of Cups you are saying, ''I can do and be pretty much what I want to do and be.'' With the Two of Swords and The Hermit, you are saying, ''I'm only kidding myself.'' It is like the duet in which one singer says, ''Yes, I can!'' and the other says, ''No, you can't!''

Look Patrick, you can't fool me. I've done your astro-numeric chart and I meant what I said when I told you it was a chart of great beauty and power. When you listen to that negative defeatist side of you, you are listening to a lie. So it is the Ace of Coins and the Nine of Cups you should be listening to for they are telling you to go out and conquer, which is the rightful occupation of all true Leos.

P: Sandor, I am not sure I know what to say to that.

SK: You don't have to say anything, Patrick. Just let out a roar which will serve notice on the world that you have recognized your kingship and are ready for a long and happy reign.

In other words, just simply do and be and what form it will take will be suggested by the yang pile. I would say this is fairly explicit, Patrick. Let's start with The Fool.

P: Is that me?

SK: Yes, it is. But because he is near the end of the spread, he is The Magus, or wise fool. He is starting on a journey but he follows the Four of Cups, which is the birth of a child. So the Tarot is telling you to stay at your parents' home until your wife has her baby and then set out for another place.

P: And it will work out?

SK: With The Chariot and the Nine of Wands it would be hard to miss. The Chariot is victory and the Nine of Wands is a new environment. But as was said before, the victory comes after you climb into your personal chariot and drive yourself to that new place in the south of France or wherever.

P: Well, that is very nice and I do thank you, Sandor.

SK: Have faith, Patrick. The Tarot has a way of topping itself. First, we will read the card on the left of the significator, which has to do with your expectations. That is really the Consultant card. And in any spread, I always consider the Consultant card a most important one for it represents the thoughts, feelings, and attitude of the consultant. And if that card is positive, almost invariably, the card of culmination will be positive.

P: I think I follow you.

SK: I know you do. Before something can manifest in outer space, it has to manifest in inner space. If a person is negative inside it is unlikely anything positive is going to happen outside. But if you set yourself a realistic goal you *know* you can attain, you will eventually attain that goal.

P: That makes very good sense, Sandor.

SK: Okay, I am going to turn over the card regarding your expectations. It is the card of Strength. And in your case, Patrick, it is rather an ambivalent card.

P: Why do you say that?

SK: As you can see, the card depicts a woman closing the jaws of a lion. She can do this in a relaxed and poised manner because she has the inner strength, which in turn gives her the outer strength to do what she needs to do.

But you see, this card is associated with the sign of Leo, which is where you live. So the question is, do you identify with the woman or the lion? If with the woman, fine and dandy. But if with the lion, then there may be problems. Because as he is depicted on this card, the lion is a loser. As you can see, he is rather moth-eaten and he has a memory problem. He has forgotten that he was born into the royal sign of Leo, king of the beasts. Once he realizes that the name of this card—Strength—applies to him as well as the woman, then he will let out a royal roar and do what he was born to do and that is, be king.

P: I will certainly work on that, Sandor.

SK: I am convinced that you will, Patrick, for the card of attainment is just that—The Wheel of Fortune—one of the most positive cards in the Tarot for it means literally a turn for the better in one's fortunes and it is usually accompanied by the undertaking of a journey or a new start in life!

NOTE: At the time of their consultation, Robin and Patrick were newlyweds.

Harriet's Life Reading

The Twelve Houses (see page 107)
Past Lives (see page 115)
Opening the Key (see page 92)

NOTE: For this reading the Morgan-Greer pack was used and the interpretation was based on the figures and scenes as depicted by that deck.

At the time of the reading the consultant was in her late twenties and living with her young daughter.

The Twelve Houses

Card #1—The Empress
Card #2—Knight of Cups
Card #3—8 of Wands
Card #4—Queen of Cups
Card #5—Page of Wands
Card #6—Knight of Wands
Card #7—8 of Swords
Card #8—Strength
Card #9—The Chariot
Card #10—9 of Cups
Card #11—6 of Swords
Card #12—2 of Coins
Indicator card—Ace of Coins

SK: For your Life Reading, Harriet, we are going to start off with The Twelve Houses, which is similar to The Horoscope Spread.

H: Isn't that one you did for me the other day?

SK: Yes, but with this difference: The one we did last time was solely concerned with the year coming up. This one is similar to a natal chart in that it takes in the whole life.

H: I see.

SK: The twelve houses remain the same but the card in each House is a prime indicator for the life rather than an event for a particular year. When I did your astro-numeric chart, do you remember the Tarot card that I felt was suggested by the chart?

H: Oh yes, it was The Empress.

SK: It appears that the Tarot concurs for in the First House of Personality is the card of The Empress.

H: That's incredible!

SK: Yes and no. Horoscopes, astro-numeric charts and Tarot cards all seem to work for the same employer, so it is only natural that The Empress should appear as the significator card of your life. She is a most beguiling and creative woman and I always think of her as the exemplification of the workings of heaven in the things of earth.

H: I can certainly identify with her in several ways—particularly by the fact that she is in the outdoors. I've always had a special feeling about flowers and the sea and just nature in general.

SK: In your Second House of Material Resources is the Knight of Cups.

H: Is that my knight in shining armour?

SK: It could be but I suspect that knight is you as you have had to fight for what you have. But this particular knight is a very generous and loving person and that goblet she is carrying is a cup of warmth for her little daughter.

H: Yes, my daughter is a very important part of my life.

SK: The Eight of Wands appears in your Third House of Communications. There is your little home out on the hill but wands have to do with work and so many wands suggest that there is a lot of work that goes on in that house just to keep body and soul together.

H: I don't know if I told you but when the place that I work closes down for the winter, I go back to being a weaver and that I do in my home.

SK: Now that I think of it, the way those wands are placed, they kind of resemble a loom. In the Fourth House of the Home is the Queen of Cups. She is all heart and exactly where she should be—in the House of the Home. And she is of course, her majesty, Queen Harriet.

In the Fifth House of Creativity is the Page of Wands. The young woman on the card is embracing her work—it is the very stuff of life for her. This is also the House of Children and so the Page of Wands is not only you; it is also your daughter.

H: Yes, both would be equally true.

SK: Now we are looking at the Sixth House of Health, Work and Service. I think I will change the name of this spread to "Pictures of Harriet" for there you are again as another knight. I take it you have done a fair share of traveling, for knights are people usually on the move.

H: Oh yes, I have lived and worked all over this country and abroad.

SK: But the knights that have come up for you—the Knight of Cups and the Knight of Wands—are more concerned with the needs and desires of others than they are with their own selfish interests. And the Knight of Wands—the "Good Samaritan" knight—appears in your House of Health, Work and Service. So that makes me feel that you derive a certain amount of pleasure by doing work that is somehow a service to other people.

H: Well, I can't argue that I do things for the money as I don't have very much to show for it.

SK: In the Seventh House of Partners is the Eight of Swords.

H: I don't like the looks of that card at all!

SK: That woman is blindfolded and bound; she does not look too comfortable. As you separated from your husband not too long ago, this may be indicative of your present situation.

The important thing is that she gets that blindfold lowered so she can see what she is about. It looks like she will for in the Eighth House of Regeneration is the card of Strength. This woman has much to contend with as evidenced by the lion trying to attack her. But she is able to handle him and a dozen more just like him if she has to for she has the strength. But it is basically an inner strength and that is truly the secret of her survival. Harriet, that is also your secret and the regenerating influence of your life.

H: It's either be strong or go crazy.

SK: I think the card in your Ninth House of Philosophy is the key to the spread and your life as it is The Chariot. In one way it suggests your Gemini sun, which is symbolized by the twins who each want to go their own way. On this card, there is a black horse and a white horse pulling the chariot but they are spirited creatures and will go galloping off in different directions if they are not controlled. However, the driver of the Chariot seems to be in control.

H: Sometimes though, I think maybe he is taken for a ride.

SK: But, Harriet, just look at his expression; he is enjoying every minute of it.

H: I guess you are right.

SK: In divination this is always a positive card for the meaning is "Victory." And the fact that the card is here in your House of Philosophy is really significant for it means that you have basically a positive outlook and know that you are going to get where you want to go.

H: On the whole, I do feel fairly positive about myself.

SK: The Ninth House is also the House of Long Journeys and the card of The Chariot is another indication that you love to travel and that your trips work out pretty well for you.

Now we come to the midheaven of your "chart" and the Tenth House of Career. That card is the Nine of Cups. You know something, Harriet; I think I am going to let you interpret this card yourself.

H: That man does not exactly look like a knight but he does look like somebody I could talk to and somebody I would like to know. He looks like somebody who would enjoy talking philosophy, like to look at art and listen to music, and certainly he would take pleasure in making love and sitting down to a good meal. I like him but I don't believe we've met.

SK: You will for he is in your House of Career. And since the Nine of Cups is known as the Wish Card, he will appear when you want him to appear.

H: I will certainly keep him in mind.

SK: The Six of Swords appears in your Eleventh House of Friends, Hopes and Wishes. There are two figures on this card and as their backs are to us, they could be men, or they could be women. They appear to be in a gondola, heading toward a town along the seacoast. I see the gondolier as you, and that other smaller figure, as your daughter. You are taking her to a seaside hideaway to make a new life. What the Tarot seems to be saying is that this particular place by the sea has some quality about it that is just right for your social, psychic, and spiritual development.

H: There is a lot in what you say. Since I have been living here, I feel like a new person.

SK: I think all of us have a home. It may be a place we do not find until we cut the apron strings. Maybe some people do not discover it until they are old and gray. But the minute we set foot on that spot, we know we are "home."

The next card, the Two of Coins, in the Twelfth House of Secret Enemies, suggests that it may not always be easy to make a living in one's home. For this individual is standing by the sea and those two coins in front of him, along with that worried look on his face, suggest that he is having a tough time getting his checkbook to balance.

H: I just applied for another loan the other day. Getting through the winter here is something of a challenge.

SK: But this fellow on the card is standing with his back to the sea. So his eyes are not looking away from his home but right at it and he seems determined to find a way to become financially solvent. And he has a strong face. I am sure *she* will.

H: One way or another I have always managed to squeak by.

SK: And this last card, which is the indicator for the life, assures us that you will. For it is the Ace of Coins, which means that money is always there when you need it although there are probably a lot of job and career changes throughout the life. But the picture on the card says it, for there is your home by the sea and coming out of the clouds is the hand of Providence dropping pennies from heaven to provide for you.

Past Lives

Throne I—Ace of Cups
The Reaper, Justice, The High Priestess, The Wheel of Fortune, The Angel of Time

Throne II—Ace of Swords
The Lovers, The Hermit, The World, The Sun

Throne III—Ace of Coins
The Lightning-Struck Tower, The Hierophant, Strength, Day of Judgment

Throne IV—Ace of Wands
The Fool, The Devil, The Moon, The Star, The Empress, The Emperor, The Magician, The Hanged Man, The Chariot

SK: Now, Harriet, we are going to look at your life in a somewhat different way. We are going to examine three areas of your life— childhood and young adulthood, work and career, love and marriage—

and trace major events in each. Then, if you like, we will take a peek at some of your past lives.

H: I can hardly wait for that!

SK: In your case, I think that should prove most interesting. We are starting, however, with Throne I, which has to do with the first thirty years or so of this present life. The Ace of Cups here suggests that you might have been something of a "party girl," or perhaps liked to have a good time?

H: I am afraid I did start rather early and that habit pattern has been hard to break.

SK: Your childhood—or at least where the Tarot chooses to begin the tale—starts on a rather ominous note with the card of The Reaper. Was there a death in the family during your early childhood?

H: In a sense there was, for my parents divorced.

SK: Oh yes, I see it now and there must have been a prolonged custody battle in the courts for the next card is Justice.

H: Yes, there was. And "Mommy Dearest" won.

SK: I guess there is no need to ask you to elaborate on that statement as your mother comes up as The High Priestess, which says it all—a woman alone who is unhappy, moody, and critical.

H: That is her all right, and she has not changed.

SK: But then later she started going with someone else, did she?

H: Yes, for a while. That was when I was in my teens.

SK: On The Wheel of Fortune card there is a man and woman partying it up but there is a third figure who has slipped off the wheel. In fact, all you can see of this person are the legs so the indication is that you felt out of the picture at the time.

H: On the card, there is a hand turning the wheel. And it was around this time that I took up weaving as a way to maintain my sanity.

SK: It is interesting how the same card can tell several stories at once. With the final card of this throne, you are truly back in the picture as The Angel of Time, a woman who seems to have it very much together. And I think the reason for that is that she is standing by the edge of a body of water. So she is where you are. It is a nice ending for a somewhat difficult early life.

H: It did have its share of lumps.

SK: Okay, now we will look at Throne II, which deals with work and career. The Ace of Swords here indicates that there have been some problems and frustrations but the rest of the cards indicate that you find fulfillment in a career. In fact, two careers.

H: Two careers?

SK: Yes, this is a very easy throne to interpret. In sequence, the cards are The Lovers, The Hermit, The World, and The Sun. The Lovers, which is, of course, marriage, was the first career. As this is followed by The Hermit it is clear that the marriage did not work out. But The World card—which is where you are now, or at least, soon will be—depicts a woman who is dancing for joy because she likes what she does creatively. And since the final card in this throne is The Sun, it looks like marriage is definitely going to be a second career for you and this time around, love will be here to stay. And incidentally, The Sun and The World are the cards I call "the happiness twins" so to have those together in the same throne is quite positive.

H: I think right now I am in between The Hermit and The World stages.

SK: Well, that is better than being between the devil and the deep blue sea. And it is nice to know that the "good stuff" is ahead of you.

H: If I could only be sure that all the "bad stuff" is behind me.

SK: Well, the "bad stuff" never entirely disappears, but with the "happiness twins" there is plenty of sunshine coming your way, believe me, Harriet.

We now go to Throne III, which is love and marriage. The Ace of Coins here is very powerful so whatever your experiences may have been to date, things are going to work out for you eventually and very well indeed.

H: That is certainly good to hear.

SK: We can see that things do not start off very well for the first card in the sequence is The Lightning-Struck Tower with two people being hauled out of their home. That probably represents the recent past; I think you are still feeling the effects of having your marriage being "hit by lightning" as it were.

H: I would say, Sandor, that describes my feelings fairly well.

SK: The next card is important because it tells you where you go from here. It is The Hierophant.

H: He looks like a priest. Does that mean I have to become some kind of religious fanatic?

SK: Not necessarily. In ancient Egypt the heirophant was the revealer of sacred things. You can see there are two large keys on the bottom of the card and what is being suggested is that for you the key to wholeness is developing your spiritual nature. This may well be a karmic testing period and consciousness-raising may be what you need to do at this time of your life.

H: I am reading *The Snow Leopard* right now and I find this book is really hitting me where I live.

SK: I think you are very much on the right track, Harriet. It is reading works like that, along with meditation, that is going to raise your consciousness and that's what it is all about for you at the present time. For you see, the cards show a real progression here: The Tower says you get hit by lightning; with The Hierophant you get "religion"; and the next card in the sequence is Strength—a woman who is strong because she has developed the spiritual side of her nature. She is also known as The Enchantress and she is enchanting precisely because there is a spiritual mystique about her.

H: I think this part of the reading has indicated "Where I am coming from" more than anything else.

SK: Also, where you are going. For the final card in this throne is Day of Judgment and it could not be more explicit for it depicts a man, woman, and child, and they form a blessed trinity.

H: This reading is really picking me up!

SK: Okay, Harriet, now are you ready for a glimpse of some of your past incarnations?

H: By all means!

SK: I should point out that this part of the reading is purely intuitive. We turn all the cards in this throne over, look at them individually and then as a whole, and just see what impressions come to mind. What is interesting is that people who have tried to trace their past lives by hypnotic regression, meditation, dreams, going to psychics, or whatever, often feel that this spread confirms what they have already discovered about their past lives.

H: If a person was a historical figure, would this spread be able to show it?

SK: Possibly. One interesting thing about this spread is that you either get an overview of several different lives over the centuries, or the Tarot takes up one past life and goes into depth on that life alone. Do you have any particular feelings about who or what you were in another life?

H: Yes, I have very strong feelings about a life in czarist Russia around the turn of the century and during the years before the revolution.

SK: Okay, let's see what comes up. The Ace of Wands here suggests that you have had some real struggles in one or more of your past lives. The first card in the sequence is the card of The Fool. That indicates that you are an old soul.

H: Others have told me that.

SK: In this spread, when The Fool comes up as the first card of this Past Lives Throne, it is invariably significant for it is usually a sign of a pilgrim on The Path.

Now, let's turn all the cards in this throne over and see what we shall see. The Fool is followed by The Devil, The Moon, The Star, The Emperor, The Empress, The Magician, The Hanged Man, and The Chariot. Hmmm, I think I see this as one life. Do you feel that you might in some way have been associated with the rulers of Russia, Nicholas and Alexandra?

H: Ever since I can remember! I went to the Soviet Union one summer and when I arrived in St. Petersburg—which is now known as Leningrad—I had the most incredible feeling of *déja vu*!

SK: Do you think you were Nicholas or Alexandra?

H: No, one of the daughters, I think. Maybe Tatania.

SK: Well, you may feel that you were one of the daughters of the czar but the life we are getting here is that of Rasputin.

H: You must be kidding!

SK: Well, see for yourself. The sequence starts with The Fool, which would be Rasputin traveling across Siberia as a *starets,* a kind of wandering holy man. The Devil and The Moon suggest the period when he was involved with the *khylsty* and satanic worship. But then comes The Star when he cleaned up his act, became profoundly religious, and discovered he was a psychic healer. Then his voices tell him he has a mission to save Russia so he journeys to St. Petersburg where he meets The Empress and The Emperor—Alexandra and Nicholas—and heals their son as The Magician. The Hanged Man tells us of his unhappy fate when he was murdered by the *boyars,* that is, the nobles who were jealous of his influence over the royal family.

H: They had quite a time killing him off, didn't they?

SK: He was poisoned, shot, and bludgeoned. But when his body was fished out of the river three days later, water was found in his lungs. So he actually died by drowning.

H: That is wild!

SK: Actually, I think it says more about the ineptness of his assassins than anything else. I mean he *did* die from a physical cause. And the tale ends with the card of The Chariot, which suggests a troika taking his body to the icy river.

H: It does seem to be all of a piece. But tell me, how does reincarnation work? I mean, is it possible to be a male in one life and then a female in the next?

SK: According to the Life Readings given by Edgar Cayce, there is no set pattern. Some people come back now in one sex, now in another, and others seem to lead a whole string of lives in the same sex. I guess that there are probably a number of things involved, including the kind of lesson you need to learn in a given life and probably sometimes it can be learned better as a woman, other times as a man.

But to get back to the spread, you may indeed have been Tatania, or one of the other daughters—or even the son—of Nicholas and Alexandra, but in order to reveal this to you, the Tarot may have found it easier to describe the life of a man who played an important role in yours and one with a number of dramatic highlights that could be pictured. What is particularly interesting is that in The Twelve Houses spread that we did for this life, The Empress came up in the First House of Personality as a covering influence for the life. It is just possible that we somehow slipped into a past life without realizing it. There are ways of finding out. It depends upon how deeply you want to go.

H: I would really like to find out more about that last life. Is there some spread we can throw that will do that?

SK: There is a spread that was supposedly favored by that incredible magician, Aleister Crowley. If any Tarot spread can give you the answer you seek about your past life, this one can. It is called Opening the Key (see page 92).

Opening the Key

SK: This should be interesting, Harriet, because if any spread can pin down that last life of yours in Russia this one should be able to do it, but we should also keep in mind that some things cannot be pinned down so easily. We will use The Chariot as the main significator as that was the final card in the Past Lives spread. We are going to leave it in the pack, however, so go ahead and cut and shuffle the way you usually do.

All right, now that you have done that I would like you to cut the pack once to your left. Now cut each of those piles once to your left. Although I said that The Chariot would be our main significator card, I also imagined two other significator cards for your last life—the Page of Cups for Tatania and The Magician for "Father Gregory," that is, Rasputin. If the Page of Cups appears in the pile with The Chariot the indication is that you were Tatania; while The Magician in the same pile would suggest Rasputin. If either of these combinations occurs we can then do follow-up spreads and really check it out. We find The Chariot in this second pile.

H: I am on pins and needles, Sandor. Tell me, which is it? Who was I?

SK: Guess what? Neither.

H: Neither?

SK: Neither! The failure of a pre-determined combination to appear in the Tarot does not necessarily mean that you were not one of those people. The Tarot is not saying that—or, at least, we do not know it is saying that. What it is saying is that for the moment it does not choose to reveal that information but rather considers other facts more important for you to know and dwell upon. You see, Harriet, the Tarot does not always tell us what we want to hear, but rather, what is best for us to know for the development of our soul.

H: And what is that?

SK: First, I have to fan these cards out and see which cards in the pile with The Chariot are actually to be read according to the numbering system of the spread.

Just three cards come up—the Two of Coins, The Hermit, and The Enchantress. They have all come up before so they have to be important. We will start with the Two of Coins, which came up before in your Horoscope Spread in your Twelfth House of Secret Enemies (known as the karmic house). I think now that we have done your Past Lives Spread, we can see the real significance of that card. Because regardless of who you were, there was a duality about that life. I think you were highly evolved in some ways but also that you were carried away and failed to keep the proper balance.

H: Can you be a little more specific?

SK: I see the duality as a pull between the material and the spiritual. That is further suggested by the next card of The Hermit, who is on a mountain top, gazing at a star. In the Past Lives Spread, he came up in Throne II after your marriage breakup and so he represents the stage where you are now. You remember that The World and The Sun are the closing stages of your career throne, preceded by the lesson of The Hermit. The Hermit teaches that spiritual wisdom is often realized after a period of solitude.

Everything comes together in the final card of The Enchantress. The Enchantress is physically able to cope with all life situations because she is *spiritually* strong. By being spiritually strong she is psychologically whole—there is no longer any duality about her for she has found the proper balance and achieved harmony with herself and the universe.

Once this duality has been resolved, Harriet, the implications for success are clearly represented by the cards of The World and The Sun.

To my memory of:

My parents, Francesco and Leitiza Marino

My in-laws, John and Anna De Angelo

CONTENTS

CHAPTER THREE
EMPLOYMENT

CHAPTER FOUR
THE MEN AND WOMEN

CHAPTER FIVE

STARTING A NEW LIFE

CHAPTER SIX

REFLECTIONS ON LIFE

add photo here

Portrait of Leo Marino 1946

Preface

I was born at the start of the great depression on December 25, 1928, back in a time of living in close proximity to other similar tenements, all with the same squalor. There were brick buildings turned black with the foul smoke emitting from the smoke stacks of the factories. My boyhood home, in which I was born, was at one time, according to my father, a beautiful home in a nice neighborhood, to which he purchased in the year of 1919.

At that time the street had wooden bricks which were in the process of being replaced with concrete. All the home owners were being assessed for this expensive work, so that was a jolt for my dad. By the late 1920s and early 1930s, the neighborhood started to take a drastic decline, partly due to the great depression. Mortgages were almost unobtainable, due to the decline of the neighborhood with the onset of the factories, which were in the process of being divided up for the so called needle trade. Walking by any of them, you could hear the hum of the sewing machines. With many homes such as ours, our backyards were ringed with factories. Ours in particular had a huge factory that manufactured quilts and mattress. Also many factories were operating twenty-four hours a day, which was not so pleasant in the summer time. All of this added to the misery of the area.

But amongst all this filth oozing from the factories, people took great pride in keeping the inside of their homes as clean as possible. The outside of their homes belied the fact of the interior. This was later attested to by people who visited these homes. The outside of the homes were for the most part, deplorable, living in a time of great deprivation, but it was with great pride that even with their meager possessions that we all perserved.

My early life was fraught with childhood illness, mainly caused by the aforementioned problems of my neighborhood. While this was a big obstacle to overcome, it also gave me the determination to persevere, in spite of some harrowing sicknesses that were challenging to me.

Growing up in New Haven, CT in the 1930s, I was dubbed a depression era baby. Born at the start of the great depression, knowing nothing but what my immediate environment allowed me to see. Our childhood was spent in close quarters, being almost confined to our poverty stricken area. As I mention in this book, it was through the good graces of good people who showed me that the opportunities for a better life can be had just by sheer determination to succeed and not blamed or excused due to the circumstances into which you were born.

As I advanced to my later teens, conscription was the stumbling block, and one in which I had and along with everyone else. It was something that we all discussed on a daily basis. Boys who were coming of age for the draft saw their childhood ending quite abruptly. Luckily, my age group was going to be spared the horrors of war, as the war ended just as I turned of age. After discussing with the many veterans of all branches of service, I settled for my choice: the U.S. Navy. I knew the Army life would not agree with my health problems, and because of my time line, I had all options open to me. I enlisted in the Navy at the age of sixteen and was sworn in at the age of seventeen, on January 7, 1946. As I write this book, one of the reasons I chose the Navy was the many opportunities that would be available to me. My first officer, who imparted a lasting impression on me was a man by the name of Chief Castle, a spit and polish man, but one of compassion.

Boot camp experience was grueling for me. With the challenges of training while weighing only one hundred fifteen pounds, and not very strong at that, if it mattered at all. A lot of the boys seemed much stronger, but had to drop out of training and were sent home. That gave me the courage to push on and succeed. My years in the U.S. Navy guided me in the years ahead, and encouraged me to have a positive outlook on life. I accepted it and was content with my service in the Navy. Having being offered a free college education on three different occasions in my life, one at the age of fifteen, one by the Navy, and the opportunity of the G.I. bill, I declined for many different, but stupid, reasons.

After my service, I settled into a variety of jobs, trolling through different factories until I found my niche in sales work, albeit a delivery salesman. It gave me the courage in later years to own my own business. I employed many people, and my business also helped me to deal with the earlier failures in life.

Part of this book could not be possible without the later part, which was my desire to meet a nice girl to share my life with. After meeting an assortment of wonderful girls, I finally found the girl who I most shared the same values with. My other girlfriends also had some of the same qualities but on a different timeline. So it was that I chose Teresa De Angelo, whose family and mine came from the same area in Italy. I then went on my journey with Teresa and began our plans to raise a family and to have a nice home. Teresa bore me three wonderful children, three gifts from God: Gail, Janet and David, who in turn gave Teresa and me eight beautiful grandchildren: Kara, Alexa, Andrew, Jaclyn, Jessica, Krista, Alyssa, and Gina. Being a survivor of my faults and failures, I am just happy that I had something to contribute to the later part of my life, by setting an example for my children and grandchildren, hoping to give them the inspiration to succeed at whatever endeavor they choose to explore.

On my journey, while not remarkable, my legacy is that I did the best I could with the talents bestowed upon me by my parents, Francesco and Leitiza Marino. The one gift that they both gave me was a love of family that I treasured the most, not in words, but by deeds. Also, my siblings Raffaela, Mary, Ralph, Elizabeth, Elvira, and Frank, who by their very nature helped to make our family as good as it was.

What I hope you will discover in this book that I was just an ordinary man, but when I was confronted with some grave decisions and extraordinary circumstances, I made a decision that I resolved to not let it hinder me. What is a man, if he does not go forward, and continue on with his life? I am glad I did, and hopefully I gave inspiration to my children and grandchildren.

Enjoy this book and my journey. It is a small piece of work, but I have put forth the many people who gave me guidance and friendship. Some were characters of a questionable nature, but also at the same time, gave me a lifetime of wonderful memories.

204 Greene Street 1960

CHAPTER ONE

204 Greene Street

BIRTH

I was born in our house at 204 Green Street (an apartment, really) at 3:00 am on a bitterly cold Christmas morning, 1928. I was the fourth of seven children, one of three boys. All seven of us were born in that house. I remember my sister Vera and brother Frank's births. Dr. Conte and a midwife came to deliver them. My father gave the doctor five dollars and a bottle of wine. Your house was used for everything from births to deaths to everything in between. When I was 12, I came down with a tonsil problem. My father called the Doctor's and two came to the house. One was Dr. Severino. He laid me on the kitchen table, then used ether to put me to sleep and proceeded to remove my tonsils. When my oldest sister, Raefalla, died, we had her wake at the house. She suffered severe burns around the neck when her frilly dress caught fire from flames in a trash dump in our backyard. A next door neighbor hopped the fence and smothered her with his body. In 1929, burn treatment was not perfected and she succumbed to infection. It was Easter Sunday. She was only five. An undertaker was called to prepare her for burial, and the body was viewed at our house. My sister told me many years later that my mother would always sing a song while she did her work in the house. The song she would hum to herself was about the daughter she lost in a fire.

HOUSE

My earliest recollections are of a life of deprivation. Sandwiched between two houses, we lived in what is called a cold water flat:

extremely cold in the winter and hot in the summer. In the winter, the windows on the house would turn to solid ice. To keep warm, we slept with our coats on and any other clothes we had. We slept three in a bed in an alcove in the front room: three boys in one bed, three girls in another bed. My mother and father slept in the back room. All together, we were eight people in five rooms. As the only source of heat, the coal stove in the kitchen was the focal point of the house. We would put orange and lemon skins on top to give the house a nice aroma. A chore that my brother, Ralph, and I had was to carry the wood and coal up from the cellar every Saturday. This included ten pails of coal and three bushels of wood. My mother would chop the wood into small units. I would go with my father in his small wagon. We would go in the back of the furniture stores and collect the old discarded wood from the packaging crates.

There were other troubles with the house, ranging from the bothersome to the dangerous. Since we did not have screens on the windows, we had to hang fly paper from the ceilings in summer. Electricity coming into the house was brought in on a very slim cable, and we had wires hanging down from the ceiling, crossing room to room. Wires were encased in walls without the benefit of cable. Also mice were a continual problem in our house. It was something we had to live with. We had traps all over the house. I remember lying in bed at night hearing them crawl along the slats in the walls. Rats were another problem, though not as severe. In those days, we dumped our garbage in the backyard and burned it. Then we'd cover up the ashes. Later on, the city started to pick up the garbage. One day, my mother started screaming down in the cellar. A rat was nibbling at her shoes. I rescued her by hitting the rat and pulling her upstairs. That's when we started putting larger traps in the cellar.

While we were poor, we were never dirt poor. There were families in our neighborhoods that were in worse financial shape. The apartments these people lived in can be described as "horrible," at best. In some, as many as three families had to share a single toilet in the hallway. Our house only had a toilet, with the water tank on top, and it flushed by pullchain. There was no shower or tub, so keeping our bodies clean was difficult to manage. We had to wash at the Boys Club on Jefferson Street or public bathhouses, the main two on St. John Street and Oak Street where the air-rights garage now stands because they had showers with hot water. Mostly everyone used this form of bathing. There were ladies' days and men's days. This practice didn't change until the 1950s. It was difficult to keep the old house, our bodies, and clothes clean because pollution and smoke made the house dirty inside with soot. To keep our clothes clean, water was heated on the stove, and clothes scrubbed on a washboard. Monday was wash day.

HOW FATHER WOULD SAVE MONEY

When we were younger, my father would cut my brothers' and my hair to save money. We did not go to the barbershop because they charged fifteen cents. The worst was in the summer when he would give us a very close haircut, like a shaved head, so it would last all summer. It embarrassed us, so we tried to wear hats so the boys would not poke fun at us, calling us baldy. My father also saved money by repairing shoes. He had a shoemaker anvil that he would put on his lap and resole our shoes. One summer, I pretty much went barefoot in order to save my shoes for school.

When my father could afford it, he would treat us by taking us out to the Savin Rock Amusement Park. This meant taking a trolley car to uptown New Haven then transferring to a trolley going to West Haven. Just travelling on a trolley car was a treat for us, since we almost never took the trolley car. At the park, we almost never got to go on any of the rides. One ride that I always wanted to go on was the boat ride with little powerboats that you could steer yourself. It traveled some distance around the area of Savin Rock. Much to our dismay, my father could not afford to send us all on the rides. The average price of admission on the rides was .10 cents. We just walked around until late in the afternoon when my father would buy us all frozen custard, which was our treat. Times like these were a bit of a stretch for my father, since the cost for the entire day was around $2.

The year 1939 brought the World's Fair to New York. It was the dream of every child in my neighborhood to go. I don't believe anybody in my immediate area went; we could only marvel at the beauty and excitement of it. We would see pictures in the classroom or at the newsreels at the movies, knowing that it would be impossible for us to go. Being poor, you make adjustments by blocking a lot of things out of your mind. As I saw things that were beyond my reach, I diverted my attention by engaging in other pursuits, such as sports (when I was physically able), the Boy's Club, and the public library in downtown New Haven, where I would immerse myself in books.

When I did not have to help my father collect wood or go shopping at the market on Saturday, I would walk downtown to the library and listen to teachers read us stories or just browse around and read a book by myself. On one particular cold day, I left to go to the library. On this day, a writer of children's books was going to give a lecture all about writing. The distance from my house to the library was about one and a half miles from Green Street to Elm and Temple. The temperature was below freezing, and I did not have warm enough clothes to ward off the cold, lacking a hat, mittens, and scarf. I started to freeze halfway there, but I decided to continue my journey to the library. When I finally arrived, my feet were frozen and I was shivering so badly that the librarian got a pail of hot water and had me soak my feet to get warm. As a consequence, I missed the lecture. The librarian gave me a book to take home to keep along with a pair of woolen socks to keep my feet warm for the walk back home. I loved going to the library to read because of its peaceful atmosphere, something I could not do at home.

Since money was scarce, I had a paper route after school, earning fifty cents weekly. This helped me pay for going to the movies, which, in my youth, cost ten cents. Twenty five cents were put to a Christmas club so I could have money to buy gifts. One Christmas, there was only one toy left for all of us to play with. It was a little carousel made out of metal. In the really bad years, there was nothing at all. I remember getting our first radio; it was a box with a dial at the bottom and a speaker on the top. Some man my father knew gave us his old one because he was getting a new one. We suddenly thought that we were rich because we had a radio. My father was so proud to have supplied his family with a radio. We would listen to all the programs. I was so happy that I could now talk about the radio to my friends, since we were the last family to get one.

I also ran errands for people for ten cents. I would go to the city warehouse and get their groceries, sometimes carrying them up four flights of stairs. In the summer, I would get ice for them in a wagon my father made. The icehouse was on Franklin Street, where I-91 stands today, and it sold ice in units for ten cents, twenty five cents, or fifty cents. My brother Ralph and I would get a twenty five cent piece for the icebox, which would last three days in summer and longer in winter, but it meant cleaning out the tray on the bottom daily. I believe it was 1942 when we got our first electric refrigerator. Before the new fridge, my mother would set the milk out on the windowsill during the winter to keep cold along with the other perishables. The cream would rise and pop out the cardboard top of the bottle.

The farmer's market where my father would go shopping for food also gave us some employment opportunities. They were always hiring young boys to load and unload produce from the trains. On one such occasion, my friend Bob Pothier called me and asked if I wanted to earn $5. I said yes. He told me that this man wanted someone to unload Christmas trees from a boxcar onto a truck. Bob, another boy named Al, and I went to the market where the railroad car was. We waited for the man to come with the truck. By the time he arrived, it started to drizzle a light rain, which later turned to sleet. As we unloaded the Christmas trees, which were tied in little bunches, it seemed to me that this was much tougher than we had bargained for. Bob and Al who were real tall for their ages and did most of the heavier lifting while I packed the trees on the truck. While we did this, we did not wear gloves, and by the end of the day, our hands were caked in sticky sap and needles.

After six hours, we were finished. Al lived in the market area, so he had a short walk home, while Bob and I had to walk home from the market to Green Street. Even though our walk wasn't that long, the sleeting made for a miserable time as we were slipping and sliding all the way home. Bob lived down the corner from me in the Schubert building. By the time we got home, our clothes were full of ice with ice hanging down from our hats. As soon as I got into my house, my mom took off all my clothes and hung them on the stove to dry. She scolded me for being out all day in that bad weather. I gave my mom the $5 that I earned. She hugged me and told me never to do that again. She said she was worried sick about me. While that was one of the most difficult $5 that I had ever earned, it was gratifying to bring some money home to my mom.

Even though we didn't have much money, my mother worked hard to maintain a functioning household. My mother was the first to rise every morning. She lit the stove with wood and paper, and then with coal. Then she'd get breakfast ready: bread and butter heated in the oven. Most of the time we had cocoa to drink. Our daily meals (lunch and dinner) consisted mostly of some sort of pasta. My father would buy ten pound boxes from the macaroni factory on Franklin Street. He would buy the ones that were all mixed and broken because they were the cheapest. Most Saturday mornings were spent at the Farmer's Market across from the Railroad Station to see if we could get some cheap food. We mostly bought what the farmers did not sell. My father prided himself on always making sure we did not go hungry, even in the darkest days of the Depression. During this time, he was out of work but refused aid from the city. Much to his sorrow, he had to accept groceries from his brother, who owned a small grocery store, and would give us whatever he did not sell. By the time we received the items, they were often damaged or expired, but my mother used them the best she could. My brother, Ralph, and I would go every Saturday afternoon to carry home what he gave us. At this time, I was about eight years old and Ralph was nine and a half. We would walk from Green Street to State Street to the store and back, carrying two bags of groceries each.

One day, we were stopped by a group of Polish boys who lived in the neighborhood. They started to harass and beat us. While we tried to defend ourselves, a man came to help us. After that, we took a different route to and from the store. It was much longer but safer. Later on in life, we became friends with our attackers. My usual taunt was to remind them they never got our groceries.

CORNER STORES

A lot of the products we now purchase at the store were delivered to us at home, including milk, bread, fish, fruits, vegetables, and housewares. Milk was delivered by horse and wagon, as were most of the goods. The milkman's horse knew the route so well that he would move from house to house by himself. After a little time, the horse automatically moved. Due to the horses on the street, manure posed a problem, especially in the summer. The city had the sanitation men clean it up. The situation cleared up toward the end of WWII when products started to be delivered by trucks. Ice deliveries were a treat in the summer because we would jump on the back of the truck, pick up the broken ice, and chew it to cool off.

Even though most products were delivered to homes, every neighborhood had its own corner grocery store. Stores carried canned goods, meats, and other sundry items. The sale of food then was confined largely to food that was in large containers. Olives were in a barrel, cookies in ten pound boxes and sold one pound at a time. Cereal was oatmeal in a seven ounce box; some stores even had corn flakes, which, at that time, were a treat. Candy was sold by the piece, one cent each.

On our way to the Boys Club, we would stop at the corner store and buy a bunch of penny candies. Some owners were not nice and mean to us. So every chance we got we distracted the owner by asking for something in the back of the store. We would walk up and down the candy case, forcing the owner to walk with us until we decided which penny candy we wanted. We would go in five or six at a time, and each one of us did the same thing. After walking the length of the aisle, my friend would say he wanted candy down the other end of the case. Every time the owner turned away from us, we would help ourselves to everything we could fit in our pockets. When the owner came back, we all bought one cent's worth of candy and he would then start to swear at us in Italian. To further harass him, we would band together our money and one at a time order a very small amount of cold cuts in which he had to go into the cooler and slice it up. To do that, he would wrap an apron over his bald head to not feel the cold. The rest of us peeked through the front window laughing at him. During Halloween, we went in the yard across the street and flipped little rocks at his window. We watched from behind the hedges as he walked up and down in front of his store wondering where they came from.

Going to the store to purchase ice cream on a stick cost three cents. To pay for it, we would pick up empty soda bottles and return them for two cents each. My friend hated the owner so much that he used every chance he got to disrupt the man's life. He managed to reach behind the counter and get a handful of ice cream sticks with the word FREE printed on them that had been returned. Ice cream companies would put the word FREE on some sticks, and if you got one, you could return the stick for another ice cream. My friend gave all of us some sticks, and we would come back later to use them, being very polite to the owner. As always, he cursed us out, but we just smiled and thanked him.

One thing that had to be store bought was American bread. It would be dropped off in breadboxes twice daily and left outside the store. The bread we ate was mostly homemade or Italian. A company called Bond Bread supplied the boxes outside the stores. They were the only ones at the time in the American bread business. One winter night coming home from the club, we stopped at the store and filled his breadbox up with snow. The next day he was on a rampage questioning everybody about it.

Grocers would order however many loaves of bread they needed for the day's business, which was the reason for the bread box. The bread companies did not have a return policy at this time, so the bread men would place their order in the bread box outside the store. Also during this time a new bread company came on the scene named Wonder Bread, and they instituted the policy of accepting returns to crash the market, and they were successful at it. They also had a line of snack cakes such as cupcakes, Twinkies, and snow balls. It was also their policy to give the grocers single unit sample cupcakes to give their customers. The policy was still in place when I got hired in 1959. This story brings back a lot of memories to me. One in particular happened at a market on the way to school each day. My friends and I would wait for the bread man to enter the store, and then we would help ourselves to the samples of cakes in the back of the truck. After I was hired, I went up to the man that had the route at that time. He remembered all the missing cakes and said, "Yes, I never caught the little bitches". I told him I was one of them and he remembered seeing them open the back door but said they were too fast for him. He said, "If I caught you, I would have given you a good kick in the ass". I had a lot of fun reminiscing about those days.

SKIN PROBLEM

For a lot of children I knew, health problems were many. When I was about eight years old, I contracted a very serious skin problem, which plagued me for the next five years. At the onset of my condition, the doctors thought it was my diet, which consisted mainly of pasta with sauce. The acidity in the sauce was causing a red, itchy rash. Tomatoes were eliminated but to no avail. I had to wear cotton gloves because it was thought to be contagious (which it was not). Various creams and medicines did not help, so a doctor told my father to put me in the hospital. I was placed in a tent of lights to dry it up, but it failed to work. Next came a very painful procedure, which, to this day, I still remember. They strapped me in a bed, and with doctors and nurses holding me down, a doctor slit my skin at the wrist and started to strip the skin off my hands until both were left raw, in the belief that new skin would heal the problem. I endured all this pain without the benefit of anesthesia. I had to stay for two weeks in order to recover. Still, after all this, my skin problem did not go away. I was always ashamed to have other kids see my hands, so I often stayed home and missed a lot of school.

I'm not sure what eventually cleared it up at the age of 13 or 14. I think there was something in the house causing it, so I would sit in the sun as much as possible, and I got better results. Later, it was diagnosed as an allergy due to bedbugs.

CIRCUMCISION

At the age of twelve I started having problems with frequent infections on my penis, so our family doctor (Dr. Severino), suggested to my father I have a circumcision which would clear up the infection. Plans were made for me by Dr. Severino to have the procedure at the New Haven Hospital.

My recollection of that day is as follows. I was accompanied to the hospital by my sister Mary and her friend Connie. My father had to be at the factory early that day and my mom could not leave my brother Frank and sister Vera home since they were less than 5 years old at the time. Also, my mom could not speak English.

The walk to the hospital was about one to two miles. The gloomy weather was only matched by my own disposition of having this surgery. Upon entering the hospital I noticed the ward where I had been for my appendix operation and there was no sign of the nurse that took care of me (a bad omen for me). I was brought into a room and soon the nurses arrived to prep me for the procedure. At this time my sister Mary and Connie had to leave. They had to get to the shirt factory where they were employed. They gave me some hugs and kisses and assurance that I would be fine.

I was put on a gurney and brought into another room and within minutes I was asleep. I awoke to find myself in a smaller room and was given instructions by a nurse to not disturb the bandages. I felt like I had a ball on my legs. After several hours I was put back onto a gurney and wheeled into the hallway along side other patients who were awaiting room assignments. That day turned into night and still on the gurney and no room. Any kind of movement was met by pain due to the expansion and contractions of my penis.

My cries of pain were met by a stern nurse who provided little comfort for me, in short, "shut the hell up". The silence in the hallway was broken up by my wailing and moaning and the shuffling of some feet. It was late in the evening when I heard some heavy footsteps approaching. I could hear female voices and they sounded familiar. Indeed it was Mary and Connie. Connie at the first sight of me exclaimed, "God this is awful", due to the sheets being soiled. She asked me, "Leo, has the nurse been here"? I said, "no, not for some time". Connie went searching for a nurse while Mary stayed with me by my side. Connie did not find anyone but she found the linen closet and got new sheets and found the medical cabinet and got new dressings. Connie takes off her coat and instructs Mary how she can help her. Connie tells me, "Leo I am going to change your dressings and sheets since they are all caked in blood". Connie put on a hospital apron and with Mary on one side, instructed Mary how to help her. While all this is going on, I am looking at Connie with some trepidation to say the least. Connie says, "Leo, I am going to start lifting the dressings off, you might feel a little sting because the bandages are stuck to your skin. She had a soapy solution to ease the pain. Connie with the precision of a professional nurse did just that, gently removed the dressings. She then went about cleaning the wound sight with Mary applying new bandages to my penis. Mary then took all the soiled linen and dressings to dispose of them. When they were done, a lot of discomfort was over. I called Connie and Mary closer to me and shamefully whispered, "I am having some pain when I am erected". Connie ever the diplomat said, "Leo, try and have a clean mind". Nudging me gently, they bent over and kissed me goodbye. Years later Connie and I would have some fun with that day, reminding me of how she took care of my package. Tell the first one I was here first!

ASTHMA

At the age of thirteen, I came down with asthma. Many days, my asthma attacks were so bad that I could not function at all. Wheezing and coughing, breathing was like someone sitting on my chest and strangling me. One night, I had gone to bed early because I didn't feel good. My mother applied a sort of pumice, then called mustard plaster, wrapped in flannel cloth and heated up, which she then rubbed on my chest. Along with cough medicine to try and stop me from choking, I usually found some relief. But on this night, nothing seemed to be working. As the night wore on, I kept getting progressively worse; every breath seemed my last. My mom held me and tried to help me breathe. It was a very cold evening in a very cold house. But I was sweating so profusely, I had to change my clothes. It was a long night, sitting up in bed with mom holding me so that I could breathe easier. My mother wrapped me in clothes warmed by the stove and continued massaging my chest. After what seemed to me to be an eternity, mom was able to get me to relax long enough so that I was able to doze off for a little while. As I awoke from my little rest and looked towards the window, I watched the sun come up shining through the ice-crusted windows. My mom was sitting in the rocking chair. The light came through the glass and glazed off my mother's gray hair, forming what looked like a halo to me. I remember thinking she was a saint, staying up with me all night long. My mother woke that morning like any other day, lighting the stove and getting breakfast ready, but without any sleep the night before. Later, I was examined by a doctor who told me that it was my mom who kept me alive that night with her sense to elevate me high enough to help me breathe. It was the most severe attack that I had ever had.

Being sickly as a child made it difficult to participate in sports with the other boys, but I did play football. Since we had no playground at school, we played in the public park, even though it was against the law. One of us watched for the police, and when they came, we all had to run away. The ball we played with was made out of newspapers rolled up with rubber bands. Having a real football to play with then was unheard of. One day, the kids handed me the ball to run, which they thought was a joke, but I ran the entire field for a touchdown. After that, I was never laughed at again.

Blame for my conditions fell on the environment because there was one other boy who had the same problem. Since his grandfather was a professor of music at Yale and his family was better off financially, he had access to better medicines. But he would share with me. As I discovered late in life, my asthma was due to my house. I was told that cockroaches, dust, and moldy wood triggered an attack. If I lived in a better house, I would not have had this problem. But since there was no money to send me away, I had to make the best of it, not over-exerting myself and trying to stay indoors on bad air days. Being in a heavy industrial area with the factory chimneys spewing out all kinds of fumes made some days terrible. We had factories all around our house, which were irritants as well. Directly in my backyard was the New Haven Quilt and Pad, which manufactured sleepwear. Working with cotton was dangerous because it is a highly combustible item. Across the street we had a gun factory called O.F. Mossberg. In the summertime, we could hear the machines running. On the next block, we had a great quantity of small factories producing shirts, dresses, and clothing. All these factories emitted an awful lot of pollution.

FACTORY LIFE

The treatment of people who worked in the factories was almost subhuman. My father told me a story of this man who got his fingers caught in the machine and sliced off. The bosses simply cleared the blood off and put someone else in the man's place. In those days, safety guards were not on any machines such as power press mills. If you refused to work under these conditions, you were automatically fired. My father was a very loyal worker at the factory by always being on time for work. He was scheduled to start work at 7 a.m., but he was there by 6 a.m. waiting for the factory doors to open. Despite this fierce loyalty, when I went to collect his personal belongings from his locker after he passed away, the foreman just pointed to a corner locker, weakly mentioning condolences before walking away. As I picked up my father's clothes, I thought of the many hardships he had to endure from this factory, and of the undying loyalty that he had for his work, only for it to end like this.

Factories harmed the people around them but were often deadly for those inside. Fires in the factories were common at the time, some small, others large. Most of the floors were made of wood and soaked with machine oil. One job I had Saturday mornings was cleaning up the threads from the sewing machines at shirt or dress shops for twenty five cents. I worked in the building where the infamous Franklin Street Fire occurred in 1954. Fifteen women burned to death on a fire escape because they did not know how to disengage the lever for the fire escape stairs.

On February 5th, 1941, a disastrous fire erupted in the factory in my backyard at the New Haven Quilt and Pad. We were awakened by this bright red glow coming in the window. The flames from the factory came halfway to our house. My sister Mary was the first to run down to the corner and pull the fire alarm on the pole. The firemen were unable to get a truck in the yards and had to run hoses through our cellar and in many cases, right through the first floor of the houses on our block. As we watched in utter horror, I remember seeing a man clinging to the edge of the window, and when he could not stand the heat any longer, he fell three floors and landed on our dump, receiving a crippling back injury. It was an extremely cold night and made everything freeze up. Other people also dropped from the second floor and were carried into our first floor apartment injured but gratefully alive. The next morning the firemen went into the factory and as we watched from the street, took out ten bodies. The bodies were laid on the sidewalk, covered by sheets. Some bodies were brought out in baskets as large as coffins. I heard one story where a man went back in at the start of the fire to retrieve his wallet but never come out. The sight of that disaster and memory of the ruins crumbling to ashes have never left my mind.

The factories that ringed my neighborhood were, for the most part, death traps, and also had some form of discrimination. The gun shop, which employed mostly Swedish and Irish, did not employ Italians. Until World War II, it was extremely difficult to get hired there since it was considered a very nice place to work. Sargent's, where my father worked, employed mostly Italians. The dress and shirt shops employed mostly Italian women who labored over sewing machines in a dinghy setting. The women were on piecework, meaning that they were paid for what they produced. Therefore, it was not uncommon for some women to bring work home to finish so they could meet their quota. A lot of times I would bring my sister Mary lunch at the factory so she did not have to take time to come home. This also was done by a lot of the women. Due to the amount of machines and clothes presses turned on, these garment factories emitted a lot of heat during the summer. Open windows and doors provided only some measure of relief. It was still very hot whenever I walked by these factories, and I watched steam rising from the clothes presses and the men who operated them perspiring with their shirts dripping wet. Some would have a towel on their neck. Women working on the sewing machines had very little time to chat with one another, not only because of their quota but a foreman as well, standing over them, making sure they did not stop. Women would complain of how mean some of these foremen were, and some of them trying to force themselves on them sexually. The molestation of women in the workplace was all too common then, but because jobs were scarce at the time, this was the only employment opportunity for a lot of young women.

Most people who worked in these factories lived within a three block radius of their work so they could walk. Some came home for lunch and had to be back at work within a half hour. The shop whistle would blow at noon, and I would watch them come running out of the shops so that they could have more time at home for lunch. Some felt it was worth it instead of bringing a sandwich to work.

Another factory that was a nice, clean place of employment was the New Haven Clock Shop on Hamilton Street. But again, to get hired there meant that you needed someone already working there to help you. I applied many times but was never hired. Maybe it was good for me because I probably would have spent my life there as so many people did. When foreign trade opened up it became the demise of this shop since watches could be made cheaper overseas. Same fate held true for the garment industry.

DOG ATTACK AND THE KIND MAN

On Franklin Street, there were a lot of small factories. We would use the walls of these buildings to play a game by throwing the ball at the wall and have someone catch it. If they missed, the one throwing the ball would score a point. One day, we were playing and a man told us to stop. We told him there were no windows on this wall and that there was nothing to break. We also informed the man that the owner had given us permission, which sent him into a fit of rage. Not thinking anything of it, we continued playing. Then we heard a dog barking. As the sound grew louder, there in the alleyway was this man again holding his dog. Then he released it, commanding the dog to attack. We started to run away, and I slipped and fell. By this time, the dog was all over me. The dog started to bite me, and I put my hands up to my neck and face for protection. The dog got a grip on my knee and started to rip my knee open when finally men in the next factory heard my screams. They pulled the dog off, and some other men came and started to fight with the dog's owner. As this was going on, one man picked me up and brought me to Dr. Conte's office on Wooster Place. He sewed up my knee and gave me an injection. The man then took me home and went back to work. Every time I went by where this nice man was working, I would wave to him, and he would wave and smile back.

Since we were of limited means, and without any good access to advice from any person in the field of law, seeking retribution of any kind would not have been productive. This incident was to have a profound impact on how I viewed dogs for the rest of my life. There were times when I would have bad dreams of dogs attacking me. As the years went by, I was able to tolerate them, but I still tried to keep my distance. Dogs on my paper route caused me some anguish, but I learned to control them.

BOYS CLUB

Despite the difficulties, we still found time as kids for leisure and fun. Located on Jefferson Street, the New Haven Boys Club provided an outlet for neighborhood kids, serving as a safe place to play. At that time, there was no place for girls. The dues for the club varied according to age. It started at twenty five cents a year for boys between the ages ten and thirteen. There were many activities that you could do. We had a reading room, room for games, such as checkers and Ping-Pong. Some nights they would show us movies which were silent films on a small screen. They had two basketball courts. There was a league composed of different teams throughout the city. At night after supper, weather permitting, we would bring our towel and go for a swim at the indoor pool. Swimming was in the nude. We did not have to have bathing suits. I guess no one ever gave it a second thought. When they had swimming meets, however, the participants wore bathing suits. You had to shower first and then get inspected by one of the club personnel. You stayed in the shower until you were clean. We'd partake in the many games offered to us. The counselors taught us how to swim by pushing us into the deep end of the pool. Because of the amount of boys using the pool, the club had time limits for being in the water. The pool times were listed so you could pick one. If you cheated and tried to get in a second pool time, they would punish you with a good slap on the butt.

If you were a troublemaker and caused unduly mischief, they would take your card away for a specified amount of time, and you would not be permitted until your sentence had expired. One day, my friend and I were causing some mischief in the gym. The man in charge grabbed us and locked us in a closet. We stayed there until the club was closing. When he let us out, he whacked our butts with a paddle. Needless to say, we did not disturb the peace again. What the Boy's Club represented to us was a home away from home. The club personnel were very strict but fair.

One of the pleasant memories I had of the Boy's Club was the day when a Yale student came to the club to ask the director if he could take some boys to Yale College to show them around the campus. I was elated when the director picked me along with five other boys to spend the day with the student touring Yale. I found out later that the student was from a very wealthy family. After touring the college, he took us to his dormitory and showed us all the nice products he had in his room, such as sports equipment, etc. Later on, he took us for lunch in the cafeteria where we thought we all died and went to heaven. We never saw so much food. During lunch, he said to save some room for dessert; he had a special treat for us. We said we thought we were dreaming and that this can't be true. Sure enough, after lunch, he took us to the ice cream plant around the corner, which was then the Sealtest Ice Cream Plant. After touring the plant, we went downstairs to a room and he said order anything you want. I felt so happy and so grateful to this person that I never wanted that day to end. And it did end, but not before he took us back to his room where he gave us all small footballs to take home. They were real but small. He took us back to the club and wished us all well. We all hugged him and thanked him for his kindness and generosity.

For two weeks in the summer, the club would take boys to Camp Clearview in Wallingford. In order to attend, you had to pay a fee, which my father could not afford. The fee was small but still out of our reach. Every summer, the boys would talk about signing up for camp, and I would make excuses and say I was going next year. But I never did. I would watch the buses pick up the boys and wonder if I would every get the chance to go to Camp Clearview. More heartbreaking to me was to hear of all the good times that the boys were having and hoping that maybe someday I share in them as well. Going to summer camp was the highlight of the summer season. I never experienced the joy of camp.

In the summer, when my father could, he would take my brother, Ralph, and I to Lighthouse Park. This required having to walk from our house to Lighthouse, which was a distance of about five miles. If my father did not have the entrance fee to enter the park, we would stop at Fort Hale Park, which was free. We had to step over a lot of rocks in the water. As we walked home down Woodward Avenue, we would see all the trolley cars passing us by. I would wonder if someday we would be able to afford a ride up and back to the park. On only a few occasions my father would take the whole family and spend the day there, bringing food from home for a picnic. We were never able to get a ride on the carousel or any other rides. We amused ourselves by swimming and playing on the beach. The dress code for men and boys required a top to our bathing suits or else a one-piece suit. Male swimmers were not allowed on the beach without complying with this rule.

Walking the five miles back home after swimming and playing in the water all day was rough. We were tired. The only times we had a chance to go to Lighthouse by trolley car was when the Neighborhood House would take us. This was a city agency with a building on Wooster Street. We would meet and depart from there. My mom would make us a ham and cheese sandwich. The people treated us very nicely, especially on hot days, by trying to make life in the city a little more bearable. For the kids who did not have lunch, the agency would provide one for them. The counselors coached some of the kids who did not know how to swim with lessons. They were separated from us. Being in such a large group, we had to adhere to strict discipline by not leaving the immediate area of our counselors. Since we did not go to camp, this was something to look forward to once a week.

APPENDIX OPERATION

Even emergencies didn't warrant a trolley ride. At the age of eleven, I had to have my appendix removed. One day at school, I started to feel sick. The teacher did not know what to do, so she went to Dr. Severino's office around the corner and brought him to school. After a short exam, he determined that I should go to a hospital. A neighbor was called and drove me to New Haven Hospital. My parents were not notified until after I was admitted.

After the operation, I had to stay in the hospital for two weeks. On the day I was discharged, the nurse on duty asked my father how we were getting home. My father replied that we would walk home from Howard Avenue to Green Street. The nurse implored my father to take the trolley car for fear that my incision would burst. But she was unsuccessful. As we descended the steps, I turned around to say goodbye, and she was crying. I will never forget that moment.

I had to hold my side the entire walk home as my mother argued with my father. It was very important that he save the ten cents the trolley fare would cost. As a young boy, I thought of how cruel my father was for letting me walk home that day. Later on, I came to accept his decision in not taking the trolley car home. My father was out of work for several years during the depression and this left an indelible mark on his mindset. To him, providing for the well-being of his family and bringing in money was very sacred.

WATERSIDE PARK

Another park, Waterside Park, was located on Water Street where the Teletrack and the Maritime Center now stand. This was the only major playground for children to play in this section of the city. To get there, we had to walk three city blocks, which was quite a way for ten or eleven year old kids. Water Street was then a major thoroughfare because it was part of Route 1 and heavily traveled. There was one stop light at the corner of Hamilton and Water Street, and some kids refused to walk down to the light and tried to cross without the light, which was very dangerous. I witnessed a number of near misses with kids and cars, but I don't remember anyone getting run down.

The park had a few swings but not much else for a playground. Many older men played Bocci, always for money. This game was played on Sunday like other sports. Sundays were a very busy time at Waterside Park. The park was ringed with factories, Sargent and Company on one side (where my father worked), and C-Cowles Company on the other, plus a lot of small factories on Water Street. There was a very large field where football and baseball games were held. The games were then called sandlot games due the condition of the fields. Football games were played under rules that by today's standards would be outlawed. Teams from different sections of the city would compete for a city-wide championship. The equipment was a leather helmet, a little padding in the shoulders, and some padding in the legs. Due to improper equipment, there were many injuries. A boy was killed when he was accidentally kicked in the head as he was rushing in to block a punt. Insurance for people playing on these teams was unheard of. The boy that kicked the boy in the head never played football again because he was so ashamed of what he'd done. The game that drew the most interest was the team from the Hill section of the city playing the team from Wooster Street. The team from the Hill section was a very tough team because they had a player of huge size. He was so tough that it would take three or four players to bring him down. Football was a very tough sport. These two teams would draw huge crowds due to the rivalry involved. There would always be a fight among the spectators.

On the other side of Waterside Park, we'd also swim off the piers in the summer. Here, again, bathing suits were not used. Only boys went swimming and jumping off the docks. The water here was not very clean due to all the industrial waste that was dumped into it. Most of the debris in the water came from ships entering and leaving the harbor and small pleasure craft. An ever-present concern was the fear of water rats. In some instances, they were as big as cats. They were not sighted that often, but we knew that they were there, especially under the docks. We were swimming late in the afternoon one day, and decided to go home. As we were going up the stairs to get out of the water, this big rat started coming after us. We all grabbed our clothes on the dock and ran to the middle of the field where we would be safe and started dressing up in front of people playing in the field. The embarrassment was nothing compared to our fear. For me, that was my last time that I went there.

Waterside Park was also a haven for lovers, which I happened to discover by chance one day. While my friends were playing on the swings, I left to go to the dock to see the fishing boats come in. The area from the field to the dock was covered with big tall weeds, and you could go into the weeds and not be seen. I was walking by the weeds, and I heard someone groaning. Fearing that someone was being attacked, I ran to the docks to tell the men, who immediately went to the area only to come upon two people making love. As two startled people stood up and started dressing, I looked on in amazement. The men said, it's all right, sonny; they were only playing. I just smiled and said sure.

Waterside Park was also a point of departure for boys hitchhiking to Lighthouse Park in the summer. The favorite corner for this was at

Hamilton and Water Street. That's where the stoplight was. In those days, people going to the beach would always pick us up. Most of the times, cars would not have enough room for us all, and as a result, we had to split up. If we had a difficult time getting a ride, we would go to Water and East Street and wait for the open-end trolley cars to come. When they would stop at this corner to turn up Forbes Avenue, we'd jumped aboard and mix in with the rest of the passengers. We got a free ride to the beach since the trolleys were always nearly full to capacity. It was not much of a risk because the conductor had to go up and down the cars to collect the fares. If they caught you, they would leave you off at the next stop.

One day as we were hitchhiking to go back home, a man stopped with a dump truck and told us all to pile in. He lived in our neighborhood and would give us a ride right to our corner. We were all very happy to be getting a ride right to our house. I jumped in the cab of the truck with the driver. The rest of my friends jumped in the rear of the truck. As we drove home, the man asked me what I did at the beach. I said swimming. While I was explaining our day's events, he was touching me on my leg. I sensed that he was doing something wrong so I slide further to the door. Then he said he wanted to see if my bathing suit was still wet and started touching me on my pants. As luck would have it, he had to stop at a light on Woodward Avenue. At this point, I leapt out and called my friends who jumped out too. I explained to them what had transpired, and they started yelling at the man. He drove off, and we walked the rest of the way home. This ended my hitchhiking days. This man and his family owned a trucking business located around the corner from where I lived. My friends and I kept our distance from him. We never played on his street again.

ROLLER-SKATING

Roller-skating was a great pastime for us. This entertainment was really inexpensive. There were several places we could go: the rink on Davenport Avenue in New Haven was the most popular, especially because it was open all year round, but we also skated at Momauguin

Beach in East Haven, which was open during the warm weather months. Travelling there was mostly walking from our houses to Davenport Avenue, which took about half an hour. Roller-skating received its name from the type of skate used mostly on the streets where roller bearings inside each wheel attached to the skates. The skates used in the skating rinks had different wheels on them because the floors were made of wood. These skates you either rented from the skating rink or brought from home. I rented the skates, as did a lot of other people. The fortunate ones had their own, including a carrying case.

Roller-skating offered young people a nice opportunity amid pleasant surroundings to socialize with no alcohol being served. There was organ music with all the latest songs, and you could ask a girl to skate much like asking someone to dance. Friendships forged here led a lot of people onto marriage; some marriages were actually performed on the floor of the rink. They ran contests in which people would ballroom dance on skates, which was a joy to watch with all the lights swirling around. They had different times for all age groups with Friday evenings and Sunday afternoons set aside for people between the ages of 15 and 18. Saturday nights were for adults. I met boys from different parts of the city in which some of these friendships still exist today. They had zero tolerance for any kind of misbehavior, and even had an employee skating around with the skaters to make sure no female would be harassed. Skaters that did not obey the skating rules were asked to leave. In this atmosphere, parents would feel safe knowing that management would protect their children.

But it was a chore to get to Momauguin Beach in East Haven. We had to transfer from one trolley line to another, but it was a much better beach with cleaner water. On many occasions, we received a ride from one of my friend's older brothers who owned a 1941 Cadillac convertible. He had paid $900 for the car in 1943, which was a huge sum back then. The car was a beauty: green with red upholstery. On the way out to the beach, we would pass all the trolleys, and you could see all the people stare at us. I guess this was our moment of glory. The one thing we prayed for was that his brother did not meet a girl. This meant that we had to take the trolley or walk home. On the order of Savin Rock in West Haven, Momauguin Beach had hot dog stands and assorted rides. The roller rink there was where everyone would go; it was probably the most popular place on the shoreline to visit. Skating here was fun since you did not have to be dressed up like the rink in New Haven. Windows were opened wide to catch the breeze off the water, making skaters visible to everyone. During WWII, this was the place for girls and boys to socialize. During WWII, East Haven beaches were filled with servicemen on leave. They would come down with their summer uniforms and GI bathing suits, which were just black shorts. This became a familiar sight. Of course, trouble would also follow them, as they would flirt with the girls who had boyfriends nearby.

ROLLER HOCKEY

The Boy's Club in New Haven had a roller hockey league in which teams were sponsored by different local businesses. The type of skates used then were ones that you clamped on your shoes. You needed a skate key to adjust the clamp on the skate to your shoe. Because the wheels were made of steel, wear and tear was a problem if you tried using them on streets or sidewalks. Replacing the wheels was a constant chore. One year, my friend Jerry and I decided to enter into the roller hockey program at the club. We formed a team but could not get anyone to sponsor us. We entered ourselves in spite of not having the equipment to play with. We were able to get hockey sticks but not much else. We had skates but needed padding for a goaltender. One boy's mother stuffed a pair of pants with a lot of material from old clothes to protect the legs and made a man's vest into a large pad to protect the chest. Facemasks were not used then. Because I did not skate fast enough, they made me the goaltender. For a goaltender's stick, we clamped boards together on a regular hockey stick. Our team's name was the Green Street Hornets. Since we had no sponsor, our practice sessions were held in the street with our little cage being moved every time a car came.

Since most teams had large stores downtown as sponsors who

purchased all the equipment for them, we stood out in stark contrast to the other teams who had uniforms where we wore our street clothes. In spite of this, we won nearly all our games in this league, which entitled us to play the winner of the other league downtown. This team was sponsored by J. Johnson Clothing Store. They were not only the best-equipped team in the league but also the toughest. The day we played them at the Boy's Club we dressed up in the gym while they dressed in the locker room. When they skated out onto the gym floor, they had nice red uniforms. The crowd was cheering them on because they were the favorites. This intimidated me, but I began to think they were not going to get to me. My teammates were coming over to me with encouragement. The best advice I got was from Victor, the truant officer, who said, "Beat them and send them back to Church Street". The boys on this Johnson team all came from streets better than ours. That gave us all the more motivation to beat them.

At the end of the second period, they were only ahead by 1 to 0. This is when we decided we were going to win. The third period they came out with a vengeance, trying to score on me. But they failed, and our guys scored two goals to win. Defeating them with all their uniforms and equipment was a crowning glory for me. I will never forget that game. We were given a certificate from the director of the club. I still have this certificate.

COLUMBUS SCHOOL

After leaving the sixth grade at Eaton School, I was transferred to Columbus School for seventh and eighth, which was only two blocks from home. Even though a lot of property in my immediate area was below par, the houses around the Columbus Green were exceptional nice since most of the families living there were involved in some sort of business. At Columbus, I met and became friends with boys who lived in these homes. It was the first time I had ever seen a furnace. It was also the first time that there were other foods besides pasta, chicken, and beans. They ate lobster and crabs.

At Columbus School, boys and girls were segregated, each in their own part of the building. We were not allowed to play together or use the same entrance. On some of the old schools, like Strong School in Fair Haven, the signs are still there, even though those rules are no longer enforced. Our teachers were of either Irish or Jewish descent. For the most part, they treated us very stern but fair. Homework was assigned on the basis that you completed it and returned it the next day with no excuse of any kind. If you did not, you had to stand up in the front of the class and felt humiliated for the entire period. One teacher, Mrs. Lowenbaum, asked me for my homework and since it was not completed on time, I told her that I did not understand some of the problems. Without warning, she hauled off and slapped me in the face so hard that I fell out of my seat. It would be to no avail to go home and tell my parents what happened. Since they did not speak English, they would only blame me. Feeling in a no win situation, you did whatever the teachers demanded of you.

Our principal, Mr. Harder, a strong, stern man of German descent, did not take any flak from anyone. If he thought you were being disruptive, it was not unusual for him to single you out by whacking you on the knuckles with a very heavy stick. I know how it felt because one day, when I was twelve, I did not feel well, so my mom had me stay home. About mid-morning, there was a knock on the door. It was Mr. Harder. Since my mom did not speak English, he told me to tell mom that he was taking me to school. He said I was not sick enough to stay home. Even though I told him I was sick from vomiting all night, he did not want to hear it. He grabbed me by the ear and marched me the two blocks back to school, reprimanding me the entire way. He took me to his office and proceeded to hit me on the hand so hard that the school nurse heard my cries. She told him to stop, and after examining me, determined that I had a fever, and she returned me home. After explaining the welts on my hands to my mom, she cried, hugged me, and put me to bed, trying to explain to me why the principal made a mistake. Mom had Dr. Conte call Mr. Harder to chastise him for his error.

The school had a tough reputation with a number of very troublesome boys. These boys were big and strong for their ages; others were simply older, fifteen or sixteen in the eighth grade, because they had to repeat grades. They had a special room for them called the sunshine room, where they would sit all day reading comic books. Toward the end of one year near graduation, two of these boys harassed the principal to the point that they challenged him to a fight. He took them down in the basement of the school and fought the two of them. This fight was witnessed by my friend Harry. The next day at graduation Mr. Harder's eye was black and blue. As he stood up on the stage to hand out diplomas, the two boys, who fought him and were expelled, came to the window of the gymnasium. They yelled out "Moonhead over Miami" because he was bald. He hated that name. The sunshine boys would walk by his office singing the song "Moon over Miami" all the time. Even though everyone in the school knew about the fight and about what happened, it did not deter Mr. Harder from continuing to be a strict task master. I talked with one of the boys involved in the fight many years later. He said he was a very tough and courageous man to fight them. Today, that would be unheard of. The two boys did not escape without any physical pain. They would always remember that fight with Mr. Harder.

One of the most horrible scenes that I have ever witnessed was a boy being raped by three other boys in the back of the school. One day, my friend Harry and I decided to play ball in the schoolyard after school. Harry helped me with my paper route so that I could finish early and have time to play before dinner. As we went to the back of the school, we heard someone crying and screaming. As we walked closer to the area of the noise, we heard voices telling this person to stop yelling. This was taking place on the back stairs of the school. We were able to observe them without being seen because the stairs were partly covered, so anyone using the stairs would not fall out. We hid behind the bushes and were able to see who these boys were. They were three older boys who had a history for being violent. They did not attend our school or live in our neighborhood, but we knew who they were. After they finished assaulting this boy, they came by where we were hiding. Standing in front of the hedges, they discussed how they should threaten to kill him if he ever talked about it. After some discussion about it, they left. We lay on the ground, afraid to even breathe or make any noise, and were so relieved when they left.

When we were sure that they were gone, we ran up the stairs where the boy was still in a state of shock. He had a fear of us until we assured him that we would help him. Harry gave him his sweater to comfort him. We helped him get dressed and started to walk out of the yard with him. This boy that was molested was a boy we knew from the Boys Club who was not a very bright boy and could easily be persuaded into things. He came from the Fair Haven section of the city. As we turned the corner of the yard to head up St. John Street, I looked back and saw the three boys returning to the stairs. Without them seeing us, we ran up to Grand Avenue where it was teaming with people. We felt it would be safer to escort him home among all these people. As we got up to East Street, we told him for his own good to stay away from the club for a while, and if he ever did want to return, to bring someone with him. He felt all this shame about what had happened. We asked him why he went with them in the first place. He said they were going to give him some sports equipment. It was his decision to not report this because he said that they threatened to harm his family. In those days, if Harry and I witnessed a crime and reported it, we would have been branded as stool pigeons. The three boys involved would later spend their lives going in and out of prisons. Maybe the decision not to report it was justified when the boy who was assaulted eventually became a repairman and married and had a family.

TRUANT OFFICER: VICTOR

A man named Victor was the truant officer for our grade school district. His main duty was to keep control of children who wanted to skip school. As a truant officer, he was exceptional at his job because he knew where he could find anybody at any time. He had a genial presence about him, was very charismatic, and could handle any situation with ease. He was on the order of a Cary Grant. He would call everyone by the name of Jasper. One day, my friend Tony and I decided that it was too hot to attend school. Tony said we could go to his uncle's shop on Hamilton Street, which was the Foxon Park soda bottling plant, and we could spend the day inside by the water and soda cooler. Tony's mom owned a small grocery store, so he got a bag of food and cookies for us to eat. Around midmorning, as we sat with our backs to the door, we both felt a hand on our necks, strong enough to keep us from turning around, and we heard a familiar voice say, "Jaspers, you are going to school, and you will never stay out of school again."

Since Tony's father was in prison for several years for what I was told was for selling dope, the grocery store that Tony's mom owned was their sole source of support. Tony and his family, which consisted of his mother and a sister, lived in three rooms in the back of the store. My mom never wanted me to play with Tony but never explained why. I found out later that it was because of Tony's father. Tony was a good-hearted boy whose problems were manifested by his knowledge of his father being in prison, which caused him great shame. Tony was just one of the many boyhood friends that I had, and as we grew older, we never saw much of each other. Tony went on to become an official with the City of New Haven and was in charge of some of the many city parking lots. I believe Tony's mom did a remarkable job of raising her son and daughter considering her husband was in prison and it was the height of the Depression.

Victor was a great influence in our lives. He was helpful in his dealings with everyone he met, and he conducted himself with honesty and class. Victor also was a counselor with the Boy's Club. His job was to oversee the senior room where boys of fifteen years or older could attend. About 1945, Victor got married, and since housing at that time was in short supply, he was given three rooms on the third floor of the club, next to the senior room. The girl that he married was tall and beautiful and was the envy of all us boys. She was a most gracious person on the order of Victor. We would say what a good looking couple they made. On cold nights, we hung out in the senior room playing ping pong and checkers, reading, and billiards. Victor's wife would make hot cocoa for us just before we went home. Everyone had the greatest respect for Victor and his wife. One of the benefits Victor and his wife had was the use of the pool after club closing. Victor spent a lot of time walking around Grand Avenue, going to all the places where we would congregate, such as little stores that had pinball machines and coffee shops that would cater to older boys, just so that he could keep an eye on us in a friendly way. He was known to be a very fair man in his dealings with people. He would get tips from various sources, including shopkeepers, as to who might be getting into trouble. The sources trusted him to straighten things out instead of the police. Some boys that Victor could not help wound up in prison.

When Victor passed away later on, his wife was so distraught that she committed suicide a few years later.

CHAPTER TWO

Doos of Life

HIGH SCHOOL

Grade school at Columbus was a training ground for what I would encounter later on in high school. The transition was a little difficult since Columbus was pretty much 100% Italian, but entering high school, I started to meet people of a lot of different nationalities. They had a variety of programs such as shops for boys' woodworking, etc. Some of my friends learned the beginnings of their trades there.

After graduating from Columbus school, I entered Hillhouse High School. They had split sessions due to the amount of students attending. I chose the morning sessions and my hours were 8:00am to 12:00pm. This would give me the opportunity to work a part time job in the afternoon.

After one year I transferred to Commercial High School, a business school, which was located right across the street on Tower Parkway. The move paid off for me later after I entered the Navy. Since I took a typing class, I was able to be placed in the office on my way to earn stripes as a yeoman third class. At this high school I met students of several different nationalities. This was a good training ground since I came from Columbus which was primarily Italian.

UNCLE LEO

My Uncle Leo, who gave my father help during the Depression, came to haunt my father for the rest of his life. Uncle Leo was by those days' standards, pretty well off. He owned his own store and never married. When I was young, I would look forward to his visits every Sunday, since he would bring Italian pastry and parcel out after Sunday dinner. Sometimes, he would give us ten cents for the movies after I did chores at his store after school.

But this was a very sad chapter in my father's life. Since my father received aid from his brother, he had to repay him with favors for many years. So when my uncle sold his store, my father offered to take him in temporarily. But he never left. He lived with us and never offered to pay for his stay. My father gave Uncle Leo a room in the attic, which was actually another apartment. He took his meals with us, and my mother had to wash his clothes and make up his room. My mom had to take the brunt of his abuse since he did not work. He supported himself by being involved in various business dealings. Always present in our house, he caused a lot of undue hardship by interfering in our lives. This servitude of my father to his brother was to stay with me for the rest of my life. Uncle Leo was constantly critical of the way my mom cooked and cleaned, and he always compared our family with others. In spite of his constant complaints, he never left. His mostly verbal abuse was directed not only at our family but others as well, always criticizing how people looked and acted, including their weight, clothes, and mannerisms.

Uncle Leo's anger and resentment stemmed from a physical handicap, which was the result of an industrial accident. In the 1930s, while working in a factory that produced wire, his left arm was severed after it got stuck in a wire drawing machine, the type where wire comes down a tube and wraps around a spool at a high rate of speed. He thought his arm could have been saved and that it was unnecessary for the doctors to cut it off below the elbow. I believe the loss of his arm accounted for much of his bitterness. He was commonly referred to by people in the neighborhood as the "one armed bandit," a name he did not appreciate.

There was a nice old man named Joe living next door to us on Green Street. I spent many hours talking to him. He had a handicap where one leg was shorter than the other, and because of this, he had to wear a special shoe. He was a very respectful man and very well-mannered. My father and he would sit on his porch and smoke cigars and reminisce about Italy and politics. One day, Joe called me over and said he wanted to talk to me. By the tone of his voice, I could see that he was troubled by something serious. He told me that Uncle Leo's taunts about his leg were bothering him. Joe said that here's a man with one arm making fun at his handicap, while his was just as bad. I said to repay him in kind, but Joe said that it was not nice to say mean things like that. This attitude proved what great character this man had. He had great respect for my father and therefore could not bring himself to discuss this with him. So I took it up with my uncle, and in a very diplomatic way, I asked my uncle if I could go with him on one of his business deals. He said yes. In the course of our walk, I made up a story similar to his handicap and related how these boys were always taunting this person, and he agreed that it was not nice for them to do that. Uncle Leo said how would they like to go through life that way? I said that poking fun at people with a physical disability was horrible. Then I brought up about our neighbor Joe and said some boys would mimic Joe the way he walked. Uncle Leo remained silent as I told him this story, and I feel that it finally reached him. After a few weeks, Joe called me over to ask if something was wrong with Uncle Leo. I said no. Joe said that he seemed a different man to him. Uncle Leo never mentioned his leg to Joe again.

My father's servitude to his brother extended to my father catering to his every whim and comfort. For us children, we had to be home by five o'clock or no supper, but if my uncle came home late for dinner, my father would have my mom make him something. I remember many nights when my father would not go to sleep until his brother came home, at which time my father would make coffee and sandwiches or whatever he could serve him. My father did not go to sleep until his brother did, and this was after my father worked long hours in the factory and was extremely tired.

To earn extra money, my father worked part-time as a pin boy in the bowling alleys setting up pins after the bowlers knocked them down.

This was a backbreaking job even for a young boy. My mother would have to put ointment on his back almost every week to relieve the soreness. A lot of boys would set up pins to earn money, which required them to stay up late, and they sometimes dozed off in school. My father gave up this job as World War II started because he was able to earn time and a half working overtime.

While not a nice person in general, Uncle Leo did have some moments of generosity. Being named after him, people thought that I was his favorite. Yet, he would criticize me for not being strong mentally and physically. But I was able to stuff this criticism in his face later in life.

Like everyone else in the area, finances created the most turmoil in my house. These arguments were commonplace. My mother and father argued constantly about money. My Uncle Leo, being a great agitator, would tell my father how other families were getting by on a lot less and were living better. Mainly, he would say that children in other families were more productive, helping to support the family by bringing home money and doing more work around the house. I proved Uncle Leo wrong because I never refused to help my father. All the aunts and uncles on my father's side were very argumentative and would argue about anything and anyone when they came over our house. We were told to be obedient, sitting in their presence but not speaking. If there was any special food put out for them, we were not allowed to touch any of it until they left. While on our trip to California, my uncle, who acted uncouth and without class, told me that his family did not want my father to marry my mother because she was uneducated and, by his definition, a lowly farmer. He would always criticize mom's cooking and general house cleaning except for some of my aunts on my father's side. The rest of them treated my mom harshly. But in her own way, mom overcame their constant harping and criticism by becoming a good mother and homemaker under these sad circumstances.

My father's entire family prided themselves on becoming U.S. citizens. We tried to encourage my mom to go to school and get her citizenship papers. At night, my sister would take mom to school and tried to teach her enough of the basics of the English language to get by. Mom resisted all efforts at trying to educate herself in speaking English. Mom became adept at understanding English but not speaking it. She would listen to the radio programs and relate the story to you in Italian and was able to look at the newspaper and somehow get a feeling of what the story was about. My father was especially proud of his citizenship papers. I remember going to night school classes with him to prepare him for acceptance. I would help him study for his exam and help teach him about our country, mostly about the English language which he learned to speak fluently. To him, becoming an American citizen was his crowning achievement. His greatest wish was for me to get an education, because without it, I would fail in life working in factories alongside many men of Irish descent. He realized then the importance of education because the English speaking men had all the good jobs in the factory while he was relegated to menial labor. Later on, he was able to elevate himself. One of the darkest times of his employment was when he had to work an extra hour every night for free just to hold his job. Due to this unfair treatment of my father from his Irish boss, which most were at the time, my father developed a great hatred for the Irish because of their abuses to the Italians.

PEOPLE FROM THE NEIGHBORHOOD

My neighborhood consisted mostly of people with Italian heritage. But we did have some neighbors of other nationalities. On the corner of Franklin and Green Street was a big brick building called the Schubert building, named after the man who owned it. He was of German descent, and the two buildings in this complex housed people of French and German ancestry. He kept his property in excellent condition and was very interested in who came and went in his building. His property was the only one in the neighborhood that had a nice yard we could play in. Unfortunately, he was very adamant about us not playing there. The first floor housed the store of my boyhood friend, Tony. After that, whenever I went to call Tony, I always avoided Mr. Schubert's yard by calling him from the side door of his apartment.

When Mr. Schubert would go out with his truck, we had a chance to play in his yard. His truck was one that was very high from the ground. It had the old fashion solid rubber tires on it. One day as we were running around his yard playing tag, along came Mr. Schubert home with his truck. As he drove into the yard, we panicked. We tried to get away from him. As I turned around to go out the front yard, I ran straight into his truck. I fell down and his truck drove right over me. I lied still until his truck passed over me then got up and ran as fast as I could. He was furious, yelling and screaming at us in German.

In the house next to me on Green Street lived the boy who tried in vain to save my sister's life as her dress caught on fire. She eventually died as a result of her burns. His family also had a tragedy of their own. This boy had a mother who was very mean and vindictive. This woman would always scold anyone for playing on the sidewalk in front of her house. Being on the second floor, she would peer down from her window and watch to see if anyone stayed on her sidewalk. To antagonize her, boys would congregate in front of her house. She then would open her window and start cursing them. Everyone would give her the Italian salute, which was the finger. This would send her into a rage. Even when we played in our own yard, she would complain that we were making too much noise. I never saw my mom ever speak to her even when she was in her yard. I was curious as to why this woman never left her house, except to venture into her backyard. I found out that she was the cause of a boy dying. They boy had stopped in front of her house to talk with some of his friends, and she threw hot water to make him disperse, but it caused him to run into the street and get hit by a car. He was killed instantly. I was told that this was the reason for her never leaving her house again.

This woman's friend, who lived on the first floor of the same house, approached me one day and asked me to watch and report to her who went into her apartment while she was at work. She suspected that her husband was having a lady over while she worked. I did see people going into the apartment before she made this request to me. I did not know until after she told me why since I never liked this person mainly for her arrogance. I played along just to laugh at her. My mom saw me talking to her and inquired about our conversations. She got upset with me because she thought that I was spying for the woman, which I was not. Mom felt that this would bring me trouble. Since the woman was desperate to catch her husband cheating, she even offered me money. To humor her, I told her that I would be glad to do it with no payment. All the while, her husband had his friend over quite frequently, and I didn't say a word.

My first lessons in real estate and business were during WWII when the defense factories were busy with everybody working overtime and earning good pays. One of the sons of my downstairs neighbor approached me one day and complained to me that my father was not taking care of the house. He thought that my father should renovate their apartment. In this apartment lived six adults five of whom worked earning good pays. I related this complaint to my father and told him what the son had said. My father said, "Well, here, Leo: you tell me what I should do. They are paying me $15 a month in rent, which is $180 a year. Between the taxes and upkeep, I am not even breaking even. At this rate, I am better off leaving the apartment empty." I knew he could not leave the apartment empty due to a rent freeze, which was the law during WWII. He could not evict them for fear of getting sued, and to complicate matters, the husband of one of the tenants would drink himself in a stupor and create a big disturbance when he came home drunk. One day, when he was totally drunk and nasty, he started to approach our porch and tried climbing the stairs. He was offered help from my next door neighbor but pushed him away. As he got to the top of the stairs, he lost his balance and fell off the side of the porch, falling on his head and splitting it open. They picked him up and brought him inside. A doctor was summoned and had him brought to the hospital, and I believe he passed away shortly after that. Of course, his family tried to blame the condition of the porch, which was in bad shape but not enough to cause this accident. The next door neighbor explained to them how their father refused help and was drunk. As to the condition of our house, my father was informed by the city of New Haven that they may be acquiring some of this property in the future and not to expend any unnecessary repairs. The war was winding down and talk of a highway coming through our neighborhood was becoming more evident. This family that lived downstairs was for the most part a very nice family.

DOMESTIC VIOLENCE

Unfortunately, domestic violence was another common occurrence in my neighborhood, usually spurred on by alcohol and gambling troubles. With the many fights I remember, some families' stand out in memory. One of the greatest riots on our street happened during the summer on a very hot evening. A man came home after working extra hours at the plant and was told by his wife that she was leaving him for another man. The man went ballistic. He went down the street to where the wife's lover lived and tore into his apartment and started a battle. This battle went down the stairs, into the street, and on up to the next block with all the relatives of both families fighting with each other. By the time the police came, they had to wade through an entire street full of people to stop all the fighting, which, by then, had become a full scale riot.

Other domestic quarrels were related to alcohol, since some men would consume their entire pay check drinking and not bring home any money. In one family that I knew, the wife would go to the factory to get the husband's pay so that she could buy some groceries and pay their rent. In another family that I knew, the husband was in a constant drunken state, so much so that he never left his apartment, except to somehow get some wine to drink. How he managed that was always a mystery to me. Yet, the children still all grew up to be very productive people. I went to school with one of his daughters who was extremely shy due to her problems at home.

Even though money was the main topic of discussion in my house, I always felt a sense of anger at the way my parents argued senselessly at the payment of bills, such as the milkman's bill, which had to be paid every Monday. And every Monday, my father would make an issue out of the milk bill. He would later tell me to emphasize the importance of money to my mother, and I would say to him it was a useless argument since the milk bill never changed. He felt that he had to express to my mother not to exceed his budget. That he was upsetting the whole house did not matter to him, getting his point across did.

My mother administered most of the discipline in my house, even though she was of the soft kind. When that did not work, my father would invoke his discipline, which was extremely harsh. When he got mad, he would take a razor strap that he had hanging on the door and hit us with it. He had this strap to sharpen his razor, which was a straight edge razor. It consisted of three separate units of leather. As he struck, it felt like getting hit with a whip. Just the sight of the strap hanging on the door was enough for me to try and not get him mad enough for him to use it on me. When things were getting out of control in the house, my brother and sisters arguing or really any disturbance that did not please him, he would issue a slight warning. My father, while not a strict disciplinarian, did not appreciate being taken lightly. He would ask you twice to do something. When that order was not obeyed, he would get up and head for the razor strap. At that instant, the whole house cleared as my mother tried to calm him down and take the strap away from him. If that failed, you either started running or got hit with the strap. Sometimes it worked, but sometimes he just went ahead and strapped us, and wherever the strap landed, that's where you got hit.

When it came time for dinner, you had to be at the table by 5 o'clock, or you would not eat. Since there were not multiple choices of food, there were no leftovers of anything else to pick from. Our menu consisted of the same item (pasta) every night, only dressed up a little differently. We did not dare voice our opinion of what we were going to eat. You ate what was on the table, or you did not eat. Many dinners were ruined by arguments over what we were eating with my father getting very upset over his choice of food. The classic ruined dinner was when my brother Ralph was out of work for quite some time when he was seventeen and came home late for dinner. He proceeded over to the stove and looked in the pot and started making a commotion with my mother over having to eat the same thing as the night before.

My father got up from the table as if a tornado hit the house. The table moved, dishes went flying, food on the floor as he went after Ralph. I went after my father to try and stop him, but he got to Ralph in the hallway and started to beat him with great force. I was able to get him away long enough so Ralph could get away. I calmed my father down, but he was in a very bad mood. He said, "I came home from work tired, and this fool comes home and complains about food, and he is not even working." My father said that it was bad enough that he was not working for a long time, but that he didn't want to hear him complain about the food. Ralph was always making excuses about how he was looking for work. My father even offered to talk to his boss about bringing Ralph in to work at the factory, an idea that was not appealing to Ralph for obvious reasons.

At this time in his life, Ralph had a problem with not wanting to rise early from bed. This was also a thorn in my father's side. My father always arose early for work or whatever else he had to do that day. Seeing Ralph in bed sleeping and not getting up would anger my father to no end. Sometimes, Ralph would arise early just to please my father and then when my father left for work, Ralph would go back to bed. Then my mom would get mad and start beating him with the broom to try and get him out of bed. She knew that my father would certainly go into a fit of rage if he came home and found Ralph in bed. It would be my mom who would have to answer to my father for allowing him to remain in bed. This always frightened my mom.

One day, my father had to return home to get something that he needed for work. My sister heard my father coming up the stairs and alerted my mom, who made a wild dash and literally yanked Ralph out of bed, forcing him to duck under the bed. With my brother wondering what was going on, my father entered the house and went straight to the kitchen to get what he forgot. He then approached my mom who by this time was making the bed. My mom let the covers hang over the bed and drape to the floor so that my father could not see Ralph hiding. We were all very nervous while my father stood there at the foot of the bed discussing the evening meal. We were all frightened to think of what would happen if he were to discover Ralph under the bed. As my father descended the stairs to get back to work, my mom looked out the window and watched him walk up the street and turn the corner heading for the factory. She then let out a sigh of relief and at the same time released her anger at Ralph by whacking him with the broom until he got dressed and left. At this time of Ralph's life, I guess the word "stubborn" would most certainly apply.

As bad as I thought conditions were in my house, I felt fortunate that my father was not a drinking man or a gambler. On Saturday nights, my father would sometimes take my brother Ralph and me to his favorite corner tavern. He would spend the night talking to his friends while Ralph and I amused ourselves by listening to the radio and best of all eating the sandwiches that were on the bar. They were FREE! Beer was sold by the pail, which I guess was enough for two men. My father never drank to excess, which, after seeing other families with that problem, I felt very fortunate. We would never stay out too late. We probably spent about three hours there. I would sometimes listen to their conversations. For the most part, their talks were about work and politics. They would all praise Roosevelt for helping them get back on their feet by the programs that the government set up for them, such as the W.P.A. This was a make work program for the people. It turned out to be that the government was borrowing money to put people to work. By the end of the 1930s, this was starting to fail. It was WWII that really ended the Depression. Another program was the C.C. Program in which young boys were put to work building roads and parks. Their pay was something like $20 per month with room and board. The age for this program was boys sixteen years or older.

TRIP TO CALIFORNIA

At about age fifteen, with my asthma kicking up, a doctor said my only hope was to go to a different climate. Uncle Leo wrote to some friends he had in San Jose, California. They said that we could stay with them, so we bought train tickets to California. The trip took five days. This was during the war, and servicemen had first priority on seats. From Chicago to Dallas we would ride in between cars and then from Dallas to Los Angeles and finally San Jose we had seats. For food, my mom fried up a stack of chicken cutlets that she wrapped in protective paper, enough to fill a small suitcase. The servicemen heading to California for shipment to the Pacific had access to hot food on the train, such as hot cocoa and breakfast, which they would share with us in the morning. For our noon and evening meals, we ate the cutlet sandwiches. By the time we got to Los Angeles, I was tired of cutlet sandwiches. We had to change trains on our trip, and we were able to get a bowl of hot oatmeal on the new train.

We left New Haven in December 1944. The ride between Chicago and Dallas was hard because we had to sit on our suitcases and cover up at night with our coats. One soldier sitting in the next car who was passing through the cars saw us along with other people huddling to keep warm and went into his car and gave us a big army blanket. When we got to Dallas, we were able to finally get a seat in the heated car the soldiers had been in. We returned the blanket to the soldier who gave us the blanket and offered him some of our food. But he just thanked us and shook our hands. I told him thank you and that I hoped for his safety.

Most of the servicemen were not much older than me, most only eighteen years old. Some asked me why I was not in the service. I had to tell them my age. A lot of them were drinking the whole time they were on the train, so I got teased about being 4-F, which was a designation for not being in the service. I believe a lot of their excess drinking had to do with where they were going. Most told me that they were being assigned as soon as they got to California, many never to return. Since the train had people from all branches of the service, there was a lot of ego backslapping as to the better branch of service. Some of it good naturally, while some of it turned ugly due to liquor being consumed. With stuff being thrown around the cars, I never stuck my head up to see who was doing it. The seats we had were upright, so we tried to sleep in a sitting position. Combined with the noise factor, it made sleep almost impossible. I guess the servicemen felt that this would be their last chance to party.

After changing trains at Los Angeles, it would take us twenty four hours to make our trip north to San Jose. This train ride was a little more comfortable since the cars were a more modern. The train was filled mostly with sailors going up to San Francisco to be assigned to ships. We arrived in San Jose at 5 a.m. We then took a bus to my uncle's friend's house, which was on Fourth Street. We were greeted well, and they gave us a room with two beds. The man's wife made me feel right at home by making us a nice breakfast of eggs with bread and butter. In the backyard, they had chickens and ducks, a lot of fruit trees, walnut trees, plus a nice garden where they grew vegetables.

I enrolled in San Jose High School as a sophomore. This was quite a change for me, and I had to deal with some cultural shock. A great percentage of the students were Mexican, but I mixed freely with them without problem. To earn some money, I was hired as a waiter's helper in a nice restaurant. My job was to set up and clear the tables and carry the food orders out for the waiter. I was given a little food at the start of my shift. My hours were after school until about 8 p.m. My pay was $2 a day. This job lasted one week. The man we were living with secured my next job, which was in a department store. My pay was .40 cents per hour working about 20 hours per week.

Since Uncle Leo spent some of his time at the courthouse listening to cases, he became friendly with one of the judges. Some days when I wasn't working, I would accompany my uncle, and he introduced me to him. I became friendly with the judge and would stop in and say hello on my way to work. After several months, my uncle wanted to return home and in conversation mentioned this wish to the judge. The judge asked if I was going back as well. My uncle said he did not know. The judge asked to see us both. He stated that if I wanted to stay in California, he would have me live with his daughter, and as an added incentive, he would send me to college. So one day he brought me to meet his daughter and family who had a beautiful home. The daughter's home was tucked away on a beautiful street almost like a movie setting. The home consisted of several bedrooms, two full baths, and a recreation room. She had two children and I would have had my own bedroom. To me it was like a dream compared to Greene Street. After several visits, his daughter said her father regarded me as a son and that I showed great promise to him. So much was thrown at me at once and I spent a lot of sleepless nights mulling over this. After I thought about it for a while, I decided that I did not want to stay. The truth was I was afraid. First, I went to see the judge's daughter to thank her and her family for their consideration. The judge's son-in-law was also disappointed that I was going back home. As I walked around his house with him, he said his father-in-law was a very generous man who spoke well of me. After meeting with the judge and explaining my plan, he was disheartened but happy for me. He said I could return any time I wanted.

While living in California, I did not have a single asthma attack. One month after returning home, I had one. Although it was mild, I realized it truly was my environment.

ST. MICHAEL'S HALL

Returning from California, my friends and I spent a lot of time at a hall on Greene Street called St. Michael's. This hall was used for sports, wedding receptions, political parties, and a meeting place for people in the neighborhood. Many nights we watched basketball games there from teams throughout the city. Since there was an entrance fee, which we did not have, we had to wait until the ticket taker would let us in. This was usually about fifteen minutes into the game after they determined that no one else was coming. What I liked best was during election times when the politicians would come and look for votes, they would have free beer and sandwiches for the men to encourage them to vote for them. While everyone was listening to the speeches, we would sneak into the kitchen and fill up bags with the sandwiches and bring them outside to eat. Then we would go back inside and get a free soda. The politicians who came were of Irish descent and would try to speak Italian to impress the men only to have us give them a good razzing when they left. The men would sit around and talk about their favorite candidate. During one such discussion, one of the men got up and called the rest of the group fools because he reasoned the politicians only came around at election time to buy your vote, and he said that you all run to vote and they do nothing for you. Improving living and working conditions were topics of conversation that would go on for hours, and still the men would wonder about their other options. These discussions would always turn to how well Mussolini was running Italy and how everyone was now prospering, when only twenty years earlier, many of them came here to look for a better life. While they would agree that life was tough for them, America still presented more opportunities for their families than Italy. Even the ones who maintained Italy was better, they still never moved back.

The manager of the hall was a man named Angelo who lived in an apartment in the hall with his wife. My father and he were good friends. We were not allowed in the hall without Angelo's permission. If we asked him if we could use the hall, he would always say no. So on days when the Boy's Club was booked for League games, we would sneak into the hall by a window. We never caused any damage to the hall and always cleaned up after we left. We did this on days when he and his wife were out shopping. Again, we had to post a lookout for him. As luck would have it, the lookout was called home, and Angelo caught us all in the hall. After he gave us a kick in the butt, he went home to tell all our fathers, and we never tried to sneak in the hall again. Since he was a great lover of Mussolini, we would go by his window and yell, "Mussolini is a fool".

The attendees of St. Michael's Church were mostly the Italians that lived in the entire area surrounding my house. St. Casmir's Church on Green Street catered mostly to people of Polish ancestry. French people, of whom they were few in numbers, frequented St. Louis Church on Chapel Street. At the time, St. Michael's had the largest parish in the city. Going to church then became a gathering place for people before and after mass, especially in the summer when they would have the Italian band playing after almost every mass. On the Saints days, the men would carry the statue of Santa Maria Maddalena through the street and people would pin dollar bills on the saint. This would happen after the last mass with the parade marching all around the neighborhood.

The nuns of St. Michael also used the hall for summer school where they'd give us instructions in religion. We would go in the morning, have a little lunch, then were forced to take a nap on cots set up on the roof of the building, which had a big fence around it. At about three o'clock, we were sent home. This was not a happy time for me because the nuns were very strict. St. Michael's Church had a policy to separate boys and girls. We had to sit on opposite sides of the church, not only for religious instructions but also for masses. During mass, nuns would be assigned to each side of the church to make sure you paid attention. It was difficult to pay attention because the mass was said in Latin. Boys who would doze off in mass felt the nun's hands twisting their ears. Prior to my Confirmation, we had to have religious instructions on a daily basis after school for a period of about six months. The Church was right across from Columbus School, so getting there was no problem. If anyone skipped classes without a valid reason, the nuns would come to our school and tell the teachers to reprimand the student. Then you had to face the wrath of the nuns the next day, which was worse. My fear of having the nuns angry with you kept me motivated to not skip class. At St. Michael's Church, I was baptized, received my First Holy Communion, and also received my Confirmation. At my Confirmation dinner, after church at our house, my father would treat us with a very large pizza made special for him by his friend the Italian baker on St. John Street named Giampapa. This special pizza was so large that it covered the entire table. It was brought to our house in sections.

GRAND AVENUE SHOPS

Grand Avenue was the main shopping area for everything from clothes to grocery stores. My father had a special shoe store on Grand Avenue where he would take us for shoes. Because he bought us all our shoes there, the owner supposedly gave him a special price. One pair my father bought me was a pair of shoe boots with a jackknife in the side pocket of the shoe. The price was to him very expensive at $1.98. These shoes I would only wear on Sundays or on special days for school. I also polished them and tried to keep them from being scuffed up. I never knew when I would get another new pair. For clothing stores, we had stores, such as Perelmutter's, where my father would take us children to buy clothes. A new suit would cost anywhere from $5 and up. But my father would always haggle with the owner over the price of the article. He would spend a considerable amount of time just to get the owner to reduce the price. It was an ego thing with a lot of people, thinking that they were beating down the owner of the store on the price of any article, before comparing the discount with that of their friends. Even after the price was reduced, people would pay the store on a weekly basis. What people did not realize then, which I would tell my father, was that he was being taken advantage of. The clothes were marked up for just this reason. Italians like to boast to their families of what a great deal they made.

I learned their business practices when I worked for a clothing store named Cohen's Department Store. I was hired for a summer job as an all-around stock clerk and sales help. One of my jobs was to price clothes for sale. The suggested retail price that was on the paper was bumped up to another 20% to allow room for customers to price him down. Many times, I saw him show one thing to a customer, and after selling the article, he would switch it with a cheaper model before wrapping it up. He always would pick out customers that were easy to fool and wait on them himself. I earned about $4 a week. He was generous to me in some ways by giving me stuff that he could not sell, but this was not very often.

My father encouraged me to work for the Jewish shopkeepers by saying that I would learn the art of retailing, which I did. That is how I was able to inform him of the way business was conducted. So with this knowledge, my father put it to the test when he had to buy me a suit for a special occasion. At Perelmutter's, the suit was $13, which was a sum in those days. After trying on the suit, on a prearranged signal to my father,

I acted like I did not want the suit. Mr. Perelmutter now did everything to encourage me to take the suit, but I kept saying no. He started to offer incentives to my father, like a new shirt with the suit. I again said no, and he then offered an extra pair of pants. Then my father who knew of the pricing policy offered to take the suit, shirt and extra pair of pants for $9. After a little more haggling, the owner relented and said yes. The $9 was to be paid over a period of three months, with me going to the store every week to make the payments. My father was elated since he probably would have paid $13 for the suit without the extra items added on. This store, Perelmutter's, was a very nice clothing store in that Mr. Perelmutter did not take advantage of people. He did have a very liberal policy of selling clothes to people on a payment plan.

Grand Avenue also had two movie houses, one named The Apollo and the other named The Dreamland. They would get the movies after the larger shows had their run with the film. These shows would employ young boys to pass out the coming attractions, which were on printed forms, to all the homes and apartments in the area. Our pay for this was one free admission to the show. Sometimes, they would offer us some free candy as well. Going to an evening show meant sitting through a double feature, which started at 7 o'clock and was over by 10. Leaving the show, especially in the winter, and having to walk home in the cold was not very pleasant to say the least. We would be shaking and shivering all the way home. When we got home, we all got around the stove in the kitchen to get warm.

Grand Avenue was also a hotbed of activity for gamblers and people selling lottery tickets, which was the Italian lottery. People were also shooting craps, which meant rolling dice. This activity was tucked away in alleyways, backyards of stores, and in back rooms of little coffee shops. People who took your bets were called bookies. They would take your bet on anything from horseracing to the daily numbers. Since betting then was illegal, it posed a problem with police always around to raid these games and arrest the men involved. Even with people who were paid to be lookouts, they sometimes did not have time to warn the gamblers of the police who were able to surround the area by hopping over backyard fences. One gambler who was caught in the raid had a basket of clothes on the ground and said he was not gambling. He said he was just hanging out the wash for his mother. All the while he had on a suit and tie and was all dressed up. The police told him that he could finish hanging clothes down at the station house. Another man crawled under a car; he too was all dressed up. He said that he was a mechanic fixing the car.

Watching these games as a young boy, I would marvel at the amount of money being wagered. Some of these gamblers had big wads of money, and some of them would also carry guns. The guns were just to discourage anyone from robbing them. Disputes during these games were commonplace with so much money being wagered. Sometimes the fights would turn ugly. The gamblers would employ young men to go and collect the daily handle from various locations. This collecting had to be done before the noon hour for the bets to be valid, such as the daily numbers, football tickets, etc. These people were known as number runners, and they were either paid a commission or flat fee for the amount of money they collected. While this was an easy living, it was also dangerous because you had all the receipts on you. Usually if the runners got arrested, the bookies would bail them out. I was offered this job as I got older but refused, due to the nature of the work. It was a very tempting job to have since you were dressed up nice all day and had a nice car with access to a lot of girls. But with all the benefits associated with that job, my only thought was getting into trouble with the law and bringing disrespect on my family. With my mother and father in mind and how they worked to nurture and feed us to the best of their ability, I knew that getting involved in this type of business would have been very traumatic for them.

WOOSTER STREET

In my childhood, Wooster Street consisted of large apartment buildings and businesses, mostly grocery stores, meat markets, and apizza places. There were six apizza restaurants to choose from. The street also had a reputation of being a haven for a lot of illegal activities such as gambling—mostly dice games and daily numbers. There was always something happening. During the summer months, the city sponsored feasts for different saints, closing the entire street from Olive Street to East Street. It was a very festive occasion with lights strung from one side of the street to the other. My paper route took me through this area of the city. The Italian restaurants that I delivered papers to were frequented by men who earned their living mostly by illegal means. On Saturdays, when I went to collect my money for the week's paper, these men who were customers would sometimes flip me a dime to see if I could catch it. I would sometimes get as much as twenty or thirty cents that way. It didn't happen too often, but I looked forward to it because it meant that I could afford to go downtown to see a first run movie.

One day on my paper route on Wooster Street, I was delivering the paper to Mike's Meat Market, and a big black sedan pulled up in front of the store and three men walked out all dressed up. Curious to see who they were, I waited while they ordered some meats. Then one of them said, hey kid, bring these bags out to the car. After placing the bags in the car, they came out and one of them said here's a little something for you and handed me a five-dollar bill. I never had so much money at one time as this. I thanked them, and they patted me on the head and said to be a good boy. As they drove away, I looked at the marker plates on the car: New York. I soon realized they were not your typical businessmen. Inside the store, a man told me they were mafia.

Wooster Street had a reputation for being a very tough neighborhood. Some criticisms were deserved; others were not. There were a lot of Italian clubs in this neighborhood with members from all different regions. My father belonged to the Minori Club, where all members came from Minori, Italy where he was born.

OFFICER JOHN AND OFFICER EARL

Throughout the city, including our neighborhood, the police were mainly of Irish descent. Some of them showed their hatred for Italians by referring to us as dagos or wops. They would walk the beat with hostility towards us. Most of our meeting places were on the corner of our blocks where we would gather and talk. This was at a time when kids my age had few places to go to socialize. Our homes were not convenient meeting places because they were so cramped, so every block or street had its own little groups. For the most part, no one ever complained of our presence on the corner. But congregating in groups like this was against police rules. To them, standing around and talking meant trouble, and trouble they hated. When the cop would come, we all had to disperse or else feel the nightstick on our legs. There was never a discussion as to why we had to move; we just did it as fast as we could.

One of the meanest cops on the beat was officer John. His fearful reputation was held by youth and adults alike; most people would say that he'd arrest his own mother. When he walked by stores on his beat, he would help himself to whatever he wanted, and no one ever questioned him. The sight of him coming towards you was enough to make you move. If you got in his way, he would push you. He was an imposing man with a large body, big belly, and swagger to his walk. His walk was so distinct that you could see him from a block away, hat pulled down near his eyes, which gave him a menacing look. But there were times when someone would have the nerve to give him a big razz. One brave boy often imitated his walk, mimicking him step by step until everybody was laughing so loud that John would turn around and try to catch him. Being big, John could not run very fast. Other kids harassed him too, calling him a fat ass or sometimes throwing water down from the second or third floors. That is why he always walked near the curb. John also walked by the Boy's Club as we waited in line to go in, staring us down. When he did, everyone fell silent—he put that much fear in us. As he walked past, he would squeeze our arms to uncover the wise guy. No one would talk. But on this one night, a boy waited until he walked a little farther and then gave him a razz and ran away as John chased after him, brandishing his nightstick. This night was truly a classic for us, and we never forgot it.

Unfortunately, our interactions with Officer John did not always end so fortunately. One evening, as we were coming out of Jason's variety store on the corner of Franklin and Grand Avenue—a store with a soda fountain that sold mostly candy and comic books and whose owner always treated us with respect—there were a lot of people in a small area, making the street appear even more congested than usual. At that moment, along comes tough guy John, yelling at us to move. With our hands full from the store, we desperately tried to put away our purchases and move away from him quickly. We knew he would hit us if we did not. As we attempted to maneuver around the people on the sidewalk, John lunges, trying to grab as many as he can. I was walking with my friend Jerry, when John appeared behind us. I moved just in time, but John grabbed hold of Jerry, shoving him into a parking meter. Jerry fell to the ground in pain as the rest of us ran off down the street. John blew his whistle to alert other cops of our fleeing attempt despite the fact that we had committed no crime. The owner of the store brought Jerry inside and tried to soothe him and his back from hitting the top of the meter. We circled the block and got back to the store and walked Jerry home. Due to his injury, Jerry suffered the rest of his life with back pain.

While John had a reputation as a very mean person, another beat cop by the name of Earl was the most gentle of men walking our area. When he came by our corner, he would sit down and chat with us for a little bit. He always treated us with the utmost respect, and everyone who came in contact with him reciprocated this respect. If he thought you were doing something wrong, he would explain to you in the most pleasant way that it was not right. Each night, he would ask us not to embarrass him, and we'd always behaved out of respect. He never gave anyone a ticket for anything, and even though (as I found out later,) he was reprimanded for this practice. One instance of his generosity was when he saw a woman driving the wrong way down a one way street. When he stopped the car, the woman became hysterical, frightened that she would get a ticket and anger her husband. Instead, she got a sermon on safety. The way he handled the situation was simply amazing. In his own folksy way, he even said that if her husband wanted to talk to him he could call him any time. Earl went out of his way to make you comfortable, unlike John, who always carried tickets in his outer pocket, ready to write anybody up for anything.

DOWNTOWN NEW HAVEN

One of the advantages of living in the Wooster Square area was being ten minutes from downtown New Haven, which, at the time, had all the big department stores and major forms of entertainment. The downtown area of New Haven also housed all the major entertainment of the day. The Schubert Theater featured live shows on Sundays with all the famous big name bands. Going to the Schubert was a real treat for most people due to the price of admission. But the big draw were the five large movie houses, Loews Poli being the best. It looked very majestic, full of marble columns and big thick rugs. The lobby was very impressive, as if you were walking into a mansion. It was so large that you could fit today's cinemas inside it. In the theater, the seats were very plush and comfortable, so you almost did not want to leave. The Loews Poli College was a smaller version of the Loews Poli but was just as ornate in its plushness and décor. The Bijou Theatre was also part of Polis chain but not as classy as the Poli or Poli College. The Bijou featured twenty two cent night on Thursday with stage shows. The policy of the chains were that the Loews Poli would get the picture first, then it would move onto the College Theater, and finally the Bijou. Each time it moved, the film dropped in price, so most times we would wait until it got to the Bijou. Another theatre was the Paramount on Temple Street, which was large but not decorated as nicely as the Poli. It did have first runs of movies as did the other independent movie theater downtown called the Roger Sherman on College Street.

Going to see a movie at the Poli was a treat because when we were young, we did not go very often. After the movies ran downtown, they would finally come to the neighborhood shows. The movie houses in our neighborhood had hard wooden seats, and in the winter, we sat with our coats on. In our little shows, the film would often break down during the movie, and we had to wait until they fixed it, which, by then, would cause pandemonium. The owner of the theater would turn the house lights up in order to minimize any damage caused by irate people throwing objects at the screen.

The downtown shows also had many movie stars make personal appearances to promote their movies. One of the movie stars I remember meeting was Anthony Quinn, who was in the war movie "Quadacanal Diary." After he made his appearance at the show, he headed for the railroad station to get the train for New York. We met him there and spent about two hours talking with him. We had a lot of fun kidding him about all the Japs he had killed. He was very interested in where we lived and asked a lot of questions about our lives.

Entering the downtown area, a large number of food stores were located on the corner of State and Chapel. Growers Outlet was the largest grocery store there at the time. It also had a bakery inside with a great variety of baked goods. Their products were so excellent that people came from great distances to purchase them. Down State Street, there was an abundance of fresh food markets selling fruits, vegetables, fish, and bakery items. One bakery made only pies, which to this day, no one has ever duplicated. The price of a ten-inch pie was one dollar.

Heading up Chapel, at the corner of State Street, there was a toy store called Rohan's. As a very young boy, I would stop with my father and look at the toys in the window. While I knew that I could never have them, it was fun to still look at the magnificent window displays and dream of someday owning a train set. My father and I would do this prior to going shopping on State Street. The next store was a major department store called Shartenberg's. During the Christmas season, it was like walking into a dreamland with all the decorations. The high point of my visit to the store was the third floor, where they had toys on display along with a stage set up as Santa land. Between the years of four and eight, I remember asking Santa for just a few things, only to find out on Christmas Day that I had received nothing. The explanation was that Santa missed our house.

Across the street, there was another department store called Stanley's. On Saturdays, my friends and I would go to the back of the store and ask the workers if they were going to throw anything away. Sometimes they would give us broken toys. Very few were in any kind of repairable condition. We would play with the broken parts. During high school, I worked at Stanley's part-time: 2:30 to 6:00 PM during the week and all day on Saturday. My pay was six dollars a week. In those days, all transactions in the store were put into a little cylinder, which was then inserted into a large tube and carried to the accounting office. Change and the receipt were then returned to the appropriate department, and the clerk handed them to the customer. Upon reporting to work, my first assignment was to bring the deposits to the bank. The money was put in a big leather envelope with a zipper on it. After making the deposit I would return the empty envelope to the accounting office. Walking to the bank with large sums of money did not faze me; I was never scared of being robbed because I tucked the money bag under my clothing.

Next door, a five and dime store, J.J. Newbury, carried a variety of small inexpensive products such as food, clothing, and jewelry. My father would stop there and purchase cookies sold loose in 10-pound boxes, where you could pick out your own. My father would buy mostly mixed and broken cookies. He would get a big bag full for about fifty cents. Whatever they were, we appreciated them. Newbury's was famous for their lunch counter, especially the steak sandwiches. Passing by after school, I would smell all that food, and I promised myself that someday I would be able to afford to sit at that counter and have a steak sandwich. After I received my first pay from Stanley's, I walked right next door and ordered a sandwich. I was 16 years old.

Chapel Street was also filled with a lot of small shops that sold clothing and other goods. One of my next jobs was working for Loehman's clothing store after school. This store catered mostly to businessmen, lawyers, and doctors. It was a store that carried a better line of clothes. Next door was Lund's shoe store where I would later on buy my children's shoes. After I got married, my wife Teresa, became very friendly with a salesman named Art. Art would dote on my children as if they were his own. He was always very complimentary on how Teresa dressed the children. He asked my wife and children to appear in the New Haven Symphony magazine advertising his shoe store in 1967.

Across the street was W.T. Grant and next door to that, Woolworth's, both five and dimes. Little did I know that my future wife, Teresa, worked at W.T. Grant at the doughnut machine. A doughnut machine was a big glass cylinder where dough was fried in oil and then they would pop out. This is similar to a popcorn machine. Each store also had its own lunch counter that was well-patronized by the public. On the corner of Church and Chapel was a store called Liggetts Drug Store, which was a meeting place for people prior to going on dates or nights out, which attributed to the success of their lunch counter. This corner was also the best in the city for the man outside selling newspapers since it was on Church and Chapel which were the crossroads of the city. Up Chapel Street stood Malley's department store, which at that time was the largest department store in the city. It carried a line of goods at a reasonable price. Next door was Gamble Desmond, another department store, though not quite as large as Malley's. On Chapel Street, a men's clothing store called J. Johnson and Sons catered mostly to boys' and men's clothes. They were very active in sponsoring a lot of teams in the city. We also had Bonds Clothes, which then featured two pairs of pants with any suit you purchased. In these days, you either had work clothes or dress clothes; there was as no such thing as casual clothes.

Downtown was also a paradise for shoplifters. Along Church Street or Grand Avenue, people were always peddling stolen merchandise. Thursday nights, the stores downtown were open until 9 p.m., which was good for shoppers and people meeting downtown, but with crowded stores, it made it easy for shoplifters. I remember once inci-dent when this guy I knew by the name of Joey (who also happened to be a prizefighter,) came running out of the W.T. Grant Store with a whole rack of silk stockings in his hands. At this time, these were hard to get and would be easy to sell. Joey ran by us, pushing people out of his way. Darting in and out of the traffic could have killed him. It was a sight to see Joey with the rack of stockings running by the traffic cop on the corner. Joey disappeared down Chapel Street then onto Temple Street. Talking to him later, we would kid him about the stockings. It was comical to hear him complain about how the salesman was chas-ing him, as if he had a right to steal but the salesman had no right to pursue him. Joey said he was mad enough to go and punch him out.

On the west end of Church Street, there was also a bar called Lips. This was a haven for bookies and a lot of what we called mafia people. I would stand outside and listen to them talking about some of their dealings. I also saw big rolls of money being transferred from one person to another. They made no pretense about hiding their trans-actions, flaunting money openly on the table, even if an off-duty cop was watching. Later on, when I was old enough to enter the bar, I would watch these mafia people sit down and eat steak and drink beer. I would wish that I could afford a dinner like that. One time they all got up to go to another table and talk to some of their friends, leaving the money stacked on the table. As we were watching, we wondered if anyone would be crazy enough to go and grab the money. I don't believe he would have made it past the door.

WALDORF AND GEORGE DAY

Next door was our hangout, the Waldorf Cafeteria. This was our place to spend a cold evening and take in the sights of the night. At sixteen, I would meet my friends there and discuss where we would go that evening. If we did not have any particular place, we would spend a few hours at the Waldorf, hanging out and getting something to eat. The counter man was a high strung man named Larry who had zero tolerance for people who did not order fast enough. Knowing this, we would take our time ordering until he began yelling and cursing. But we never paid for our food; we had the whole system figured out. At the Waldorf, you took a ticket out of the machine as you entered. We entered on both sides of the machine, and one of us would grab an extra ticket. Being a cafeteria, you went up to the counter and ordered your food, and the counterman would punch the amount on your ticket. Each ticket went up to five dollars. Then on the other ticket you would order a cup of coffee for ten cents and just pay the lesser ticket. This cafeteria also had some people who would fall asleep. We would grab their ticket and order from them and then put the ticket back in front of them. I recall many nights as they got up to leave that they would argue with the cashier. This would cause a ruckus, and the restaurant would throw them out.

A lot of boxers and streetfighters hung out at this cafeteria as well. Some of our nights were filled with teasing them about how they fought in their last fight. One fighter was a man named George Day who fought before I was born. He was a fighter we would call "punch drunk" from having too many fights. When he walked, it looked like he was going to tip over with each step. But he also had a great personality and would delight us with his ring experiences, so we never treated him with disrespect. Every time you saw him, he was always dressed up with a carnation in his lapel. One night, as Georgie was talking to one of his friends prior to ordering at the counter, Larry kept asking him to hurry up and order. But Georgie continued talking to his friend. In a fit of anger, Larry threw water on Georgie. Georgie, taking great pride in his clothes and appearance, went ballistic, reaching behind the counter, grabbing a pie, and hitting Larry in the face with it. Then Georgie's friend pitched in and started throwing food at Larry. By then, the kitchen help came out and a good fight was on. The hysterics of it all had us laughing for a long time. We, of course, helped it along by cheering for Georgie Day. When the police came, they knew George and only ushered him out of the building and sent him home.

This cafeteria was also where I would meet a lot of men who had just come home from the war. A lot of boys approaching the age of seventeen would think about enlisting in the service or waiting until they got drafted, but by then they would have no choice but to go to whatever branch they were assigned. One veteran, listening to us debate about which branch was better, Army, Navy or Marines, sat down and quietly told us about the horrors of war. No matter which branch you picked, he said, it was nothing like the movies. He had seen men get blown to pieces, like they were toys. He said, when you are in battle, you just keep moving forward with the flow, trying to duck and hide and not get shot at. This man was on leave, recuperating from shrapnel wounds, waiting to be reassigned for another tour of duty. He advised us to stay out as long as possible. Listening to him talk about war as a soldier and how horrible land wars can be made me start to think about enlisting in the Navy instead of being drafted in the Army. One of my decisions was made for me as the war ended in 1945 when I was sixteen. But with the draft still on, I was eligible at eighteen when I graduated from high school. So I enlisted in the Navy at sixteen and was inducted at seventeen, Christmas, 1945.

WHY AND HOW I GOT INTO THE NAVY

I was 17 years old, so my father had to sign a waiver for me to enlist. He had to come with me on his lunch hour, and on the way to the navy office, he kept asking me why I was enlisting. I told him that with my asthma, I would get excellent medical treatment, and that I would not be a burden on him. Because I would be on my own, for the first time, he was concerned about me getting in trouble with women. My father's only advice was that there were a lot of sick women out there, and I should be careful. I did not know what he meant by that, but upon entering the service, I soon found out what he meant since we were shown a lot of movies on the subject of sexually transmitted diseases.

On my day of departure for the Navy, January 7, 1946, I remember it as a very cloudy and cold day. I said goodbye to my mother, brother, and sisters—my father had already gone to work—and I walked to the railroad station. As I approached the station, I saw all the families seeing their sons off for the Navy. Standing there, I wondered why they had come down here. The train ride down to Norfolk, VA was on an old coal train, and it was so dirty, you could hardly see out the windows.

On arriving at the camp, we were told to take off all our clothes, and place them in a bag that was going to be shipped home. We were taken to a large hall and measured for our Navy clothes, and as we glided down a long table with our sizes taped to our shirt, we were given a bedsheet to put all our clothes in. I had been notified by my friend Louie who had just gotten out of the service not to drag the sheet on the floor, since that would be the sheet that I would sleep on. It was very heavy to lift and keep off the floor. I tried to tell the other boys with me to pick up the sheet, but they laughed at me. They soon found out about the bed sheet when the officer of the day came in and told them, that it was their bed sheet, and that there would be an inspection of all bedding, prior to sleeping. Anyone with a dirty sheet would have to wash their sheet before sleeping on it. I did not have the heart to laugh at them. They were given new sheets after they had washed their old sheets, but they certainly learned their lesson.

After being up all day and traveling to Norfolk Training Station and putting our clothes away, it was not until 1 a.m. when we got to sleep. At 4:30 a.m., the bugle sounded for us to get up and be dressed by 5 a.m. That meant in full uniform of the day and ready to do exercises for one hour before breakfast. There was a lot of moaning and everyone bitched about everything, but we soon found out who was in charge. In came our officer named Chief Castle, and his first words were "I am now your lord and master. You will obey every word I say, and do everything I tell you to do. For the next eight weeks, I will work your ass off. You will be a man when I get through with you."

After my first week, I was having second thoughts about enlisting. The training was very tough, but I was determined to finish. Every week was a different kind of training, and we spent a lot of time being submerged in a very deep tank, told to ascend to the top of the tank in a matter of seconds. They showed us how to tie our pants legs at the bottom and make a life preserver out of it. They told us that it would last for about an hour. We were also trained to help ourselves in case of a gas attack. That was done by having us go into a container and to put on our gas mask, each one of us helping one another to make sure that our mask was on properly. Then they would open the gas jets to check to see if we all got them on right. If you did not, you would soon find out. Even then, as we departed the container, we could smell the putrid gas. They told us to always have a buddy to check your straps.

A lot of the time they had us on the drill field marching for hours at a time, sometimes with a full field pack, to teach us how it would be to carry someone for any length of time. We also had to learn all the rope knots, and we were to be tested on them.

The name for this training in the Navy was called Boot Camp because we had to put on leggings that extended from our ankles to our knees. They were very cumbersome to say the least, and they also had to be kept clean, which was a problem due to our training program. They gave us a brown soap to wash our boots with, and it was very coarse and smelly. Because they were so hard to clean, I was able to obtain a second pair that were brand new, and I kept them in a separate part of my locker. I would take them out only on inspection days, which were Saturdays. I also had a second pair of white hats and tee shirts for Saturdays. A lot of the guys would wear all their clothes all the time, and when it came for inspection, they would fail because the clothes were very hard to clean with the soap they gave you. Passing inspection was very important in that they would grade you. A lot of bad marks meant you would wind up in the deep sink in the mess hall, and some of the cooks were sadistic, making you wash pots and pans over and over. They would mess them up on purpose and laugh at you. I had to do it once, and I said never again. That's when I learned to never step out of line and make sure that my bunk and locker were always kept neat. They would inspect them when we were out on the marching field. One time, my friend Lopez and I messed up by not saluting an officer as he came into the barracks. For punishment, we had to clean a whole floor, which included forty toilets and sinks, on our hands and knees with a scrub brush that did not have a handle. We had six hours to clean up the place. As he was leaving, the officer said have a lot of fun and that he would be back in six hours. To make matters worse, he was a rebel from down south, and he had no love for a Spanish and an Italian from the north. He had a grin on him that said we would never finish the job, but we did. He had hatred in his eyes for us, but it was a good thing that he came back with another officer to verify that the place was clean or dirty. I still remember the shocked look on his face when he saw the place clean and spotless, and he could not say it was not, because of the other officer present. Lopez and I could not stop laughing all the way back to our barracks.

One of the worst nights was when they called lights out at 9 p.m. As a rule, there was to be strict silence. Some of the guys started talking and carrying on about the day that we had just gone through, which was a rough day. The chief heard the talking down in his office and he came into the room and said everybody up and dressed: we were going for a walk. It was now about 10 p.m. when he said get your sea bag and fill it up with your gear. It just so happened to be a very cold and rainy night, so we had to get our ponchos on and also our leggings, and down to the field we went. This was called the grinder where we marched from about 10:30 p.m. until 3.30 A.M. And the bugle still sounded at 4:30 a.m. After that, lights out meant lights out. The guys that were responsible for this chaos were given a very strong calling out by everyone in the barracks. On top of this, we were to march in full uniform because of some very important visitors. Needless to say, we were a very tired bunch of recruits. As we were preparing to end our training and get our assignments for which ship or station we were to serve on, I met Chief Castle in the hallway and he invited me into his office for a talk. I told him that I appreciated being instructed by him and that he was the nicest bastard that I had ever met. He had such a laugh about the way that I approached him on that, and he then said that he hoped I liked the duty where he was sending me. Hopefully not in some rotten ship I said. No he said. He put me on the list for duty in San Juan, Puerto Rico. I told him that I had learned a lot from him and thanked him for considering me for that duty. He said that I was one of the guys who always showed him the greatest respect. I said I did because I did not want to get on his shit list. He then said that I will go a long way in the Navy because I was a great con artist.

AFTER BOOT CAMP

When boot camp was over, I was given a ten day leave and was told to report back to Norfolk, VA for transfer to San Juan, Puerto Rico. I was assigned to a ship that was going to make several stops on the way to Puerto Rico. The ship was a class of ship listed has an L.S.T., which was what they used during WWII to bring men and materials to the battle areas. It was a flat bottom ship and therefore not a very pleasant riding ship. When the ship would hit the big waves, it would come down with a very large bang. The first day out at sea we were all very seasick, due to the weaving and bobbing of the ship. As we passed through the Cape Hatteras area, we encountered a great big storm with the waves completely washing over the ship. It was to be a very horrible experience for us. As the ship was been tossed around like a toy, all hands were to secure their stations. Then came the distress call from the captain; one of the men was late in coming back from the bow of the ship. Since my crew was assigned to this area, we were close to the man who was trapped up at the bow. With our life line tied to our waists, we hooked on to one another for support, and inched our way to the bow by holding onto the railings, and were able to throw this man a large hook with a line attached to it. He tied it around his waist, and we were able to pull him toward us, and secure him. I can vividly remember the way the ship slipped beneath the waves, and then bobbed up again. It left me with a profound respect for the sea.

We stopped at Trinidad and were told not to venture too far inland because of problems with the natives who were great at mugging the sailors with all kinds of offers, from sex to great bargains of fake materials. They were a very scary lot of people, so we stayed in the dock area close to the ship. Still, the people would try to get your attention any way they could. Our next stop was S.T. Thomas Island which was a very nice place to spend a day. After several more stops, we finally arrived at San Juan, Puerto Rico. It was May 1946. The trip from Norfolk, VA took us exactly 30 days. The Navy did this quite often to save transportation expense to move large groups of people. It felt good having finally arrived at our destination, and I lucked out by being placed in a barracks with a great group of guys from New York. Our work assignments were going to be passed out to us, and as luck would have it, my friend Al from basic training was in the same group. We were mostly from the same area of the east coast, so we had a lot in common. Al said for me to register for the commissary store, since that would be a good job. I had to tell them that I had a lot of experience in retail, which, in truth, I did, having worked in my uncle's grocery store and in clothing stores while I was attending school. Because of my low rank as a Seaman 1st class, I would have to work on the docks or in the machine shops, which were dirty jobs.

Working on the docks meant loading and unloading ships at all hours of the day and night. I had to do that once when there was a shortage of men. The day that I had to work the docks they had an ensign in charge who was about the same age as the rest of us. It did not take long before the catcalls started to ring down on the poor ensign from Lopez and the N.Y. crew. The ensign said that he was going to put us all on report for failure to obey an officer, but as he was talking and trying to instill some fear in us, the laughter only got worse. We saw him go over to the lieutenant and point at us. The lieutenant told us to knock it off and leave the ensign alone. The problem with the ensign was that he trying to show his authority by pushing the men to work faster when we were already at full speed. The lieutenant already knew this, and that's why he did not follow up with the report that the ensign had suggested. In the Navy, we called ensigns the 90 day wonders.

Working in the store with me was a person from New Haven who was working in another department whom I got friendly with. His name was Ralph and he came from the Fair Haven section of the city. Ralph lived in a different barracks from me, so outside of work, I did not socialize much with Ralph because we each had our own friends. But after I got discharged, I met Ralph when he had a gas station in Fair Haven, and as it turned out, he was getting married and asked me to be an usher at his wedding. Being from different parts of the city, I would see Ralph from time to time. We met again when I belonged to a bowling league, and we bowled against each other. His team consisted of all his brothers.

While the work in the commissary store was hard, it was at least a clean job. Our officer in charge was a man named Donaldson. He was a good man who we all became friends with. He introduced us to a very nice lady who ran a hotel and restaurant. She would have us meet some very nice girls who came from some of the best neighborhoods in San Juan. From this group of people, we were introduced to a person who was going to put on a variety show on the base. I got on the committee to put the show together and along with five other people, had to select the talent that was going to perform. It turned out to be such a huge success that it was going to be repeated every year after that. Standing on that stage and receiving the applause for our work was my crowning glory. It was a moment of pure excitement, and to say the least, a great rush. Out of this show, I dated this girl named Mariana. Since she was Spanish and I was Italian, it was not an acceptable situation for her parents in those days. Still, they allowed me to date her but were very cautious in accepting me into their home, since they did not want the situation to blossom further. If they only knew that it was the same for my family as well: my father would have killed me for bringing home anyone that wasn't Italian.

Since I enjoyed being on the show and able to get out of my regular duties, Al and I were asked if we wanted to enter a boxing program, which was called Smokers. Boxing was with sixteen ounce gloves, so we thought, what the hell? We can't get hurt with that size gloves. Besides, we would spend about two months preparing ourselves, trying to get in shape for the boxing match. Al was always trying to figure out ways to get out of work, and of course, I was always interested in doing the same thing. Little did we realize who our opponents would be. It turned out they were from a different part of the base, and they did not spar in the same gym as us. We were matched up by our weight, which at that time I was about 120 pounds, but my opponent, as I quickly discovered, had some ring experience. At this point, I started having reservations about going on with the program, but Al said not to worry since it was only three rounds lasting two minutes each. As I got into the ring and saw the huge crowd that was on hand, cheering and howling, I started to get very nervous. I did not want to embarrass myself and let my section of the base down by not putting up a good fight. As the fight progressed, I got my bearings on the guy and did what my manager said, staying inside of him and not letting him get a clear shot at me. It might have been only three, two minutes rounds of boxing, but to me, it was the longest six minutes of my life. When it was over, the two of us shook hands, and I told him this was the last time that I would ever think about being a boxer and he laughed. To satisfy everybody they called the fight a draw. For me, the sad part of all this was I lost all the photos of that night.

One of the most pleasant experiences was the day that I was selected to spend a day on a submarine. The day lasted about 12 hours, and they had us do light duty stuff to give us a feel of working on a sub. Next to San Juan was an island called Vieques, where the Navy held landing drills in bombing and the landing of troops. We were supposed to be a target for aircraft to locate us and try to bomb the sub, trying to hit us using large bags of white powder for markers. The sub was very successful in eluding the aircraft, since I believe we got hit only twice, but not directly. When the aircraft could not locate us, the commander would surface and entice them to locate the sub. This meant that we had to go on the deck of the sub, and wait for the signal to submerge. When the planes were coming, the buzzer would sound, and you had to slide down the ladder with both feet on the outside of it. With a man coming right after, you had to be very fast or you would get stepped on. On this day, we made thirteen dives. While we found it very exhilarating, it was also very scary to think of what the submariners had to endure during the war, being in such a small space with very little room. The commander of the sub had been a prisoner in Japan, and his body had stab marks on it. I asked him why he did not get discharged after the war, and he said that this was his life. He never said how he was captured. I could still picture him in his shorts, standing by the periscope, as if he was just a member of the crew.

As time went on, people were getting discharged, so many of us had an opportunity to advance ourselves to a higher position in the commissary store. The person that was in charge of all the refrigeration units was named Bernie. I was friendly with him, and he gave me an edge up on everyone else. Bernie recommended me to take over his position to the captain of the store. The position called for me to handle all shipping and receiving of products, in and out of the units. I shared two of the units with the meat department of the store. Along with a man named Mac, who was head of the meat department, we had all the keys to all the units. We had to keep all the inventory for the base but were mostly confined to our units. My units contained mostly grocery products, so I was responsible for billing departments for products they ordered. We had some civilian workers whose job it was to keep the grounds around the store clean. I noticed that they would go through the dumpster and look for food to take home. They were a bunch of nice guys, and I did not want to see them picking through all that garbage, so I said to my friend Jose to wait until the trucks came in with all the food items. Then I would give him all the damaged goods and a pass so that he could get the goods off the base. Jose was forever grateful to me. Of course, I extracted a little extra work out of them, which was work that I had to do.

For several months, the store was having a very bad inventory. After checking where the shortage was but with no success, the Navy security team came to the store to ascertain where the problems were. They said that everyone was to be interrogated. Since I, along with Mac, had control of most of the inventory, we were selected to be the first ones to be called in. They called me in first. There were three men in a back room set up with a chair under a light. Two men would question me, and the third one would just stand in the corner and not say a word, just looking at me, watching and listening to my answers, analyzing my expression as I gave testimony to the questions. I was very truthful with my answers as to my duties and the handling of my inventory. I told them that I took all broken candy boxes and other damaged goods that the store got credit for and gave them to the men in the barracks for snacks as they were playing cards. To be honest, I sold them to the men for fifty cents each, but I knew that they would not say they paid for them as they were all my friends.

THE TRIAL OF MAC

In the ensuing days of the investigation, the security team finally got a lead, even it was all by accident. One of the security men happened to be in Mac's office when calls came in from several stores in town questioning when their meat was going to be delivered next. The team went to visit the locations and found out that Mac was selling them products from the commissary store. They got all the information as to the amount of products they were purchasing, when the delivery days were, and all the pricing of the products they purchased. The security men did not let on that there was an investigation going on of Mac; they simply said that they were only bringing all the records up to date. This is how they were able to secure all the information they needed to indict Mac. The evidence was overwhelming against Mac. Little did Mac know that he was standing on quicksand. As he came to his office, they confronted Mac with all the paperwork of all the missing products, the dates, and the locations of his customers.

For the upcoming court martial, the Navy appointed Mac a lawyer to represent him. His attorney set about calling each one of us to prepare Mac's defense. Since I had the most contact with Mac, working in close proximity with him, he called me to his office first, and wanted me to give testimony as to Mac's daily schedule. I did not want to put myself into Mac's daily schedule, I told the lawyer that I only saw Mac making his usual stops around the base. I told him that Mac would load his truck and give me what time he would return. He asked me how long he would be gone, and I said that sometimes he would be gone for quite some time. I said that I felt that he was goofing off somewhere and never gave it any thought as to what he was doing. The lawyer asked if I ever noticed if the truck had an overabundance of products, and I said that yes, he seemed to be carrying a lot more products lately. Mac's lawyer was trying to ask if maybe I misjudged the amount he was taking, but I said no, because some of the products came out of my units. I was responsible for my inventory and made notes of all the products that were taken, and they matched up with the security team's information. I knew that my information would not be helpful to Mac because it would coincide with the prosecution's evidence against him. The lawyer was trying get me in a position to change my account of the events, and as much as I did not want to hurt Mac, I also did not want to give false testimony since I knew what the Navy had for evidence. As a gesture of friendship, Mac later told me that he understood and that he did not want me to get into any trouble because of him.

In questioning all the other people in the store, they tried to cover up for Mac the best they could without giving any damming evidence against him. The trial of Mac went on for about three weeks, and when it was over, the news spread fast that he was guilty as charged and would be sentenced in one month. On the day of the sentencing, it was very somber in the barracks, as all kind of rumors were going around as to how long Mac would have to serve. We soon found out when a bulletin was posted for all hands to appear in the court yard that Saturday at noon. All the officers were seated at the center of the yard, with all personnel standing on all sides of the yard. A court martial is a very somber military trial, in which the accused has to stand in the middle of the court yard in their full dress uniform, with all their decorations and whatever medals they were awarded. Then, as the sentence is read to the accused, including each article of wrong doing that was he was accused of, an officer standing in front of him removes one item at a time from his uniform, virtually stripping him of all his medals and decorations, leaving him with just a bare uniform. The sentence was for Mac to serve a twenty years to life sentence. While it may have seen a bit severe to us, it was explained by the commanding officer that this was government property, not just some grocery items taken for profit. That is why it had to be such a severe punishment. As Mac was being marched around the court yard by the sentry, he stopped by me and said thank you. He wanted to give me something to remember him by, so he said to me, "Remember: a bird in hand fools no man." To this day, I have tried to figure out what he meant by that. The only meaning I could come up with is whatever you have, you have, be it friends or money.

A SMART DRUNK

In my barracks, a sailor had a habit of always drinking quite a bit whenever he went into town. He was more or less the joke of the barracks, noted for always being drunk. On the rare occasions when he was sober, he would come up with all kinds of investment schemes. One day, he presented me and several of our crew with a grand opportunity to buy up a lot of the land that was known as Condado beach, an area that was swampy at the time but had a lot of shorefront attached to it. His proposition was for six of us to put aside half our pay every month until we got enough for a down payment to purchase the land. The money was to be held in a Navy bank account under all our names, with any withdrawals to be signed by all of us. We went to look at the land many times, mulling over the offer of purchasing the property, since the down payment was about three thousand dollars. He said that this shorefront land was going to be very valuable because as people have more disposal income, they would be traveling to these islands for vacations, and that there would be hotels that would have to be built to satisfy the huge amount of people arriving in San Juan. He said that he was giving us the opportunity because he could not get the down payment in time, and that it would be a great investment for all of us. After studying the proposal for some weeks, it was decided that we would have to make payments for some time before there would be any chance of making a profit off it. And since it was mostly swampland, we were very hesitant about the deal. He pleaded with us as to what a great opportunity this was, but we did not buy the land. On that land today stands some of the largest hotels in San Juan.

BACK TO THE STATES, THEN BACK TO PUERTO RICO

Around the summer of 1946, I started to have some breathing problems due to working in cold areas and then warm spaces outside of the units. After undergoing a lot of tests to get at the source of the problem, it was decided to send me stateside for more observation. It was about October when I arrived at Jacksonville Navy Base hospital to begin my treatment of my breathing problems. The doctors could not find any one thing that would cause me to have these breathing problems, and after several weeks of all kinds of testing, it was decided to send me back to duty. I spent the Thanksgiving holidays at the hospital in Jacksonville, Florida.

After being discharged from the hospital, I was ordered to report to Norfolk Navy Base, via South Carolina, but the Navy would not give me a train ticket, since they said they had a ship going there, and I should take this ship, along with four other sailors who were also being sent to Norfolk to be reassigned. The ship was a class of small vessel that the Navy used for short distance travel. After the five of us went to see the ship that we were going to take the next day, we all looked at each other in disbelief. We thought that they made a mistake and were joking. We went on board and met the officer in charge, gave our names, and he instructed us as to the time of departure. The officer was a L.J.G., not much older than us. We said holy shit, are they kidding? Along with the officer was a crew of three, and at five o'clock the next morning, we reported to the ship. The officer of the ship wanted all of us to get to know all the positions of the ship, even the wheelhouse, where you take control of the wheel and keep the ship on course. Since there were nine of us altogether, the officer gave us our time slots for when it was our turn to go to the bridge and take control of the ship. This trip would turn out to be a trip right from hell, since it was November and the weather reports were not very promising. We were all a little bit nervous about the bad weather we might encounter to Norfolk, as we had to sail through Cape Hatteras, North Carolina, which is always very stormy, even on a good day.

As we approached the Cape, the weather started to get very stormy, the waves washing right over the ship. I felt that this was it and that we would never make it to Norfolk. Because of the bad weather, we made very little headway. As night started to fall and the storm grew in intensity, the five of us were below deck and strapped to our bunks, holding tight to whatever we could get our hands on. Then the officer called to us to come topside and help him on the bridge. We were all very seasick by now and vomiting, but it was then I learned a new word, which I still recall the officer saying. He opened the hatch and shouted for us to come up on deck and DEVIATE your mind. This was supposed to somehow make us feel better, but the guy next to me shouted, "Deviate this" while grabbing his testicles. One of the crew members who had stayed in the wheelhouse all night, along with the officer, somehow managed to stay with the wheel and had his hands all blistered from trying to keep the ship on course as the storm pushed the ship farther out to sea and way off course. We finally came up on deck only to find out that we were off the coast of Bermuda, where we docked, and the officer was reprimanded for failure to have control of the ship. Another officer was put in charge to take the ship to Norfolk.

Because of our bad experience at sea, the Navy gave us all a seven day leave, so we had a chance to go home for Christmas. I went from a storm at sea to one of the worst snow storms in New Haven. In December 1946, we had twenty six inches of snow. The low point for me was getting transportation home. Since my pay records were not processed in time, I had no money to take the train home, so I went to the Red Cross for a loan. But it was denied because it was not an emergency situation, even though I knew men right from the same base who did get advances from the Red Cross for this type of leave. I always believed that it had something to do with me being from the north and the man from the Red Cross being from the south. The Navy office was at least able to get in touch with my father and have my father wire me the money for the train ride home.

After my leave, I reported to Norfolk Navy Base for reassignment and was surprised when I was given orders to report to San Juan, Puerto Rico to a Navy Air Station in San Juan. It was a navy squadron base whose duty was to patrol all the islands in the area. During WWII, this base was very important since it was the security of the east coast of the southern part of the U.S. The ship I was assigned to was a vessel that was used to transport heavy materials. Our first stop was at Gitmo Bay, Cuba, where a lot of the material was off loaded. We tied up in Cuba for two days, but a lot of the men were disappointed that they could not go to Havana. That was where all the big night clubs and night life was, and all of the stories they had heard was this city of sin, with girls, girls, girls. There was a lot of moaning to the officers about why we could not get a twenty four hour pass, but we were told to be patient. After we got settled in San Juan, we would have the opportunity to get a weekend leave and go to Havana.

After a few more stops, we finally landed in San Juan. Lo and behold, on the dock were some of the guys I was stationed with in San Juan. They gave me a great cheer and also a lot of ribbing for returning to San Juan. After we were processed off the ship, we were all assigned a different mode of transportation. Mine was by a large carrier truck with racks on the side to hold on to. The road to the base was very narrow and curvy, with just enough room for two vehicles to pass by each other. The people on the island had a bad habit of driving at top speed along these roads, and they would not slow down, even at the sight of oncoming vehicles.

The first person to greet us was a man named Chief Hall. While he was very friendly, he also gave us the impression that he was a stern man and went by all the rules that would apply to us. We had to fill out forms as to any qualifications and experience we had, and what our education was. I looked at some of the type of work that was available to us, and I noticed a line for any clerical experience you've had. Since I went to a business school and had some typing experience, I highlighted it on the form to get the attention of my interviewer. It just so happened that there was an opening in the leading chief's office as an assistant to the chief. It just so happened the chief was Chief Hall, and he asked me about my clerical experience. I told him that I could type, but not very well, and that my typing speed was about thirty words a minute. He said that would be sufficient as I would be in charge of typing up the plan of the day, which included making up the watch list, and assigning men to their time of watch duty. I then had a lot of friends of all of a sudden because nobody wanted the 12 to 4 a.m. slot. The plan of the day was all the business that would take place the next day, and I then had to distribute a copy to each department in the hanger. The downside to this job was being called a titless wave because I worked in the office, which was not considered manly. But the advantage of the job was that I never had to stand guard duty. The class of ratings for this work was called Yeoman's service, and I worked alongside several other men, who worked in the main office. I met a nice guy from Springfield, MA. His name was Al Gentile, and we became close friends. Because of our friendship, the other guys would also question why Al never got the 12 to 4 a.m. as often as they had, but they knew that if they complained too much, I would stick them on weekend duty. I had some power, but I did not want to take advantage of them, so I had to walk a very fine line.

COMMANDER JOHN MILO

Working in close proximity to the commander's office was also an advantage. The commander's name was John Milo, a very tall and imposing man. One of my duties was to inform him of all his appointments for the day and tidying up his desk before he came on duty. He treated all the men with the greatest respect and would close down the base every Wednesday and take us all on a beach party with all the food we wanted, including beer. We only left a small crew to take care of the hangar, which rotated every week. We had a lot of different aircraft stationed there, which the mechanics had to service, or in some cases, completely overhaul, depending on the plane's condition.

Many times, Commander Milo would take us to St. Thomas Island to pick up supplies for the officers' club. He took mostly clerical personnel and did not disturb the people working in the hangar. It would be a fun day but also a work day. We had to carry all the whiskey and fine foods aboard the plane. Milo was a great pilot flying his two engine plane, called the S.N.J., which was a forty seated aircraft. It was very comfortable to ride in, unlike the transport planes we had to ride in, which had bucket seats along the bulkhead with straps to hold onto. The old prop planes were not smooth to fly in because if you hit an air pocket, the plane would fall rapidly, and in a manner of seconds, it could drop as much as a couple of hundred feet, which was not very pleasant on the stomach.

JAY WESTBROOK

One of the most colorful and charismatic men that I met in San Juan was chief petty officer Jay. He gave me a lot of advice and mentored me in the ways of the Navy. He was a career man and tried to instill in me the great opportunity of staying in the service, telling me about all the wonderful advantages of being a twenty year man, which meant getting a pension after twenty years of service. Jay was in charge of all the machinists in the hangar, a rather demanding position with a lot of responsibility for the care of all the aircraft in the fleet. Jay had seen a lot of action in the Pacific, but I had found out from talking with his buddies that he never made a big deal of his war experience, as a lot of people who fought found it hard to discuss the trauma that they endured. Jay had a strut about him as he walked, almost as if he was the captain of the base. Not in any offensive way, just that he was very noticeable whenever he went. He was well liked by all hands and was even allowed by the commander to have a mustache, even though at that time, the rules were that you had to be clean shaven.

Being a chief petty officer had a lot of advantages. They had their own club, almost like the commissioned officers. Although Jay said he was offered a higher rank many times, Jay explained to me that his rank was as high as he wanted to go. He did not want any more responsibility than he already had. As an officer, he was an exceptional person in that he always favored the enlisted men of lower rank. I believed that he felt more comfortable with us peons, and that he did not have to always be careful of what he said and how he acted. He preferred clowning around, acting foolish, and confiding in us all his actions in his private life. Jay would regale me with stories about all the parties at the chief petty officers' club, and how the wives were always very receptive to his advances. Jay was a charmer and therefore constantly hounded and harassed by the husbands of the women. I told Jay that someday you will meet the wrong lady and that he better concern himself with all the single women that were after him instead.

Jay would sometimes meet up with us on liberty (his time off,) while we were in town, and go bar hopping with us. He knew all the hot spots, which was good, because we were only looking for a good time and did not want to get into any trouble. My friends and I really did not want to go to any bad areas, such as a place in town known as skid row. Here, prostitutes would walk the streets and almost pull you aside and force themselves on you. They knew when it was payday for the sailors and would come out in full force, so we avoided going into town then.

One night, Jay said, "Let's go to this bar where you can go dancing and have a good time." He assured us that it was nice place to spend the night and that it would not cost us too much. As we approached the area, it didn't look too bad, so we entered the bar and had a few drinks and some nice conversation. Jay looked across the room and saw a lady he was having relations with, and it just so happened that she was with someone, who was a civilian and did not look like a very sociable person. Jay wanted to go over and talk to her, and we said, "Are you crazy?" The guy looked like a wacko, so we said not to go over, but Jay said, "Hey, he don't own her." We told him to let her be and to try and pick up someone else, but when Jay got his ass up, he was hard to convince otherwise. To make matters worse, he had had a few too many drinks. But Jay said all right, he would wait until she had a free moment, all the while telling us how beautiful she was and how he was taken by her. Looking at her, we agreed with him how striking she was but that it was not worth getting cut up over.

We started to engage the women in the bar, asking them to dance, and if they were having a good time. We brought the girls over to our table and introduced them to Jay. They said that they were familiar with Jay and had seen him many times in the club, especially with the lady Jay was interested in. The girls said that the guy the lady was with was her on and off boyfriend and that he had a very nasty temper and were not very fond of him. Jay said a lot of guys talk tough just to scare people, but the girls said not him. He was a bad hombre, and on this particular night, he had some of his pals with him.

As the night progressed, Jay started to get agitated and kept looking over at her table and said, "That son of a bitch is not going to have her." The lady knew Jay was looking, and she returned his glances, flirting with him. I said, "Jay, she is only breaking your stones." The lady was in a full mode of teasing, and she kept egging him on by lifting up her dress and really teasing him, all the while the guy she was with started to get mad at the way she was flirting with Jay. One of his friends came over to our table and point blank told us to leave the club. The girls told us that they were not to be taken lightly, as they were always carrying some kind of weapon, mostly knives. Jay, in a mocking way, told the guy that he was very scared and told him to tell his asshole friend to go and take a shit. Then Jay said, "Do you want me to say it in Spanish?" After the guy left, we said, "Jay, are you crazy?!" Although there were a lot of Navy personnel in the club at the time, we were still outnumbered.

Before we could grab a hold of him, Jay said he was going to call his bluff and started to cross the room. Lopez, Cabby, A.J., and I went chasing after him. Jay got to the man's table, grabbed him by the shirt, and cold cocked him flat out. The guy did not know what hit him. His friends all got up and started after Jay. As we dragged Jay away from the crowd of men, all hell broke loose in the club with the sailors in the club warding off civilians who started to get involved, helping Jay and us escape from the club. By now, it had turned into a free-for-all with the place being literally torn apart by all the fighting.

As we started to descend the stairs holding Jay in the middle of the pack of us, a group of guys tried to cut us off from the stairs. They were hitting us from all angles, but God must have been looking out for us as no one got cut from any weapons they were supposed to have on them. I got punched in the side of the face, and it staggered me. As I bounced against the wall, I held onto the railing so as not to fall down. The five of us tried to get down this narrow stairway to the street with the men behind us yelling curse words, still throwing punches.

Just as we got to the bottom of the stairs, we heard the sounds of the shore patrol. The men behind us ran away, so as not to get arrested, and Jay told the shore patrol there was a riot going on in the club and that we had escaped just in time. Since he was an officer, it gave us a great cover, since they had to respect his rank. But we knew that all the turmoil and all the damage was caused by Jay. As we walked away without any problems, we said what about your girlfriend? What if she turns you in as she knows who you are? Won't we all be held accountable for all the damage? Jay said not to worry as he knew of her association with a lot of drug dealers, and she was not about to turn him in.

We hailed two cabs to take us back to the base, since the base was quite a ways from where we were, and in the cab, we took stock of who got hit and how bad. In our cab was Jay, Lopez, and me. Lopez told Jay all this shit just for a piece of tail and that we could have gotten killed, or just as worse, we could have been cut up like a piece of meat since these Puerto Ricans like to chop people up. He told Jay that he knew that and still had to challenge them. Jay took all of this in a nonchalant way, then said, "Don't ever be afraid of anybody." We said but not when you are outnumbered and the other guy has weapons that could kill you. That's when you must be afraid and walk away. Jay said that these are life experiences and that you must face them head on. Lopez said that not when you manufacture them. I said defending yourself is one thing but sticking your nose out is another. Jay said, "Did I not say we were going to have a nice time?" as if nothing happened. Lopez said, "You must be the craziest chief in the navy."

JAY AND COMMANDER MILO

Jay was always pushing the envelope, and he never seemed to care about anything, while Commander Milo was just the opposite: easy going but always leading by the book. He had a strict set of rules, and he expected everyone to obey them. Cmdr. Milo taking us to the beach every Wednesday was a royal treat, and he did not spare any expense. But the way he treated us was also the way he wanted us to reciprocate by turning in a good work week and doing our jobs and meeting our goals in whatever department you were in. All the officers under him always told me that Cmdr. Milo was someone to be admired, as they were in a lot of commands and they were never treated with the respect that Cmdr. Milo gave them, especially with providing them with full support in any decisions they made.

Cmdr. Milo's wife was a very tall, statuesque blond. She was about six feet tall and always dressed very nicely. Every time she came into the hangar, the noise of all the men working would suddenly seem to come to an end. She would always have a big white hat and dress to match, and she would acknowledge the silence with a great big smile, walking up the stairs to Cmdr. Milo's office. When she got to the top of the stairs, she always turned around and gave a little wave of her hand to the men below in the hangar, toward the envy in their eyes. It was something to see as our office was next door, and we had a front row seat to the whole show.

Cmdr. Milo was very proud of his wife and under the glass of his desk, even had a very revealing photo of her, almost topless, in a very sheer blouse and no bra. The first time I entered his office to give him his reports, he pointed out the photo to me and said, "Isn't she beautiful?" I stood there with my mouth open, then said, "She looks like a movie actress." Since all the men had heard about the photo but none were allowed in his office, they would ask me if it was true. I said, "It's only a photo…" And to edge them on a little further, I told them that I had to clean his desk every morning and that I had never noticed it. Al said that he must have the cleanest desk in the whole office: "You must spend an hour cleaning his desk." Such are the perks of the job I said.

Per usual, Jay was always looking for a way to circumvent the rules set down by Cmdr. Milo, including having women invited to our picnics on the beach. With all the officers attending, Cmdr. Milo was strictly against any problems arising from any such behavior that might cause a scandal. Jay figured out a way to invite some women but to keep them out of our area of the beach. One of the girls, named Frenchie, lived nearby and was a friend of Jay. Frenchie took us to deserted part of the beach, and Jay said for her to show us a little skin. Frenchie removed her top, and I took pictures of her with Al and two other men. One of the guys said that he wanted the negatives because he felt that later in life it might come back to bite him. I said not to worry; I won't blackmail him. Frenchie posed for us and said that was all she was going to do. Then Jay went off with her and we did not see him for a good part of the afternoon.

JAY'S BIG MISTAKE

Al called me one day and said he heard rumors about Jay and Cmdr. Milo's wife spending a lot of time together. I said, "Yes, so what?" They would come to the office, and I would hear them discuss matters pertaining to the upcoming refitting of Cmdr. Milo's plane. This wasn't out of the ordinary because Jay was involved with the mechanics of the retro fitting and the interior of the cabin. Jay was very knowledgeable about how to make the interior more soundproof but still be able to keep the interior according to Navy specifications. The Cmdr.'s wife wanted to put something like a curtain on the windows, to dress the plane up, and make it more luxurious, and yet still keep it within the parameters of the specifications set down by the Navy. Since that was not allowed, she agreed to have shades installed, but with one caveat: she got to pick out the material for the seats. As I had never heard Jay and Milo's wife having any intimate discussions, I told Al I thought the rumors had no merit and that Jay was not that crazy to even entertain any ideas about fooling around with the Cmdr.'s wife. Well, Al said, with Jay, anything is possible. When it came to women, Jay had no scruples. Besides, Al said, how many times did we see the way Jay would admire Milo's wife. Well, gee, I said. Who the hell didn't look at her with lust and say what a beautiful woman she was?

Cmdr. Milo would leave on business and be gone sometimes for about two or three days, and this is when the rumors became more prevalent. As to the accuracy of the information, I was always given the reports as to where all the officers would be in case the leading chief needed them. I noticed Jay would be marked off base with no time of return stamped on his sheet, which he could get away with because he had that much clout in the hangar. I asked my friend in the office of Cmdr. Milo, named Charlie, who kept the log of all the officers and their mates, as to where they could be reached in case of an emergency. Charlie gave me the log and told me to place it back in his desk when I finished with it. Since my duty was making the plan of the day, this was not an unusual request, and I would ask Charlie for it from time to time to report on any upcoming events associated with the personnel on the base. Usually, I would scan it and not give it second thought unless there was not something that was newsworthy I could report. This was not my only source of supply for news to print, but there it was: Jay's absence from the base always coincided with the Cmdr. being away. Although Jay did not leave the base, he had marked himself off because of official business. All the while, as it came out in the trial, he was holed up in the Cmdr.'s house having an affair with Milo's wife, in Milo's house situated on a hill overlooking the base.

On this trip, Cmdr. Milo had a short stay and decided not to inform his wife because he had bought something special for her and wanted to surprise her. In short, he got the surprise of his life, when upon entering the home late at night, he very quietly tiptoed into the bedroom and saw two bodies in his bed. He turned on the lights, and lo and behold, there was Jay under the sheets. All hell broke loose, with the sounds of sirens going off. Nobody knew what was happening, but we soon found out, since shore patrol headed to the Cmdr.'s house, thinking it was a false alarm or malfunction of wires. In the morning, we found out that Cmdr. Milo had Jay arrested and hauled off to the brig, and Al said to me, "I knew that son of a bitch was fooling with her." It was very sad that morning in the barracks, since the respect of the men under Jay's command ran deep, despite his faults. A week later, Jay's court martial was set to begin and already the rumors were flying as to what the punishment would be, since it involved adultery, but we figured a change of duty would be all he would get.

We were told to report in the court yard the next morning at 10 a.m. in full dress uniform, to be witness to the execution of the findings of the court. The court martial lasted about two hours, as the lead officer read the charges against Jay, which included adultery, abuse of the code of conduct, neglect of duty, and unauthorized use of Navy materials, which was, in short, a bunch of bullshit, but they had to lay more than one charge against Jay to give him the punishment that he received. After all, the charge of adultery was all they had against him, which was a charge that everyone knew could have made against any other officer because of the exposure they had to each other's wives, whenever they were away for any extended amount of time and the parties they had at the officers' club. This was a well-documented fact by the personnel that worked there. While Jay was a chief petty officer, he mingled well with the other higher ranking officers, often attending a lot of their social gatherings and even going on excursions with them and their families. Jay's personality was something that was admired by the higher ups; he knew how to swing between us and them.

It was very sad to see Jay standing in the middle of the court yard and hearing the charges against him. As each verdict was read, they disassembled his uniform, from his hat on down to the arms of his uniform, which had his rank on them. The punishment was a demotion to third class petty officer, a fine for use of unauthorized Navy materials, and to be assigned to a new post, designated by Cmdr. Milo. We all knew what that meant: some crappy duty on some old ship. The thing that he worked so hard for was gone; the position he held and was admired for was taken away. He made the biggest mistake of his Navy career by getting involved with the Cmdr.'s wife, and in the end, it was his devil may care attitude that did him in.

After the trial we sat around and told Jay stories, of which there were many. Lopez said one of Jay's famous sayings: "Life is a horse race; you have to know how to pick winners." Lopez joked, "You should never pick the captain's wife."

CHIEF HALL

Chief Hall was a great influence on me. Chief hall and Jay were polar opposites as to their approach of lifestyles in the service. Chief Hall was a remarkable man, who was a great mentor and family man. We had a lot of discussions about being a twenty year man, and he was very honest and told me about the many hardships as well as the advantages of a Navy career. He asked me if I intended to someday marry, and raise a family, then told me of his experiences, as to how many times he was transferred around the world, and the many years he spent on sea duty, away from his family, for an extended period of time. He said in the Navy, nothing is permanent. He said if marriage was not in my future, a Navy career would be an acceptable way of spending twenty years, and that I would be only thirty seven years old and have a nice pension. Chief hall said all you have to do is look around this base, and ask yourself: do you want to bring up a family, knowing what the pitfalls can do to long separations from your family. He was obviously referring to the many cases of marital infidelity, which, though he never had any of those problems, many of his friends did. Chief Hall spoke of his three children, who all seemed to be well-adjusted, despite the uprooting of their father's many different assignments. But they were looking for him to retire from the Navy, so they could finally get a home of their own, instead of living in Navy housing. Chief Hall and I discussed my education, and I told Chief Hall that I did not finish high school and asked if that would hinder me from advancing my rank to a higher grade. He advised me to get involved in a correspondents course, of which many were available through the Navy offerings. Hall said even if I did not stay in the Navy, it would help me when I got discharged. At that time, my enlistment would be up in about six months, so unfortunately, there would not have been enough time to complete the course.

LT. CMDR. MILO

Six months before my discharge date, Cmdr. Milo called me into his office for a conference to discuss my discharge date. When a superior officer wants to talk with you, especially when you know it has nothing to do with your everyday work, it is quite out of the ordinary. Most matters, including reenlistment or discharge, were taken care of by a leading chief, like Chief Hall, who would make an interview before sending the results up to the Cmdr. for review. Chief Hall and I had many discussions on the subject, but not anything formal, so I was very surprised when I was asked to meet with Cmdr. Milo. Not really knowing what the meeting would be about, I was kind of caught off guard when he brought up the subject of reenlistment, not expecting Cmdr. Milo to be discussing reenlistment with me. Milo had all my records on his desk and started to discuss the offer of reenlistment. His offer was for me to enlist for six more years, with an offer to send me to college for four years, and after graduation, I would be moved up in rank. Milo discussed the possibility of making the Navy my career, and he said by the time I have all my time in, which would be twenty years, I would be receiving a pension. I would only be thirty seven years old and still young enough to start another career. I told Milo, "You have my education background before you, so how do we reconcile the fact I did not finish high school?" Milo said with a big wide grin, "By giving you a crash course. It's only paper work; I will handle all the details."

We discussed all the advantages and disadvantages of a Navy career, mainly centering on having a family, and that some of the problems of trying to raise a family in an atmosphere of constantly being transferred from post to post. These were some of the same talks I had with Chief Hall. Milo praised me on my work record and stated that I had the potential of attaining a good rank before the end of my career. I thought that he was trying to be a good salesman, but at the same time, I knew that not many people were given that offer. The fact that I was being given this opportunity really surprised the hell out of me, especially with what had just occurred in the family of Cmdr. Milo, with that mess with Jay and my friendship with Jay. But Milo never even mentioned Jay in any his remarks about my work record, or in my relationship with Jay. Sitting across from Cmdr. Milo, I thought what a true gentlemen this man was, in not mentioning my association with Jay I always believed Milo truly was looking out for my best interest. Milo said to give this offer a lot of consideration and to get back to him with my decision.

I went back to Chief Hall, and we discussed the offer from Milo. Hall said, "Think it over and remember what we always discussed." Hall said that he had to make the same decision many years ago and that he did not get an offer like that. After much soul searching and speaking to my buddies as to what I should do, I pondered the request by Cmdr. Milo for some time. I had to give him an answer by the first of October, since my service time would end by the end of the year. This would be the second time in three years that an opportunity like this was presented to me. Believe me, I spent a lot of sleepless nights thinking about the college offer of four years. But I would have to spend six more years in the Navy, which, at the end, would have a total of eight years. Then

I might have to give some consideration to making a career in the Navy, being a twenty year man, but I'd have a nice pension at the age of thirty seven. There was so much to think about, especially when you are eighteen years old, but I had already gone through this before when I was a fifteen year old in California. The time being away from my family was kind of scary, being on my own, even if it was with a nice bunch of people that welcomed me into their home and treated me as a member of the family. Still, I was a little uncomfortable, feeling like an outsider in the midst of such a lovely family, and so it was then that I decided to forego the offer and give Cmdr. Milo my answer: I felt that my family back home needed me to help out supporting them and that maybe I could take advantage of the G.I. bill and continue my education back home. My friend, Charlie, told me I could take night courses and have a job during the day, like a lot of the other veterans. It sounded like a good idea, and it would not cost me any money, and that way, I would be home and almost have the same offer.

Going in to tell Cmdr. Milo my answer was not an easy thing for me as I believed Milo went out of his way by electing me for this honor. Upon entering Milo's office, I felt very nervous, and Milo, being the gentleman that he was, got up from his chair, and walked over to me, putting his arms around me and said, "Whatever your decision is, I will respect you, as I know that you gave this offer a great deal of time, so sit down and tell me." I had the feeling that Milo had talked with Chief Hall, so I think he was appreciative that I approached his offer very thoughtfully. I explained to Milo that my family could use me back home to help out and that maybe I could further my education with the G.I. bill. I said to Milo, "Believe me, Cmdr. Milo I feel very proud that you considered me for this, and for that, I will always remember you. I just hope that your expectations of me will prove right." Milo got up and put his arm on my shoulder, walked me to the door, and said, "Leo, I will expect nothing less than to someday hear about you being successful in whatever field of life you choose." Walking down the stairs of his office, I had a feeling of relief, but also doubt about whether or not I made the right decision, since this was my second offer of college in three years, but it was then Milo said, "Go with your decision and run with it." Still, it was a very traumatic time after weighing all the pros and cons, but I finally came to grips with the reality of my decision and accepted whatever life would hold for me.

The route of passage for my discharge entailed me to go to San Juan Navy base and start the process of release from the Navy. I was put on a small two engine plane along with five other men, who were also being discharged. The flight to San Juan was a very short flight, about thirty minutes flying time. Since the flight did not require a great altitude, we felt like we were skimming the ground, and we actually felt close to the roof tops of the homes below. The crew member who was responsible for securing the aircraft for takeoff did not fasten the door properly, and ten minutes into the flight the door swung open, and it was flapping against the bulkhead of the plane. He tried hooking it to close, without luck, but the pilot cut down on air speed and swung the plane over the water and decided to continue on to San Juan, in case the door came loose and fell, it would go in the water. We were about ten minutes from landing, and we heard the pilot radio a distress call to the tower. Upon approaching the air field, we could see the emergency trucks lined up on the side of the runways, as the pilot tilted the plane slightly to the right, favoring the broken door, so it would not fall off. After we landed, we saw the door had quite a bit of damage to the hinges, hanging by a thread. The guys joked that we should sue the Navy for our trip and demand to be compensated. After landing, there was a truck to take us to the Navy base for our transfer to Charleston, South Carolina Navy Base to be discharged.

At Charleston separation center, I had to surrender my dog tags and I.D. cards since my two year enlistment was over. With it came a sense of relief and sadness at the same time, as I passed through the base, carrying all my gear to the bus stop. I stopped and looked at the building in front of me, which was a ward of recuperating servicemen who were still recovering from their war wounds, sitting in chairs and wheel chairs. I felt very lucky that my time in the Navy was during peacetime, and here I was going home, while these poor boys, who were not much older than I, still had to spend more time in the hospital.

CHAPTER THREE

Employment

BACK TO CIVILIAN LIFE: Looking for a new house

On the train ride home, I reflected on all the good times, and not so good times, and I felt that the people who made my journey in the Navy a pleasant experience would forever be encased in my mind. I felt a great joy of coming home, and yet, there was this overwhelming sadness about leaving the Navy, leaving behind all the wonderful friends and memories as well as an offer of continuing my education. Much later in life, I came to regret missing out on this opportunity. When I got into the work force, sometimes I wished I had made a better choice, especially when the choices of work offered to me were limited by more demanding qualifications. This is when I decided to go to night school and get my high school diploma, which would help me in obtaining better employment. At this time, I believed that the opportunity of earning better pay was in the work force, than, say, becoming a teacher. This would prove wrong again at a much later date, but when I came home, the only motivating set of circumstances that interested me was earning as much money as I could. I felt that I had to help out the family as much as I could, which was a problem faced by many returning servicemen. And many of them also made the same mistake of choosing employ and earning money over education. I had the opportunity to take advantage of the G.I. bill and further my education, but at the same time, the pressure of helping out the family was still an overriding issue in my home.

As I took stock of the family home, such as it was, I realized it was in need of a lot of repairs due to the fact that the Great Depression took its toll on my father, trying to raise six children, as well as my mother who tried to make do with whatever she could. One night, I sat my father down and had a serious conversation about our living conditions, which, in my mind, were deplorable at best. Seven people living in just four rooms, with no bathroom to bathe or shower in, and not to even mention that three boys slept in one bed, two girls in another bed, and my father and mother in a small room in the back of the house. At this time, my older sister Mary had gotten married and was living in the attic, which consisted of four rooms, which they split with an uncle of mine. We would all eat together in our kitchen, which, at times, was very chaotic. My father and I both agreed on the poor condition of the house, but what I did not know was that he had received a letter from the city stating that our property might be in the plans for a redevelopment project at a later date. At this time, the first floor had become vacant, and my sister Mary talked my father into rehabbing it so, she could move downstairs with her son and daughter, renting it as an apartment for twenty five dollars a month.

One of the areas of discussion that I knew that my father would not like was the subject of his brother, who was the biggest pain in the ass in our family. Knowing that this would bother my father, I choose to put it on the table first. My suggestion was simply that the home was not worth spending money on since the family needed a larger living quarters. He agreed, and we decided to look for a home in a better neighborhood. My father was worried about having to take on debt at this stage of his life, which I understood, but with the sale of the house on Greene St., we could find a home in the amount of the sale, and we could all help pay for the home. But he was afraid that when we all got married, he would get stuck with something he could not afford. I said we could look for a big house or a two family, so someone will always be with you. He liked that idea and was happy with my suggestion, but then I said that this will only happen with the exclusion of your brother.

I knew this would be a big problem for my father because of his devotion to honor his brother for his help during the Great Depression. For my father to go along with my proposal to severe ties with his brother was something that I knew would be a great strain on him. At the outset of our conversation, I knew I had to be forceful, but without seeming to be too combative, about laying out our plans for the future of the family. Yet, I did not want to give my father any wiggle room, in case he wanted to make any other suggestions to change our plans that would include his brother moving in with us. I told my father that he did not owe his brother anymore compensation than what he had already done for him. I realized the great pressure my father was under but said that he was put there by a bully of a brother, who all but demanded his undying loyalty to him. My father said that his brother was a big crap thrower, but being his older sibling, he still felt obligated to provide for him, in spite of my father knowing the stress his brother put on our family and him.

I told my father, "Well, Pop, this is what we are going to do," and we have decided to make a clean break and start a new life without his brother. We had all taken his shit, and we were all tired of him and his crap, and I said that we would have had a much better life had he not been living with us, messing in our lives, and dictating as to how my father should run our family. My father could not disagree with me and said he knew that he was a pain in the ass, but as in a lot of Italian families who also had the same problem, the obligation to repay almost sacred; not only with money but a lifetime of servitude, by including that person in all family functions and having them give input in the lives of the children, as if they were the family breadwinner. I told my father, "When you borrow money from a bank, that's all you owe them, not a lifetime of servitude." Pop said, "Being the youngest member of a family, you have the obligation to help out the oldest whenever you can." At that I said, "That was your generation, when help was used as a club to put people into submission for a lifetime. Look," I said, "Here I am eighteen years old, and talking about moving our family to a better neighborhood, and helping my brothers and sisters have a better life, with no discussions of any repayment. Maybe we can all have the life where no one intrudes in our family matters." I let my father know how deep my commitment was and how I was determined to fulfill my dream of making all this come to fruition. Most guys my age were talking about dating girls, sports, etc., and here I was talking as if I had a family and were ready to settle down. At that moment, as I looked at my father's face, I could see that I was making some progress toward him accepting my offer.

My father finally agreed and said we would quietly look for a new home, without telling anyone until we found what we wanted. I knew what he was worried about, and I respected his wishes, but foremost in my mind was the fact that I would take the heat from his brother and tell him myself. Nothing would give me more pleasure than to tell that son of a bitch to go to hell. We started the process of looking at different neighborhoods as to the proximity of bus lines, stores, etc. since my father was getting ready to retire someday and did want to venture very far without bus service. We were not looking for a place full time, as we had a lot of restraints on our time, since my employment was not secured. I wanted to make sure I had a steady job because I did not want to disappoint my father and fail on our mission to leave Greene St. and to be successful with the purchase of a new home.

At about 1950, the people living in the first floor apartment moved out, and my sister Mary saw an opportunity to move into the apartment. She was living in a third floor walk-up, where the rooms were very small, and she figured by moving into the first floor, she would have the best of both worlds: my mother upstairs would be a built-in baby sitter, and my sister would be able to go out to work. At this time, she had two children, and the school was only a block away. My father was talked into renovating the apartment for Mary, which I told my father was a big mistake. By bringing Mary here, he was setting himself up for a lot of misery, since Mary was a very troublesome person, who always had money problems and would infringe on the rest of us. Also I did not want to lose sight of our plans to move to a better neighborhood. Mary, in my mind, was as bad as my Uncle Leo, always causing my father to fight with her over any and all matters, money being the number one problem. Mary could spend money faster than she could earn it and was always in some kind of debt. In addition, she had an undue influence on my mother pertaining to finances. Mary's only redeeming quality was that she was a good housekeeper and kept her apartment in a very neat and orderly fashion.

Between Mary and Uncle Leo, it was a combination of constant turmoil. When only one of them was home, you could almost feel at ease because you feel you could handle one of them at a time. I had always felt that without those two pains in the ass, our family would have had a better life. Now with Mary living in our house, moving out would now pose a problem for my father, since he now had two people that he felt obligated not to abandon. I now had to really convince my father to accept our plan of moving away, leaving both Mary and Uncle Leo to fend for themselves. But my father's loyalty to his brother ran deep. And now with sister Mary in the mix, the problem ran twofold, so I then had to reassess my future plans and start to lay out my own life. Sadly, this went against my true desire to help the family obtain a better life. But this chapter of my life taught me that sometimes you cannot control the forces that circumstance throws at you, and I now had to look at life with a different perspective.

After my discharge in November 1947, I started to look at what my options were for the future. To go back to school and get a high school diploma was something that I knew I needed in order to compete in the job market. Since the G.I. bill offered veterans a free college education, a lot of returning veterans took advantage of, so I went to night school, and took a one year course to get enough credits for a high school diploma. It turned out to be more of a social gathering, with the teacher more interested in listening to stories of the veterans, their experiences in the service, etc. At the end of the school year, we all got our GED with a passing grade. Now with a high school diploma, I could start thinking about furthering my education and to go on to college, but the decision to do this meant I could not take a day job and would therefore not have enough income to live on, especially with family commitments, etc., even with the small stipend veterans received. Despite wanting to take advantage of the G.I. Bill and further their education, many veterans made the difficult choice to remain in the work force, maybe forging a career in one of the trades, which, at that time, were paying more than what teachers were earning, to just give one example of education versus what a good paying profession in the trades was earning. There were, of course, a few industrious veterans who took advantage of the night courses being offered and held down a full time job, but it seemed impossible to me.

SOCIAL LIFE AFTER THE SERVICE

My life goals after being discharged from the Navy were not only in attaining good employment but to have a good social life, which, to me, I felt had somehow passed me by, due in part to my not having the best of health with my asthma always kicking up from time to time. In 1948, my friend Tony and I decided to purchase a 1930 Ford Roadster. It was a small car that had a rumble seat in the rear, enough to seat four people. The price was one hundred fifty dollars, and we put in seventy five dollars each. We had to share with each other whenever one of us had to go somewhere. We purchased the car so that we could go places out of town, such as dances, shows, etc. In those days, there were not lot of cars to be had because this was right after the war and the inventory of used cars was at an all-time low. But with the servicemen returning home and everybody wanting a car, the new cars were just starting to roll off the assembly line. To purchase a new car, you had to put your name on a list, and hopefully maybe wait a year to get one. Since we could not afford a new car anyway, this was the best we could do. There were lots of stories of people paying the salesman to put their name at the top of the list, which just showed how competition has a way of making people greedy.

The car was seventeen years old when we bought it. It needed some work, but luckily, Tony's uncle was well-versed in fixing Fords since he had owned one. This car had mechanical brakes, which you really had to press down to stop it. There was no heater or defroster because in those days, the cars did not have any of the things in cars that you take for granted today. We even had plastic windows that we had to attach to the doors whenever it rained. Thinking about that car today, I wonder how in the hell we drove through some of the worst weather, without even giving it a second thought. I guess youth and being stupid go hand-in-hand.

One of our worst experiences with the model A Ford was the time we decided to go to a dance hall in Derby. This hall was on top of a steep hill, and it was connected to a large park and was frequented by all the people from Derby, Ansonia, and Shelton, CT. The model A Ford only had a four cylinder motor, not very powerful, especially with four people in it going uphill, but we made it slowly but surely. Coming down the hill after the dance, we were all laughing about how easy this was going to be.

In the car with me that night was my brother Ralph, Tony, and Joe Balls. We called him that because his last name was Bolognese. Joe and Ralph were in the rumble seat, Tony and I in the front. I was driving, and as I started the descent down the hill, I felt the brake pedal go all the way to the floor. "Shit," I said, "No damn brakes." I pulled up the emergency brake but that too was not working. By now, the car was picking up speed, and I was trying to hug the side of the road to slow the car down. In the back of the car, Joe hollered, "Leo, apply the goddamn brakes! Apply the brakes!" "Joe," I hollered back, "There are no brakes!" By now, we were going at full speed down the hill and in front of us was a two lane highway that had an island in the middle of it.

When I approached the bottom of the hill, I made a right turn and spun the car on two wheels, hugging the side of the island. We went a good fifty yards on two wheels along the side of the road, then, when the car righted itself back on all four wheels, we came to an intersection and came to a complete stop. Joe got out of the car and said every curse word he could think of, blasting us for not having the car checked out. Tony yelled at Joe telling him his uncle worked on the car and gave us the okay for us to go out of town with it. All Joe kept saying was how we all could have died, or worst still, maybe be banged up for the rest of our lives. Luck was with us that night because of the late hour and very little traffic. If a car was coming down the road, there would have been no way to avoid an accident. To this day, every time I drive by that hill, I still think about how close we all came to being killed. I do not know how people live up there on such a steep road. It gives me goosebumps just thinking about it.

This was not the end of that night because we now had to drive home from Derby with no brakes. Now Joe was really shitting his pants, but the guys said, "Joe, shut the fuck up. Leo, got us down the hill, and he will get us home." It was no small feat, as it was a late hour, about one in the morning, but what I did was I went down Route 34, doing the same thing as before: going very slowly and hugging the side of the road. Luckily, there were no more hills in our way because if there was any kind of traffic like there is today, I would not even think about trying to drive the car home. It took us about one hour to get home from Derby.

The next day, Tony's uncle came to check the car and found that the brake cable had snapped. When Tony's uncle put in new brake pads, he checked the cable and thought it was not necessary to change it. Tony's uncle sat down and put his head in his hands, thinking how he had put us all in a terrible situation. Tony's uncle put his arms around me and thanked me for being the cool one. He said, "Leo, I cannot thank you enough. I do not know how I could have lived with this if anything happened. I put the lives of you four guys in jeopardy because of my stupidity."

As my finances improved, due in part to getting better employment, I told Tony that maybe we should get our own cars. He agreed, so I started to look for another car, maybe a little later model. I had seen this ad for a 1934 sedan. The price was one hundred dollars, and I purchased it after getting it inspected by Tony's uncle. The motor was not the best, but Tony's uncle said he could work on it for me. One thing that sold me on the car was the braking system: it had a braking fluid system, which made it much easier to stop and more comfortable by not having to press hard to stop the car.

With having my own car, I now felt a lot easier to go out to the dance halls, knowing that if I met anyone, I could drive her home. In those days, if you had a car, the ladies would be more agreeable in having you take them home, and not having another man in the car. A lot of guys would go together in one car, and no ladies would even think about going home with all of them, so when I did take anyone with me, it was with the understanding that if I met someone, they would have to get a ride home from the dance hall.

The first girl I met at the dance came from the area of Ansonia, right next to Derby. "Shit, I said, "That's the town that has a lot of hills." Here I was trying to avoid that area, and the first girl I meet comes from there. Since I spent the whole evening with her, I could not refuse to take her home. We were having such a nice time that when the dance was coming to an end, I told her I would take her home along with the friends she came with. She agreed, and after dropping off her two friends, she told me what street she lived on. It turned out to be a steep incline.

Now I felt a lot more at ease with having a much stronger car, and that I could really test the strength of the motor and also the braking system since this part of the valley area has nothing but steep inclines. After securing a future date with her, I dropped her off at her home and started down the hill. On applying the brakes, I noticed they felt a little soft, so I started to pump the brakes to get a better brake bite. Now again, the car started to pick up speed down the hill. It was not as fast as the model A Ford, and this time I was able to control the brakes better. Still, it turned out that the system was low on brake fluid, and if I did not pump the brakes, I would have been in the same predicament as with the model A Ford. After I got back home, I went to Tony's uncle, and he inspected the lines to the brakes and found a leak. Now I did not know what to do about calling this girl about our next date. When I called her, she said she would be sleeping over at her girlfriend's home, and I could pick her up there. Great, I figured, since her friend's home was at the bottom of the hill.

After a few dates, I decided that dating someone from that area would be a problem because of not having a good car, and I did not feel safe driving up and down those hills. In those days, driving more than ten miles out of town was considered a long way. When I told Marie about my problems of having to drive this distance to go out with her, and that I did not think it was going to work out for us, Marie suggested maybe I could meet at her friend's house, which was at the bottom of the hill. I did not want to impose on her friend, but no matter what I said, Marie did not want to stop seeing me. She advanced all kinds of reasons to continue our relationship, but at this time, the distance was too great for me to overcome. If I had a better car, it would have made all the difference in the world.

Marie and I dated for some time, in fact, a period of several months. We had so much in common: a mutual love for the movies, spending many hours comparing movie stars and going to the dances. Marie had never been to a barn dance so one night I gave Marie a treat by bringing her to Sea Cliff. Marie was fascinated by the gracious reception she received from complete strangers. Marie said she did not like the modern dances due to the way some men treated her but at the barn dances the friendliness of everybody amazed her. She did not have the feeling of being stared at by the men. Anyone could get on the dance floor and join the group. Our conversations about her home were that she thought her home was below standard. I told Marie that her father has provided a nice home for her and it is in a very dense area of homes in impeccable condition. She said, "Leo. I know you are just saying that to make me feel good". On the contrary I said, my home is like a garage compared to yours but my father like your father did the best he could with what he had. Since coming home from the Navy, my father and I are contemplating on purchasing a better home. Marie looked at me with a wondrous look, "You and your father, not your mother?" "Well," I said, "that is another story, I should have said my siblings also. As bad as my home is, changing locations will be a problem for my mom." Marie's parents came from the same locale in Italy. Her grandfather came from the same town as my father. Her parents invited me into their home for a few dinners. The chemistry was there but on the many nights I had to drive home from where Marie lived gave me a great deal of time to consider continuing the relationship any longer.

I made my decision to end this relationship before Marie and I got to be more vested in each other. My reasons were the car and the distance. On a balmy summer evening after going to a local dance hall, Marie had me park the car some distance from her home. Marie overwhelmed me with passion and at this juncture I could see releasing her was going to be a problem. To lessen the shock on Marie I made up a story of taking on another job and my visits would be curtailed.

She offered up all kinds of scenarios as to how we can overcome this. I went on a few more dates but then finally ended it.

Other than going to the dance halls, we also would drive up to the State Theater in Hartford. There, they would have all the top entertainers, the big bands, singers, dancers, and all the people who were at the top of the entertainment world. The price was about one to two dollars. We would see a movie, along with a stage show, but there again the cars always came into the picture. I had a 1934 Plymouth, my brother Ralph had a 1935 Dodge, and Tony had a 1938 Ford, all which had some problems, but we ventured up to Hartford using Route 5. This was before I-91, so we had to allow a good hour and a half of time for us to make it up there. These cars had no heater or defroster, so in the winter, we froze our asses off.

One Saturday night, the State Theater had booked the Tommy Dorsey band, and this was a band we really liked. My car and Tony's car were having some problems, so Ralph said we were going to go up to Hartford in his car. Tony and I were not too happy about going up in Ralph's car because he had a habit of always running low on gas. His gas gauge was not working properly, and he never wanted to get it fixed. He said he knew how much gas he had and not to worry.

The night we had to go to the show happened to be one of the coldest nights in January. We left New Haven about five o'clock, figuring we would be there about six or six thirty. About halfway to Hartford, Ralph's car started to sputter. Ralph pulled over to the side of the road, and the car completely stalled. The needle on the gauge was on empty, so we got out of the car and started to look for a gas station. Tony had grabbed the gas can that was in the car. Walking up the road, Tony turned to Ralph and said, "Did you put any gas in the car today?" "No," Ralph said, "I put a dollar of gas in the car on Monday." Tony turned to Ralph and said, "You dumb son of a bitch. Here we are freezing our asses off, looking for a goddamn gas station, and you forgot to gas the car up." With that, Ralph saw Tony's anger boiling over, so he started to run up ahead of us. Tony chased him, throwing the gas can at him, cursing him out with every curse word he could think of. I ran after Tony and tried to calm him down, yelling, "Do not lose the can. The hell with Ralph; we won't be riding with him anymore."

As I said this was one cold night, and all we could think of was finding a gas station and getting the hell on the road again. After about a mile or so, we found a gas station. Then we went back to the car and tried to get it started again. Tony was pretty mechanical minded, so he put a little in the carburetor, and the rest in the tank and got the car started. To add insult to injury, Ralph blurted out again, "I cannot understand it; a dollar usually lasts me all week." "Ralph," I said, "Keep your big mouth shut. Because of your being stubborn about not fixing the damn gas gauge, we could have been stranded here for the night." This night with Tony chasing Ralph on the road, flinging the gas can at him, was something you would see in a Laurel and Hardy movie. Funny now but not then.

One of our prime pieces of entertainment was the dance hall's places where you could meet someone and socialize with your friends. We ventured all over the state, looking to meet girls and have a nice time. One night, my friends decided to go to Bridgeport. I told them I wanted to go to the Y.W.C.A. in New Haven, and I was not in the mood of having to travel all that distance. But one of my friends at work said he would meet me there, so I had someone to chum around there with.

At the Y.W.C.A dances, which I had attended pretty regularly, I was pretty familiar with a host of people, and we were all more or less from the same area. On this one particular night, I felt that I had made a mistake by not going to Bridgeport because it was turning out to be a drag because I had not met anyone I cared for. As I was just standing by the door thinking about calling it a night, I felt a tap on my shoulder, and a girl called me by name. Looking startled, I did not recognize her. She said she had gone to the same school as I had, Commercial High School, and that we always crossed paths in the hallway. Then I remembered who she was, but she looked different to me. She was dressed a lot classier than when we were in school.

Her name was Roseann, and the conversation was about our mutual friends. We then danced until the dance hall closed. She had come with her girlfriends, so I offered to take them all home, but they said they would take the bus home, which was only about two miles away. They wanted me to just take Roseann home. I guess this was all pretty much arranged, almost like the arrangement I had with my friends.

On the way home, Roseann told me how she just broke up with her boyfriend due to his bad gambling habits, and then she mentioned the part of the city her boyfriend came from. Before she mentioned his name, I almost knew who she was talking about. Roseann said that her boyfriend's name was Jim, and I then filled in his last name. "How do you know him?" she said. "I went to school with him," I said. "He lived right around the corner from me on Greene Street." Jim's father owned a tavern and also a lot of homes. The family had a lot more income than the rest of us, and Roseann's father owned an oil business. Jim and I were pretty close when we were kids, playing on the same hockey team at the Boys Club. Jim was a lot of fun to be with due to his devil may care approach to life.

Roseann and I started to date pretty regularly; we really enjoyed each other's company. She introduced me to a lot of nice people. I took her to all the dance halls that she had never been to, and she appreciated it, saying, "Jim never took me to these places." Since I was going pretty steady with Roseann, my friends were asking, "What the hell are you doing with this girl? Are you thinking of marrying her?" At this time, I was nineteen years old, and I told them, "If everything keeps going the way it is, maybe."

I had to attend a stag for a friend of mine who was getting married. At the stag, I ran into Jim, who was also a mutual friend of the groom. He broached the subject of me dating Roseann and said that he also dated Roseann for some time. I said to Jim, "If you want me to back off from seeing Roseann, I will." At this time, it was an unwritten rule that you would never try and take another man's girlfriend away, but Jim said that he was no longer interested and that it was okay for me to keep on seeing her. At this time, I had invested about two months of time with Roseann. While Roseann and I were seeming to get along very well, I had felt that maybe Jim still had feelings for her and that he was not being truthful about the relationship ending.

On our next date, which was the next Saturday night, we were going to go to a movie at the Lowe's Poli's on Church Street. This was going to be a night that will forever be embedded in my memory. We had plans to go out to Savin Rock after the movie and spend some time out there, but the inevitable occurred. As we were leaving the theater, walking down Church Street the three blocks to the car, Roseann started to stumble. I grabbed her by the arm and looked down at her feet, and saw some kind of cloth entangled in her feet. She let out a crying moan, all the while trying to take her shoes off so she could untangle it. I was holding her by the arm so she would not fall. The article was her panties that came loose and had fallen down.

Talk about being in an embarrassing situation: this was it. The crowd leaving the movie all stopped and stared at us. Roseann picked up the panties and put them in her pocketbook. She said, "Leo, please take me home." We could not get to the car fast enough for her; the expression on her face was of total shock. When we got to her house, we sat on the porch for a few minutes and then Roseann said she wanted to go in the house to get herself together again. Being a gentleman called for not even mentioning the situation, and I never did.

After about six months, our conversations turned to what I had in mind concerning her. Since our feelings were mutual, we discussed about being together for a while. She was pleased with that, but several dates later, Roseann told me her father felt that I was not a good fit for his daughter. For one thing, I was a factory worker with no visible assets, and the father felt that Jim, whose family had a business and a lot of real estate, was a better catch than me. I did not want Roseann to go against her father wishes, but she pleaded with me to maybe talk to her father, who, by the way, I had never met before. But what could I say? I only had two nickels in the bank and the other guy had a load of money. I was not in a good position to present myself, and I understood the father's side of the matter. The only thing I had going for me was my work record.

Life sometimes takes curious turns. Years later, after I got married and had two children, I took my family out to a restaurant, and after we were seated, a waitress came up to our table. I looked up and it was Roseann. I introduced her to Teresa and Gail and Janet, and she looked at the two girls and gushed over how pretty they were. She told me she had two boys. Roseann was to experience a bad turn in her life. Jim had gotten into a serious accident and died after driving the wrong way up the highway. Stories went around that Jim owed a lot of money to the bookies, and they were after him for payment, so he committed suicide.

My next move was to get a better car. My 1934 Plymouth was giving me a lot of problems, so I purchased a 1941 Dodge four door sedan. While it was a much later model than my 1934 car, it too was not in the best of condition but still a great improvement over what I had. To begin with, the car had been hand painted, the color was black, and it had the shift on the wheel instead of the floor. I actually felt good about driving around with the car. I paid about two hundred dollars for it. When my father saw the car, he was very impressed with the size of it. I told him, "Now I can take you shopping to the stores you could never get to." Here it was 1949, and he was sitting in a 1941 car, but to my father, it was a new car. Because of the rough finish of the paint job on the car, I spent a lot of time polishing it to make it look good. I felt now I did not have to worry about traveling any distances. Used cars at this time were what the terminology meant: used. Mine was no different than most cars of the day because they all had a problem of burning oil. My car burned about a quart a week, so I had to keep checking on it all the time.

As the months passed after I purchased the Dodge, it started to be more of an oil burner. I took it to the garage and was told it needed a ring job in the motor. The cost of repairs was to be one hundred dollars, half the price of the car. To me, it was not an option. I felt I would drive it until it broke down. My friend Tony said, "Let's put an ad in the paper and try to sell the car." "Are you crazy?" I said. "This damn car is an oil burner, and the car smokes like hell. Who the hell is going to buy it?" But Tony put the ad in the paper, and I then got a call from an interested buyer. He told me to bring the car to his house, so he could look at it. I told the buyer in two days I would bring the car to him, and

Tony and I then set about giving the car a cleaning. We then got all the papers together and went to the man's house. He asked if he could drive the car around the block, and as he did, the car smoke was coming out the back like a smoke stack. "Oh shit," I said, "There goes the sale." The man came back and asked how much we wanted for the car. Tony told him the price was four hundred dollars. Standing there with Tony, we had never discussed how much we were going to ask, so I was completely caught off guard would be an understatement. Thinking this was crazy, the man, to our amazement, said okay and went into the house and came out with the four hundred dollars. I signed the papers, Tony removed the plates, and we actually ran down the street, as if we had just committed a robbery. To see the car coming back after the man took it for a drive with all the smoke coming out the back, I was hoping to just get maybe one hundred dollars for the car. Tony said, "All it takes is a little balls." And I added, "And also a dummy to buy the car.

My next car was a 1946 Chrysler, a two door coupe with a straight eight cylinder motor. In my mind, I was upgrading myself, getting nearer to a new car, since this one was only four years old. At this time, most people were driving ten year old cars. Since I was making a lot more money at the rubber plant, I could easily afford the price of the car, which was six hundred dollars. Now having to travel a great distance to some of the places of entertainment that I enjoyed was no problem. Not to mention, the ladies really liked the car. This was the time when if you did not have a car, it made it difficult to get a date, but having a nice set of wheels made it all the more easier.

The smooth ride the car gave you was also sort of a bad thing because I could not hear the bumps on the road. It was the most comfortable car I had owned up to that time. Driving this huge car, people would just stare and admire the beauty of the body with its long hood and huge tires. One man in particular was at the Chinese laundry where I took my shirts. Especially if I had a date on a Saturday night, he would always come out and look at the car. He asked me if he could sit in the car behind the wheel. As he was sitting in my car, I kept thinking about what my father would say if he had seen a Chinaman sitting in my car. When I was a little boy, he told me to watch out for the laundry man. He said, "The Chinese liked to chop people up with a hatchet." For years, I would never walk in front of his store, I would walk across the street because of what my father said.

I started going to this laundry after I had gotten out of the Navy, but I had never had a conversation with him. But the car fixed all that. As I became friendlier with him, I felt it was time and told him about people's version of the Chinese, about chopping people up. He got such a fit of laughter, he said, "His family told him not to open his store in an Italian neighborhood because the Italians went around carrying knives and would want to rob you." We sat down and laughed our asses off. This was the second time that this subject came up in my lifetime. The other time was when I was attending Commercial High School. One boy that I got friendly with was of Irish descent. Jimmy would always joke about how his father told him to be careful when he was around Italians, as they always carried knives and would cut you up. "Jimmy," I said, "Go ahead and search me." And he did. Laughing, Jimmy explained that he never met many Italians growing up and that was the topic of conversation he had with his friends.

At this time, especially during the football season, I sold football slips that people gambled on, and which I got a commission. You had to pick at least four teams and could go up to ten teams, which paid a big payoff. It was surprising how many times people picked ten winners. I sold them in the school to all the boys and was known as the bookie for the school. I was earning about ten to fifteen dollars a week for the duration of the football season. Jimmy always joked about winning and hitting on ten teams, wondering if he was going to get paid. "Paid with a knife stuck in your back," I said, and then the jokes about the Italians would start all over again.

The year 1949 had me changing jobs. I went from the radiator shop to Armstrong rubber. Prior to getting hired at Armstrong, I was offered a job overseas in Saudi Arabia, for which starting pay was ten dollars an hour, with time and a half after eight hours, and people doing double shifts. The presentation left me with the impression that I could earn enough money and leave after maybe two years, and be set to start my life with a good amount of money. This was when they were building pipe lines, storage tanks, etc. What stopped me was when I was told in some areas I would have to carry a gun to protect myself. There were a lot of different tribes that had disagreements with each other, and I was told sometimes they would start shooting at the workers.

At this time, a lot of jobs outside of the contiguous United States were available, such as up in Alaska and the Middle East. Alaska did not entice me, due to the horrible weather people had to work in, but a barber friend of mine went up there and made a lot of money. In fact, Dom the barber is the one who got me interested in overseas employment and set me up with an interview at the agency. The person that I met with laid out for me all the employment options I had, but I told him I didn't like freezing weather and having to worry about getting my ass shot at for money did not interest me. For quite a while, he pursued me to try and change my mind.

MY RECORD OF EMPLOYMENT

Jan. 1948-Mar. 1948: **N.Y.N.H. & H R.R.; car cleaner**

Mar. 1948-Nov. 1949: **G&O Radiator; packing radiators**

Nov. 1949-Nov. 1951: **Armstrong Rubber; mixing chemicals for the Banbury mixers**

Nov. 1951-Jun. 1952: **Working for a Feed & Grain Co.**

Jun. 1952-Nov. 1954: **Sheet metal**

Nov. 1954-Nov. 1955: **Dugan Bros. Bakery**

Nov. 1955-Jan. 1956: **Chambrelli Bros.; bakery route work**

Jan. 1956-June 1956: **Laundry delivery to factories**

Jun. 1956-Jun. 1959: **Sealtest Dairy, milkman**

Jul. 1959-Jun. 1982: **Wonder Bread Hostess Cakes**

Jun. 1982-Aug. 2012: **A.M.I. owned Retail Bakery Distribution**

From age 12 through age 17 I worked in various part time jobs, such as delivering newspapers, cleaning sewing machines, retail clothing stores, Cohens Dept. Store, Lowenthals Shirt Shop, Stanley Dry Goods.

JANUARY 1948 - MARCH 1948: Car Cleaner

As a car cleaner for the railroad, I had to clean three passenger cars every night, which entailed turning all the seats toward New York, sweeping the car, cleaning the windows, cleaning the bathroom, and washing the floors. Whatever we found left behind by the passengers was placed in a bag and turned over to the lost and found department. The only important thing that I ever found was a set of blueprints for an airplane, which was marked with a French government sign. My hours of work were 11 p.m. to 7 a.m.

MARCH 1948 - NOVEMBER 1949: Packing Radiators

My next job was working for the G&O Radiator Co. The hours were more pleasant, from 7 a.m.to 4 p.m., and my pay was forty dollars a week for a forty hour week. This was less than I was earning for the railroad but at least the work was not as demanding. My job was to pack automobile radiators in cartons. It was piece work, and you had to pack twenty radiators an hour to make a dollar. My hands would be black from handling all that metal. We had to put slats of wood on the bottom of the carton and the top of the box, and slide heavy cardboard on the sides of the box. At least we did not have to work in the factory and smell all those fumes from the chemicals they used for the radiators, since we worked in a warehouse outside of the factory. As it turned out, the company consolidated our operation and put us in the building where the factory was, and we were in the next room to the finishing line. It made sense for the company because they did not have to transport the product to our warehouse anymore, but for us, we were now under the constant supervision of all the bosses, which was not a nice situation as we were used to having a lot of privacy and the opportunity to take rest periods without any bosses around.

NOVEMBER 1949 - NOVEMBER 1951: Armstrong rubber

In Nov. of 49, I left G.O. Radiator to seek a better paying job. At this time, I was not satisfied with the pay at G&O, and the prospects of advancing to a better position were not very promising. I applied for a job at Armstrong Rubber, makers of auto and truck tires. I was hired almost immediately and given a job working in the department where the crude rubber was. My job was to supply the men working the Ban Bury machines with the product and to rotate the stock by grade as all the tires did not have the same quality of rubber. We made tires for a lot of different companies. I had to put Vaseline under and around my eyes, so that I could wash all the lampblack off my face at the end of my shift. All the men had to take a shower at the end of the work day. In this department, I was one of only four white men, two foremen and two workers, the rest being all black men. We all worked together, ate together, and all showered and dressed in the same locker room, I must say there was a lot of nice banter between everyone in this department with a lot of black and white jokes. At the end of the day we would say, we all looked alike. And when we said that you guys don't have to put Vaseline on your eyes, they said, "See, there is an advantage to being dark." We all worked hard for our families, making the same money to do the same job, and we respected each other as equals.

One day, my foreman called me into his office and told me that a cleaner position was going to be available, and that I would not have to work handling all that crude rubber and get as dirty anymore. The job was mixing the chemicals that go into the Ban Bury machines where the rubber was being mixed up. I had a chart to tell me the exact amount of products to put in each bag, since they had to be the exact weight. The scale was under a hood that was supposed to remove the smell of chemicals that I was working on, but it was not very effective in removing the odors from the chemicals. I got to know the chemist who came to see me on a daily basis to check my work and the scale and make sure all procedures where being followed. One day, he said to me, "Do you know what you are mixing here?" I said, "It looks like flour to me." He said, "If you stay here on this job and keep ingesting all these chemicals, it will affect your lungs. Try and get off this job and get in another department. I know you can do better than this." The job was the easiest job I ever had, just standing near a scale and putting mixes in small paper bags, but with the warning from my friend the chemist, I got into a much cleaner department, working on a production line folding cartons for rubber that was being sold for retreads, even though the hours where from 11 p.m. to 7 a.m.

With overtime, I was earning over 100 dollars a week. Plus, the job was in a very clean room, and I felt very happy working there. People that worked in some of the other departments of the factory had jobs that were horrible at best because of the oppressive heat generated by the rubber compounds. I believe it was the proofing room that was the worst, and I had even seen men being carried out and laid on the ground, given smelling salts to revive them and send them back to work.

The problem at Armstrong Rubber was the company tried changing the work rules set by the union. They were constantly having labor problems in some department, which would have a ripple effect throughout the plant. If one department shut down, then everyone else would walk out until the problem was resolved, and this happened quite frequently. When they wanted to bargain from strength, the company would have a large inventory to back them up. The real problem for us was that the contract would expire around January, right at the beginning of the winter season, so that way they had the upper hand in the negotiations. After one strike that lasted for about four months in the winter, the union was successful in changing the date of the contract to end in the spring of the year, just at the beginning of the driving season, so that sort of put a halt on any future advantage the company had. After that long strike, the company had the names of all the people that had participated on the picket lines, including film of everybody on the line. My whole crew that I worked with was given a notice that the operation that we were working on was going to be shipped to the Norwalk plant, and if we wanted to stay with it, we could transfer to Norwalk. This was a way to get back at us after the strike because they knew that nobody was going to transfer to Norwalk. The company would have had a fight on their hands to outright fire us, so to make us pay for the strike, they did a lot of transferring of people and their positions.

The company offered me a position on a production line, cementing the ends of the tire treads. There were six of us on the line, and we stood there for eight hours with two ten minute breaks and one half hour for lunch. This was a very boring job. To get a rest every once in a while, we would let the rubber jam up so the line would stop, and the mechanics would come and undo the mess. I was then placed in the department of tire builders but in the truck tire division where the product was far heavier. In building a tire, you had to slip the fabric onto a rotating drum, using a tire rod to guide the product into place. If you did not hold the rod correctly, the rod could snap right back at you. There were quite a few times it just missed me. Then, after the fabric was in place, you had to slip the rubber treads on, which was the tricky part since the rubber was heavier than the fabric.

After being shuffled from one department to another, I decided to leave Armstrong and look for something that was not as demanding. The company knew that by giving us all these crappy jobs, a lot of us would up and leave, and by not firing us, they would avoid having to fight the union. It was hard for me because I was being brought along to obtain a position with the union, and was urged to stay on by the union president of our local chapter. The union was trying to get me into the warehouse office since I told them I had a lot of shipping experience in the Navy. But the work and the night hours were starting to get to me, especially my social life, and it seemed all I was doing was working and sleeping. Being twenty one and single, and having to refuse dates that were set for me by my friends, was the turning point in my career at Armstrong. I told the union president about my desire to leave, and that the prospect of my getting advanced to the warehouse would take too much time. He said to "hang on and be patient" and that I would have a great future with the union.

Then, this one night, as I was building this huge truck tire, I held the rod a little too loose, and the rod came out of my hands, just missing my head. I told the foreman that I wanted to go home as I was very upset by the incident. He agreed with me and told me to come in the next night and that he would find a regular job for me to do, like setting up the work spaces for the workers. He did not want me to quit, and neither did the union steward who was constantly in touch with me, urging me to hang on and to not get disgusted and quit, saying the future was very good for me with a chance for a union position. The union wanted to reward me for all the cooperation that I gave union, including the time I spent on the picket line and having to lose the job on the camelback line.

After weighing all my options as to my future with Armstrong Rubber, I had a meeting with the union president of our local, a very well-respected man who I got to know extremely well during the months of the long strike. He had spent his whole working life in the rubber industry, and he told me what it was like twenty years prior to the time I was hired, and how bad the conditions were, and of the many advances the union made. He said, "Leo, we need people like you to help us stamp out the horrible work place conditions people are working under." While I felt very flattered by that statement from the president, I also was aware of tires being imported into the country, which I felt was going to have a big impact on the industry. Having that knowledge, and seeing the trend of tire sales going to foreign countries, I told the president that "the future did not look good to me for the tire industry" with all the cheap imports coming in. The president laughed it off saying, "Nobody can beat American made goods." I said that "the majority of people are very price conscious, and time will prove me right." "Leo, he said, "you should never believe all the crap in the newspapers." I told him my decision to leave and thanked him for thinking so highly of me. He said, "If you ever need any help in obtaining work in any other industry, call me," and with that, my time in the rubber industry came to an end. And it turned out, I was right: Armstrong Rubber closed about ten years later.

NOVEMBER 1951 - JUNE 52: Feed and Grain

I wanted to try a different type of work by getting out of the factories and working on the road, maybe delivering products to stores. I felt being out in the fresh air would be a good change for awhile, being able to meet different people and not to be tied down to one location for eight hours a day. I applied for a job at a feed and grain warehouse in North Haven, which entailed working in the warehouse and delivery to farms in the area. I was sent by the company to spend a week in school to learn about the products that I was going to be working with, so that if the farmers had any questions, I could answer them. I soon learned the value of having an education, and since this was a large corporation, to advance from my position as a warehouse worker, I would need something more than a good work experience to better myself. All the manager's positions were filled by college educated people, mainly people from the University of Connecticut. They had degrees in agriculture, including dairy, farming, livestock etc.

By delivering to all kinds of farms, I met some of the nicest people who had grown up on farms. As city kids, we used to call them "hicks," but I quickly gained a different perspective of what their lives were like. They would tell me what they had to do before they went to school, which included a bunch of chores, like getting up at four a.m. to milk the cows. This paled compared to what I had to do as a young child, and I developed a great admiration for them. They returned that admiration to me and invited me to all their social events, such as their Saturday night square dances, graciously accepting me into their inner circle where I got to meet all their family and friends. Most of the farms that I served on my route were all small by comparison to the large corporate farms that operate today, and that is why they could not turn a profit to keep the farms profitable. It is a sad commentary that so many good, hardworking people had to sell off their land just to keep from going bankrupt.

I remember the Augur family in Northford. Some of them had a turkey farm, some had a dairy business, and on Thanksgiving, I would order a turkey from them. I would go into the shed where the women would be plucking the feathers off the birds. You could not get a fresher bird than that. These were all free range birds, well fed and very clean. Since I delivered the feed to them, I knew that they were buying and feeding the birds the best products from our company. The many families I knew from my route were mostly all related to one another. I would sometimes do favors by dropping off parcels. Even if they were competing for the same customers, they were still friendly with each other. They always would lend a helping hand to one another, and that to me was something that was lacking in the area where I grew up. Country people were the most hospitable people that I ever worked with, and they gave me a different perspective on relations with people. While my time in the feed business was not very long, the lasting friendships with the families that I served remained. I continued to attend their square dances long after I left the feed and grain, and they would always try and match me up with one of many available ladies. But the life of farming did not sit well with me, not after I had seen what they had to endure during the cold weather and very hot summers.

This one girl that I dated tried her best to interest me by baking me all kinds of baked goods and having me over to her house for some dinners. The family treated me as one of their own, but I would sit at their table and think of how I could fit in, since they had a different religion and nationality than me. Her father was always messing around, telling me jokes about the difference between city people and country folks. As a warning of good faith, he said, "Don't believe all the jokes about the farmer's daughter; my daughter is not one of them." I said, "With all due respect, sir, I value my life." And with that, the ice was broken. He cracked up, laughing so hard, he fell off the chair, and the family came running in the room thinking that we had a fight. At first sight, with him on the floor and me standing over him, they looked at me menacingly, and I completely froze. But after his son helped him up, he told his daughter, "This little Italian is a good man."

Since marriage was not in my immediate future, I had a long talk with Mary, and I told her of my future plans, which were to establish myself in something that was lasting, to maybe get into a trade, and that meant maybe going to some school to learn something. I did not want to stop her from her goal of taking over the family farm along with her brother. She said that I could help run the business, as her father was aging and would someday give up the farm, but I said, "My asthma would preclude me from being a productive member of this business."

JUNE 1952 - NOVEMBER 1954: Sheet Metal

As this chapter of my life was coming to an end, I started to look for a field of labor that earned a better income, but with no skills in any of the trades, I knew it would be some time before I could decide which one to pursue. In the meantime, there was a sheet metal shop that produced all different metal products used in the home and offices. I knew the brother-in-law of the owner who encouraged me to make out an application, and after the owner read my application, he called me in for an interview and offered me a job. The job entailed working on all different types of machines, such as a power brake. At the time, all the positions in this factory had some degree of danger attached to them. The shear machine that I was a helper on, was one in which you had to be very alert, as the blade that cut the material had no guard on one side of it. The operator would feed the large sheets of material into the blade, and the helper would catch the metal as it came out of the machine, which was the end that had no guard.

The man who had the job of machine operator before I was hired was out on a disability leave because he was involved in a horrible accident. The accident happened because the large sheets of metal were placed on a wooden table, prior to being fed into the machine, and the area where he was standing did not give him any room to move around. As the story was told to me, despite the limited space, he decided to place more metal than usual on the table. This was because every job in the plant was on piece work, so every step you could save meant extra money in your day's work. The day of the accident the load of material was heavy as usual on the table, but since the table was old, it just gave way, and poor Joe was pinned under all the metal, crushing his legs. The pain was very excruciating, and one of his legs was badly damaged. All the men in the factory ran over and tried to remove the sheets of steel off of his legs as quickly as they could. But being in a tight place, it made it very difficult to remove the steel, as they had to hand the sheets of steel over the shear machine one at a time and be careful not to injure themselves in the process, only having cotton gloves covered in oil between them and the razor sharp steel. As quickly as they could take the steel off of Joe, it seemed it was not fast enough, the agony of his pain from his injuries were heard all over the plant and also outside of the shop. Firemen were called, and police and ambulances arrived at the plant to help get the material off of Joe. They brought in a large jack and slipped it under the material, enough to slip Joe out from under all the steel.

I was told one leg was so badly broken that mostly all his bones were damaged. I was hired when he got hurt and needed a replacement to help on that particular operation. Joe was out on disability for about a year, and on returning to the plant, he was given a different job, but he did not want to stay in this work. He told me he was going to go into the heating and air conditioning business. I worked with Joe on a number of different projects in the shop, and we had a nice working relationship. He was very friendly and always joking around, teasing me about getting married, etc. I would pick him up for work sometimes as he and his wife had one car and sometimes she needed to go somewhere. He never talked much about the accident, except to remind me that the machines were very old and to be careful.

One of the machines Joe was talking about was the one that I had an accident on. It was called a power press, which is a machine that stamps out material, and it did not have a safety guard on it. How it works is the operator slips the product on a little top, and the die comes down and stamps out the material with a crushing blow. When the die rises up, you took out the piece, and placed another one in its place. It is a very boring procedure, and yet you had to be alert and fast so that you could make your quota for a day's pay. Your hands were always under the die placing the product, and even though the operator did have control as to when to release the die to stamp out the product, the routine of it made a lot of operators lax in keeping their mind at the task at hand.

One day, after not having a good night's sleep due to staying out late with friends, the foreman, who was a nice man, took pity on me and gave me some easy material to do. He said, "Don't get used to this; I do not want spoil you," and I thanked him as he knew I would make up for this favor. The machine that I worked on had a makeshift guard on it, which was very flimsy at best, so my foreman said to be careful until he got some time to make a better guard to protect my hands. The guard was designed to come down with the die and keep your hands out from under the die. The work the foreman gave me were all small objects to place on the platform, from which the die would come down and stamp out the product. I felt very happy to have such an easy day ahead of me, but after about three hours of work, the unthinkable happened: the guard broke off as the die was coming down. With my right hand under the die, the guard that broke off pushed me off balance enough to have only my fingers under the die. My fingers were by now on the edge of the platform, and the top of the die caught my right forefinger, pushing the other fingers out of the way but flattening my finger badly. The pain that I felt and the shock of almost losing all my fingers on my right hand caused me to jump up from the machine and run away from the area, but my shop mates came over to calm me down and started to apply ice over the hand and some pressure to stop the bleeding. To this day, the little scar that I have on my finger is a reminder of how fragile life can be.

Industrial accidents were commonplace in the factory of years ago. It was almost routine to hear of people losing parts of their hands or arms, due to the negligence of the owners to protect the workers. The sheet metal factory that I worked in was no different because of the indifference of the owners who always looked out for more profits and did not worry about the safety of the workers. I had an uncle who lost his arm in a wire drawing machine. The arm got mangled and twisted with this heavy duty cable that he was working on, and it severed him up to the elbow. As far as I know, my uncle did not receive any compensation for his accident. My uncle was always very bitter because he felt that they did not have to cut off his arm. As for my injury, which came many years later, I was rushed to the emergency room and had the good fortune of having some good doctors attend to my wound, sewing up my finger and putting it in a cast.

The owners of the sheet metal factory were so different in their approach to the plight of the workers. All my problems were with one of the owners who had no compassion for the workers because he was only interested in how much profit he could make, whereas the other owner always treated me and the rest of us with the utmost respect. As the time study man, Frank would always give us a fair price for the work we were on, unlike one of the owner's, whom shall remain nameless because I really hated him and believe he does not deserve a name. His own brother hated him, and I could see why, since when I worked for the brother in another factory, he was kind and treated me fairly. But this owner was a mean man who had no compassion for anyone or anything. If I were to meet him outside of work, he would not acknowledge me. In fact, we belonged to the same athletic club, and I could sit in the same room with him and not know it, such was his disdain for anyone he thought below him in class.

My friend Rocky and I devised a system to get back at him. Since he was always trying to cheat us on our pay, we did him one better by charging him for work that we had already done a week ago, and he ended up paying us twice for the same work. Even though he thought he was so smart, we had found that he would forget the previous work from the week before. We reveled in the fact that he actually looked upon *us* as peons. One job that I really enjoyed cheating on was the time after my accident. This boss put me in the basement of the factory stenciling the name of a local dairy on milk boxes. It was very humid and smelly down in the basement, and such a boring job that he thought I would get disgusted and quit. This way he could get rid of me and get someone else who did not have a handicapped hand. As it turned out, it was the most profitable work that I was ever given to do. The owner's partner, came downstairs to time study me and give me a price for each milk box that I stenciled. The price he gave me was ten cents a box. The operation called for me to clean the boxes of any oil and grime before stenciling the name on the box, then having to mix the paint to get the right mix of color, and to keep the spray gun and parts in a clean and working order. When the boss saw what his partner gave me for this operation, he came running downstairs like a madman and demanded that I be retimed by him, as he said the price was too high. He retimed me by doing the job himself, but being as clumsy as he was, and not being organized and getting everything in order before starting, the paint started to run and drip out of the spray gun. He said, "Did you have the right paint here?" and I said, "Here, look at the label." In his haste to bring the price down on the job, the dumb bastard did not look at the mix to see if it was the right one and also did not check on the procedure for preparing the milk boxes for painting. After he did ten boxes, he had to come up with the same price as his partner did, and with a look of great disgust, he thrust the spray gun back to me and swore at me that he was going to figure out a way to do it cheaper.

What the boss didn't know was that before the boxes came down to me, my friend Rocky's operation was to solder the ends of the boxes and clean all the grime an oil off of them, which was in his time study. So when I got the boxes, they were all cleaned and ready for painting. Now the shop had a full time painter on staff who would do all the spray painting on all the finished products, but the shop felt this was an operation that would be cheaper for me to do. Still, Roger the painter helped me with the paint by having it all ready for me, so all I had to do was put the stencil on the boxes and spray the name on it. I was able to spray fifty boxes in ten minutes. I would line them up on the back wall away from the door and stack them up, so the owner could not see me working. This was one of the methods that Rocky and I had to get back at this miserable human being by having him pay for the same procedure twice.

Since I had more slips to turn in for my pay, and it would put me over the limit for the day, I gave Rocky some of my other work tickets to turn in, and he did not have to work as hard to make his day's pay. Rocky always said, "We have to beat this bastard every chance we get," but sometimes I would feel guilty, until I remembered the meanness of this creature, who would not send us home on the hottest days of the summer when the temperature was hovering around the one hundred degree mark. Since the roof of the factory was covered with asphalt, it was liking working in an oven. What he had for cooling off the factory was to have water being sprayed on the roof of the factory; that was his idea of air conditioning. He did have large fans on the floor of the factory, but all they were doing was moving the hot air around, making it worse. Luckily, that finally ended when we all got up one hot summer day and just shut down all the machines and started to head for the doorway to cool off. The creature came running downstairs and wanted to know why we closed off the machines. We said, "Stand inside by the power presses and see how hot it is." He finally relented and sent us home.

The conditions that I am describing were the same ones that all workers who worked in various factories were experiencing at the same time as I worked, but not like the slave master that I worked for. To him, you were a body who could be replaced at any time. His favorite expression was "I am going to bring in some chinks from china who will do the work cheaper." Fine, we said, go right ahead. If he was around today, he would have all immigrants in the factory. I don't think that they would put up with his type of working conditions. One of them would probably put him in one of the power presses and flatten him out.

The brains of the factory was the head layout man, a quiet man also named Joe, a low key kind of person, who had to design and figure out all the different cuts and bends in the material, so that the boss could bid on the job. Then after they got the job, they tried to get it made as cheaply as possible. The boss had to figure out how much each part of the operation would cost and try to reduce the cost of manufacturing the product. All the while, they had a lot of leeway to give us a better price on our work. We found out from the lady that worked in the office how much they had figured in for labor, and then they would try to reduce that by half of the cost. When the steel came to be delivered to the factory, we had to unload the steel from the truck. The ones that were picked for this were mostly the ones that did not have a priority position, meaning whatever you were working on could be put off for the time being. The steel came in large sheets that took two men, one on each side of the material, and one at the end of the sheet, to guide it onto a skid. For this operation, we were paid a day rate.

Sometimes, we would go through two pairs of gloves, since unloading the steel was not only oily, but very sharp, and had to be handled with great care, or else you could give yourself a bad cut, which happened quite often. I learned to handle the steel by putting my hands under the steel, trying not to touch the edges, as it would cut right through the gloves. As we were unloading the freight, I would always think of poor Joe and how he got caught under all that steel. We tried not to put too many sheets on one skid as it might topple over and fall on us, much to the dismay of the owner, who did not like to have to use too many skids.

I finally got a break and was put on a power brake machine. Although it was a smaller version than the large one that another man was operating, this machine was designed to make small bends in the material. To bend the little pieces of material that went with the product, it was a lot cleaner, but you still had to put your hands in position to place the material under the blade to make the bends. Since this was still piece work, you had to work at great speed but with great care and focus on the job at hand. One day, with a very boring routine of bending the same parts over and over again, I turned to talk with the man next to me. We were having a great conversation, and joking about how we got a great price for the operation we were on, and in a split second, I inserted one piece the wrong way, and the machine spit it out right pass the right part of my face. Had I been looking straight at the machine, it would have taken out my eye.

I knew at that moment that this kind of work would not be my career, as every position in the factory had some risk to it. I did like the hours, working eight to five and earning about one hundred twenty dollars a week, which, in 1952 dollars, was a pretty good pay. But the constant arguing with the owner over how much he would pay for every job was starting to get to me. Every day, it was a battle for everyone that was on piece work. The owner was constantly trying to get people to work for less money, and he was never satisfied. Even after he timed you and got you to work cheaper, he still thought that he was getting screwed, which made me figure out ways to get even with him. Joe, Rocky, and I finally worked out a system to pile up work in the corner of the room, and make it look like it was all part of the production being processed. Then every Monday, we would mark the same work on our work sheets to make up for any shortfalls we would have that day or any day that we came up short for our quota. Talk about skinning a cat, this was the highpoint of working with a piece of shit.

I did have some fun with guys that I worked with, by telling them about my days in the Navy, and my being a middleweight champion of the Navy. They knew that it was all bullshit, and they would have a great time teasing me about it. Since most of them came from the Fair Haven section, and I came from the Wooster St. section of the city, there was a lot of banter about who was the tougher fighters. This friendly talk back and forth about what section was the toughest, with me always telling them how I was the middle weight champion of the Navy, always got a lot of laughs about how tough I was. That set the stage for my friend Ralph to see how tough I was by offering to engage me a few rounds every day during our lunch hour and to hold the title fight at the end of week. Now Ralph could break me in two just by walking by me as he was a very muscular man, but he offered to make me look good, and just spar around for laughs and not tell the other guys about it. I agreed.

The first day of our boxing match, we would use clean gloves so as not to get any oil or grease in our eyes. After a little ceremony orchestrated by Joe, we started to box, and as luck would have it, poor Ralph, in a moment of not looking where he was, stumbled backwards and fell. It looked like I hit him, which I had not, but was given credit for a knockdown. So as not to rile Ralph up, I helped him up and dusted him off, much to the laughter of all the guys. As I said, this was supposed to a friendly boxing match, but I did not want to embarrass Ralph. We did this for about ten minutes every lunch hour. It was good clean fun, and everybody had a good time with it. This went on for four days, with each of us winning two days each. Friday was set for the title of the sheet metal shop, and the guys were taking bets as to who was going to be the middle weight champion of the shop. The foreman gave us a new pair of gloves, but when I say gloves, these were our work gloves, not boxing gloves. Again, Joe gave a rousing speech and held up a little trophy that was going to be awarded to the winner. I have to mention that there were no punches thrown, just little jabs that were going to be scored as points. No way in hell would I even entertain anything else.

As the boxing match started, I had the advantage of knowing Ralph had a weak spot, especially in the area of the midsection. I had worked with him on some projects in the shop, and at times, would poke him with the material, and he would double up and laugh. Having not used it before, I saved this for the last day, my secret weapon. As I worked Ralph into the corner of the room, with my back to the rest of the room, it would look like I was hitting him with a series of hits in the midsection, when it was only my fists digging into his midsection. As Ralph started to fall, mainly from laughing and growling with pain from having fallen on the floor, he was stuck in the corner of the room and had a tough time getting up. Joe counted to ten very rapidly and declared me the champion. When Ralph got up, he said, "You son of bitch, I knew you were going to cheat somehow." "Ralph," I said, "I always told you that I was the middle weight champion of the Navy." The guys had a lot of fun with this and would tease Ralph about this from time to time. Ralph said he wanted a rematch, but Joe said, "The contract calls for no rematch."

NOVEMBER 1954 - NOVEMBER 1955: Dugan Bakery

Rocky, my friend from the shop, was getting disgusted working in the shop and said, "There was no future for him there" and that he was going to try something else. So he applied for a route man's job in the Dugan Bros. Bakery, which was based in Bridgeport CT, with their main plant in Long Island N.Y. This bakery was primarily a home delivery service, in which you had to sell baked goods to the homeowner on a daily basis, such as bread and cakes. It was a straight commission position with the incentive to earn more money reflecting your sales. Dugan Bakery had a program that they sent you to school for a week to learn their product line, and also test you on your skills, on sales, math, etc. They stressed the point of always being very neat in your wardrobe, which was a uniform of the bakery.

Rocky said that they took you on location to see how you performed and presented yourself to the customer, then graded you and gave you the results at the end of the week. Many guys were turned down, not being what the company wanted. All this, for the great sum of one hundred dollars a week, with some route men making as much has one hundred fifty dollars a week, as well as a lot of benefits thrown in. Rocky would stop in from time to time and keep me posted on how he was doing, as his route was in the vicinity of the shop. While the hours were longer than his hours at the shop, he said he felt more gratified with his potential on earning more money and that the work was cleaner. He had to get up at five in the morning and work until he finished the route, which was somewhere around five in the evening. Many nights as I was on way home about four thirty or five o'clock in the evening, I would see Rocky making his rounds to his customers. Twelve hour days were the norm for home delivery in those days, but Rocky said that "it was nice not to have a boss around you all day" and that you could work at your own leisure and not have to meet any deadlines. Rocky kept trying to sell me on the idea of leaving the shop and going to sell bread and cakes. He said how nice the company treated him, as a person instead of a piece of meat, and that he did not feel just like another body in the room. At this time, I had just gotten married and was reluctant to give up a steady job, and for a sales job which I did not have any experience for. But Rocky said, "For Christ sakes, you are a good bullshitter; that's all you need."

There was another friend of ours who worked in the shop and was interested in leaving, whose name was Frank. Frank and I would discuss Rocky's new job with the pros and cons of it. We were both undecided as to what our future would be, since he also had just gotten married, and was in the same situation as I was with payments on furniture and car payments but with no children yet. The day came when Rocky came bursting into the shop during our lunch hour when the boss was not there and said, "When that asshole comes back, go and tell him to shove the shop and the job up his ass." I said, "I think I should talk this over with my wife." Rocky said that there will be several openings soon, and that I could get a good route. After I spoke with her, Teresa agreed that I should take this opportunity and try it. If it didn't work out, I could always go back to the factory. My generation was always looking for a steady and secure job, especially after just coming out of the Depression. With the stories of my father's generation still fresh in my mind, everybody was concerned with building a dependable and lasting job, especially if you were married and planning to raise a family. So it was a little agonizing having to ponder the question of leaving.

The very next morning, I took one look at my boss's creepy face and that was it. Up the stairs I went and told him I was all through at the end of the week. At this time, the shop was swamped with work and he begged me to not quit, even promising me more money, but I knew as soon as the shop got caught up with all the orders, my ass would be out the door. It was kind of sweet to see him beg, but I knew he would get even with me and fire my ass as soon as he could. And so began my life has a route salesman. I did not know at that time, but it would last sixty years. I always have Rocky to thank for that moment when he all but dragged me out of the factory. He always said that it was me who influenced him to leave the shop, but that we would always be talking about doing outside work where the opportunities were much better. Maybe I put the idea in his head by talking about making the change, as we were always comparing different areas of employment.

Along with me leaving, Frank also gave his notice the next day and that really set the asshole to go off his bonkers, cursing Frank about leaving with me. Suffice it to say, it was not a good time or a good last week for the both of us. Our boss knew we were both going to work for the same bakery and that we had somehow conspired against him. It was nice to see him have a long face every day. Such was our revenge for all the agitation he gave us for the last three years.

We had to spend a week traveling back and forth to Long Island to attend the school. Frank and I were both surprised at the training that we had to go through. Rocky did prepare us for the work they were going to give us, but when it came to the field training, and actually having to knock on doors and try and sell to the lady of the house, that really took our socks off. It was cold selling, but they taught us how to arrange the basket of baked goods, so as to make it appealing to the customer seeing the products.

After I passed the test at the school, we were told to report to the Bridgeport CT depot and get assigned to a route. I really lucked out by getting a route based in the Branford area and parts of East Haven, so it was not much of a large area to cover. This home delivery route was a lot different than working in the factory, and not having to answer to a boss for eight to ten hours a day, gave me the opportunity in meeting all classes of people. It also allowed me the freedom to sit down and have a cup of coffee whenever I wanted, which was nice, not having to wait for the ten minute break twice a day. The hours were also a lot longer because I had to drive to Bridgeport, pick up my truck, and load it for the day. Most drivers reported to work at five in the morning, which I also did, so getting up at four in the morning and working until maybe five in the afternoon was a normal day. Some of the drivers worked until seven or eight in the evening, especially the routes that had a heavy shore presence. I had some in the Indian Neck region of Branford, and I had to call on all the summer people who had rented cottages for the summer.

There were areas of Branford that had my worst customers. They always questioned the price of the products, and to add to that, they would pay me once a month, so I had to leave them a statement and then collect on my next delivery. One day, after receiving an order, I pulled up to the front door of a club and entered the kitchen, placed the order of bread on the counter, when suddenly this man grabbed me by the arm and said, "You are not supposed to enter through the front door. Pick up your order and go through the back door." I walked around the side of the building and picked up some mud on my shoes and scuffed up the floor before I got to the kitchen. That was my last delivery there. I turned the account over to another bakery delivery service. As the saying goes, "the rich think their shit does not stink."

I had several nice customers who lived on the fringe of the area that would always give me a lot of business, especially when they had parties and needed a lot of baked goods. They would never question the price, but instead they were more interested in making sure that I would be able to fill their order. My commission from the Dugan Bakery was twenty five percent, so an order of maybe a hundred dollars was a very good order. Since I had to sell four hundred dollars a week to make one hundred dollars, I wished I could get those orders every week. It was not easy to sell my quota every day as the price of bread was just twenty cents. But the cakes and pies were a lot more expensive and that would help me make my day's pay. I would have to average about eighty dollars a day in sales, since my route averaged about four hundred and fifty dollars a week. Some routes would average about six hundred a week in sales, but they also put more hours in every day, working from about five in the morning to about six or seven in the evening.

One day, a route man received an order for a large birthday cake, and then as he was about to leave for his route, a call came in from his customer to cancel the order. The manager had everybody pick a number and put it in the box, so he could raffle off the cake. I had gotten home about six in the evening, which was a long day for me, but not for most of the route men. At nine o'clock that evening, we heard a knock on the door, and it was my friend John, just coming home from work. John helped me a lot to make my route a success, and later on, I would be working with his son in another bakery. He had this large box in his hand and said you won the cake. We had enough cake for a whole week, and I shared it with my in-laws who lived downstairs.

Having a home delivery route brings you into a diverse area of distribution. On my route, which covered quite large area of town, I went to some pretty wealthy homes and to homes of people who were in my income bracket. I also had a lot of what you would call mom and pop farms, which were small, considering the size of large farms of today. One day while I was out looking for some new customers, I came upon this house that was set back from the main road and did not look too promising, but I went ahead and drove in the driveway. Coming out of the house was a man and his wife. He had a large shovel in his hand and appeared menacing to me. Just as I was thinking about turning around and getting the hell out this yard, his wife motioned to her husband, "It's the Dugan man." The man told me they were glad to see me and asked if I would come into their home. They offered me some iced tea and wanted to know how much the price of bread was. After a little chat about my products, I started to notice all sorts of farm animals coming in the kitchen, such as chickens, and even a pig. It seems they had the full run of the house and also the odor that came along with them. They said they had eight children, and most of them were busy with the chores of the farm. When we finally got around to discussing what they wanted to purchase, they gave me an order for twelve loaves of bread three times a week, plus some pastry. They were also feeding some people next door to them, in which the man of the house was sick and could not work. People that you sometimes think don't look like what you perceived turn out better than the so called "swells" on the other side of town.

Home delivery in those days was the norm, as pretty much everything was delivered, all sorts of food products, such as baked goods, fish, fruits and vegetables. You could even have a person come to your home who would sharpen knives. They also delivered bleach for washing clothes, named Star Water. I got the crazy idea of trying to manufacture it our cellar, which was my in-laws' house. I went and got the necessary products, which I researched from the label on the gallon jugs, and I got my father-in-law interested in the project. He started to figure out how much profit we could make by under cutting the product already on the market. On the sales end, I already had access to a readymade route on my bakery route. After we assembled all the necessary items needed for this operation, we went and got started to test out our new bleach. One of the products in the mix was something like an acid. Not knowing when to add the items together, we filled up this mixing jug, and it started to boil over and smoke. We shut everything down quickly, for fear of blowing up the house. When we resumed retesting the mix, one item at a time, it came out, a very gray color, not nice and clear like the Star Water we were purchasing. We had on our hands about fifty new gallon jugs, plus everything else, and we had figured a profit of about thirty cents a gallon with sales of about five hundred gallons a week. I was completely frustrated by not succeeding in this venture. Pop said to me in Italian, which I can translate into English, "Leo, doing something is better than doing nothing." So back to concentrating on my route and seeing how else I could increase my income by selling other products to my customers.

I knew that I wanted to stay with this route work but not putting in such long hours. Home delivery was a very satisfying line of work, in that I met such a wide range of people, from all income brackets, people who had some good jobs, and who gave me encouragement on how to better myself. One of my customers named John said, "Don't look at what you can't do but go with your strengths because you are a ballsy type of guy." Then he said, "I wish I could do what you do, and go and greet people, and to make a cold sell like you do. That's a rare talent that very few people possess." Coming from a person who had a high level job with the government gave me a lot of confidence to stay in the field of selling, not only of a product but also selling myself. John said, "Leo, you are great at that. You have learned the art of selling yourself first; the product is secondary."

One of the most interesting customers on my route was a man by the name of Johnson, his first name I do not recall. He owned a real estate company in Branford, and I would deliver to his office. He always purchased a good amount of products because he was always entertaining large groups of people at his home. One day, he said to me, "Leo, what are your plans for the future?" I said, "To have a steady income and maybe purchase a home someday. Then the conversation turned to this:

Johnson: Leo, you should be thinking about investing in real estate, income-producing real estate.

Leo: Mr. Johnson, I owe money on furniture, plus my car, since I just got married.

Johnson: Leo, you have to look ahead to the future, for future income.

Leo: Where the hell am I going to get money to invest? I owe out money.

Johnson: This is what I call creative financing. You come with a small amount and leverage.

Leo: Leverage what? Johnson, you must be kidding.

Johnson: Let me tell you how I got started in income-producing real estate. I started with a three family unit, then borrowed money on that property and purchased another, winding up owning fifty units of property.

Johnson was very generous with his time, taking me around and showing me his investments all over town. On one our trips around town, he took me to Indian Neck and pointed out an Island with a house on it that was for sale. The price was five thousand dollars.

Leo: Johnson, you are the either the nicest guy or the craziest bastard I have ever met. What the hell am I going to do with a house on an island?"

Johnson: Sit on it for a while and maybe you can unload it for ten thousand in a few years. These island homes will be in great demand in the near future."

Leo: You gave me all this talk about income-producing property, and you want me to purchase this?

Johnson: What did I say about leveraging? I will show you another way to look at investing in property.

Johnson took me to Branford Hills and showed me land on the right side of the hill going west. It was a good size lot like the rest of the hill.

Johnson: Leo, commercial property on the hill will be very attractive in the future. The price of the property was fifteen thousand dollars.

To me, it looked like a wasteland. Johnson also took me to some property in the center of town and told me of its potential, just to show me where I could get started in investing in real estate without much input from me. In hindsight everybody is smart, and that piece of property that I said was a wasteland turned out to be leased out to a

Burger King, which is still there today.

Another work friend of mine named Robert had a way with the women customers on his route. He was quite the charmer, and they would buy more than they needed. He said it was "salesmanship," but I called it what it was: seduction of the first order. Because Robert had more than selling baked goods on his mind, I guess it was his looks and his swagger that the woman loved. One day, Robert told me this story about this woman on his route, whom he had become very friendly with, who would invite him and his wife over for dinner. Her husband and Robert had a nice rapport, so I never gave it much thought. It was nice to see Robert enjoying the company of one of his customers. He was always telling me about how generous they both were, with themselves and their home. Then Robert told me that the woman was pregnant and was expecting her second child. After several months, Robert said he had to go over and bring a gift for the new baby. "What do you think I should buy?" Robert asks me. "Boy or girl?" I said. "Girl." "Have your wife pick out the gift," I said. So Robert and his wife went over to see the new baby, and upon seeing the baby, Robert's wife said, "Robert, the baby looks just like you." I told Robert, "Are you serious? You mean to tell me that you were spending a lot of time with her, and you were not surprised at this at all? Robert, you must have the biggest pair of balls, or else are the craziest asshole I have ever met."

I believe that Robert's wife knew something was amiss with this situation, but to her credit and compassion to keep both marriages intact, let the matter drop. But, as Robert said, his wife gave him signals that she knew and would not tolerate anything like this in the future. Robert dodged a bullet on this one. Robert went on to become a very successful distributor, and eventually left the route sales work to open a gas station and grocery store about the time I started my bakery distribution business. It was Robert who gave me a lot of customers, people he had done business with, and it opened the door for me to get started. I could not ask for anything more than what Robert had bestowed on me as far as friendship goes. Over the years, we kept in touch with each other, meeting at social functions, business matters, etc.

NOVEMBER 1955 - NOVEMBER 1956:
Chambrelli Brothers Bakery District Restaurant Suppliers

This was a bakery route that serviced restaurant and private clubs. The delivery part of this job was the easiest job that I had because everything was pre-ordered. The part that I did not like was after you had finished the route, you had to call all your customers for the next day's order. I did not want to stay in the office for another two hours making calls after I finished the route, especially since my customers usually ordered the same products and the same amount every day. Therefore, I told my customers I did not want to bother them when they were at their busiest part of the day, so I said, "I will give you a standing order, and you can change it as you wish." They all went for it. Of course, I was the one who was really going to benefit from this. Sometimes, you have to tell people that you are doing them a favor, even when it is you that will be gaining the most. At no cost to them, all my customers thought it was the best idea since sliced bread. The only ones I still had to call were the private clubs, whose menu would change daily, but that was only a few phone calls. I would come in to the driver's room, make a few calls, and put my order in for the next day.

One of the craziest stories was told to me by one of my good customers who sold a lot of pies every day in his restaurant. On my first day on the route, the owner said to me, "One thing that I demand is honesty." I said, "No problem with me on that, as I need you to help me make this a successful route." "Good," he said, "when you make your deliveries here, make sure you always give me fresh goods." "Why do you say that?" I said. "All my products are delivered fresh daily." He then went on to tell me about the man who had the route before me, and he felt that he was not giving him fresh goods. So to test him out, he had marked a lemon crème pie on the bottom of the box and told him to exchange it for a fresh pie, as it did not smell good. The driver went out to the truck and came back in with the pie. The owner picked up the bottom of the box, saw it was the old pie that he had given the driver to exchange, opened up the box, and slammed the lemon crème pie in the driver's face. The driver was fired the next day because what he was doing over-ordering to see if he could unload the extra product on his customers. But apparently, he did not rotate his product, or he took it back from another customer, and did not want to lose any sales. The owner of the restaurant told me this story so that maybe I would not do the same thing. When I checked out the story with the boss, he said every word of it was true.

They wanted me to purchase a truck, and they would pay me twenty percent, but I did not think it was a very good deal, as the expense of running the route did not warrant an investment by me. I had gone to an accountant, and he told me it would be a bad deal, as it would take at least thirty percent to earn a good living, based on the current sales of the route, plus the route covering a great distance. The route started in Westport and ended up in Greenwich CT.

JANUARY 1956 - JUNE 1956: Cheese and Laundry Routes

I had a cheese route delivering to pizza and grocery stores, mainly in the Waterbury CT area. Being January, it was not a nice place to work in, due to the fact Waterbury is a very hilly area. Steep inclines mixed with icy streets during bad weather meant you had to be careful not to lose control of your truck. As luck would have it, I had the misfortune of having to do the route in a horrible snowstorm. I was up in Torrington when it started snowing, and as I saw the snow start to pile up, I canceled the rest of the route and started to head back to New Haven. This was about eleven o'clock in the morning, and as I headed back and the storm grew in intensity, my vision was limited because of the blowing snow. At this time, I was lost right in the center of Waterbury, and I had to stop at a gas station, which was just closing, to direct me to the nearest road to New Haven. It was a road that ended up in Westville, and as I drove down this back road, my vision was so bad, I could only see the front of the truck. I got home at ten o'clock that evening, then phoned the owner of the company and told him I had the truck at my house. To this day, I do not know how in the hell I got home that night. Suffice it say, this would not be a long term job, at least not in that area.

After a short stay with the cheese company, I got a job with a laundry company, which was just down the street from my house. I took this job only to earn money as I continued looking for something more stable, probably with a national company, so that I could have some security. The route started in Meriden and would take me all the way up to Enfield, servicing mostly factories, such as Fuller Brush, Kamen Aircraft, Colt Firearms, Royal Typewriter, Fafnir Bearing, Stanley Tool, and a lot of small factories. I would sell the workers aprons and towels. They would rent an apron or towel for twenty five cents for the week. They had to hand me their old aprons or towels in exchange for new ones. You would be surprised at how many men would try to get two weeks out of their aprons so as not to spend the twenty five cents. It was kind of interesting to see all the different kinds of work people did to earn a living. I had seen people work in some of the worst conditions that you could possible see, but there were also a lot of departments in the factories that were exceptionally clean, where people worked with white shirts on. But they too used aprons so as not to soil their clothes.

Fafnir Bearing, probably the noisiest factory, manufactured ball bearings. I had to put on ear plugs before I entered the room where the huge tumblers were spinning the ball bearings around. It was a clean room, but the noise was horrible. Even with the plugs in my ears, I stood in the doorway and had to raise a flag they gave me to get the workers' attention.

The worst factory that I had was Colt Firearms, particularly the room where the buffing machines were located. It was so dark in there that I could not see the people working due to all the dust and grime that was generated from the machines. I never entered the room. I had to blow my whistle, and they would come out to where I was. Seeing them come out to me was something out of one of those space movies. As they moved toward me, coming from the dark to the light, was very eerie. Reading about that kind of work, I felt bad for those workers many who came down with lung problems, like black lung disease.

The conditions that I saw in the factories were similar to the ones that I encountered as a young boy working part time in the factories, and later on, in my working career. It seemed normal, in some sort of way, as if this was an accepted way to earn a living. One of the bad jobs in the factories was the job of working on the cleansing tank, where they would clean all the finished material. The worker had to dip the material in the tank that contained a strong solution, and the heat from the tank would steam up the room. The worker would be working there with no mask on and breathing in all those toxic fumes. At that time, nobody knew how bad it was for the worker to breathe all that foul air. I personally knew of people who did that type of work, and they all had contacted some sort of cancer, mainly prostate cancer.

This experience of seeing all types of factories and actually working in them too cemented my desire to stay out of the factories. Since this laundry route was just a way for me to earn money for the short term, I knew my future had to be in something else. My goal was to get hired by a large corporation and have a secure future for my family, but I had to work around my problem of not having a college education. So I believed that sticking with my plans of going into sales would be my ticket to security.

Being on the road and meeting different route men delivering all sorts of products opened me up to all sorts of possibilities of employment. One such man was a man named Nick, who, when I had the cheese route, I would exchange my products for his. He was working for Sealtest Dairy at the time as a milkman, and from time to time, I would run into him, and we would talk about me going into that organization. He stressed how I would have a lifetime job as everyone needed milk delivered to their homes. This I thought would be my life's work, a nice steady job with a lot of security. This was the thinking of people of my generation because of the effects of the Great Depression. One day, Nick stopped me and said, "Leo, get your ass down to the dairy right now; I told the sales manager about you. There will be an opening soon because this guy is going to retire." I went right down that day and did not go home to change my clothes. I told the sales manager, whose name was Earl Pall, "Mr. Pall, please excuse my not being properly dressed. I want to apply for the job, and I will come back tomorrow, after the introduction of myself." He said, "Leo, you did it a little bit backwards, but you seem to be earnest in working here. Nick already called me. Come back Friday, and don't worry: you have a good friend in Nick."

JUNE 1956 - JUNE 1959: Sealtest Dairy

And now started what I had perceived to be my lifetime job, a steady pay and good benefits, which included someone washing and pressing my uniforms on a weekly basis, just like a dry cleaners. You deposited your soiled clothes and picked up your clean ones. In my time, having a steady job was considered to be the best thing anyone could hope for. As I said, that's what people who lived through the Great Depression lived for. Having a high school diploma was the same as a college education today: you needed a high school diploma to get a decent job, such as any kind of sales or a position of management, so being a milkman for a national company was a great step up.

My friend Nick was promoted to being a supervisor when I got hired at Sealtest dairy. He gave me the inspiration to be a good salesman, so that someday I could advance myself to be in that position, since it was something worth working for.

The job of running a milk route was in itself a very easy job as the route took me about three hours to complete, but the hours were brutal: I had to awake at three in the morning to get to the dairy and get in line to pick up my order. All the drivers had a set time to arrive to get their load of milk. It was the practice then that customers wanted their milk delivered no later than eight in the morning, so there was a lot of pressure for being on time. I actually had customers waiting for me to deliver the milk, so that they could feed the family breakfast. The routes were set up to deliver milk every other day, so that meant I had two routes. My route was a city route, which meant a lot of stair climbing, and I had buildings with as many as five flights. As far as territory, it only covered six city blocks and that is why it only took me three hours to complete.

In order for me to get a vacation, I had to build up credits by working six days a week for five weeks in order to have a week's vacation.

Looking back at it now, the company actually did not really give me a paid vacation because we had to put extra time in, so really, we paid for the time off ourselves. As I started to settle in at Sealtest, the men started to have meetings to stop the company from this practice. As times were changing, so too was the company's policy of this part of their business. They knew the men were not happy by having to work an extra day for five weeks just to have a week's vacation, and the company relented when confronted by the men, who overwhelmingly voted to do away with this policy.

Sealtest had as one of their top executives a man by the name of Albie Booth, who was a standout football player while at Yale University. They called him "little boy blue" because of his small stature, but he was a great athlete. His exploits on the field were legendary, and because of his presence with the company, we had almost all the business in the city, especially Yale.

Sealtest was a family-oriented company and would hold a Christmas party at the Hotel Taft in New Haven and have all the employees and their families attend this great event. In my second year, when Gail was over one years old, I was very proud when we were able to take Gail to this great party. Sadly, I do not have any pictures of Gail meeting Santa Clause because we forgot to bring the camera.

Being the junior man in the group, my days off were Monday and Tuesday, which was not so bad, since Sunday was a short day with no collections, just delivering milk. I was home by about eleven in the morning, and it felt like a three day stay. In those days, most people did not have to work on Sundays, so that was a little bit of a bummer.

On Saturday, when I went to collect the bill for their delivery of milk, they would ask me if I could have somebody deliver soda to their homes, since most of my customers were on a biweekly basis for paying their bills. I felt that this was an opportunity for me to earn extra money. So I went and inquired about the possibility of purchasing soda from a small soda company to see if it would be a profitable venture for me. I felt that since Sunday was a very short day on my route, I could have the time to deliver soda to my customers, who were all my milk customers. I made a deal with the owner of the soda company to purchase the soda for one dollar a case, and I could sell it for two dollars a case. I purchased a little pickup truck for one hundred dollars, and even though it was not in really good condition, I just wanted to test myself and see if I could make a go out of it.

At this time on my milk route, I was earning about one hundred twenty dollars a week, so on a Sunday morning, I would sell well over one hundred cases of soda, making this more profitable than my milk route. It would take me four hours to deliver the product. What I would do is take my milk truck home and pick up my truck, which was already loaded from the night before. After finishing my soda route, I would then bring my milk truck back to the dairy. Of course, I had to keep this from my supervisors because I don't think they would have approved of this. I only took on this side venture to earn a little extra cash because I felt my future was with Sealtest, but it did start to make me think about going into a business. The thought of not having to answer to anyone was very tempting.

Being a milkman was easy, but the book work was not so pleasant. Having to keep records of maybe three hundred customers and to tally up just the day's receipts on all your sales had to be accurate, or you would have a shortage in your books at the end of the month. That's the part I did not like. The people who had a wholesale route, which was delivering to stores and such, tallied up daily with their money, and knew if there were any mistakes right away and could have rectified it quickly. But the home delivery people had to wait until the end of the month when an accountant would add up your purchases and had to match up with the money you turned in. If there was a shortage, you had to make up the difference, or you could find out yourself by going over all the books, which, either way, was nerve racking.

Delivering milk in bad weather was a real challenge, especially snowstorms. There was no way you could postpone deliveries. The motto was milk had to go through no matter what. There were snowstorms when I left my truck at the end of the block and walked up and down the street, sometimes in snow up to my knees. To make matters worse, some assholes would complain about me being late with their milk. The milk trucks were designed for the milkman to drive standing up; there was no sitting down, and in some snowstorms, the snow would actually be inside the cab.

One nice thing about the winter was that you did not have to deal with putting ice on the milk. It made it a lot easier to handle the milk bottles, as they were not wet from the ice. I would drive my route in the winter with both doors open. There was no such thing as having a heater in the truck, and wearing gloves was a pain in the ass because you had to write in the book any changes in people's order, so constantly off and on with the gloves was not practical.

On a milk route, you get to experience a lot of unusual happenings, such as the time I was delivering to Yale doctors' building across the street from Yale New Haven Hospital. It was a residential building for the staff, and on this one morning, I noticed the hallway was a little dark, which was very unusual for this building. With my flashlight shining the way, I noticed some dark figures standing at the end of hallway where I was supposed to deliver the milk. I directed my light to the milk box near the door, and there in front of me standing right near the milk box, where two people groping one another. She had her dress up, and the pair were in the act of making love, his pants down to the floor. As I placed the milk in the milk box, they did not even stop to address my presence. They were so close to the milk box that I had to move the box closer to me. I do not know if that was my customer because the money would be left out on the milk box, and I never got to meet any of my customers in this building. Today, that scene would be on Youtube.

There were always a lot of jokes about milkmen getting romantically involved with the ladies on their route, some of which was true, but mostly, it made for some good chatter. My route consisted of mostly Italian families, with the women at home taking care of the children. I would get to meet the husbands only on Saturday when I went to collect the money for my deliveries. With the hustle and bustle of the job, I do not know how anyone had the time to even think about getting involved with anybody, but I guess some people made time for that. Some women were very sloppy the way they came to the door with their clothes, not fully dressed and not caring about their appearance, not thinking how they made you feel very uncomfortable. I had this boy working for me to help me in the morning before he went to school, like so many other milkman had. His name was Butch. There were some apartments he did not want to deliver to, and I got mad at him one day and said, "Butch, you can't pick out the stops you want to do." "Leo," he said, "some of those ladies come out almost bare ass." What I did was change the time of the route so we would get there earlier. I did not want to do these stops either because of how many flights of stairs you had to climb. That's when it was nice to have a helper. Actually, kids on a milk truck were not approved, but the company did not make an issue out of it.

In 1956, soon after I started with the dairy, there were a lot of people that came over from Europe, especially from Hungary and Russia. I had a six family building on Columbus Avenue, and there were two apartments on the third floor that these people rented. Because of the way they had to live in the old country, they brought all their fear with them. When I went to collect on Saturday, I would knock on the door and there would be silence. Then a man would come to the door and ever so slightly open it just a crack to see who it was. Through the small opening of the door, I gave him the milk bill, and he would then shut the door, before sliding out the money. I never got to see the man, even when I delivered the milk, and I never heard anybody walking around the apartment.

Another incident that happened to me was the time I delivered to a woman who had three children, all quite young. This one morning, she was waiting for me so she could feed her baby. I brought the milk inside and put in on the table. She was very grateful that I was early that morning. The milk bottles in those days had the tops of the bottles covered with just a hard paper wrapping. There really was no protection about the tops of the bottles. Well, the unthinkable happened: the woman poured the milk into a glass for the baby to drink, and then the baby started to scream, blood coming out of her mouth.

It turned out the top of the bottle, under the paper cover, was apparently chipped, and little particles of glass went into the child's mouth. When I got back to the dairy, they told me what happened, and I verified what the woman said, that she took the bottle from me after I left, and it was not something she had left over. The bosses went to see her and offered her compensation in the form of a free week's delivery, plus all the ice cream she wanted. To my amazement, she accepted. I tried to tell her she should not have settled for such a small amount, since she had me to back her up, but her response was they also paid for the doctor's bill. Seal Test dodged a bullet on that one.

I did have a famous person that lived on my route that I never got to see. His name was Dominic Frontier, who I believe played the accordion. He went out to Hollywood and wrote for a lot of movies. His arrangements of music made him famous, and he married the owner of the then Los Angeles Rams.

I had been given some new territory to do, and it centered around the center of New Haven, near Yale University, so I inherited a lot of Yale people for customers. Most of them I never ever met; most paid monthly, and they would leave their order and the money in the milk box. This one professor I had was three months in arrears, and my efforts to contact him proved fruitless. My supervisor at that time was a man by the name of Joe, who we used to call J.J. He was going through my books and wanted to know why this man was not paying his bill. I told him my other supervisor said he was an important professor at Yale and that he would pay his bill, so J.J. said he would meet me at the customer's apartment and help me collect. When I tapped on the door, this tall man with glasses came out and looked me up and down. He had the look like I was disturbing him. J.J. then pushed me aside and proceeded to tell the professor that he was in arrears on his bill and that he needed to pay. The professor looked at J.J., who was short and robust looking, like he was built to the ground, and the professor said to J.J., "How dare you insult me by demanding money? I will pay this bill when I decide it is time to pay you, and keep in mind to whom you are speaking." J.J. then let loose with a tirade of abuse at the professor, saying, "I don't give a rat's ass who you think you are. In my eyes, you are a piece of shit. You pay this bill, or I will go to the university and turn your ass in." With that, the professor went in and came out with the check, and J.J. said, "You are a monthly account; one more missed payment, and I will put you on a weekly basis." When we left, I said to J.J., "This is not the projects; this asshole could turn you in to the office." "Did I not get the goddamn money?" J.J. said. "You can't let these people shit on you. They are nothing but educated assholes anyway. If poor people pay their bills every week, why can't they pay like everybody else?" Well, it worked. The professor was not late anymore, so every time I had problem of someone not paying on time, I would send J.J. He loved to break the balls of the eggheads at Yale, and I think he got his fix just going after them.

When J.J. was a route man, his route consisted of the public housing projects in the Wooster square area. He had two boys assisting him every day, so in that respect, J.J. dealt with mostly blue collar people as the mainstay of his customer base. Going from that area of the city to Yale was quite a leap for him, having to deal with mostly white collar customers. J.J. was promoted to supervisor about the time that I was hired. There were a lot of stories about him, how he would go and collect from his customers with a little black bag and carry a gun with him for protection, and also how he would give the poorest of his customers a free turkey on Thanksgiving.

When my brother Frank was a young boy, he worked on a milk truck as a helper, and he would tell me to go and try to get a job as a milk-man, telling me about how much money that I could earn and that it was better than working in the factories. At that time, the hours did not please me, being single at this time, and my mind was on having a good time with my friends and dating the ladies.

As a young man, I could remember the Brock Hall man delivering milk with a horse and wagon and how the horse would move from house to house by himself as the man delivered the milk. The horse had the route all timed down. That's where the terminology for where we housed the trucks came from: it wasn't called a garage but a barn because of the days when horses were used, before the advent of trucks.

One of the funniest times was when the dairy ran contests for different products that they wanted to promote and push up sales on an item that was not selling well. I say funny because this one man did all kinds of crazy stuff to win most of the contests. The one that stood out from all the rest was when they were having a chocolate milk contest. What he did was order all chocolate milk for his customers, telling them that there was a shortage of white milk, and for the next two weeks, they would have to use chocolate milk. Some of his customers called the dairy and said their coffee did not taste well because of the chocolate milk. The prize for the contest was a Lazy Boy recliner chair, and he won it hands down, but not without getting a lot of flak from the manager. He was told not to pull that shit again, or he would be fired. He did not intend to make this his life's work, so losing this job did not seem to worry him.

JULY 1959 - JUNE 82: Wonder Bread

At about this time, late '58 to early '59, sales on milk routes were going down due to the arrival of the milk stores, brought on by the legalization of the gallon jug. This made it possible for the stores to sell a gallon of milk cheaper, which was nearly half the price of purchasing four quarts. Most customers who were purchasing four or more quarts every other day decided to go to the milk store, and so it was set in motion, ending the home delivery system. The job that I thought was going to be a lifetime job suddenly started to come to an end. As route sales started downhill, the dairy started to take off routes, combining them with other routes.

I heard Wonder Bread was going to start putting on routes just to sell snack cake. This was a separate venture from the bread routes because the bread routes were handling the brand of Hostess Cake. They wanted to increase sales on their bread routes by having the bread men just sell the bread. Not having time to sell both, a whole new business was started by having cake routes and bread routes.

At this time, the procedure was for a person interested in sales to spend time working in the bakery, and then apply for a sales job. I knew a lot of the people who had to do that, but because they needed so many people with some route experience, they were bypassing the system they had in place. I found out the name of the sales manager, Pete Martin, who was doing the interviewing for the new positions, and on meeting him for the first time, I got the impression he was looking for someone with a little more experience than I had. After several trips up to Wonder Bread, he said, "Leo, I have your phone number, and I will call you as soon as something breaks." I was used to being told that by this time in my life, but I told Pete, "No, I will be seeing you," which I did. Whenever I would run into him on his way in and out the markets, I would approach him. Sometimes, the conversation would be about nothing, but I let him know of my desire to work there.

My big break came when I told my good friend Nick, who was my supervisor from Sealtest, how I wanted to get into Wonder Bread. He said, "Why the hell did you not tell me? My brother is a supervisor there, and he is the supervisor for Hostess Cake." "Nick, you bastard," I said, "Now you tell me. I must have worn out a pair of shoes going up to Wonder Bread." Then Nick set up a meeting at his house for me to meet his brother Sal. On meeting his brother Sal, who was more formal than the fun guy that Nick was, I was not too pleased, since Sal had this air of superiority about him. But I wanted the job badly and was going to overlook that quality about him.

Sal then set up a meeting with Pete Martin, and after talking with Pete for awhile, Pete turned to me and said, "I am sorry for the problem I caused you. I misunderstood your qualifications and did not understand how much of a desire you had to work here. I know you won't disappoint me." This is the bullshit I had to go through just to get a route man's job, knowing someone who could open doors for you. After all this trouble to get into Wonder Bread, and having to pester Pete Martin for such a long time, and even needing a helping hand to land this job, I said, "Pete, I am here to earn a good living, and you will not have to worry about me breaking your balls." With that out the way, Pete shook my hand and looked me in the eye: "I think you will be one of my best hires." Indeed, he became my mentor and best friend.

On starting out on the job, I had to go through a program teaching me all about the products that they sold. I had to spend two days going through the Hostess Plant, showing me how all the products were produced, and the other three days in a classroom. At the end of the week, I was tested to see how much I had learned. I passed the test, but one of the other fellows who went through this with me failed. He also had someone to help him get the job, but I could see the interest in him was not there. The training program continued with having me ride with different route men, and they would have to report back to Sal the supervisor, grading me in how well I did. I always got a good report because I would really help the route man do all the heavy work. Just a little trick I learned was that "a little grease goes a long way." I hit it off really good with all the cake drivers.

Hostess Cake was in its infancy when I arrived. To start with, the process of relieving the bread routes of this product caused a lot of dissension from the bread men. This was part of their sales on the bread routes, and they did not want to give it up, so the bread men did everything to sabotage the program by telling the grocers, "Now you have two people coming from the same company, and that's one more person you have to put up with" where before all the product came in by one man.

The training that I got from this would serve me later on when I had to start my own business. I actually had to go out and build up a route where none existed. The customers I was given from the bread routes were not enough to sustain a route. Ten to twelve hours daily was the norm, and I left home in the dark and returned home in the dark. I had to fight for space in every store just to place my product. That was part of the job; some stores where so small that the allotted space for my cake was on top of canned goods that were on display. This was all before the arrival of the chain stores. We dealt mostly with mom and pop stores. My product line was five snack items and a box of doughnuts.

Some of these stores had a cash flow where all the vendors would try to get to the store, before everybody else, because if you did not get there in time, the grocer would not have any money to pay you. To see all the vendors going from street to street, bypassing some stores and jumping around to who has the money to pay you, was very comical, to say the least. Looking back at what I had to do just to sell my cake was crazy.

Later on, as the routes were building up, the company would cut your route, taking some of your customers and some from another route, and making a new route. With me, it meant that I was being pushed more out to the towns into the country, which, at first, I did not like because it meant more driving for me, but the best part of it was I did not have to worry about beating anybody to store just to get paid. It was like a different world where I did not have to fight for space, and the treatment from the grocers was nice. They talked to you like a gentleman and did not shout at you, like the city grocers did.

I think back to the time when I had a store near Yale, and how this grocer treated the vendors like crap, even telling us to wipe our feet before we came into his store. The store was owned by two brothers and a sister, and the three were a bunch of bastards in their treatment of us. One week, a son of bread man from a private company was running the route for his father who was sick, and the son had heard from his father about all the problems he was having with this account. He needed the store because of the sales he was getting from the store, but he was tired of all the bullshit he had to take from these people. I was standing at the counter getting checked in by one of the brothers, and standing next to me was John the son of the man who was sick. John was listening as I was getting checked, hearing the brother breaking my balls about me bringing in too much product. This was normal for me with this asshole, so I just took it in stride, having to get my money and get out of there. No sooner had I left the counter and started to put my cake on the shelf, when I heard John being questioned about his delivery. In an explosive second, John grabbed the little shit head by the neck and pulled him clean off his feet and across the counter. John, who by then was choking the grocer, told the asshole, "My name is John, and the next time you see my father, you so much as raise your voice to him, I will come back and beat the shit out of you." John then threw the grocer on the floor and walked out. If this had happened today, the driver would have been arrested for assault and battery, but after that, the word got around the route of what transpired in the store, and all the vendors were delighted by what they heard because that family was a hateful gang. I was treated well after that; they even called me by name.

The price of a Hostess cupcake was ten cents when I started for Hostess cake. The wholesale price was eight cents to the grocer, so to sell one thousand dollars a week of product, you had to handle quite a bit of cake. In the summer months, selling five hundred dollars a week was considered good, since ice cream and soda were the top sellers.

CHAPTER FOUR

The Men and Women

JOHN THE GROCER

On my route I had a wonderful relationship with a customer of mine named John. He was my mentor of sorts; I would ask him for advice on many subjects, especially during the time I was looking to purchase a home. John was very helpful in pointing out the many flaws with today's homes and on the other hand, what he considered to be a well-built home. Being a city person, my knowledge of building materials was little to nothing.

John had a wonderful family that was very close, and most of them were also involved in the business. I admired the family greatly; our friendship went beyond buyer and seller, so much so that, I became part of the fixtures in the store so to speak. John told me of the many pitfalls of his experience with owning a home but also the joy of giving his family a nice place to live.

John, on occasion, would convey some of his personal problems, which had to do with family and business. Mostly they were of a minor nature, and so it was one day, during a slow day in the store that John asked me to sit down and have some coffee with him. I pulled up an empty crate while John sat on a bench, and he said he wanted to tell me a personal story that transpired many years before.

We always talked about our time in the service, mine being during peacetime, after the war, and John's time during the early part of the war. He was never one to personalize his achievements in the service; we mostly talked of his anxiety of going overseas and other general topics. I know many men who had seen battle were reluctant to discuss their fears and the horrors of war.

Normally I would make John laugh as I made light of my peacetime service, being stationed in San Juan, Puerto Rico, and regale him with sea stories of bullshit, but on this day John was in a somber tone. He said he had a story to tell me that bordered on the insane, and he knew he would have confidence in confiding in me. Since this bizarre story happened early on in his life, he just felt the need to express it.

Here is the story of a young man who was confronted with a problem of the highest magnitude. When John got his draft notice, he was notified to report for duty in the early part of 1943. His brother was already in the service, preceding him by about a year, and at the time his brother got married to his childhood girlfriend while on leave from the army.

After John got his basic training, he was given some time to go home but was told he would have to soon report to New York City for deployment overseas, mainly to Europe. He then planned a "last fling" weekend with his buddies. At that age, young men were trying to get as much as they could out of life. In such a short time they were going from boyhood to manhood. Time was moving quickly for them, but they were trying to savor life as much as possible.

The first place that most soldiers frequented was the bars. They wanted to have some drinks and not think about the future that lay ahead of them. All the rumors of death and destruction were on their mind but this weekend was for fun and games, perhaps finding a girl to share some time with and go dancing or listen to music. Anything to not think about what was in front of them. John and his two buddies decided to go to clubbing in this nice location that was on the main floor of a hotel, which was a favorite place for servicemen due to the many groups of available girls, everyone just looking for a good time.

As John and his buddies sat at the bar, just drinking and joking around, forgetting for a moment why they were there, but knowing this would be their last weekend, they see these two girls sitting at a table. They noticed the girls were not paying attention to anyone in particular, so they decide to go over and join them. The girls asked them to sit down, and after several drinks and a lot of fun conversation, the girls said they wanted to go dancing. Since there were three of them and only two girls, John begs out and tells them to go on ahead without him, and he will catch up with them later.

The girls tell John to come on along and say they will find him someone for him, but he still declines. So now John is left sitting at the bar and was getting friendly with the bartender. The bartender, Dave, asked John what he was planning for the rest of the evening, so John says, "Hopefully I'll try and meet someone to have a good time with." Dave then tells John, "If you are looking for a lady, I will be able to help you out." Nervously, John responds, "How so?" Dave tells John, "Go a secure a room upstairs, and I will send you up a nice lady."

Now here is John, who never had an experience with a lady of the evening. He was mulling over in his mind, and eventually John decides yes. He tells Dave he will right back and gives him the room number. So now John is going to have his first encounter with a hooker. Dave tells John the password will be his name so that John will know it will be the hooker knocking at his door.

As John goes up to his room to await the arrival of the hooker, he pulls down the shades of the window and turns down the lights. As time goes by, John is now pacing the floor, as this is his first time with a complete stranger, or with anyone for that matter. John's mind was racing with thoughts of what he should say or do when he meets her. He was told she was young and beautiful so he could relate to her. Dave told John, "Let the lady go about her business, and you will be happy." Dave sensed John's hesitation so he tells John to relax and just enjoy his encounter, and he will see him later. As the hour of his appointment approached, John started to perspire a little, and he kept toweling himself off so that wouldn't be embarrassed when he saw her. While he waited, he looked around the room to take in the moment. He noticed the hallway had a carpet only in the middle of the hall with wood showing on both sides, the lighting of the room kind of dim, and although this hotel was not considered a "fleabag", but also not a four-star hotel. John was all of eighteen years old, and his life was about to change.

John hears very faint footsteps coming down the hallway, but they were increasing in volume. As the footsteps became more pronounced, John went from sitting on the bed to sitting on the chair and back to the bed; the anticipation of meeting the hooker was now at a fever pitch.

Then like a bolt, there was pounding at the door. John jumps from the bed, gathers himself, then slowly goes to the door. With his hand on the doorknob, he inquires the person to speak, waiting for the password. When the person gives the name, "Dave the bartender," John slowly opens the door. The vision he is confronted with is of a girl with black hair and a bright yellow dress. The lighting in the hallway being was very dim but it cast a shadow over her, illuminating her from behind.

As John swings the door wide open, the shock that is before him is without question one of sheer disbelief. Two people frozen with surprise, both had the expression of a deer caught in the headlights, a moment in time that will forever be framed in their lives. Their eyes now were locked in an expressional stance, both not knowing what to say, John stumbling for words, the lady's face now turning ashen white with guilt.

The hooker at the door is none other than John's sister-in-law.

John pulls his sister-in-law into the room, closes the door, and sits her down on the chair, "Ann, what the fuck are you doing?" Ann is now crying and trembling, trying to answer John. John begins stomping around the room, the shock still reverberating throughout his body. He started banging the furniture to make sense of this encounter, all the while asking, "Why, why, why?" All the while, Ann was crying out trying to answer.

Finally controlling her emotions long enough to answer: "I wanted to have some money for when Sal comes home, so that we can purchase a home." She shows him the money to prove it, then goes into a rambling story of her love for Sal and how she started doing this a short while ago. Fumbling over her words, she continues to profess her love for Sal, and explain how she was planning to have a nice family when he got home.

Now John was faced with a decision. Should he tell his brother or keep this between the two of them? What the hell is he going to do? With Ann begging John to let this slide, refreshing John's mind with the many good values she had, which at the moment were questionable. Ann was asking for something so great for a brother in law to give her a pass. In addition, a brother was hiding a shocking revelation from his own brother. As I mentioned earlier, John was only eighteen years old, and now faced with the prospect of keeping this grave secret.

Knowing Ann, John was trying to remember her from the time Sal started dating her. How she adored Sal and doted on him as if they were married. Of the many times Sal had Ann over at the house, this would be a tough nut to swallow, but John then tells Ann, "For now, until I get back, this will keep." Ultimately, John felt he did not want to burden his brother with this news, especially since he was in some serious battles already.

After the war, when Sal got discharged before John because of the point system, he and Ann were in the process of purchasing a home, and Ann was pregnant with their first child. As John entered the flat where Ann and Sal were staying, greeting everyone, John and Ann locked eyes, and John knew then that he would keep the secret. The manner of love Ann bestowed upon Sal was genuine; John knew it was not fabricated. Ann and Sal went on to have three children, and it turned out to be a secret well kept; Ann was a wonderful wife and mother.

Ann, John, and Sal have now passed away, but this story of a young boy who some would argue did or did not do the right thing, has stayed with me. It is a statement of compassion, and of loyalty, but also it was a story of love and intrigue.

This next strange story is of a woman, who by today's standards, would be put in jail. In my neighborhood, there was a great variety of grocery stores, but this one was exceptional. It was a small store, which catered to the needs of little grocery items. Mary lived in the back of the store with her family. Upon entering the store, she would size the men up with a look of mischief written all over her face. She was clearly a woman intent on causing pain to men in the crudest fashion.

So it was at the beginning of my career with Wonder Bread, and

I had the misfortune of having a pain in the ass train me, but I was soon to repay this guy, big time. Since he did not know the territory well, and never been in the area, he only had the list of stores we were supposed to do.

On the other hand, this was my old neighborhood that I grew up in. I told the trainer, Pete, that I would show him around the area and introduce him to all the grocery store owners. At the time he was trying to become a supervisor, so he wanted to make an impression on everyone in the area, so I agreed to help him. Pete was about to have a life changing moment. I positioned the route so that by the time we got to Mary's store, the truck would need to be rearranged. As I stated, it was a small store that we were not expected to leave much product. Pete, being the lazy bastard that he was, ordered me to fix up the truck and said that he would go in and see how much product to bring in. I could not wait to see what would happen next.

Pete goes in the store, and I go to the side window. I told Pete the woman's name is Mary, I said, "Call her by her name, she likes that." From the side window, I would have a perfect view. I would be able to see Mary coming down the stairs into the store, and as she usually did, stop at the top of the stairs, with that shit eating look on her face to survey her prey.

Pete was standing there waiting to greet Mary when she came from behind the counter. Mary was no more than five feet tall, but she had the strength of a bull, and she had this nasty habit of going for the balls of men, even with her husband in the store. So like a serpent, she grabs Pete by the testicles, and gives him quite a squeeze. Pete jumps into the air, screaming, but Mary refused to let go. Here was Pete, all of six feet tall and over two hundred pounds, wiggling his arms, trying to push Mary off. By this time other people from the neighborhood, all laughing their asses off. They had heard the screams, which was Mary's way of greeting the men.

Naturally, when Pete finally came out of the store, I knew what he was going to say. He was not a happy camper, stating, "Leo, you son of a bitch, you set me up." "Pete," I say, "I have not been in that store for quite some time. Mary must have gone crazy. What the hell did she do to you?" He screams back, "You son of bitch, you know damn well what she did!" Pete was walking around like he had a crooked back he could not straighten up. "Honestly Pete," I say, "It has been years since I was in that store." All the while, I was trying my best not to laugh in his face. Anyone who lived in the area knew about her nasty habit, so naturally the wives would never send their husbands into that store, but as kids, we would taunt Mary.

Today that scene would be played out on YouTube, and most surely, some kind of social punishment would be administered. Mary was one crazy bitch. It was many years later, after the fact, when I fessed up what I had known to Pete. By then, we had a working relationship, and for the most part, a cool but friendly atmosphere. But just to make sure he didn't get to be too much of an asshole, every time Pete was in a good mood, I would remind him of Mary.

Whenever men from the area had to go into that store, they knew enough to keep their distance. She did go after me one time, but I was able elude her by waving an empty basket in front of her. After a while you knew not to let her get to close to you. I pitied the new salesmen who went in there and got baptized quickly. That little bitch was as fast as a snake; she would spring on you even by a distance of say a couple of feet.

On my route, there was a grocer who of German decent, who spoke with a hard to understand dialect. I believe he made it more difficult on purpose, especially when it came time to pay you. All the vendors warned me about him, as he always would try to get your attention away from the transaction at hand. What he would do is keep talking to you while paying for the product you brought in, all the while he had his hand on the money that was in front of him. Then he would ask you some stupid question about the product. This day in question I kept my eye on the money and watched him at the same time. He would start to slide the money back towards him and divert your attention to something else. He must have had success with this many times for him to try and pull it off with me. It was a little like three card Monty.

Snowstorms were a blessing and also a curse. The good part was that all the stores would sell out all your products, but the bad part was trying to get around the city to do your route. When we had a forecast of an oncoming storm, we would load up the stores with extra product. One of the worst storms occurred about the early 1960s. It was so bad that Pete Martin, the sales manager, came in early that morning and advised us not to jeopardize our safety and to get back as soon as possible. He truly was worried about anybody getting injured, but he did not have the authority to have us forego not going out that day. In those days, the routes always had to go out no matter what. Pete came up through the ranks and never forgot what it was like to work in bad weather. He stood on the platform that day, telling everybody the same thing. Pete Martin was the best sales manager I ever worked for.

The snow started to grow in intensity almost as soon we left for our routes. My route at that time was centered around the Fair Haven section of the city. I started to unload more product than usual in the first stops that I made since every store got a double order. Around about ten o'clock in the morning, with the snow staring to pile up, and the streets started to become impassable, I was on the corner of Haven and Grand Avenue. My truck was in the middle of the street because I could not get too close to the curb for fear of being stuck. The rear end of my truck was on Grand Avenue, but I could not turn the truck around. As I decided to head back to the garage on Goffe Street, the snow was hubcap deep. I drove the truck backwards down Grand Avenue towards East Street where I figured it would give me room to turn my truck forward. The distance was about the size of four city blocks, and I opened the back doors of my truck so that I could have some better vision. When I got to East Street, I had just enough space to turn the truck around and head towards Goffe Street. A trip that would take me about fifteen minutes normally turned into a two hour ordeal.

I arrived back about noon and was met by the manager of the bakery. I was one of the first to come back, and he had the audacity to ask me about how my sales were that day. This man's name was Jack, and he had no compassion for anybody. In his eyes, you were a commodity that could be replaced, and he wanted to know if I had finished the route. At this time, Pete came down to the platform and heard the conversation and told Jack the manager, "This guy is one of the smart ones because I told them all this morning that I did not want anyone getting hurt. We can make up for the lost sales another day." Jack just looked at Pete saying, "We can discuss this in my office." Pete would defend his workers to the death. To Pete Martin, he valued the lives of his men above all else.

As I was able to get in early enough, I decided to try and make it home. After some two hours, I finally got home from a distance that usually took about twenty minutes. The men that came in later from their routes had no choice but to spend the night up in the attic of the bakery, sleeping on the floor or on chairs. For food, they had plenty of bread and cake to eat.

My friend Ralph Barrie was stuck up in Hamden and had a hard time traveling the short distance to the bakery. Being out in the snow for a great length of time and having his clothes get wet, Ralph came down with pneumonia, which was to plague him for years because he had caught a virus and it settled in his eye. He was out of work for three months, and it literally took years to correct his eye sight. After much exhaustive visits to doctors, he was able to finally find an eye surgeon who helped him restore his eyesight to a better level than he had before.

Ralph and I often have conversations about all the crazy stuff that went on in the bread business. We both had the same supervisor, and after Sal our supervisor got fired for bad mouthing a manager of a supermarket, Sal had been replaced by what we in the service used to call ninety day wonders. This man's name was Al, and he wanted to make a name for himself and advance as quickly as possible. He would work long hours and wanted you to do the same. We would say, "Maybe this creep does not have a home to go to.' He would be out until seven or eight in the evening after starting at four in the morning.

One of the funniest things that Ralph did was when Al rode with him one day. Al had this habit of talking to the grocers, not seeming to care how long he spent in the store, or how long the job took. All the while, Ralph was worried about getting to the next stop. I know how Ralph felt because I argued with Al about the same problem. I told Al, "I have a family waiting for me, and three children who have places to go in the evening. I do not want to keep them waiting for me to come home, as we have supper around five in the evening." Al looked at me like I was crazy. Then this one day, when it was Ralph's turn to have Al ride with him, Ralph had a large amount of product to sell. In short, Ralph was in no mood to waste any time listening to Al bullshit with the grocers. After a few stops, Ralph decided to fix Al for good. He waited until he got to the part of his route which was a great distance from the Bakery, and while Al was in the store talking to the grocer, Ralph gave a toot on the horn. Al did not respond, so Ralph left Al stranded out on the route, and Al had to call the bakery for a ride back. As Ralph was driving away, he looked in the rear view mirror, and he saw Al standing on the corner looking for the truck. Ralph just laughed his ass off.

When we all found out what Ralph did, everybody was elated to say the least, but the bosses at the bakery did not find it funny. Ralph was marched into the office and had his ass reamed out. Al said, "I want this man fired," but according to the rules of the union, this could only happen in the case of a shortage of money, or not keeping his product up to code, and you still had to be given a written warning. At this, Al was fuming that he could not get Ralph fired.

My bad turn was when Al had to run my route when I had a two week vacation. I left the route in such a beautiful condition so that Al would not have any problems. Instead, what the bastard did was he told the bakery manager that I was underselling the route and not getting the sales that Al said that I should. In short, he wanted to make me look like a fool. On my return from my vacation, when I went to get my order, I found a double order. Al knew that this would create a lot of returns and make me look bad because he told the manager the route could easily sell that amount, even though the son of a bitch knew better. I guess my friendship with Ralph had a lot to do with Al coming after me.

At this time my mother had just passed away a few months earlier, and I was in no mood for any of this crap, so when I got back to the sales room, Al was in his office and gloating over the fact that he was making me work my ass off. When I looked at the smirk on his face, I could not take it any longer, and I went into a wild rage and flung all my books at him and called him a dumb ass. At this time, the sales manager came out of his office, and all the route men tried to calm me down.

Frank was our new sales manager, and he called me and Al into his office and wanted to know why I had gotten so mad. After Al and I told our versions, Frank said that Al was only trying to help me. I proved to Frank my sales were consistent with my returns. Frank told the both of us to apologize to one another, but that was not end of it. Al spent all his time trying to discredit me, which thankfully did not last long because the company got rid of him.

Our new sales manager Frank was brought in to replace Pete Martin solely because the company felt that Pete was too friendly with the route men and did not serve the best interest of the company. Pete never forgot where he came from; he knew the many pitfalls of having to deal with the pressures of route sales, and he always kept that in mind. Whenever there was a problem on your route, he would call you into his office and speak to you in private. He was truly a great gentleman, and he treated you as person, not as a number.

When Ralph got sick and was out of work for three months, Pete would visit him often. I was to find out myself later on when I fell on an icy sidewalk and was in the hospital for two weeks, what kind of a man Pete really was. One day, he came to the hospital and kidding around, tried speaking what he called Italian. I said, "Your English is just as bad." With that, he laughed and reached in his pocket and pulled out a wad of money and offered it to me, saying, "I want to help you out because I know you will be out of work for a while." "Pete," I said, "At this time, I am alright because the union is giving me seventy five dollars a week. If I need it, I will accept your offer." Pete then said, "You call me, and I will come right over your house." I was also out of work about three months at that time, and Pete would come over or call me to see how I was doing. He said, "I will hold your route for you as long as I can." The union rules were that as long as a doctor verified your problem, the company had to abide by that ruling.

PETE AND THE BAKERY MANAGERS

One of the first bakery managers that I worked under was a man named Gordon Woodward. He had come from a wealthy family, and it showed in his approach to the men and the business by his gentleman manners and always addressing people with a lot of respect. He appreciated your effort no matter what position you held in the company. Gordon gave Pete a lot of leeway in letting Pete make all the decisions as far as the sales force was concerned. He was smart enough to know that Pete knew the bread and cake business, and he never interfered with Pete. He would sit in his office and take care of the financial part of the bakery. He and Pete made for a great team. One day, Gordon called me into his office as I was going into the sales room and wanted my advice on a new product that he wanted to push. The product was a new box of donuts that he called an elongated box and was excited about the sales of the donuts. I felt proud that he singled me out for my opinion, which was one of his ways to make you feel important. Gordon also gave me permission to arrange for a Christmas party for the sales force, and I took advantage of his good nature and arranged the Christmas party.

Our next bakery manager was a man by the name of Lou. He was a loner and not very friendly. Most of all, he and Pete locked horns on many occasions, as he did not like the idea of Pete having full control. The policy of Wonder Bread was to change managers every two or three years and move them up to the corporate office. It was a stepping stone for them, and they had to improve on what the previous manager did. Lou was making a big mistake by sidestepping over Pete. When it came time for me to go into his office to tell him about the upcoming Christmas party, I had all the information and pricing for the party, but he looked at the cost of the party and said, "Are you out of your mind? This is way too much. I will offer only one hundred dollars." I told him, "Lou, I have over forty people that want to come. This is unacceptable, and we will do this on our own." When I informed everyone, they responded by hanging a picture of Scrooge on the wall.

Our next bakery manager was a very outward and gregarious person, who really got involved with the sales staff. Bob also had the good sense not to interfere in the way Pete was getting good results, which made Bob look good to the front office. All the sales people would joke about how there was never anything on his desk. Pete had the whole bakery producing at top level, and the morale was excellent, both in the production and sales, so this left Bob to concentrate on super promotions. Bob was great at that: he was like a kid in a candy store in the way he would dream up ideas to promote the product. There was a time he had to promote a new loaf of bread and had the meeting located in a television studio with all the bread men present. This was to be a special event, and with cameras rolling, Bob came riding in the large door of the studio on a white horse dressed as a gladiator, saying, "Where can I find the new wonder Bread?" The place erupted in explosive laughter and cheering. Another promotion was with the product known as Twinkie, and he came in dressed as Twinkie the kid. It was a child's program on Channel eight. Bob was not afraid to spend money to promote the sale of Wonder Bread and hostess cake. One way was to take the grocers who were giving us the best location in their stores along with a bunch of sales people to Yankee stadium to see the New York giants. This was in the old Yankee stadium, a far cry from Lou..

During the time Bob was the bakery manager, he and Pete put together a great team by bringing management and labor together, and setting the stage for a wonderful workplace environment. It was truly a pleasure to come in and see Bob. Sometimes, he would arrive early and watch us load our trucks and inquire about our families. While Pete and Bob had a great rapport, there were forces in the front office that wanted to get rid of Pete because of his attachment with all the personnel, both in the bakery and the sales force. What they wanted was a more robust approach towards all the workers. Bob knew this and protected Pete, but from what I learned later on, this took a toll on Pete, just the thought of him being replaced by someone in the front office, his position that he loved more than anything else taken away. This was his life, and now it was slipping away from him.

As the months went by, I, along with everybody else, noticed a change in the way Pete was doing his job. He seemed to be so preoccupied with this problem that his manner of speaking was noticeable in the way he addressed you. We knew he was drinking. You could tell by the way he walked: he had lost that quick step and was sort of dragging his feet. This was a man who came up from the ranks and attained a position of sales manager, which was at the time considered a lucrative position. Pete coming in late for work on some days was a telling sign that something was going to happen. Even with Bob covering for him, you knew it could not last. The demise of a great individual brought about by some jealous people who wanted him out and replaced with one of their cronies was a tragedy.

The shock came when I got a call from one of my friends that Pete Martin had passed on. The excuse from the company was that Pete died from an enlarged heart, which was true, but also caused by his heavy drinking due to his worrying about losing his job. It was a shame to see all the people from the main office come to Pete's wake. What a bunch of phonies. I along with most of the sales people ignored their presence. I went up to Mrs. Martin and expressed my condolences. She embraced me and inquired about my back. I was a little bit surprised about the inquiry. Mrs. Martin said, "Pete always had your interest at heart" and that he would discuss all the problems any of his men had, be it financial, or for health reasons. She made a note of asking me about my two daughters, even remembering their names, Gail and Janet, because at that time, Wonder Bread had a policy of giving baby blankets whenever a baby was born, and she was the one who made out the cards. She was a carbon copy of Pete Martin.

While the death of Pete was bad, the other shocker came when Bob was promoted, and we had to have a new sales manager named Frank, and a new bakery manager who was strait-laced, one of those guys who wanted to run everything by the book. He was only interested in numbers and did not care about anything else. A very cold man, he and the sales manager made a good pair. The new bakery manager's name was Tom. His last name rhymed with a man's package, and that's why I am omitting it here, but we did have a lot of fun with it. I was one of the first guys that he decided to use as his pet project, wanting to upgrade my route and show everybody else how he can get more sales out of a route. He also felt that I had more potential than anyone else because of the area that my route covered.

Little did he know that I already had all the best locations in every store, and that he would be wasting his time. But he found out in a hurry when he and Frank spent the better part of a week trying to poke holes in any weakness that I had. Every store told them the same thing that the service was great, and their stores were never out of product. Not to come away empty-handed, Tom and Frank went into one of my biggest supermarkets and started to dismantle my display. When the manager of the store, Mr. Johnson, approached them and wanted to know what the hell they were doing, they introduced themselves as representatives of Wonder Bread and told Mr. Johnson that they were placing the product in the order that it said should be. Mr. Johnson looked at the both of them and said, "You guys put the product back on the shelf and leave this store. I am totally satisfied with Leo's service and his display, and do not come back to this store unless I call you." When Mr. Johnson told me what happened, he said, "Their faces turned beet red; they were totally dumbfounded by the way he lectured them in front of the customers in the store." That ended the debacle of trying to discredit me. Johnson treated his employees and vendors with equal respect because he never forgot where he came from. But that did not stop Tom from every once in while giving me a jolt or two whenever he could. You know that old saying: "You can win the battle but lose the war."

A good family friend who worked in the bakery named Sid was a hardworking man who never missed a day of work, even coming in during the worst storms to get the bread out to the route men. He was fired by Tom for taking two loaves of bread home. But this bread was what they called the rejects because it was going to be discarded anyway. As Sid was leaving to go to his car that day, Tom had happened to be passing by the parking lot and saw Sid with the bread. The union tried to get Sid his job back, but the rules were you cannot take anything out of the bakery without paying for it, no matter how bad the product was. Tom was steadfast and would not give Sid a break, which made all the employees have even more hatred for this creep Tom. Tom could have given Sid a two day suspension, thereby Tom would still be able to say that nobody is going to get away with anything. But Tom would not have any of that. He wanted to set an example with Sid.

So to stick it to Tom, a lot of the bakery employees brought in all of the products that Wonder was not selling and made it a point to leave all the wrappers where Tom would see them, especially in the break room. Now that really got Tom mad. We did a lot of crazy stuff to antagonize Tom. I would put the empty bread racks in the doorway leading up to the sales room and just jam the platform so that Tom had to go around to the front of the building to get into the bakery. This got Tom fuming mad and he said he was going to find out who was responsible for this. Of all the guys to address this to, it was ironic he told me. When I told the guys about this, we had such a laugh to think I made such a fool out of him.

Another time to harass Tom was when we had a sale's meeting in another town, which was quite a distance for us to travel, knowing we had to listen to two hours of bullshit and then have to drive home, getting home at a late hour, and get up early the next day for work. As the guys and I left the meeting with everybody really pissed off about attending this meeting, I found a pair of wooden horses that were used for construction sites, and I picked them up and placed them on Tom's car. The parking lot cleared out fast because nobody wanted to be the last one to leave. Again, Tom came into the sales room and addressed all of the route men about the incident. And who the hell was Tom standing next to but me. I don't know how the hell I did not burst into laughter. I had to quickly make some excuse about having to go to the men's room. Everybody had a hard time containing their composure. The little bastard never found out about the racks or the wooden horses on the car.

The morale was at an all-time low with this combination of Tom and Frank. They had the whole bakery and sales force in a very bad mood. At a meeting of all the supervisors and heads of the departments, Tom asked the people present why this was so, but nobody in the room had the nerve to tell Tom what the problem was. But the head of all the mechanics in the garage got up and told Tom, "You are the problem. Ever since you got here, you run this place like an army camp. These are all good people, trying to earn a living. Try being a little more compassionate with the workers." And with that, Nick, the head mechanic, sat down. We feared Tom was going to go after him, but instead, Tom went up to Nick and thanked him for his honesty and standing up to him.

As it turned out, another problem was on the horizon: Wonder bread decided to close all the small bakeries and open up a large bakery up in Massachusetts, and close New Haven, Hartford, and Bridgeport. My route was either going to Milford or Meriden. I was hoping to go to Milford, as it would be a lot closer to home, and mostly all the guys that I worked with were going there, but the company decided to send my route and my friend Dick's route to Meriden, since our routes ran along the shore line, and they felt it would be better for them.

One of the nicest things that happened for me was when the agency manager, Stanley, said the people in New Haven did not give you and Dick a good report, but as far as he was concerned, we were starting here with a fresh page. "All I want from you guys is a good day's work, and I will be in your corner no matter what," he said. We shook hands, and from then on, it made for good working terms between Stanley, Dick, and I.

As the months went by, I had picked up a lot of new business, and now my route was up at the top of the charts. Stanley called me into his office one day and said, "Leo, this is the report that they gave me on you. I'd like to tell them to shove this up their ass, but instead, I am going to tear it up." And with that Stanley shook my hand and said, "Leo, I think this is the beginning of a great friend ship," to borrow a line from the movie Casablanca.

Indeed, Stanley and I had such a great time working together that one day after work, he invited me over to his home and introduced me to his wife and family. Stanley was of Polish decent and his wife was

Italian. On meeting his wife the first thing, I said, "Stanley! I knew that's why I liked you! You are half Italian." Stanley then told me, "They also told me that you were a ball breaker, but a nice one."

Having to travel thirty miles just to get to work was starting to get to me, especially in the winter. I had to get up at three in the morning, arriving in Meriden about three forty five a.m. to start the truck and let it run for a little while. It was a diesel motor, which was a pain in the ass to start, but at that time, we did not have electric plugins to help start the damn motor. Our trucks had a cold running motor, so the heater and defroster were just about useless. It was so bad that one cold morning with the temperature hovering around zero, it took me over thirty minutes to just get the truck started. I was already freezing my ass off when I got to loading up the truck, but when I finished, the first thing I did was get as much cardboard I could find and put in and around my seat to keep whatever heat there was in the truck. I along with the rest of the men would put some of the cardboard in front of the radiator to try and make the truck warm, but it only help a little.

On this one particular morning, which is still seared in my memory, after I had loaded up the truck, it was now about five a.m. I started to drive to my first stop, which was from Meriden to Old Saybrook, and the forecast for that day was that it would not get past ten degrees. Driving down route nine to Old Saybrook, which normally took me thirty to forty minutes, took me one hour to arrive at my first stop. I was shaking so bad from the cold, even with two pairs of socks on and two sweaters and a jacket, because the cold was going right through me, my fingers numb by this time.

When I finally arrived at the store, which was a supermarket, it was about six in the morning. The door to the store was locked, since they did not let anyone in until six thirty. I banged on the door and pleaded for them to let me in as my feet were so cold that it was painful. Upon seeing me, the night manager opened the door and yelled to the clerk to go and get a pail of hot water. Then he removed my socks, got a chair for me to sit on, and put my feet gently in the hot water, and started to massage my feet, one at a time. I was so cold by now that tears were streaming from my eyes. It was the coldest day of my life.

The men even went into the truck and got the order for the store. The manager made out the bill for me and let me stay in his office until I was able to stand up and move my feet. He even offered to send one of the clerks to help me do the stores in the vicinity of his store, but I had to decline the offer because the company's policy was no riders unless sanctioned by the company. Now to make matters worse, a light rain started to fall, and it was turning icy. The windows were icing up, and I had to stop every few miles just to clear the windows. This was to be one of my longest and coldest days that has remained with me forever, and yet, it was a day that was so gratifying because of the way people came and tried to make me as comfortable as possible.

It took me three hours from Old Saybrook to Meriden that day because of having to stop and clear the windows. I never got to finish the route because I got rid of all my product as fast as I could in the first few stops, which were mostly all supermarkets. I decided to drive down I-95 to 91, since the back roads to Meriden would be all iced up. It wasn't much better, but at least I was moving. I would stop under bridges and get away from traffic as much as I could to clear the windows. Upon arriving back at the bakery agency, the bastards had the nerve to ask what I was doing back so early, since it was only about one in the afternoon. These two supervisors were setting out to go and check on the routes, and see how sales were going. At this time, traffic was almost at a standstill because of the icy conditions. The highways were a little better because of the highway department. To think, even in the most adverse weather, the company was only interested in how much you were selling.

That day, I was thinking of my friend Pete Martin, who only had the interest of his men at heart. I believed he would have called all his men back to the bakery as soon as they could. He was of a time when people came first, and he would worry about getting you home to your family. But now that Wonder Bread was taken over by a corporation, we were addressed by a number; they never referred to us by a name. It was a shock to me to think they did not know me. The people that were now in the front office I would classify as number crunchers: they wanted to know how much you were selling and how were your returns. They had a figure of returns of baked goods at five percent of your sales.

So to them, no matter how inclement the weather—rain, snow, or shine—you were expected to produce good sales. But with Stanley, I always had a feeling of being protected. He was a good family man, like Pete in a way; if you gave him a good shake, he would go all out for you in any situation. But as they say, all good things come to an end.

Next up came a new agency manager, a loser if there ever was one. According to the men who worked with him over the years, he was one of the worst route men in the agency, but because of his close ties with people in the front office, he was picked to be the agency manager. Stanley was transferred to an agency that was having problems, and the company picked Stanley to get the agency in shape.

One of the worst storms to hit was in the winter of 1978. At this time, the company was introducing the use of computers for the route men to use because they said that it would make all the bills more legible. The computers would print out a three part bill, which supposedly made it a lot easier to read, and it would also regulate how much product to put in the store according to the store's last sale.

The day they picked for the introduction of the computer was the day we had the big blizzard. All the route men had someone from the front office to show us how to use the computer, along with a little training they had given us. I was unfortunate in having one of the men who was in charge of all cake sales, a real go-getter, who was looking to make more of a name for himself. The day they picked was a Monday, which happened to be my busiest day because I had to do all the schools, along with the stores on my route. Usually on Monday, I only did the chain stores or else I would be out all night. It was about eleven o'clock when I had finally wound up at all the schools, but the man said now we can start doing the stores.

At this time, the snow was piling up on the roadways, and the going was very slippery. The man's named was Bob, "I think we can finish the route before it gets worse." We then got stuck in front of store. By now, the snow was really coming down, and I was saying, "Bob, after we get out of this ditch, I am going to go back to the agency." He, being a company man and all gung-ho, wanted to finish the route. But I said, "Not with me"".

After we dug out from that store, I started up the roadway and was heading into snow drifts that had the snow covering the wheel wells. I took the back roads from Clinton to Meriden because all the highways were having a lot of problems with people getting stuck right in the middle of the highway. It was about one o'clock when we got back to the agency, and the first thing I did was to figure out if I could get home by the highway, since at that time I-91 was still passable. I unloaded the truck and cashed in as fast as I could, while this asshole tried talking to me about the computer and sales. I had a little car that I bought to save gas because there was a shortage of gas, and it was then I decided to chance it and head for home. I did have worries about making the trip home, but I felt it was early enough, and maybe I could get through.

From exit 16 in Meriden, I started home. I got as far as exit 15, but the car was now struggling even in the middle of the highway. That was it, back to the agency. I no sooner parked the car in the yard and got stuck along the fence, when two men I worked said, "Let's go up to the hotel and get a room." One of the guys had his car near the roadway, and up the hill we went. We rushed into the hotel and was told it was all sold out.

Back to the agency we went, figuring we were going to spend the night in the garage, maybe having to sleep on the floor of the trucks. Then as luck would have it, Marty said he was going to take five of us to his house, which was two blocks from the agency. We were able to fit into one car that was not stuck and go to Marty's house. The only thing Marty did not do was tell his wife he was going to bring five guys home with him, and we all walked in shaking off the snow off our shoes. The look on Marty's wife as we walked into the house was priceless: her jaw just dropped, and she said, "Marty, why did you not call me?" Marty was the kind of guy who really never worried about saying or doing the right things. Marty's wife could not be more generous with herself to us. She tried to make us as comfortable as possible with the space she had. Marty and his wife set about trying to place us around the house. Marty had at that time two small children, and his house was not that large to fit us all in, so everybody picked a spot on the floor. That was where we were going to spend the time in the house. I was given a spot on the kitchen floor. I was given a heavy blanket and made a mattress out of it.

The first thing we did was to order a lot of takeout food, and load up the house with as much as we could. One of the foods I remember was about twelve large pizzas and plenty of beer. Two guys went out into the storm and got the food for us. After we all ate, the four other guys started to play cards. Since I was not a card player, I sat and talked to Marty and his wife and children. I asked Marty's wife if I could use her phone to call my family. "What the hell are you waiting for?" she said. "By all means, go right ahead. Same for the rest of you guys."

I spent the next two days and nights in Meriden because of the horrible storm. The first day after the storm we all went over to the agency and started to shovel our cars out of the snow, which was quite extensive. Since the Governor closed all the highways, we had to leave our cars at the agency. The best thing about the storm was that the bakery was not working, and they told us to take the rest of the week off. This was a surprise, since if there was a chance that they could produce the product, they would have sent us out on our routes.

To compensate Marty's wife for being such a generous person in making us feel as comfortable as possible, we gave her a little gift of forty dollars each and thanked her for putting us up. We all pitched in and cleaned up her house as best we could. She tried to stop us from cleaning the house, saying, it was her pleasure to have us over and that she would see us in the next snowstorm. We all had a good laugh, and as we all walked out the door, she gave each one of us nice hug, saying, "Thanks for stopping by," triggering more laughs.

BILL

While I was employed at Wonder Bread, I met a character named Bill. At that time I was running a route for Hostess Cake and Bill was working on a bread route. He was a very jovial and impulsive guy. He did things first, then surveyed the consequences. He was a ladies man of the first order; he had such a great personality, it was easy to see how he could charm the pants off any girl. But he also acted with such class, which was one of the reasons he was so successful on his route. He dealt mostly with the women who did the buying for the restaurants he delivered to.

The buyers would always favor Bill whenever they had a big party and he would get the orders instead of the other bakery people. The competitors hated him. Bill, on top of having a good amount of large restaurants, also had a great many luncheonettes, which were mostly small breakfast and lunch spots (very few of them today because of places like Dunkin Donuts). One of the small coffee shops that Bill delivered to was a place I used to stop and have coffee in the morning. This one was on my route and sometimes other drivers would also stop there. It was a nice coffee shop, and it gave us the opportunity to have a conversation about the days' happenings.

My sales manager Pete called me aside one day, and asked me if I would do him a favor. Pete said he had a problem and wanted to keep it from getting out of hand, as Pete was always trying to protect someone from losing their job. This was a serious matter and it involved Bill. Pete explained to me what the problem was and wanted me to start serving the coffee shop instead of Bill.

This was indeed a serious problem. It seems Bill was having an affair with the waitress, and to make matters worse, they were having assignations right in the kitchen area. Now, the owner was a fastidious person about keeping his kitchen clean. His name was Dan, not necessarily a neat freak, but he kept a clean place, especially his kitchen.

I had to go and see Dan and told him I would be bringing him his product. At this point he was not a happy camper and I asked Dan as a favor to Pete if he would not make an issue out of this; Pete did not want it to get back to Bill's family,

"Dan," I say, "If you could cut Bill some slack on this, Pete would be forever grateful," Dan responds, "Leo, how the hell do you think I feel? That son of a bitch was using my kitchen table for a bed, the table that I use to prepare food on," Dan was really incensed about this, so I told Dan that this was all the more reason you do not want this to get around. People would have a different view of the situation and not want to patronize your shop. Eventually, Dan relented, but he was still seething mad and he still wanted to punish Bill somehow. I said to Dan, "As a favor to me, let it go. After all there is a job and a family at stake here." We shook hands, and I finally got a smile out of him.

This was one bullet that Bill dodged, but there was another one more serious that was about to come to light. This story Bill told me is something that movies are made out of. It seems Bill met this woman, who according to Bill, came on very strong. She initiated contact with Bill wherever he was delivering and although she told Bill she was married and that her husband was away for long periods of time, she was in fact lonely, according to her, and living in a very secluded, wooded area and had no children.

So Bill gets invited over to her house and to be cautious, Bill had parked his car down the road from her house. This happened to be after a snow storm, and quite a bit of snow was still on the ground, especially in the woods. As he entered the house and went to her bedroom, she was already waiting for him. He no sooner got prepared, when she jumped up, saying, "My husband is home! I just heard the garage door being opened!" Bill gathers up all his clothes, in his arms, opens up the window in the bedroom, jumps out stark naked. Running through the woods to his car, barefoot in the snow, gets to his car and could not get dressed fast enough. Bill said he put his pants on and drove away from the house, down the street, parked the car, and finished dressing. It was this episode, I believe, that cured Bill of any future dalliances.

TOMMY

The next character that I met was a man named Tommy. He was hired to train for a supervisor's position, seeing his lack of interest, into becoming a sales person. I figured he would not be long for this type of work since he did not fit the description nor have the dedication. The company had Tommy ride with me to get some experience and to have him go on all the other routes to do the same.

In our conversations, I learned Tommy was quite the prolific gambler, not in betting huge sums, but still too large for me to manage. He was into all kinds of betting. I had experience with these types of guys before, always looking for the pot of gold at the end of the rainbow. Now, for Tommy, having access to a lot of cash money, was not a good thing. I figured it would not be long before he would start using the company money for gambling. We had to turn all our money in by the end of the week, so this would give him a week to play with the money.

Now after he got his own route, I noticed he was holding out some money. He started using the money for betting. He started out making bets in the one hundred dollar class, and yes, he would hit it big sometimes and pay the company back for the money he used. He did this by saying that some of the accounts did not pay him, so in effect he was paying Peter to pay Paul, a nice little Ponzi scheme.

By now, Tommy had developed a friendship with a lot of heavy betting gamblers, so it was ripe for Tommy to come up with the idea of having the gamblers over to his apartment for the purpose of gambling. Tommy told me he was raking in the sum of about two hundred dollars a night. Since he was the host, he would get a percentage of the money that was gambled, and for that he would provide the gamblers with sandwiches and beer.

Tommy told me that he was going to make enough money to retire at an early age (seems I heard that one before). Tommy would berate me for not gambling, but the thing that intrigued me was how much he was making by raking (term for percentage). What this ass was doing wrong was that he was getting involved in playing and he would lose some of the money he made.

So one day Tommy and I sat down, and discussed the possibility of operating an apartment strictly for gambling. Tommy had connections to all the big gamblers, and he attracted quite a following. My desire to earn a lot money in such a short time spurred me on. Tommy needed a partner because he could not devote full time to the project, same as me, so it would have been a good fit.

One thing we had was a lot of trust in each other, as far as handling the receipts of the evening. At this time I did not even think about getting raided by the police, since this would be in an apartment setting, but the snag came when Tommy was getting a lot of flak from his neighbors, due to the limited amount of parking spaces in the complex. So we then decided to rent a building for that purpose, but after looking at the possibility of having being exposed like that, I did not want to venture any further. Making money was one thing, but the thought of getting arrested and shaming my family was another thing. Tommy eventually had to stop using his apartment since the neighbors were threatening to call the cops.

As time went on, Tommy was getting into making huge wagers and not even thinking one bit about betting three or four thousand dollars on a single event, whatever the sport was. I would hear him many times placing the bets from the office phone.

Tommy, to my dismay, was in deep debt to the people he was placing bets with, but he hid this from everybody. We knew he was betting heavy, but at the same time, we knew of his winnings, so I for one did not give it second thought until Tommy confided to me he owed the bookies three thousand dollars and that his winnings did not cover his losses.

Tommy said that they were pressing him for the money and he needed it right away because they were on his ass and they were getting nasty with him. He asked me to loan him the three thousand dollars and he would give it back to me by the end of the month. I told Tommy, "You should know how I feel about people gambling. You dug a hole for yourself by over betting more than you could lose and I have to remind you of your boast, about going to retire early with the winnings. If you needed the money for your family, that would be something else. We are friends up to a point, but I will not loan you money for any gambling losses."

Tommy was very disappointed with me, but I held my ground and as we continued the conversation as we headed down the stairs from the office, two men dressed in dark suits were standing by a car. They were very menacing looking and they called us over, "We are looking just for Tommy. You, (pointing to me), you can step aside." They pulled Tommy over to them and slammed him up against the car. I overheard them tell Tommy, "Tomorrow we will be here. Have the money ready." These two goons were sent by the bookie.

Now Tommy knew he was in deep shit and that these guys play rough. He did have a lot of warnings from the bookies, about paying his debt. He looked at me and said, "Leo, what the hell am I going to do?" "Go and borrow some money from members of your family," I tell him. He said, "They will all refuse me, as I already owe my brother one thousand dollars."

With his sorry predicament, one in which he put himself in, he now was faced with the problem of having to tell his wife about his gambling losses, which was something he did not want to do. She was already fed up with his gambling so he goes home and gets his bank book and cashes in some securities and comes in the next day and pays off the two goons, who were, as they said they were, there exactly at the appointed time.

I was surprised at how easily Tommy came up with the money and I soon found out how he got it. A day or two later, his wife called the office and said she wanted to talk with Tommy when he got in off the route. The sales manager gave Tom the message as soon as he sat down to cash up. Now Tom gets on the phone and I hear him arguing with his wife. She found out when she went to do some banking and saw how much he had taken out of the book.

It was right after that his wife had enough and filed for divorce and Tommy lost his family. This was something that had to happen. He then left our company and bought himself a cookie route, which he was successful with, but that too eventually went by the wayside, due to his continuing gambling. A man who thought he could beat the odds, instead lost everything dear to him in his life.

JUNE 82: Leaving Wonderbread, researching own business

Another bomb was about to drop on me, another decision that I was to be confronted with. Rumors were starting to surface that the

Meriden agency was in danger of being shut down and consolidated with another agency. Rumors were that we might be sent to Rocky Hill, CT., another twenty minute drive for me. As this was going on for some time about moving, here I am thinking about putting in three more years, at which time I would have my twenty five years and could collect a full pension. So I started to think about the future without Wonder Bread. Maybe I could get a job closer to home, or start my own business, mainly doing the same thing of delivering products to stores. I started to do some research on what I could sell the stores, such as products that they were having trouble getting. The small stores could not purchase packed cookies from the big suppliers, since they had to have a certain amount of products to have it delivered.

A great change was coming for me, in the form of rumors of another move by the company. There was talk of the closure of my agency in Meriden, CT with the company wanting to relocate me to the agency in Montville, CT. This would add many hours to my day in the form of traveling time, as the distance to Montville is exactly one hour from my home Branford and in inclement weather that time would double. At the age of 52 I had to make a decision: to stay on the job which would add a lot of stress for me or leave.

After making a dry run up to Montville and my route, it was a no brainer that my health would not permit me to continue this job. I started to make plans to look for new employment, but at my age I would have resistance from any future employer. In a discussion with my brother, Frank, he said, "You have all this experience in retailing. Put it to good use and maybe you can start your own route business". This sounded good to me so I went about thinking of ways to start a route business.

After some time, I came up with a plan to service all schools with a cookie product line. The man that was servicing the schools left much to be desired from my conversations with people at the schools. I gather they were not happy with his service.

I contacted my brother Frank and briefly told him of my plans. He asked me to meet him and his friend, Tom Basti, at his friend's restaurant and bring my business plan with me to discuss. At this time,

Frank was in a slow period of his business and ready to close up shop. Tom was selling real estate and was not happy with his progress.

That evening we decided to start the business based upon my plans. The first order of business was for me to give my two week notice. It was kind of scary for me to leave a company after 22 years and go out on my own, especially with three teenagers at home and having to start all over again. I took the position to forge ahead and not look back. To continue on with the company would have caused me a great deal of stress. The first week Frank contacted a cookie company and secured the product and we had my son, David, deliver the product. The start of a business or any business is fraught with a myriad of problems. Our plans were to sell to the market items that were not presently available. We serviced small markets with products that the major suppliers would not deliver due to the amount they required.

Our first three years were an adventure. To do it now, I do not know if I could do it again. It was so much work to obtain grocery items for the small retail market. It was a learning experience for me such as putting too much trust in people. I contacted a company with a line of snack cookies and small bags of potato chips. These items were being distributed by a major company. In speaking with the grocers who were selling the product, they gave me no negative feedback and said the products were not being displayed properly. Following up on my research of the products, I knew with the proper merchandising and with limited product line, this would be a great start for us.

I contacted the company and they sent two representatives to my home. They were interested in my business plan and a display rack I designed. The drawing of the display rack was done very professionally with the help from one of my closest friends at work. They praised me for the rack and were very excited to present this to their home office. They left with my drawings and gave me assurance of doing business with me. I never heard from them until one day about 6 months later in my travels through the markets, I saw the rack I designed. I learned my lesson when the reps left my house and took my plans with them. In short I had no signed agreement, which taught me a very valuable business lesson.

When I left my old job, the least the company could do was to give me a letter of appreciation for my years of service. A cold feeling enveloped me as I left the building for the last time. On the drive back home, I thought about all the work that I had done to help build up the routes, along with everybody else, the many hours of labor, starting at around four a.m. and finishing up at around five in the evening, and then to not even be granted the courtesy of a sendoff. I was instrumental in recognizing that when someone retired, you should give them a little party. Along with two other men, we would arrange a nice retirement party for them because a long time ago when I first was hired, a man retired after forty years, and the only thing they did for him was to take him up to the third floor of the Wonder building and have coffee and sandwiches. I sat there and thought how cruel this was to not even have a time for him. The men were in the process of doing something for me, but it came as the agency was being disbanded, and people were being transferred to other agencies. I was to be sent to Montville, but I left just before the deal was to go through. The man that took my route lasted only six months. He lived in Meriden, and the toll of the hours and traveling to Montville finally caught up to him. The poor guy came down with a brain tumor and passed away.

This chapter of my working career was now coming to a close, and I was embarking on the next phase of my life by starting my own business. I was a little apprehensive, to tell the truth, but also excited at the same time. For me, there was no turning back: failure was not an option. It was also to prove to the bosses at Wonder Bread, who I know where waiting for me to fail, that they were soon going to see how much they were wrong in evaluating me.

1950-1954 My Friend Jimmy

This next chapter in my life was to be one of the most memorable and rewarding times of friendship with a new set of friends. While I knew of Jimmy and Joe from the neighborhood, we really never hung out with each other; he mostly concentrated on Grand Ave., an area that catered to gambling and a lot of mischief. I also visited with the people that I went to school with, yet never really got involved in any underhanded and illegal problems, but I was offered the opportunity of working with the bookies. Essentially, I would be what they called a number runner, a person who would have to go around and pick up all the day's action for the bookies, with the understanding that if you got caught the bookies would bail you out. At that time the earnings were about one hundred dollars a week, which was a good amount of money. These people were always wearing nice clothes and didn't have to get and up and go to a full time job.

Jimmy and Joe were primarily sports bettors. They hung around a coffee shop that was a front for the gamblers, and the characters that inhabited that shop would make for a full length movie. The shop was known by the police and from time to time the cops would come around to break up the crap games that were always in progress. One such time that stuck out in my memory was during a big crap game that was taking place in the backyard of the coffee shop.

As my friends and I were on Grand Ave. heading to the boys club for the day, we heard the sirens of the police cars coming down the street heading to the coffee shop and soon they were surrounding the building. The gamblers started to run in every direction to get away from the police. We seen this man running towards a parked car and slid under it to try and hide from the police. A policeman seen his feet sticking out and dragged him out from underneath the car. The man gets up, looking bewildered and asking what the policeman wanted. The policeman said, "You are arrested for gambling." The man answered, "Are you crazy? I am repairing my car!" The policeman responded to the man: "I never seen anybody fixing a car with a suit on."

The raids were the reason Jimmy and Joe wanted to get away from that area. They were becoming more frequent and they did not want to get arrested, especially Jimmy, who could not afford to give his family any more problems. So since they knew that Tony, my brother Ralph, and I hung out on Church St. and were not involved in any social problems, they got in touch with us. They liked what we had going for us, such has attending dances and just having a good time, so we bonded together and formed a great friendship. Eventually another friend of Joe's, Ray, who worked with him in the factory joined our group. Jimmy's reputation preceded him, so we let him know we were only interested in meeting some girls and having a good time, and we did not want any trouble.

On meeting Jimmy for the first time, we saw that he was a really fun guy to be around. All of the rumors about him seemed to disappear from my mind. He was the most charismatic person I had ever met, and there was never a dull moment. He was always agreeable to any and all suggestions about where to go and have some fun (part of which was probably due to his not knowing how to drive, and not having a car of his own).

We would usually meet each other on Church St. at a bar, but it was not like on Grand Ave. It was also where most of all the big money gamblers in the city stayed, along with the bookies who controlled most of all the gambling in the city. The characters could have been right out of a Damon Runyon novel. Lots of prizefighters, gamblers etc. but people never had to worry about any problems with the police because this area was a little classier. Jimmy knew most of the people in the bar because of his gambling, but he also knew his place and did not cause a disturbance. He knew this was not Grand Ave. Jimmy would take the bus from West Haven to downtown New Haven and meet us at the bar and most nights one of us would take him home.

I found out later one of the other reasons he wanted to get away from the Ave. was a man named Donald who was a bad influence on him. Donald was also a kid that I went to school with. He came from a great family, but he was also the black sheep. While I hung out with Donald I knew enough not to get involved with him due to his crazy way of living. I will get to Donald later on.

We had a great bunch of guys now in our little circle, all just wanting the same thing: a good time. We would meet up in either the cafeteria next to the bar, or at a dance hall, and when there was nothing to do on the weekends, we would take a ride to N.Y.C. Jimmy knew all the places we could go. One was the Spanish Club, where they had the flamenco dancers, and of course Jimmy had his eye on one of the dancers and wanted to get friendly with her. In a nice way she told him she was not interested and to get lost. As a response, he puts on a show to mimic the flamenco dancers, but again she tells him to go home and lose some weight.

One of the funniest stories that Jimmy ever told us was the time there was a bus accident in front of the coffee shop on Grand Ave. As the police came to investigate the accident, Jimmy noticed the back door was opened. The driver was busy talking to the police, so he tells everybody to go in the backdoor of the bus, and out the front door, because the driver had to take down the names of all the people on the bus. Because of the accident, they were all going to be rewarded with a check for five hundred dollars each. Unbeknownst to the driver or the officer, Jimmy jumped in line and got a check.

On one of our excursions up to Hartford to go to a dance hall, we had what I call a most surprising evening. After the dance we decided to go to restaurant and have some food and a few more drinks before heading home. It was then that Jimmy told us the story of his army career. He seemed to be in a reflective mood and wanted to tell us his story of why he got a dishonorable discharge. We all heard rumors of it, but never from Jimmy himself.

Jimmy starts off his story of getting drafted at the age of nineteen, and being sent to basic training, which was to last about eight weeks. During this training, Jimmy had a hard time adjusting to army life and did not fare well with his superiors. He was constantly being reprimanded for disobeying orders. Jimmy's M.O. did not go along with authority, and he was a bad influence for the rest of his unit. Jimmy explained how he hated when his sergeant would come busting into the barracks at all hours and tell everybody to stand up for inspection.

On one of the times his Sargent came in for inspection, to aggravate the sergeant Jimmy stood up and did not put his underpants on, sort of letting everything hang out. Now a fair description of Jimmy's body and skin color was on the dark side and very hairy. We sometimes to tease him, called him, "the hairy ape man." Jimmy always had a lot of fun with that. To discipline him for mocking his tour of inspection, the sergeant grabbed a hold of Jimmy by the back of the neck and marched him right into bathroom. The sergeant tells Jimmy to wash all the walls and toilets and sinks, and tells Jimmy that he will be back in the morning. He gave Jimmy a tiny scrub brush to do all this work. In the army, the toilet is called a latrine, and one of the most unpleasant jobs you could get, especially when you have to clean up after about fifty people using it, was cleaning duty. Jimmy could not start to clean the latrine until all the men used it before bedtime which was ten o'clock. It took Jimmy until three A.M. before he was finished. Revelry was at five o'clock in the morning, and Jimmy said he no sooner got to bed when the bugle sounded.

The next day they were all going to go on a long hike, with full field pack, but before Jimmy could go the sergeant said not until I inspect the latrine. The sergeant puts on his white gloves and runs his hands under every toilet. He tells Jimmy when the march is over, you have to clean under all the toilets again because he found some dust under one of the toilets.

By now Jimmy said he was ready to choke the bastard. Sensing Jimmy was ready to explode, his friends calmed him down. The march ended around three P.M. and dinner was at five in the evening, which gave Jimmy a little time to rest. By now Jimmy said his ass was dragging, and could barely move around. Jimmy was not one to hold back his emotions, and as tired as he was he let out every expletive he could think of at the sergeant, not in his presence of course. His buddies said they would help him after the lights went out, so he could get to bed and rest. The next night before taps, the sergeant comes in for an inspection, hoping to catch Jimmy again. This time Jimmy had his underpants on and all zipped up. The sergeant remarked to Jimmy, "By the time I get through with you, I will show you what good manners are."

Now with all the bad news coming in about the war, the rumors were relentless about where they were going to be deployed. Jimmy said at this time the troubles with the sergeant seemed pretty small compared to what he was going to be confronted with in the future. Jimmy's training was coming to an end and the thought of actual combat scared the hell out of him. Like most eighteen and nineteen year old boys, going from playing sandlot ball to going to war was pretty terrifying.

After his training they gave everybody a week to go home and told to report to an embarkation point at a pier in New York City. Jimmy had already made up his mind to go A.W.O.L. He was scared shitless about going overseas for combat, and at that age a lot of boys had the same feeling. On the other hand, being a deserter was akin to embarrassing your family. At this time the movies portrayed war in a different manner, never showing the true horror of the experience.

And so the day came for Jimmy to report for duty, a day that was going to be remembered for the next year. This was the day that he dreaded about not showing up and the consequence he knew he was going to have to face. Having to hide his plan from his family was especially hard. Once he made his decision, Jimmy then had to deal with the stress of playing a cat and mouse game with the feds, hiding out with friends and associates. The feds were making a lot if inquires around the places where Jimmy was known to hang out and let people know that they were on his trail and would get him. They left word to whomever they spoke to that to tell Jimmy to give himself up before they have him arrested for being a deserter.

With so much bad news coming back about all the casualties, it was not hard to feel sorry for people like Jimmy who had to make the decision to be a deserter. The fear of the unknown is a powerful thing, and since most of boys who had to go war were at a very young age, their fright was understandable. Yet the thought of running away was also to be a great embarrassment, one that supposedly would haunt you for the rest of your life.

Jimmy decides to give himself up to the feds, and not go through a trial. He hoped to get redemption from the judge and maybe return to active duty, but the army courts gave Jimmy the full punishment and sentence of life in an army stockade. When I quizzed Jimmy about how he felt at that moment of being sentenced to a life term, his answer was typical Jimmy: "I did not give a shit because somehow I was going to get out before my term." I know from seeing men get long terms for doing crimes in the service, and watching their faces as they were being let away, Jimmy certainly was of a different mold in not being frightened of serving a long sentence. Jimmy's rationale for doing what he did was that at least he was alive. He said that all of the men in his unit were killed after about two months in combat. This also, I believe, had a lot to do with his attitude. He might have had a guilt complex about his dishonorable discharge and of the many buddies he made in the army, in his unit who were killed.

As Jimmy stated, his plan was not to spend the rest of his life in an army stockade. He said he would escape and leave the country, which was the same idea a lot of prisoners had. Based on how Jimmy described it, the stockade was very loosely guarded by two wire fences with a little barbed wire on top of it. At the camp, Jimmy met prisoners who had the same thought about escaping. So Jimmy and his cohorts started to make plans for an escape. They ruled out going over the fence because of the two layers of fencing they had to go through, plus all the guard posts at the corners of the stockade. The guards were armed and would shoot to kill anyone trying to go over the fence, so an elaborate scheme was proposed to tunnel under the fence, about a distance of twenty feet. The tunnel was designed to go under the barracks and under the fence with the excess dirt to be piled underneath the barracks. This operation took about several months to complete, and since quite a few people knew about what was about to take place it was inevitable that someone would inform the officers about the plan, all in the hopes for a reduced sentence for themselves.

The night came when the breakout was to occur. Jimmy and his friends started to crawl under the fence, helping each other as they went along the tunnel, and when they got out on the other side, they helped pull each other up out of the hole. When the last man got out and they were assembling to leave, they were hit with floodlights shinning on them, guards coming out of the woods, rifles aimed at them and shouting to the prisoners to get on the ground. Someone had given them up to the officers about the plan. The prisoners were punished very harshly for the attempted escape, so that other prisoners would get the message and not try it themselves. After spending time in what they called "the hole", with just about enough room to lay down, Jimmy and his friends were released back to their barracks.

When they returned, they soon found out who the person was that informed the army brass about the escape plans. This guy was transferred to another part of the compound, but not so far away that he could not be reached. Jimmy's contact with the prisoners in the barracks that held the informer was told that Jimmy and his friends wanted to get even, so they agreed to help set him up for a severe beating. The informer was given the task of staying inside to clean the latrine, and the escapees were given the time that the informer would be inside. They would have ample time to punish him, but were also told not to injure him beyond recognition. Jimmy and the other guys decided on giving him a "G.I. shower", which was with a hard bristle brush. The man's rear end, legs and feet were where they inflicted the most damage. These areas were as red as a beet. They did that so he would feel it for a long time by not being able to sit down. Jimmy said they left his face alone so the marks would not show. The officers questioned the man after he was found on the floor of the barracks, moaning and groaning. The man said that he had fell down and scrapped his body on the floor. The officers did not believe him and wanted to know exactly what had happened, but he knew if he had told them who did it he would have been in for more of the same or worse.

Jimmy told us how the guards would only be to glad to punish them for any little infraction, because of the nature of their crimes of running away from duty. Every day was very stressful because they had to figure out ways to stay away from the guards and not anger them. Being a deserter was a stigma that regular army personnel looked upon with scorn.

I knew what Jimmy was talking about, because when I was being transferred, and had to go through Charleston, South Carolina to be processed for another place of duty. I was going to the mess hall one morning and was told not to go in. I had to wait because they were bringing some prisoners in for breakfast. The guards were all marine personnel, and the prisoners came in a marching two by two, and they responded to the commands of the guards, shouting, "yes, sir" and "no, sir." They marched over to the table and waited for the guards to blow a whistle, indicating when they could sit down.

As the prisoners marched into the mess hall, I saw the guards whack some prisoners on the ass if they did not move fast enough. Charleston was a transfer point for prisoners being routed to their places of incarceration. Essentially, it was a holding pen and not designed for any long term confinement. While there we were awoken one night by loud horns and floodlight. Two prisoners tried to escape by going over the wire fence. It was a scene that you would see in any movie about prison. I ran out into the yard with the rest of the people in my barracks and saw a large crowd of people near the fence. They had the prisoners on the ground, with all the marines standing over them. The marines quickly disbursed us, so now I knew what Jimmy meant about being in confinement.

As the war was winding down, rumors were flying around about what the army was going to do with all the deserters. Some rumors had them being sent to a regular prison, some were saying that the army was going to put them a military prison, which everyone said was just as bad, if not worse than what they had. About six months after the war ended, all the deserters were given a dishonorable discharge and sent home. Some had to endure a lot of ridicule because of their stance of not taking part in the war. Jimmy only spoke very little about this episode in his life. I did not meet him until about 1950, so my knowledge of this part of his life was sparse.

Jimmy did tell me about his problems finding work because of his dishonorable discharge. At the time, employers wanted to see your discharge papers before they hired you. If you misrepresented yourself on the application and were found out, it called for an immediate firing. Some men said that their papers were all tied up because of a back load and would bring them in as soon as they received them. Most of the time employers needed workers and told them to bring them in as soon as possible, and for this reason, Jimmy was able to slip between the cracks.

When I met Jimmy he was employed at a defense factory, which was changing over to peacetime production. He was able to get that job because he had connections: a family member who was a lawyer and then became a judge. At that time I never really gave it a second thought, and neither did anybody else.

One of the main characters that Jimmy wanted to separate himself from was a boy named Donald. Donald and I went to school together, and he had trouble written all over him. There was never a dull moment with him; he was always getting into some kind of mischief, but like Jimmy we had a lot of laughs together. Yet, Donald had a temper and a vicious streak that would get him into a lot of trouble. Donald came from a hard-working family. His father was held in high regard in the Democratic Party and held a good job. This is the one reason Jimmy wanted to get away from Donald's influence, and started to hang with us. Donald's life almost mirrors Jimmy's, but with one exception: Jimmy didn't want to get into any more serious trouble. If he stayed on the Ave, that would certainly would have been the case. Donald was so crazy that he would have a baseball bat and chase black people down and try to hit them, albeit with always some back up to protect him.

Once at the beach Donald picked a fight with a boy who he claimed made fun of him. We were with a bunch of guys, so Donald felt brave and went after the boy. He beat him so viciously that he took a bite on the boy's chest, and that's when we all stepped in and broke up the fight. The boy was bleeding profusely, and he had to be given first aid from a restaurant owner nearby.

This boy Donald would later on spend twenty five years of his life in prison for the murder of a man he had a disagreement with. His temper cost him a third of his life, and yet the Donald I knew as a young boy was not the same one that Jimmy could not deal with. Donald never tried to be a bad influence on me, as he knew I would draw the line getting into any serious scrapes with the law.

Jimmy took us to a bar and restaurant on upper Chapel St. in New

Haven that was a great location for stag parties. The owner was a man named Ted, who ran the place along with his sister Miriam, and they made for a great pair. Miriam was in charge of organizing the stag parties, like providing strippers who were brought in from New York City and having rooms for assignations. On the other hand, Ted took care of the bar and restaurant business. Ted and his sister were on the hefty side, with Ted looking like Jackie Gleason and Miriam was a spitting image of the late Sophie Tucker. Miriam was never at a loss for words, and she could stand toe to toe with any of the toughest guys that came into the bar. She had a booming voice, and she would curse any ass who got out of line. Ted and Miriam had some respectability since their establishment was frequented by quite a few business-type people in addition to the regular blue collar workers. A lot of people from my neighborhood had their stag parties there and they were to be sure quite raucous.

Jimmy was on a first name basis with Ted since he brought him a lot of customers and bookings for these parties. Jimmy loved to break Miriam's balls by always insulting her on her choice of show girls. The banter between Ted and Jimmy would sometimes get out of hand, with Miriam making a lot of obscene gestures to Jimmy, and as usual Jimmy would love when she got mad at him. Jimmy would make fun of her body by walking in back of her, and mimicking her walk and shaking his ass just like Miriam. This bar was the type of place we would frequent when we had a slow night and not much to do. We always knew we could go there and have some fun.

One night in particular happened to be a slow night for business. Ted welcomed us in and gave us all a free drink. As we were joking and drinking, this drunk at the bar who was regular was giving Ted a hard time. The drunk could hardly stand up and kept asking for more drinks. Ted refused him and the drunk started to curse out Ted, even mentioning his mother. That crossed the line so Ted told us to take the drunk out in the alley and leave him there.

When Jimmy heard this request, his face lit up with one of his shit eating grins. He replied, "Sure, Ted. We will take care of him." Jimmy motions us to help him dispose of the drunk. We were about five of us and carried the drunk out the back door of the bar, which let out into a little alley. It was very secluded, and Jimmy said, "Let's grab this guy's money." Jimmy felt he had a lot of money on him by the way he was throwing around twenty dollar bills.

We laid the drunk onto this cardboard box and Jimmy started to rummage through all his clothing. When he got through and the man was down to his underwear, Jimmy comes up with 15 dollars. When we walked back into the bar, Ted knew what had occurred and did not care as the drunk was a big pain in the ass. Jimmy said, "Let's go out to Savin Rock and have some seafood." Then someone said, "We should go back and put some blankets on him, the son of a bitch got so much booze in him he will not even feel the cold."

The very next night we go back to Ted's place and the drunk was there. He wanted to know who the hell had took all his money. Ted turns to us and said, "Did you guys see anybody outside last night?" We all said, "There were three kids standing on the corner when we left." Ted shoots back and said he recalls the kids, and chastised them for causing a lot of noise. Not missing a beat, Jimmy goes up to the drunk and shakes his hand and tells him, "I will look out for those three little bastards myself."

One night Jimmy had his eye on a waitress that he was talking with all night. She gave him the impression that she was interested in him, but she also said she was seeing someone else. Jimmy kept pressing her for a date, but she kept putting him off, so Jimmy tells us he wanted to see who the hell she had a date with. Tony and I stayed with him until the bar closed and waited outside to see where she was going. Out she comes and who the hell was waiting for her, but a guy who looked like he did not have a good night's sleep. He was crummy looking, and this got Jimmy all riled up, thinking she passed Jimmy up for this piece of shit.

The waitress gets in the car with the man and as the man starts to drive away from the curb, Jimmy opens the driver's door and starts to hit the man in the face. Now the car is heading down the street with Jimmy hanging onto the door. The car finally pulls away, and all we could do was laugh our asses off with Jimmy cursing up a storm. Jimmy was enraged that the girl ditched him for this ragamuffin. The waitress never came back to work at Ted's place.

We were pretty much regulars at Ted's place, and Ted put up with all our crap, but he still liked us. As long as we did not disturb his business, we could always spend the night at his bar. It was always a fun place because it was so lively. We always had Miriam to joke with, teasing her about her girls, who she said were her friends, but we knew she was pimping them off to mostly business men who could pay for her services. So that's why we busted her chops: we were too poor to pay her prices.

One night Jimmy somehow got into a rather heated discussion with Ted. They were I believe talking and arguing about baseball, and Jimmy had a few to many drinks in him and started to curse out Ted. That was it. He throws us all out, and tell us to go home and cool off. This was one hot and steamy night, very muggy, and the air was so stale that it smelled. Across the street Ted had his small coupe parked. Jimmy said, "Let's all go and take a piss in Ted's car." We all did, but Jimmy decided to do one better. He said he had to move his bowels, so he relieves himself on the front seat of the car, then Jimmy said. "Let's roll up all the windows and close up the car."

We did not go to Ted's place for some time after that, but we heard from people that smoke was coming out of his ears he was so mad. He had to have a company clean up the car since it smelled so bad. When we did go back one night, Ted relates the story to us and wanted to know if we had heard about what happened to his car. Jimmy yells out, "Jesus Christ! What kind of animals would do something like that?" We put on a good show, with Jimmy really laying it on thick, asking, "What kind of car did you have?" and "Where was the car parked?" Ted really bought our act.

One of our most favorite dance halls was in a Polish American Club in Wallingford that had a nice mix of music, and a lot of people, mostly from the New Haven crowd. It was like we were out of town but were still able to meet our friends from our area. The owners were very friendly but also made sure to let you know that they did not want any undue disturbance. Upon bringing Jimmy there, we made sure to let him know this, as we had been going there for some time and were respected by the crowd from Wallingford. This one night Jimmy was not having much success in getting girls to dance with him, partly because he spent too much time downstairs in the bar and smelled of beer. I told him to chew some gum, but he did not take kindly to hearing that. So the inevitable happened: Jimmy wanted to dance with this girl all night. She told him that maybe later on she would, but in other words she was not interested. She tried to put him off, and I kept telling him, "You asshole, you stink of beer so leave her alone. Maybe next time you see her she will dance with you." But Jimmy wouldn't listen and he had to make a statement by letting her know he was mad at being refused.

So Jimmy goes down to the bar and comes back with some ice cubes. He had this shit eating grin on his face, which was almost normal, but we did not see the ice cubes since he hid them on his side. Jimmy goes up to the girl who was talking with some other people, in the middle of the hall. He pulls away the back of her dress, and slips the ice cubes down her back, causing her to let out a blood curling cry.

The boys who were with the girl started to punch Jimmy. We were trying to get Jimmy away from the crowd, who by now were all against us, and the hall erupted in a free for all, with everyone hitting any-one they thought started the commotion. We were dragging Jimmy down the stairs, all the while the guy was hitting at Jimmy, with Jimmy trying to return the punches. The fight went all the way downstairs and out into the street. By now we were hearing the sirens of the police cars, so we quickly got Jimmy into one of our cars and had him taken away because he could not afford to get arrested due to his trou-ble in the army. Also, his family would have been furious with him. Tony and I stayed behind to talk to the hall manager and try to make amends for what happened. The damage to the hall was minimal, and we offered to pay for any damage, but all he said was he did not want to have Jimmy back there.

When the guys and I confronted Jimmy the next day, we told him, "Jimmy, you are not on Grand Ave. anymore, and you cannot do this.

You have to show some restraint and curb your temper. If you keep doing this, we will have no place to go." Jimmy thanked us for getting him out of there just in time, and he gave us his word that there would be no more problems like that. But with Jimmy that was only to being taken with a grain of salt. Like I always said, this all goes back to his army days and was maybe the reason for his aggression towards people.

One other time at another dance hall in the city of Meriden, we were having a few drinks with the girls we knew from the area and just joking around with Jimmy. So Jimmy suggests to go down into the yard where we could have some privacy. This hall was located in a nice residential area and a very quiet neighborhood, so the hall put the lights on for us and told us to keep the noise at a very low volume. Jimmy and one of the girls started to dance to the music coming from the hall, then he started to sing and all of the girls joined in. We were given a warning from the hall because the people were complaining about the noise, not the music. As usual Jimmy was in all his glory with all the attention he was getting from the girls. All of a sudden, two police cars show up, but they did not have the sirens on. They informed us of the neighbor's complaint and that we had to break up the party. The kicker was we had to be taken down to the police station for questioning.

I guess they took us down to make the neighbors happy because all they did was give us a written warning so that the next time if we get pulled in for the same infraction, we could be arrested. When I looked around, I did not see Jimmy. I asked Tony and Joe, and they did not see him either. They thought he was in one of the other cars, but the son of a bitch slipped out of the back of the yard and waited for us to return. He said he slipped under the table, and did not get noticed. The army taught him good.

With Jimmy, any night could turn into laughter or sorrow. He really was a fun guy who could make you laugh just by his expressions. He was on the order of Lou Costello the comedian, and if you were to close your eyes you would think it was Costello you were talking to. A night that comes to memory, well many nights now that I think of it, was the time we met the New York Yankees broadcaster Mel Allen, who this one night was a little tipsy himself. We met him in the Phyliss restaurant in Savin Rock. Mel Allen had some of the players with him, which at that time I did not know since I was not interested in keeping up with baseball; I always liked football. But Jimmy knew all the players by their name and position since he was great at betting on baseball. He always knew all the scores for the day, so in conversation Mel Allen makes the mistake of asking Jimmy of all people of the previous day's game and what he thought of the errors that were committed. Jimmy goes into a tirade calling the Yankees a bunch of assholes because they lost the game and cost him a bundle, a bundle being about twenty dollars.

The players just laughed, but Mel was a little drunk so he goes head to head with Jimmy, who by now was on his feet, and in front of Mel, calling him out for making mistakes in his reporting of the game. Now everyone in the restaurant was laughing their ass off at the antics of Jimmy's description of the game. Mel Allen looked foolish for even trying to argue with Jimmy. Mel looked like an asshole since he was drunk and slobbering. Now Jimmy to make his point and actually ran up and down the aisle of the restaurant to show how the play should have been done. The players with Mel Allen were having the time of their lives. They did not take offense to the way Jimmy was portraying them. This scene should have been in an Abbot and Costello movie.

Our favorite restaurant in Savin Rock was Philly's, where we spent a great deal of our time, especially during the week when there was not much to do. We would hang out there, and meet up some of our other friends, and occasionally see Mel Allen. The place had a very lively crowd. One particular night we were just sitting in our usual booth and not discussing anything of importance, and Jimmy says, "I am going to help clear the tables for the waitress." We all looked at Jimmy wondering what the hell he was talking about. So Jimmy goes around to the tables and starts to take the salt and pepper shakers off of every table and brings them to our table. I was sitting on the end of the booth, and Jimmy hands them to me and says, "Hold these. I will be right back." One customer was still using the salt shaker, so Jimmy goes up to him and says that he will be right back with some new ones. The guy was in the process of using it when Jimmy takes the shaker out of his hand.

By now we knew Jimmy was doing something stupid, and we were laughing at the way he took the shaker out of the guy's hand while he was using it. Jimmy takes all the shakers and puts them in the closet with all the linen. He then goes back to the tables and removes all the napkin holders and puts them in the linen closet, too. Then he sits down in the booth and calls the waitress for more napkins. She starts looking around the tables for napkins and then goes looking in the kitchen, all the while the guy was waiting for his salt shaker to return. He then calls the waitress for his salt shaker, but she could not find any around the tables. Since our booth was in the back of the restaurant, the customers could not see Jimmy so they tell the waitress that the waiter took their shakers and napkins and never returned. At this point, the customers were wondering what the hell is going on. They also wanted more napkins since this was primarily a fried food restaurant, and people would be eating quite messy finger food. Jimmy calls the waitress again, "Where the hell are the napkins?" Jimmy hollers. "Please be patient," the waitress then tells Jimmy. When the waitress leaves, Jimmy takes all the napkins out of the closet and puts them in an empty booth. She comes back and finds the napkin holders and starts to bring them back to all the booths. All the while, she had the look of amazement on her face on how the napkins got there. The customer who was waiting for his salt shaker to arrive left the restaurant. Jimmy now takes all the shakers and puts them in the same empty booth and waits for when the waitress comes back. Now she is going crazy as to how all this stuff was happening. Back into the kitchen she questioned everyone as to how this was occurring, but no one knew what the hell she was talking about. We were watching all this unfold through the glass door of the kitchen.

We were laughing so hard that the waitress looked at us. Jimmy tells her to come over and to listen to this dirty joke he just told, which was a cover for our laughing. She declined, but Jimmy had the balls to go up to the waitress and ask her what all the commotion was about. She then explains about the missing products and how they suddenly surfaced back on the table. Jimmy put on a good show, looking and listening to her story, suggesting maybe someone in the back room was playing a joke on her. She aggress with Jimmy, and starts to try and figure out who would pull that shit on her. Jimmy stares at the dishwasher and suggests to the waitress, "Maybe that piece of shit."

It is said that people sometimes laugh so hard that they could pee their pants. This was one of those times. It turned out to be all in innocent fun, but at the expense of the poor waitress. For her trouble we did leave her a very generous tip and waited about three months before telling her who was behind that evening. She cursed us out and then gave us all a hug, "You guilty bastards. That's why you guys gave me such a nice tip. I should have known."

One Saturday night Jimmy and I decided to go to a dance hall in New Britain while our other friends went to Sea Cliff in New Haven. The reports I received from people I knew gave this dance hall in New Britain some good marks. Jimmy and I both had put in a full day at our factories and I had to do the driving since he did not have his license. After a fun night of dancing and drinking we decided to call it a night around 1:00am. As we were heading home on the Wilbur Cross Parkway, Jimmy fell asleep. With no one to talk to I put on some soft music. As I approached Yalesville, I felt drowsiness coming on and after a little while fighting to stay awake I fell asleep. I crashed into the fence posts on the parkway. I wake up just in time to avoid going down the embankment and knocking off my right front fender and damaging the right side of my car. Jimmy wakes up quickly with a startled look. I bring the car to a halt and as usual Jimmy jumps out and yells, "between you and your brother Ralph you are going to kill me".

The police came almost immediately and gave me a ticket. I lost my license for 6 months. Lawyer John Maresca represented me and the fine was $110.00.

We had a very funny experience one night at the bar on Church St because of the clientele that the bar catered to. There were a lot of book-ies, gamblers, lawyers, prize fighters, etc. It was a great mix of people, and just being there and watching the crowd was better than going to a movie. The characters that came and went during the evening was sometimes hilarious, especially the ex-prize fighters, who would relive all their fights with us. One such man was named Georgie Day, who always wore a fresh carnation in his lapel. He had the walk of a guy who looked like he was always walking on his heels, and Jimmy had a field day with him. Jimmy liked to tease him about all the bouts he lost and then Georgie would go into a stance as if to fight with Jimmy. Georgie was always good for a laugh since he never took any of the ribbing personally. He always said he could have been a champion and that he never had a good manager. Well as Georgie was talking, this guy who had some ties with the mafia and was into a lot of illegal gam-bling and loan sharking, comes down the aisle. This guy was also an ex-prize fighter and punch drunk just like Georgie; a real bad ass. He pushes Georgie aside, and goes up to the front of the bar where there was a booth. Georgie goes after him because he had pushed him aside. The guy grabs Georgie by the neck and tells him to beat it. We took Georgie back to our area and said, "Leave him alone."

Jimmy's interest in politics was very sparse. Between gambling and always looking for women to date, he didn't have much time for any-thing else. One thing with Jimmy if you mentioned either baseball or girls you would have his attention, and as a matter of fact sometimes just to test his reaction, I would make up a story about going to meet some girls, but I really was not really interested in them. His eyes would light up and badger me, and ask me questions about where they were located and what they looked like. I always got a charge out of teasing him that way. One night we heard there was going to be a big shindig at the hotel Taft. We walked up there to see if we could get in. It turned out to be a political gathering and naturally we figured we could at least get some free drinks and food. We were turned away at the door because we did not have the credentials for entrance. So as we waited outside trying to get in the door, out comes a large group of people, with a lot of state policemen making a clearance for this man to get into his car. It turned out to be the governor of CT, Chester Bowles. Jimmy said, "Who the hell is that?" We said, "Chester, the man from Hartford." We laughed because of Jimmy didn't know who he was. "Oh," Jimmy says, "So it's Chester. Let me go and say hello to him." Jimmy goes up to the car as the governor was entering it. The policemen got in the way of Jimmy to head him off. Jimmy calls out to the governor, "Hey Chester, how the hell are you?" and extends his hand to the governor. The governor waves the policeman off, to let Jimmy get through. By now Jimmy had his shit eating grin, and repeating the name of Chester, instead of calling him the governor. Jimmy turns around and says to us, "Hey guys! Look over here! It's Chester!" Now the governor stops from entering the car, and asks Jimmy what his name is. After Jimmy tells the governor his name, the governor shakes Jimmy's hand, and tells him, "I must say you have an unusual way of greeting people, but you have a nice evening and hope to see you again." Jimmy keeps up the Chester shit until the governor gets into his car, with Jimmy now standing in the street waving him goodbye. Jimmy says, "See, this is how you get to know people. You have to go right up to them and stick out your hand." We were laughing so hard because of who he was talking to and we said, "Yes, the man now knows your name. Watch out you do not get a phone call from the state." The fun we had with that lasted the rest of the night. We were calling Jimmy "Chester, Chester". It was a sight to see Jimmy in the street that night waving the governor goodbye.

On the same street there was a policeman named Earl, who had the downtown beat that night and was in front of the hotel Taft. He was watching the scene unfold with Jimmy and the governor. Earl knew Jimmy from when he had the beat on the Ave. Earl was one of the kindest of human beings, who not give a ticket to anybody, and instead he would lecture you on the rules of law. "Jimmy," Earl shouts out, "Behave yourself! You should know better than that. Do you want to make me look bad by making a fool of the governor on my beat? Shame on you." Jimmy responds, "Yeah, but now I got to meet Chester, and he knows my name!" Jimmy tells Earl the cop.

As this was unfolding, a woman was driving down the street the wrong way in front of the hotel Taft. Earl was giving Jimmy a lecture on manners and this woman is going down a one way street the wrong way. Earl stops talking to Jimmy and stops the car being driven by this woman. He tells her to pull over and starts giving her a lesson on how to read the signs. Jimmy, not to let any opportunity go by to have some fun, walks with Earl near the car. Jimmy tells Earl, "Maybe you should have her get out of the car." Earl snaps at Jimmy, "When did you become a cop? You do not even drive a car!" Now the lady is confused as to what the hell is going on— a policeman and a civilian asking her questions all at once. Earl gets Jimmy to get on the sidewalk and out of the way. Now the circus really starts to heat up. After Earl gives the lady one of his friendly talks, he then goes into the street and stops traffic so he can have the lady turn her car around and head in the correct direction. Jimmy now gets in the street up a little ways and stops traffic in the other direction. Jimmy tells the driver of the first car to wait until the cop says it is okay to go on. Now Earl does not see that the traffic is stopped in the other direction and is not moving. Earl finally walks up the street and asks the driver why he is not moving his car. The driver tells Earl, "I was told to wait until you came over." Earl says, "Who told you that?" The driver points to Jimmy, "That short dark man told me to wait for you." If this was any other policeman, Jimmy would have is ass in jail. No matter what beat he was on, Earl was a very beloved cop in that he would not give anyone a summons. His way of policing was to interact with the youth of the neighborhood and be their friends. According to some of the policemen I knew, Earl would get his ass chewed by his superiors because of his lack of not issuing even a parking ticket. Earl knew Jimmy from when he had the beat on the Ave. and the way Earl would talk to Jimmy was more like an associate than a civilian. The banter between them was hilarious. I never ever seen Earl get upset with anyone; he had such a low key approach to a problem, no matter how serious, and managed to defuse it in a matter of minutes.

During the 1950s with bars having to close at 1.A.M., a string of bottle clubs started to open up. These were set as private clubs and members would have a locker in which to store their alcohol. Most of the members in these establishments were upper middle class people who had the means to afford this pleasure. One night, Jimmy and I met our barber Louie when we were leaving Church St. and I was taking Jimmy home. Louie says, "Where you guys going? Come with me. I have some friends who belong to a bottle club on Orange Ave. in West Haven. We could go and spend some time there." So we go and meet these guys who turned out to be professional golfers and lived in Waterbury.

Louie the barber was a character on his own. He owned a lucrative barber business on the Ave. along with his partner Dom. Their shop was always busy since there was such a great concentration of people in the area and the place was well liked. Also it was a meeting place for the men who would just come and talk about gambling or sports.

His partner Dom had a bad experience with his wife, who ran off with another man. This left Dom in a state of depression that was to plague him for a long time. Dom was the more likeable of this partnership, but he got so desponded in his personal life that he up and left New Haven and went up to Alaska to work. We heard he did very well working on the pipeline for the oil company.

Louie, on the other hand, was known to be a frugal person, which we translated to be a cheap bastard, so much so that Jimmy and I found out the hard way. These two men that Louie introduced us to at the bottle club were very generous and hospitable with entertaining us with their liquor. After two times that we met, they invited us to a party that was going to be attended by people in the sports world. They said they would introduce us to some nice women. This was right up our alley, as Jimmy and I were not that interested in just sitting around drinking, and Louie being a married man was only interested in sponging off these guys.

Jimmy tells Louie, "When the hell are we going to return the favor and furnish these guys with some liquor, since we are always drinking their booze? Now they even invited us to a party." Louie says, "The hell with them. They have a lot of money. Do not say anything to them." Listening to his advice was a big mistake.

The party that we attended was at a very nice night club in Waterbury. The crowd was as we expected all professional people, and true to their words they introduced us to a bevy of women who were all associated in some kind of business. Jimmy and I were definitely out of our league. Louie, in the meantime, was having the time of his life because he was not paying for a thing. To my surprise, Jimmy did not make any bad moves toward the women. He was behaving himself until one caught his eye and he zeroed in on her. It was like watching Mutt and Jeff. The girl was about two inches taller than Jimmy and while he was dark and short, she was of a very light complexion.

After spending some time with the girl, Jimmy asked her for her phone number, but she declined. Jimmy comes back to me and tells me what had happened. I said, "Good. How the hell were you going to date her? You do not have a car." Well Jimmy says, "Maybe she has a friend and we could both go. I just felt this night was a night to meet some different people and have a good time." I was having a drink with one of the men that brought us there, named Pete. He said to call Louie over and that he wants to have a discussion about us donating to one of his favorite charities. It had something to do with a hospital fund, but after Pete tells Louie what the amount of the donations are, Louie tells Pete he was not interested in donating.

Pete now goes into a tirade with Louie, calling him a cheap bastard and how in all the time he knew him he never offered to pay for anything. I grabbed a hold of Jimmy and told him what had happened. By this time Pete was really lacing into Louie at the bar and causing a scene. Jimmy and I really liked the crowd. It was very different from our circle of friends, so we tried to not make a scene. We eased Louie out of the bar and away from Pete, who was steaming mad at Louie. Louie squeezed these people and now they were disgusted with him, so that ended our fantasy of mingling with the upper class.

The guys and I brought Jimmy to an Italian club located in the hill section of the city. On Friday nights the club gave permission to have a meeting place for young people to socialize. They had a juke box so you could dance, but alcohol was limited. The club room was in the next room if you wanted to drink. This was like an association of the sons and daughters of the club to have an outlet for them to meet someone. They would also organize day trips to various places such as hay rides in the fall and ice skating parties in the winter. They put together a nice social program, and it was well attended by a very diverse group of people from all parts of the city. The only drawback was that if you wanted to join the main club, your parents had to come from the northern part of Italy. The old timers did not encourage their children to marry people whose parents came from the southern part of Italy. It was a well-documented fact about how people from the northern part of Italy did not take kindly to people from the southern part of Italy. They felt the southerners were inferior to them because for the most part people from the north had access to a formal education, while the southern region was denied the same opportunity, mainly because of political lines.

Jimmy had some fun with that. At one of our meetings they had us fill out a questionnaire about your family's birthplace in Italy. I put down that I was born in Rome, my brother, Ralph, put down that he was born in Naples and Jimmy put down that he was born on the Swiss border. The girl reading the applications in front of all the members wanted to know from me how I was born in Rome and my brother was born in Naples, so I said, "My father was a traveling salesman." That cracked the room up, but Jimmy was worst since he could not name the town his parents came from. All of this because of the old world suspicions of people from the south. I must say the members of the main club treated us very well. We would go there on a Saturday and drink beer and have what they called "shiners" or "little fishes".

But I found all of this out the hard way when I met a nice girl from the club and asked her out for a date. We decided to go to a movie, which was a short walk from her home. The movie had a starting time of seven o'clock in the evening, so I arrived at her home at six-thirty to pick her up. Upon entering her home I was introduced to her father and mother and was asked by her father to step outside on the porch with him.

The interrogation began with the usual, "Where was my place of employment, where did I live, my father's place of employment," etc. The girl's name was Louise, and she had informed me not to give her father too much information about were my people came from. Louise tried to break up the conversation by saying we did not want to be late for the movie but Louise's father kept asking me for more information than I wanted to give. I told her father I really did not have too much knowledge of my parents' birth place in Italy. Louise comes out and tells me, "Leo, it's time to leave or we will be late for the movie." At that the father turns to me in broken English, "Hey, boy, it's now seven o'clock, and I want you home by nine o'clock." After the movie we had to run home because we got out about eight forty five. Louise said she was sorry about our date and hoped it would better the next time. She said she would be looking forward to seeing me at the club. On the way home I am thinking, I do not believe there will a next time, not with that father of hers.

The next day Jimmy wanted to know how the date went. "Jimmy," I say, "How did the date go? I will tell you how the date went. I was questioned by her father who I thought was an F.B.I. agent. He looked me up and down and shot several questions at me all at once. Christ, this was only a date, not a marriage proposal." Jimmy says, "Well, did you make out with her?" I yell, "Make out? I got to shake her hand when I dropped her off. Her father was waiting for her on the porch." How ironic when I had the milk route this is where my route was, up in the hill section of the city where most of the people from the northern part of Italy lived. I found them to be very hospitable and generous toward me.

Some of the funniest times I had with Jimmy was when there was not much going on and Jimmy would suggest we go to some of the gay bars and have some fun with the gays. Upon entering one of the bars, Jimmy yells out, "You should all be ashamed of your selves, you bunch of sinners!" This little gay guy struts up to Jimmy, and in a very feminine way, admonishes Jimmy for being so cruel. That was a big mistake on this poor little guy's part. Now Jimmy goes into his gay routine and is talking just like this little gay guy. The hilarious part of it was the gay guy puts his arm around Jimmy and welcomes him into the bar. With the both of them welcoming each other, the gay says, "See, we are not so bad. I think you are one of us." After visiting several more gay bars, we decided to call it a night. We were all laughed out. As we were leaving our last place of call, this gay guy comes up to Jimmy and says, "May I have a moment with you?" "Not tonight. Maybe in the next world I will see you!" Jimmy exclaims. I told him, "See, we said you keep coming here and they think you want to be with them." But while Jimmy had fun teasing the gays, he was never vicious with them.

On the opposite side of Jimmy's character was his love of the boxing game. We would attend all the boxing matches at the New Haven Arena. This sport was more in keeping with his persona and of the rough and tumble life he led. Well we were all great boxing fans for that matter, and in fact some of the fighters hung around the same places we did. Jimmy would have a field day discussing with a fighter about his latest fight. One was a fighter named Mike. Mike and I lived in the same neighborhood. Mike's brother was also a boxer who had many professional bouts. One most notable was with a boxer by the name of Jake La Motta that would have given him star power, but he lost. Mike had an impressive record and he was also an up and coming fighter. He was moving up the ranks which I thought was too quickly. It all came crashing down one night in Waterbury, CT when Mike fought a kid from Maine. Just looking at him we knew Mike was in for a tough night. He fought a grueling ten round bouts with this kid and Mike gave his all but came up short. Mike lost the fight and would never be able to fight again due to the injuries he received. The boxing commissioner would not renew his license. Mike hung up his gloves and got a job as a truck driver and was employed for many years. Mike and I spent many an evening dissecting the present boxers of that week. Being an avid fan of boxing we would compare different styles of boxing. One of Mike's favorite pastimes was getting me to shadow box with him. I had to be careful due to the fact that Mike would forget himself and let loose on me.

In West Haven there was a bar that catered to transvestites. When we would be in the area, we liked to stop in and see the shows they put on. It was quite hilarious, and as usual Jimmy was in his glory talking to them. This one night Jimmy really got fooled. He goes up to this nice looking blond and strikes up a conversation. We remarked what a beautiful girl Jimmy was talking to and wondered what the hell is a girl like that doing in this place. Jimmy asks the girl to dance, and she says, "Look honey, just so that you do not get any ideas. What I am is only an illusion." She then lifts up her dress and shows Jimmy who she really is. Well, not only Jimmy but all us assholes were mesmerized by this person. The shock on Jimmy's face was worth a million dollars. His jaw dropped and his mouth was wide open. We knew what kind of a bar this was but this person was more like a woman than a real woman. She (or he) was the ultimate in drag.

Little did I know that when I met Jimmy, he would have 12 more years to live.

Jimmy's days as a single man were coming to an end. After I got married in 1954, Jimmy told me that he felt it was time to meet someone and settle down. When we talked, all he kept asking me about was my life now that I was married. I did not think much of it at that time, especially about his future plans of marriage, since I really could not envision Jimmy being married.

Well, in about 1955 Jimmy meets a girl at Ted Hilton's, of all places. Jimmy was pretty well known at this place mainly for his penchant for a good time, but he meets a girl of German-Irish descent who lived in Long Island. They started a long distance courtship, even though Jimmy did not have a car and would have to travel by train to see her on the weekends.

When he told me about this girl, I was happy for him but at the same time reminded Jimmy about the girl I met in Atlantic City and how and why I did not pursue her. At that time Jimmy said the distance was too great. I said, "My, how the worm turns. You are doing what you told me not to do." Jimmy laughs, responding, "But for me it's different. I am a little bit older."

After about several months of courtship, Jimmy decides to marry Helen in 1956. We just had our first child, Gail, and Jimmy invited all of his friends to the wedding. It was mainly us that he associated with and had a great rapport with. His family gave his friends their blessing since they appreciated us for bring good friends with Jimmy. Jimmy's family treated us all like we were part of the family. We enjoyed going over Jimmy's house. His mother was very hospitable, putting out a spread for us every time we came over. She was overly generous, and sort of grateful that Jimmy met us.

There were eight of us and we went to Jimmy's wedding in two cars. I was the only married guy at that time, and Teresa did not feel at ease in going as the only woman there, so I went with the rest of the group. The wedding was on a Sunday, and it was such a happy occasion for all us guys, seeing Jimmy with his tuxedo on and not believing that this was happening. Jimmy had the look of contentment and was in such a jovial mood, like he was in another world, a world in which he probably never thought of being.

Helen turned out to be his lifeline. I was told that she knew of whatever short comings Jimmy had, and told him, "What you were, you were. From now on you are starting a new life." Helen accepted Jimmy has he was, maybe a bit fragile, but a good and decent man. Helen had some family ties that got Jimmy a job working at the airport. His first job was in cleaning the airplanes, which he enjoyed, and later on he was promoted to a better position. I think it was in the hangar were they worked on the airplanes.

Jimmy invited my wife Teresa and me to his apartment in Long Island for a Sunday dinner. We brought along our daughter Gail, who was about one year old at the time. Jimmy and Helen's daughter was six months old. We took a picture of them on the couch, which I always treasured. Not only was Jimmy married, but here he was a family man. Jimmy helped Helen set the table and take care of his daughter. I said,

"Jimmy, you are doing better than me." Jimmy always had that sly grin, "If I don't do this, she will kill me." Although Jimmy changed, he did not lose his passion for humor; he had that way about him that made it hard for you not to like him. At the end of the dinner, I helped Jimmy straighten out the table and put away the extensions of the table back. He then says, "Come with me. I have to take out the trash. It is down the hallway." I could not believe my eyes on the transformation of Jimmy. He was so domesticated; he actually was better at it than me.

We went to visit Jimmy and Helen twice, and they came to visit us whenever he came to visit his mother. By this time Jimmy had learned how to drive and had his own car. Jimmy had come full circle. He was a real family man. We now talked about our jobs, our pays, and how tough it was at times making ends meet, but he was happy and so was I. It was not too long ago that our conversations only centered on where we could go to have a good time, now here we are talking about comparing our different lifestyles and where we will go from here.

Jimmy came into my life and brought me a great deal of joy, mixed in some times with a little sorrow, but he gave me the courage to speak up and not be afraid of the consequences. It would serve me well later on when I went into sales and had to learn how to make a cold call. Over the years I often would think of Jimmy and of all the good times we had, especially at times when I had to drive long distances on my cake route. I would reflect on those times and start laughing to myself, and it made the drive seem a lot easier.

The day I got the phone call that Jimmy had passed away was a day that still lingers in my mind. Jimmy died of an enlarged heart. We never knew he had any kind of heart trouble, not with the way he carried on his life, a life he lived with abandonment. I could not believe the news. He was so full of life and had so much going for him—a wonderful wife and a beautiful daughter, a good job, and for this to end this very sad. Helen had Jimmy brought to be buried in New Haven to be near his family. That showed Helen always thinking not of herself, but of others.

Jimmy passed away at the age of 40 years old in 1962.

FRANK'S BEST FRIEND, CHICKIE

This next story is of one of my brother, Frank's best friend. You might say they were joined at the hip, friends almost from birth and most people thought they were brothers. They were a year apart in age, and lived just a few doors away from each other. Chickie and I were separated by about eight years, and I went to school with his brother Mike. Mike and I also were very close, actually life-long friends, as I have already written about him earlier.

Chickie was born on March 4, 1936, while Frank was born on March 5, 1937. Chickie's life at home was more severe, and full of hardship due to the being born into a family of nine other siblings- five boys and five girls. They were all living in a four room cold water flat with the shared toilet in the hallway. Five boys were sleeping in one room and five girls slept in another room, while the mother and father had their own room, and they all shared the small kitchen. Our home was spacious compared to his: we had an attic we could use and our family, while we numbered eight in all, shared four rooms, but we had a toilet in our flat.

From the time Chickie was born, and as far as I could remember, he always had that mischievous, spur of the moment, cavalier attitude toward life. Chickie's father was sick, almost from the time he was a young boy. His mother and older siblings had to raise him, so this is where Chickie's life and personality began to take form. He constantly wanted to be accepted by someone, thence his desire to do and say outlandish things just to bring attention to himself and to be admired by others.

He acted this way during a time of great poverty for his family. They received very little assistance from anyone, which was a tremendous feat in and of itself for a mother with ten children and a sick husband. I have written about Chickie's mother earlier, and to this day, I still have memories of her, unlike any other in my neighborhood.

He always worked at some kind of job, such as a helper on a milk truck, and whatever menial work boys at that time could find. The one job that Chickie excelled at was selling himself. He did have the personality to offer, always making jokes, imitating people, and of course disguising his voice, which I will get to later on.

At the tender age of twelve, Chickie got a job working in a small restaurant that was primarily a hangout for gamblers and bookies. The place had a battery of phones on one wall so it was convenient for the bookies to conduct their business. Chickie was a helper in the kitchen area, and I might add the food was pretty good. All of the food was being made from scratch, and there was always a big pot of tomato sauce on the stove.

One day the restaurant received a tip that a raid was going to be conducted and that the police were on their way. Now the bookies had to hide the betting slips containing the day's action, and there was no time to bury them in the yard. They give the slips to Chickie, thinking the police will not search him, which ultimately was a bad decision.

In walks the chief of detectives, who had a vendetta against this establishment. Actually he hated them. The police storm the place and find everyone sitting in the booths, eating, drinking, and just making conversation. They welcomed the police, although with a smirk, so the police started to shake down all the so-called "customers", but they found nothing.

Now the guys were worried and became desperate to find something. The chief went over to Chickie, who was in the kitchen stirring the sauce, and started to question him. The rest of the guys were squirming, and Chickie tells the chief, "I don't know. Maybe they are in here," as he points to the sauce. The chief pats Chickie on the head and tells him to be a good boy. He even offers the chief a taste of the sauce, which he declines.

After the shakedown, when the police leave, the bookies run up to Chickie and yell, "What the hell did you do with the slips?" Calmly, Chickie said, "Not to worry." He grabs the big spoon, and scoops out the slips, which were wrapped in wax paper, and were on the bottom of the sauce. They raise Chickie up, and march him around the restaurant, like a conquering hero.

Chickie was all of twelve years old, but he was growing up fast, and deception was now part of his act.

When Chickie was a little boy and he had to wear glasses, but the ones they were able to get were a little too big for him. The glasses made him look comical, and also kind of weird. One day Chickie and some of his friends stopped off at the pizza place, and as they were sitting in the booth, making jokes, and just having a good time, the owner came over to them, and told them to stop with the chatter. The owner, Peter, especially singled out Chickie, and mocked him, for his appearance, making a comment, "You little four eye little shit. I will be keeping an eye on you," making Chickie feel uncomfortable in front of all the other customers. This would start a twenty year vendetta, between Chickie, and the pizza owner.

As Chickie got into his teen years, he started playing phone tag with the owner, placing crazy orders and harassing him for his lousy pizzas. But the best was yet to come. Chickie found the owners Achilles' heel: the owner's wife. She was a rather good looking waitress in the restaurant, and for those days she dressed rather risqué, such has low cut blouses which drew the attention of the male customers.

Chickie would go to the phone booth across the street from the restaurant, and ask Peter if he could speak to his wife. Chickie knew of the strong jealousy Peter had for his wife, due to the male customers always commenting on her looks. On the days when Peter's wife was out doing some shopping along the avenue, Chickie would see her and that would be his moment to go and call Peter. He would rush to the phone booth, call Peter, and start the conversation with how he was with Peter's wife, even going so far as to describe her clothing to Peter. Chickie would speak Italian to Peter, all the while he was watching from across the street, and see Peter slamming the phone, getting enraged with every word. He would say to Peter, "Listen to us while we are making love," and make slurping sounds in the background. By now Peter is beside himself with uncontrollable rage, demanding to know who the hell he is talking to.

Peter in total anger, responding in Italian, "Chi Da Stramorte, Stu Pizze Strunze," [in anger, and you little shit,]. Such was the jealousy that this man had for his wife. He would constantly monitor her every movements. After the phone calls, Chickie would wait for the wife to come home and watch their exchange from across the street, reveling in the turmoil taking place in the restaurant. His wife was innocent of all the accusations thrown at her by Peter, but she struggled to account for her every hour she was away.

The scene that just transpired was another notch in Chickie's belt, making atones for the years ago insult, and he knew no ends. What was to come later was even more devastating, the insult of all time, especially for an old world Italian like Peter.

As was mentioned Chickie had a flair for imitating peoples voices, especially women's voices. I should know as I was on the receiving end of one of those calls. It's not funny when it's you, but with me and his friends, he had a way of not offending the wives of his friends to the degree of anger, but he knew no bounds when he wanted to mess with Peter.

Chickie called the restaurant, and as usual Peter would answer. Chickie, in his very seductive female voice, husky in tone, would ask for Peter's wife, Mary. Peter asks for the women's name, she responds, in a throaty voice the name. Peter does not confirm the name, but he asks what it is she wants. Chickie now goes into a beautiful profession of love that she has with Mary and wants to confirm their next date.

For Peter, now the shit really hits the fan. He was used to having to deal with attention of men, but now this, a woman calling his wife for a date to make love. Peter's face was by now a glowing red, and his neck veins were about to burst. Chickie, kneeling down in the phone booth, peeking out through the side window, hearing Peter yell to Mary, "Che Fa" [what are you doing] what kind of a " Putaun" [whore] are you, a woman calling for a date! "Che Spachine".

Chickie would not let up on this guy, and the problems he caused between Peter and his wife were legendary. We died of laughter whenever he told these stories, and sometimes with my brother Frank chiming in to be an accomplice in the mayhem. Chickie would call people that aggravated him and disguise his voice to irritate them. If it was a man, he stir things up. He called this his "AT&T Hour"! He would also repeat the reverse if it was woman, but always with the same M.O. (adultery), which was a sure subject to stir things up.

Another one of Chickie's habits was his way of looking for flaws in the character of people he met. If he noticed the littlest bit of perceived slight towards him, and he would go ballistic. Such is the story of when we would frequent the Railroad Y.M. It was there where we would often go and take our showers since the R.R. maintained a very clean shower room.

This facility was primarily used for the men who worked on the railroad, and when they had to layover between stops, they would stay there. But they also allowed the public to have full use of the premises. The man behind the counter could sometimes be a little brash with us, using Italian slur names, so we would call him the big Mick to show the feeling was mutual.

This one particular day, as Frank related the story to me, the big Mick rubbed Chickie the wrong way by refusing to give Chickie an extra bar of soap. The bar they gave was small but just about enough to take a shower. Now after being refused the extra bar, Chickie goes into a sorrowful explanation, but the Mick says he will have to make do.

Now the stage is set in the mind of Chickie. The Mick has to pay for this insult, but to what degree? It has to be awful, and lasting, but what? After he and Frank take their showers, a light goes on in Chickie's head; he came up with something really stinky and something that the Mick will remember for a long time. Unknown to Frank, Chickie excuses himself, and tells Frank that he will be right back. Frank had no idea of what was about to transpire.

Chickie goes into the stall and relieves himself of a bowel movement. He takes the excrement from the bowl with a board, wraps the stuff in paper towels, and places the crap in the highest locker and shuts the door. At about that time the place was getting busy, and a lot of men were entering the shower room. Not many low lockers left, so they started to use the high ones.

Chickie and Frank were in the next room sitting down, waiting for someone to open the locker door with the surprise in it, and when they did, Chickie and Frank heard a loud scream. The big Mick runs into the shower room with everyone else staring at this scene. The Mick is mystified: "How the hell did this asshole take a crap in this locker?" He could not figure out how someone could put his ass in there so high.

Chickie tells the Mick, "When we were in the shower, we heard these two guys, laughing, and slamming the locker doors." Mick responds, "I knew I should not have let them in; they looked shitty to me." Another day in the life of Chickie.

One of the characters in my neighborhood was a man who owned a restaurant, and who was a pretty good singer in his own right, but he fashioned himself after the famous Italian singer Enrico Caruso. He even dressed like him, especially wearing his large brimmed hat the way Caruso did, tilted to the side, and even wore the cape Caruso wore.

The restaurant was a pretty popular place and was doing well, until the 1960s when the highway system was coming through. Outside of one business deal I had with him, I really never knew him, but he was the butt of many jokes made by a lot of people. One my dear friends Chickie, made such a great impersonation of the owner of the restaurant. That was something that should have been on tape.

Chickie came down the street one day wearing a big white hat with a large brim on it with a cape over his shoulders just like Caruso. Chickie had the strut of the restaurant owner down to a science; he even tried to mimic the singing. Chickie had the peppers to even go into the restaurant, but without the Caruso attire, and actually imitate the owner inside the guy's restaurant. One day while I was sitting at the counter, I saw Chickie do this. He came up to me and strutted just like the owner, waving his arms and gesturing like he was Caruso. The owner just stood there giving Chickie the long and hateful look.

Another character was the owner of another restaurant in our neighborhood. He also was a sight to see. This guy thought he was God's gift to women, and he also would dress accordingly, always being in style with lots of very big flamboyant hats. Chickie also did a number on this guy. Chickie had no reservations about mocking him to his face. He'd walk into his restaurant, even talking to him in the same tone of voice. I could still see Chickie walking down the street doing an impression of him.

These two restaurant owners were cut from the same cloth, both living in a fantasy world that only they could envision. One thought he was the great Caruso, the other fashioned himself a great movie star with all the women adoring him and not being able to live without him. They left themselves ripe for ridicule, especially from a guy like Chickie, who was the master goof artist. Chickie looked for flaws like that in people like them; he was obsessed with these kinds of characters.

Once, I invited Chickie to a dinner party with a group of people that I knew. At this dinner was a person who had a great passion and love of wine. As the wine was brought to the table by the waiter, this guy who was in my club took the wine bottle and examined the label. He then had the waiter pour a small amount to taste it. He accepts it, then goes into a series of wine babble, explaining how the origins of where the wine comes from is very important. All this time I am looking at Chickie's face and checking his expression. I could see Chickie was conjuring up something. The guy then proceeds to explain about how to pour a glass of wine properly, by holding the glass slightly on an angle and to pour gently. Then he starts to demonstrate how you only pour a small amount in the glass, and ever so gently start to twirl it around the bottom of the glass, smelling it for taste. He then he tells us to inhale the aroma as you do this. At this time I am saying to myself, all this for a glass of wine?

He then drinks a small amount and swirls it around his mouth. He lets out a smile of satisfaction, raising his glass in the process. Now Chickie gets up and says, "Oh I know how to do that!" Chickie grabs a water glass and fills it up to the top. He then drinks the wine like it was a glass of water, all the while making slurping sounds as he is drinking it. The table now erupts in laughter, and the guy gives Chickie a look, like who the hell is this asshole, then excuses himself and goes on to another table.

This was Chickie's normal behavior. Anyone who knew Chickie knew you do not do anything in his presence that you do want duplicated, as my friend from the club tells me on the way out the door, "You better get that guy some help; he is one crazy bastard." In a crowd of people you did know what Chickie was contemplating. If anyone did anything that to him was out of the ordinary, you knew Chickie would seize upon it.

On Grand Ave. a man named Sal was made for Chickie's antics, and he owned a small breakfast shop which was one of many restaurants that this man owned over a period of years. Sal was noted for being well groomed and very neat in his appearance. In fact, he looked almost as if he was not working in the restaurant. He always had a white shirt and neck tie on, all this even while he was doing the cooking. Sal was a great foil for Chickie. I mean who the hell gets behind a stove with a white shirt and neck tie on, especially a small coffee shop in a blue collar area full of factory workers? The place was kept immaculate, which was a sight to see in this area. Sal's other establishments were all the same, but they were in a much better part of town.

Chickie meets me one day and said, "Let's go and pay Sal a visit. I have not seen him for a long time, but first I have to go home and change." Change he did. Chickie came out of his house wearing a white shirt and neck tie on. He said, "Now let's go and have something to eat at Sal's."

Chickie was now primed and ready to go into his act. Upon arriving at Sal's, the first thing Chickie does is give Sal a great big greeting, all the while walking just like Sal with his arms spread apart so has not to get his shirt dirty. Sal always had that distinct walk about him with his arms spread apart, giving the impression to people to not get near him. Sal was meticulous with that clean white shirt on.

Chickie, on the other hand, was the total opposite of Sal. The moment Sal hears Chickie's greeting, Sal turns around with a skillet in his hand and the look of disgust on his face. I thought Sal was going to fling the damn pan at him. Sal tells Chickie, "Get the shit out of here and go and break balls somewhere else." Chickie responds, "That's no way to treat a customer!" All the while, Chickie is walking around the shop with his arms spread apart, gesturing to me, "Wipe that table, I think it is not clean."

Not to take any chances, I was near the door. The expression on Sal's face was not pretty. Sal comes out from behind the counter, with the pan in his hand, and he had the look of extreme anger on his face. Chickie still did not move, "Sal, what the hell? I just came in for some food! Is this any way to treat a friend?" Sal yells out, "Move your ass!" As Chickie is talking to Sal, he is still mimicking Sal, with his arms spread apart and dusting off his shirt as he is leaving the shop.

Another night I remember was one that ended in utter chaos. We were at a stag for one of my brothers in law at a club in Milford. My brother Ralph, and my brother in law John were of the same cloth, both happy-go-lucky type of guys, so it was no wonder that they would team up with some crazy idea of going into show business. They wanted to be the next Martin & Lewis (a far cry believe me). On the night of the stag, they were going to try out their routine, which was their first mistake, without Chickie there.

John was supposed to be the song and dance man with Ralph playing the foil. They had rehearsed for this night for some time, lining up all the jokes and songs. As the show started, with the master of cere-monies introducing the acts of the other performers, John and Ralph were busy backstage honing their act. John and Ralph would be stuck following the act everyone was waiting for- the stripper.

The owner agreed to let them have some time on the stage. This club had a stage that would rise up about six feet off the floor so that the performers would have great visibility. This was a night made for Chickie but unbeknownst to John and Ralph, Chickie was already conjuring up his reply to their great show business entrance- a night to remember. As the stripper was in the process of finishing her act, we could see John and Ralph through the curtain, with John holding his straw hat and cane, doing a little dance step as Ralph cheered him on.

The scene unfolding in the club was one of sheer laughter because everyone was waiting for the big act to come on. Most of our group made up a great part of the audience, and we all had seats right near the stage. John and Ralph were about to get the reception of their short show business lives.

As the master of ceremonies started to introduce John and Ralph's act, Chickie was already conjuring up some bad mischief. The build-up was tremendous, with the emcee really laying it on, saying this next act has bookings in all the major cities. The club was generous in allowing them to perform and went along with the gag.

Now the lights go dim, and the spotlight is thrust upon John, who came on stage, singing his favorite song, "Penny Serenade". John was flipping his hat and cane in tune with the song, doing his dance shuffle, and as the song is coming to an end, Ralph casually struts onto the stage. John stops the song, and asks Ralph, "Hi Ralph, where you been? I have not seen you in a long time." Ralph responds with the corniest answer, "Hey John, I just flew in from California, and my arms are tired!"

With that joke the audience went into an uproar, booing the shit out of them, and that was the cue for Chickie to throw an avalanche of material at them. First Chickie threw all the towels on the tables, and then he started to fling the chairs and anything else that was not nailed down. Everyone else began to join in, all laughing their asses off.

In the midst of all this, John kept right on singing, oblivious, to all the catcalls from the audience until the owner put an end to their misery. As John and Ralph left the stage, they came up to us and said we spoiled their act. Chickie interrupted them by saying, "You two assholes should be ashamed of your selves," and the booing did not stop. Remember, this was a stag, and by the time they went on, everyone was pretty well lit up, so it did not take much prompting from Chickie for the place to get out of control.

Chickie, as is my understanding, was inducted into the Army but initially I did not know he was even in the service, because it was of such a short duration. I believe the timeline was just a few months, and knowing Chickie, obeying authority was not in his D.N.A. Just to picture him being told what to do was something I could not see; he regularly would do the opposite of anything that he was ordered to do, especially by a top sergeant, who by nature always came from down south and was ripe for Chickie to mimic. He was a quick study in the character and mannerisms of people, not always for the good, and he would openly display his interpretations right in front of his subject. During his time in the Army, Chickie came to a quick decision: he was not cut out for any service. His whole life was centered upon doing exactly the opposite of what was excepted of him. Conformity was not on his strong suit.

Being the class clown sometimes will follow you all through life. People that knew him would expect him to say or do crazy shit, and he was always good for a laugh. In that sense, he was trapped with this personality: one of merriment at all times and never to be taken seriously. He worked as a waiter in a pizza restaurant, and he did bring a lot of business to that establishment due to his vibrant personality.

Whenever I would enter the pizza place, I made sure to have Chickie wait on us. He had a way with my children. What child does not want to be entertained? The other two male waiters were foils for Chickie. He would imitate their walk and speech and my children could not stop laughing, always begging to return.

Chickie and Gaetano, the waiter: Chickee worked at the pizza place on Wooster Street with Gaetano. Gaetano had a severe hearing problem so he had to use a device which had a dial that would hang from his neck to control the volume. He would have it tucked under his apron.

Chickie would seize this opportunity many times as a way of angering Gaetano. Chickee's favorite was calling Gaetano from one end of the room, just by moving his lips. Gaetano would keep turning up the volume but still could not hear, even pressing closer to Chickee. Between these two was the rivalry of securing the best tables, so Chickee would unleash a torrent of lip reading at him, then mixing up the tickets on Gaetano's tables as the wrong orders.

He was very successful in this endeavor. The job was a great way to showcase his talents of mimicry. He and I talked at length many times about his opening his own place, of which I know he would have been successful, but he told me he was earning a good pay, and without the headaches of ownership. Well, after some time, he did give thought to owning his own restaurant, but it was not a just pizza place, it was a full menu restaurant called Salvatore's, his full name. It was a place with white tablecloths and furnished beautifully.

I was so proud of him; he now had fulfilled his dream, but as it turned out, much to my chagrin, he also had two partners, who were actually the money men. The restaurant became extremely successful.

After some time, the rumors started to surface that Chickie was not able to meet his obligations with his partners. Chickie was out of his league and the restaurant was dissolved.

After the restaurant went belly up, Chickie got a job as a bus driver, another job in which he was well suited for. He had the perfect personality- a very affable people person. He greeted the passengers as if they were his family, and of course that made a big impression with them.

At about that time I started my own business, a retail bakery distributorship, so it came to pass that our paths would cross again. My first warehouse was on his route, so I knew many fun days were about to begin. One of them was when Chickie would drive his bus off his route and park in front of our office to stop in and have coffee, even while he had a bus load of people who just sat there staring straight ahead. He would call us and tell us look through the keyhole in the door at the scene. That would give all of us a fit of laughter, and the passengers did not even notice that he was not on his route. He would say, "Look at those fools!" Every once in a while he would pop out the door and wave to them.

One day as Frank and I were driving back to our office, and we encountered Chickie at the corner of the street. He stops the bus, gets out in front it and shouts to the passengers to get up and all go to the back of the bus, explaining that something was wrong with the front of the bus. They all got up and followed his directions, but then he gets on the bus, and tells them to all keep going past the middle of the bus, thereby having them all bunched up together. He then drives down the street with all the passengers standing and squatting together. It was quite a sight.

Another one of his quirks was to mimic the passengers, and since most of them were steady customers on his line, they took all his jibes with a grain of salt. In fact I think they enjoyed his portrayal of the passengers. He would sometimes even give them a song. Before the buses had a handicap ramp to help people get on the bus, he would go out on the sidewalk and help the elderly people get on the bus, all the while poking fun at them in a good mannerly way. Now his route was primarily in the section of the city that had a large population of African Americans and as was stated before, it was never boring on Chickie's route. He had a penchant for imitating voices and manner of speech, but while doing this, he made sure to never offend anyone with personal remarks. He would have the whole bus laughing at his jokes. He sometimes would stop the bus and have everyone join him in song. No one ever complained to the bus company about Chickie. While going through his act, he made damn sure not to do any off color jokes. To make everyone feel at ease, he would even make fun of his own heritage just to make it even.

One day in particular involving Chickie is burned into my mind. I was on my way back to my office, and I had to go past the huge garage of the bus company depot that housed all the busses. It was also the office all of the drivers had to report to and from there they would be assigned a station to wait for some transportation to their respective routes.

Well, on this day I encountered Chickie waiting at the corner of his garage, along with a group of other drivers. As I turned the corner and had to slow down because of traffic, Chickie sees me and runs out in front of my car, shouting obscenities at me, waving his fist saying, "You dirty son of a bitch, you better leave my wife alone, I know you are screwing her!" Now he is banging his fists on the hood of my car and traffic has now stopped. People started gathering, office windows were opening up to see what all the disturbance is about. Now Chickie starts to really put on a show by running all around my car, shaking his fists. All the drivers on the corner are trying to get Chickie off the street and Chickie's swearing, "You lousy bastard, I will get you!" It was hard for me to contain myself, driving slowly away and laughing at all the commotion Chickie had caused. Looking in my rear view mirror, I saw all the drivers centered on Chickie. They knew it was a bunch of bullshit because they knew he was not married, but the asses on the street did not know. Today this would for sure be on the Internet and probably go viral.

Eventually Chickie did get married and to a very lovely woman. She was the daughter of an owner of a successful Italian pastry shop. This marriage began and ended way before Chickie started working for the bus company. It was one of the largest weddings I had ever attended, and the brother of his wife spared no expense. It was a first class wedding. At that time most people went to a hall and had a catered affair, but this was in a huge restaurant, and well attended by over four hundred people.

There was a difference in ages, with the girl being a little bit older than Chickie, and horrible rumors went around that he married her just for the money. The truth was far from it, he was not like that, but it was a union that was doomed to fail for no other reason than that Chickie was not prepared for married life. Chickie was the so outgoing and gregarious; he seldom took anything seriously, because he always gave more than he received.

After several years, the marriage dissolved and he wandered through several different relationships, mostly of a physical nature. All the while he was still searching for someone to extend himself to, and every time I met him, he seemed to have a new girlfriend. He'd say he was satisfied but not for long.

One of Chickie's great talents that many people did not know about was his mastery of the organ. He learned how to play the instrument without ever having taken a lesson. He never learned to read music, but he was masterful at it. He purchased one for the sum of thirteen thousand dollars, many times calling me and having me listen to his rendition of any song. Every time I had the occasion to visit his apartment, he would entertain me with his playing. When Chickie started to play, you could see the expression of his love of music. Gone were all the crude jokes he was noted for; the joy of his playing the organ captured him like nothing else. Sitting there one day listening to Chickie playing, I kept thinking of the little pain in the ass he was when he was a little boy, and yet here he had this talent that was hidden away from society. Playing the organ for people gave him a great pleasure, and yet he never had the strength to follow through with this gift. In life they say you must go with your strengths, but it somehow eluded him.

The one of his great moments in life was the day he told me that he had purchased a two family home for his two sisters, who were not married. Because of their status in life, the obligation to help them was overwhelming. His family was a pretty close knit group, helping one another was common, but this was beyond the ordinary relationship between siblings. For that period in time, his gesture was extremely over the top generous, which was something a lot of people did not know about this man.

As life went on for Chickie, he developed some bad health problems. He had high blood pressure, just like his father. This condition caused his father to have a stroke and become immobile. He became a burden on himself and his family. Besides that, Chickie also had some other health problems that were going to have a devastating effect on him and create one of the strangest meetings between two very close friends.

After undergoing is annual physical, my brother Frank was diagnosed with a severe blockage of his arteries. As a result, he was informed that he would have to undergo open heart surgery to relieve the situation. Frank could not believe the findings of the tests, as he always had a regimen of walking about three miles a day and lived without any dis-comfort. But with our family history, our father and I both having the same problem, blocked arteries, Frank knew he had to take it seriously.

Now to get back to Chickie and his worsening health problems. To help him, he had to take some pretty strong medications, which gave him a lot of side effects. One in particular was not being able have an erection, which gave him grave concern. This was before Viagra, so the spiral of decline of his health woes was taking hold to the point of having to undergo major surgery to clear the blockage of debris setting in veins leading to his head. The meeting of these long-time friends who used to be almost joined at the hip was about to take place.

Frank was scheduled for his surgery, not knowing that Chickie was also to be operated on. Frank knew of Chickie's admittance to the hospital, but not of his surgery. Frank goes to the hospital and as they do with these types of surgeries, there are lots of tubes and medications to numb the pain. After Frank had his operation, he goes through the usual procedure of the recovery room, and after some time was placed in a regular room. By now, Frank was oblivious to anything or anyone. He was sedated quite well, and the room they assigned him to was with another person. When he awoke the next day, he only saw a curtain closed between him and the next person, never hearing a sound from the person because the person was in a coma that was induced by the doctors. Frank's wife Carla, who sat beside him throughout the surgery and recovery, motioned to Frank, "Who do you think is in the next bed?" Frank, in a state of numbness, eyes half closed, did not have any clue.

So Carla parts the curtain to have Frank have a look. Frank, peering through a haze of medications, made an effort despite the pain. He saw the features of a very familiar person. After some agonizing moves in bed, he finally had a better view, and saw it was Chickie. How in all the world could this happen? Two life-long friends united by sheer happenstance to wind up in the same room.

In the same room was Frank, who made a great effort to keep a healthy body, and Chickie, disobeying the doctor's orders to stay on his medications just so that he would be able to perform whenever he wanted. Chickie made a bad choice- pleasure before his health, and so with Frank feeling he did what he was supposed to do, he could not believe they both ended up in the same place.

The surgery Chickie had was to relieve the pressure of blood cloths in his head. After this he would never be the same. On visiting Frank, I was told of Chickie being in the next bed, not being able to speak, due to the induced coma. It was not a pretty sight; a man so outgoing, full of life, now being reduced to a vegetative state. On my second visit to see Frank, I refused to have a look at Chickie. Frank was being prepped to come home, but not Chickie. He would now be on a downward spiral of poor health for the rest of his life. It was hard for me to not see Chickie, but I didn't want to have that memory.

After Chickie finally was released from the hospital, I saw him at a dinner function, and the scar of the surgery was quite large. It covered almost the whole side of his head. He was now subdued, moving very slowly, his words slurring, and his eyes in a fixated position, staring straight ahead. He was not able to view people on either side of him. The image was quite shocking to those who knew him before the surgery.

From time to time, I would see Chickie at different gatherings and every time he seemed to have less mobility. Upon seeing me, he would ask me for my name, as he did with everyone else. The deterioration was excruciating to encounter. Whatever faults this man had, leaving life in that state is not pretty. Finally he had to be confined to a facility since he was no longer able to care for himself. He spent his last days sitting in a wheelchair, with his head slumped over, not knowing of his surroundings.

This man, who at times, carried on with his antics too long and ruffled a lot of people the wrong way, was a great supporter of his siblings. He constantly saw to their needs and this aspect of his personality took the edge off his foolishness. One might say, as a lot did, that Chickie, was in an Italian expression, a "chovone" translation: "a boorish person", but to me, I overlooked that, because along with that bullshitting expression of his, he did give me and others a lot of humor, mostly at the expense of others. But as I mentioned before, his dedication to his friends and family was beyond reproach.

Sadly, Chickie passed away September 2011.

CHICKIE'S SISTER, RAE

This next story is not in the category of characters, but of a great family friend: Chickie's sister, Rae. She was a few years older than me, but we had a lot interaction over the years, due to my friendship with her brothers. As I stated previously, Rae was one of the eldest siblings, and helped her mom with the raising of her younger sisters and brothers. She actually became a mother before her time, as so many young girls did in the large families in my neighborhood.

In trying to gather materials for this book, I was involved with many people who had the materials that I wanted, such as photos, maps, information. I also interviewed anyone who could help me in my endeavor. This journey would cover quite a bit of ground, and this is one such story that would carry me back in time.

One day I met Rae's brother Fred, and in the course of our conversation, I discovered Fred and I had the same interest in our past history of our neighborhood. It was during one of our chats, that Fred told me about his sister Rae, who also had some photos of our neighborhood, in fact quite a few of them. One in particular was a photo of a neighborhood movie theatre, one that I sought after for quite a while. I even went to the New Haven Museum, but to no avail.

The photo was of the Dreamland theatre, one in which I spent a great part of youth, especially the Saturday matinees. It was a place where we could escape for a few hours a week and get lost into a different world. The price of admittance was only ten cents, but it was a huge sum for us kids. Most kids did just about anything to come up with the money; this was the treat of the week.

So for all the photos that I collected, the movie theatre was the one that I coveted the most. So when Fred told me Rae had a copy of the theatre, I was completely overjoyed. I felt like I was finding a lost love or a jewel almost. After Fred gave me Rae's number, I called her, and she was so happy to hear from me. That the conversation went on for some time before Rae asked me, "Leo, what are you presently doing?" I said, "Rae, I am in the midst of gathering material for a book, such as photos, etc. and in speaking to your brother Fred, he told me that you had a picture of the Dreamland theatre, which is one that I have been chasing for a long time."

"Oh Leo, yes I do, and you are more than welcome to come and see it." We set up a date for me to come and interview her and see the photos. I was so excited after searching for so long and here it was right in a home of a friend of mine. Rae lived in the town of Orange, a nice suburban enclave of beautifully kept homes. Driving down the street to Rae's house, my mind wandered back to when we were young and living in the exact opposite of this street. This was a world away from the dust and grime we grew up in, and I imagined what it must be for Rae to come from a four room cold water flat with twelve people. We had a lot in common, and I saw that we probably had the same sense of joy in purchasing our homes.

Pulling into Rae's driveway, the first thing that struck me was the beauty of the yard. There were lots of flowers, and I felt so far removed from both our previous dwellings. Going up to the door, I walked on a little pathway that was so picturesque and displayed lots of love and tender care. To the outside surroundings, as I approached the door, the splendor of the door struck me as very beautiful.

I rang the doorbell, and it was answered by Rae's husband, who welcomed us graciously. His name was Dallas, and after introducing my wife, Teresa, to Dallas, he led us to a nice room and had us sit down, as Rae was still dressing. I had been informed that Rae was in ill health but to what extent I did not know. I did not want to overstay my visit, so I kept thinking how to make this visit as short as possible, and yet not give the impression, of just coming over to obtain something.

Entering the room with our host Dallas gave me such a warm feeling. The light was shining through the blinds, and it was just a beautiful family room. The picture that I wanted was in this room, but my sightline was hindered, as I was facing the window, and did not want to seem too aggressive. I stared around the room as Dallas was making small conversation with us and offering us beverages. We declined at first, but then I did not want to also be rude, so we had some soft drinks. I almost felt like an intruder, as I have not seen Rae in quite a few years, and here I was, sitting in her home, looking for a picture, but that notion of fear was soon dispelled.

As Rae enters the room, she throws out her arms and gave me a warm embrace, as if time had stood still, I got the feeling as if it was yesterday that we had last seen each other. She was that kind of person. After introductions to my wife Teresa, to whom she also greeted warmly, being slow of foot, she asked us to all sit down, I understood, and we chatted.

Rae was eager for information about my family and she was just digesting all she could in such a short time. Dallas was also very conversational and I almost forgot why I came. Then Rae points to the opposite wall: "Here, Leo, is the picture I have of the dreamland theatre, and also buildings on St. Johns St." But looking at the picture, which was mounted on a wall with had a large piece of furniture in front of it.

Rae asks Dallas, "Bring down the picture so Leo can get a better view of it." Dallas had to step on this huge couch to bring the picture down, almost falling in the process. He gives the picture to Rae, and she in turn asks me to hold it. Together we are holding this picture and reminiscing like two kids, sharing our memories of the many Saturdays we spent there. So many memories of a time when a few hours in a movie theatre would lessen the burden of the deprivation we faced at home. We would be transported into another world, one that was near and yet so far.

After some time chatting, Rae gave me the pictures to take home, so I could make copies of them and return the originals. For Rae to do this was very generous on her part, and a gift that I would definitively not abuse. With my experience in obtaining photos, you had to give this transaction a lot of respect. I had copies made and sent her the pictures back as soon as possible, with a note of extreme thankfulness.

This next tidbit about Rae was given to me by my brother Frank. She overcame obstacles in her early life through her education. The influence of a teacher inspired Rae to concentrate on the skills she had, which was excelling in clerical work, to rise above her circumstances at home, and study has best she can, which was a feat in itself.

After graduating high school, Rae went to work in the office of a large manufacturer, and due to her devotion to succeed, went on to work her way up to being the manager of the office, something I was proud to hear.

Having this information about Rae, and seeing her conduct herself with dignity with her illness was beyond my expectations of her. As we were getting ready to depart, Rae rose slowly from her chair, embraced

Teresa, and gave me a hug has best she could. She thanked me for coming over, and said she was so happy to help me with my project. Her husband Dallas, also extended himself to me, and said he hoped to see us again. As we got into our car, Dallas and Rae, were in the doorway waving to us. Unfortunately the repeat visit was not to happen.

Rae passed away a short time later.

ATLANTIC CITY

This was our vacation of choice for the years of 1949 through 1953. Every 4th of July we would go there for a week. In comparison to Coney Island in New York, Atlantic City offered more in the way of entertainment and the crowds were more diverse. Instead of all from New York, we met people from all along the east coast. It was the place to go in the 1950s. This was a place for a lot of socializing, and the night life was really fantastic. There were so many choices, and we did not have to spend a lot of money to do so. We took the Garden State Parkway all the way down and the trip took us about five hours.

Tony had just bought an Oldsmobile 88 convertible with a rocket engine, and the car was two years old. He purchased it from a doctor who wanted to buy another car and was in a hurry to sell it. Tony got it for a very low price, and we thought we were in heaven gliding down the parkway to Atlantic City.

The hotels on the boardwalk were out of our reach due to the prices they were getting for a room, so most people stayed on the side streets leading up to the boardwalk where the hotels were more reasonable. The hotels on the boardwalk were all very classy. We would walk through the lobbies and just look at the well-dressed people who had rooms there. Those hotels had cabanas for the guests, which was only a short walk under the boardwalk for them.

One of the things that attracted us to Atlantic City along with the entertainment was the expansive beach. We loved the water because of the huge waves and would ride them into the shore. We would plank our towels near where the cabanas were located, feeling maybe we could meet some of the swells that patronized the hotels. Our hotel of choice was the sea gull hotel located about five blocks from where the large hotels were. In those days we never had to make a reservation because the owner always had a room for us. He would charge us three dollars a day each, including parking the car which was in a lot next to the hotel. We never had to use the car once while we were there because it was within walking distance to everything we wanted to do.

Once when a bunch of guys that were friends of my friend Ray wanted to meet us in Atlantic City. They asked us how much we were paying and thought it was too much. They came down in two cars and slept in their cars to save money. They wanted to use our bathroom in the hotel to wash up, but we told them to go and take a walk. Talk about being a cheap bunch of bastards. They washed up in the outside showers that were located right off the beach and used the bathrooms in any restaurant they could find. Jimmy would do a number on them every chance he got, calling them every name under the sun, but they just laughed it off. Jimmy said, "How the hell can you pieces of shit sleep in the car?" One guy was quite tall, and we couldn't figure out how they all fit.

The hot spot in Atlantic City was for us the 500 club. All the top entertainers of our era would perform there, such as Dean Martin, Jerry Lewis, Frank Sinatra, Jerry Vale, etc. The 500 club was owned by Skinny D. Amato and was on the same status as the best night clubs in New York by drawing all the top notch entertainers of the day. To bring a date there would be a very expensive evening, but being single you could stand at the bar and not have to spend much money and still see the show. The week I remember best is when Al Martino performed (Al Martino is the one who played the part of Frank Sinatra in the first godfather movie). It was a sold out week when he was there. Now to get inside the club was one thing, but to get to see the show was another. They had a man standing at the door to the showroom, holding a rope line. We were told that we had to give this guy five dollars each to enter the show room.

Jimmy yells out to no one particular, "I called Skinny about one hour ago, and he said he would meet us at the door." The doorman hears this and wanted to know Jimmy's name. "Jimmy from New York," Jimmy says with an air of authority. I thought the guy was going to throw us out on our ass, but instead he lets us in. On the way in Jimmy slips him a five dollar bill. But Jimmy being Jimmy he had to prowl around and look over the crowd and see if he could find any single girls. He did not have any luck because of the prices the club charged. It was mostly couples and single men. We said even if you met someone here, how the hell can you afford to pay for the bill? We know because any girls you met always suggested that they would like to go to the 500 club.

It just so happened that my friend Frank and I had gone down to Atlantic City about two days before the rest of the guys, and we met a bunch of girls who were staying at the home of the aunt of one of the girls in the Jewish section of Atlantic City. There was five of them, and I said in two days the rest of our friends would join us, so Frank and I dated two of them. This friend of mine Frank was a very shy guy and did not talk much so the girl that Frank was with was very leery of him. She said to me, "I do not trust him, he scares me, and he just smiles and does not talk much." I told the girls, "Hang on. The rest of the crew would be arriving soon." I did not want to lose contact with them because they were planning on having a big party at their house.

When Jimmy and the rest of the guys arrived, I told them about the girls I met and we would be invited to their house. Jimmy's mouth was watering. I said, "Hold on Jimmy, this is not what you think it is. They wanted to spend the day with us at the beach and then go out at night, maybe to a club or something like that." We did spend the day at the beach and I took a lot of pictures. We had a really nice time, and now I realized the girls were testing us by saying they would like to go the 500 Club. We suggested a different club which was not too expensive but nice. They were a little disappointed because here they were inviting us to their house for a big party, and we did not want to take them where they wanted to go.

The sad part of this was when Jimmy at the end of the evening starting making a lot of jokes about the Jewish people. I take Jimmy aside and tell him to lay off the Jew jokes because the girls were Jewish, but they had a fondness for Italian boys because they grew up in the city. At the end of the evening I knew we were not going to be invited to their house, and the girl I was with told me as much. Our group had plans to maybe spend the rest of the week with them, but it was not to be since Jimmy screwed it all up. Tony yells at Jimmy, "Asshole, we could have eaten all week at their house, you and your big mouth."

The next day I was supposed to meet the girl I was with. She told me she would meet me at the Steel Pier, but she never showed up. I waited for one hour past the time we agreed on, and by then I knew the party was off. All the photos of that day and in the night club were somehow misplaced in my house, and sadly the photos of a nice group of friends have been lost. To add a little salt in the wound of this whole fiasco, we saw the girls later on with some other guys. Naturally Jimmy wanted to go and punch their lights out. With Jimmy it was like a bull in a China closet—you had to keep a tight rein on him.

Jimmy redeemed himself later on in the week by taking us to a new club where we had the time of our lives. This club was known as the Jockey Club and was a gay bar for women. All the women in the bar were lesbians, and some were dressed as men and others were dressed as women. Now Jimmy was in his element since this was an audience he could be at ease with because they would not even pay attention to him, and he could say whatever he wanted and no one would listen. He did not have to hold back anything.

The bartenders were dressed like men, and they let Jimmy know in no uncertain terms that they would serve him drinks but not take any shit from him. The way Jimmy used to look when someone talked him down like that was so comical, like he was choir boy out for an evening. He would go into one of his stances, like to say, "Who me?" He would mimic the bartenders by telling them what a nice bunch of people they had in this establishment.

Jimmy spots a couple sitting at the bar and saddles up to the one who had a dress on. He tried to strike up a conversation, but they both look at Jimmy and tell him to go home and play with his trains. Jimmy would greet women by calling them "dolly" with a smile of his, but these girls were not in a mood to be greeted. Jimmy then extends his hand to the girl and wants to dance with her. The girl who was dressed in a manly fashion tells Jimmy, "Get your hands off my girl or I will kick you where the sun does not shine."

Now the bartender comes out from behind the bar and yells at Jimmy, "Hey, shithead, what the hell did I tell you? Now you and your posse get your asses out of here or I will break your little stones and shove them in your mouth." The bartender was a women but built like a truck driver. I believe she could have beaten the shit out of us with no problem. Jimmy had a penchant for teasing the gay crowd, and this was not to be the last one.

At the Sea Gull hotel came one of our funniest moments. Our daily routine was to go to the beach for a few hours, walk along the board-walk, and more or less mingle with the crowd to have a few laughs. It so happened this one day, Jimmy decides not to go with us to the beach. He said he just wanted to sleep late and rest up for a while. We all thought it was kind of strange of Jimmy not joining us for the day, since he was the one who enjoyed the beach the most, mostly due to the girls on the beach.

At around two o'clock Tony says, "I think that bastard has something up his sleeve. This is not normal for Jimmy not to come with us today." We said, "Leave him alone, maybe last night with the bartender shook him up." Ray comes back with, "When the hell did Jimmy ever worry about shit like that?" So we all looked at each other, and said okay, "Let's go and check his ass out." So back we go to the hotel. It is now about three o'clock in the afternoon, a time when Jimmy knew we would not be coming back since we never left the beach until around five o'clock.

Jimmy was nowhere in the lobby of the hotel or on the outside of the hotel. Now we all came to the same conclusion, it was like we all had the same mindset. Instead of taking the elevator up which was right across from our rooms, we walked up the stairs. The stairwell was down the hall from our room so we quietly walked to our adjoining rooms and slowly inserted the key into the door.

We pushed opened the door and there was Jimmy in bed with one of the maids. The maid lets out a scream, thinking maybe we were burglars or something. She grabs a sheet in a hurry to cover herself up and falls down in the process. Jimmy stands there butt naked, yelling at us with every expletive he could think of. We mocked him by calling him a dirty pig and a cheater. We said, "Jimmy, you sly son of a bitch. You should be ashamed of yourself by not telling us." That was only followed up by Jimmy with his devil may care attitude, doing whatever came to his mind. Jimmy never gave much thought to his actions. He brushed off our comments and we moved on. We were relaxing on the beds and catching up on our day at the beach, including who we met, etc.

Jimmy was the last one to shower up that night, but nobody was really paying any attention to him. We were deep into our conversation deciding our meal and the night ahead. All of a sudden we heard a lot of screaming coming from the hallway. We ran out and there was Jimmy standing by the window completely naked, looking out the window. We found out that what happened was when the elevator door opened, a bunch of guys and girls came out and saw Jimmy naked. To make matters worse, he turns around and wants to know what all the fuss is about. Jimmy, who had a dark complexion and was very hairy, would scare the shit out of anybody. According to him, he just wanted to look out the window. While we were laughing our asses off, the people did not think it was so funny. Some ran back into the elevator and some ran down the hallway. This was typical Jimmy. After all this commotion Jimmy calmly walks to our room and says, "What the hell are they yelling about? They are making all this fuss for nothing!" It was a wonder nobody called the management and reported this, as I know they would have us thrown us out of the hotel. To this day I often relive this moment. I can still see Jimmy standing by the window and looking around in amazement at all the people like they were the crazy ones. There is an expression that resonates with this incident: nothing is as precious as the innocence of a child. Not that I am putting Jimmy in that frame, but just his expressions of surprise when something goes wrong, like saying, "who me?"

This one day when the waves were really kicking up, and we were all excited about splashing around and riding the waves. We could not wait to get into the water. I would say the waves were about five feet in height. Once you got out past the beach and turned around in the water you could get a nice ride back to the beach. This day the water was really packed with people and you had to be careful not to bump into anyone. The water was so rough that we had to hold on to our bathing suits. The waves would just smack you and throw you down. As Tony, Ray, and I were coming down off a large wave, we heard this girl screaming near the water's edge. She had a two piece bathing suit on and the top came off in the waves, so now she was covering her chest with her arms and did not want to stand up. Who the hell comes up with her top is nobody but Jimmy, who was in the water nearby. Jimmy now tells her, "Here, Dolly, is your top." Of all the people in the water, Jimmy comes up with her top. In a nice gesture, women nearby came to stand around the girl while she got the top on. On this day, Jimmy proved himself to be gentleman by not staring at her. Although, Jimmy later commented, "She looked good from the top down."

In Atlantic City there were two piers, one was the steel pier and the other was the million dollar pier. The steel pier featured an attraction with a person on a horse jumping off a tower into a large vat of water, plus a lot of other attractions. The million dollar pier was also a place of entertainment, but not as gaudy; it also featured a lot of merchandise for sale.

One night on the million dollar pier, Jimmy and I went walking around taking in the sights. On this night there was an automobile display on for a number of different makes of cars. I happened to have on a seersucker sport coat on, which was mainly fashionable in the summer. I was interested in looking at the cars and Jimmy said he was going to look around and see what else there was. As I was standing near one of the cars, people mistook me for a salesman because of the way I was dressed. These three girls came up to me and starting asking me questions about the car, assuming I was a salesman. I went along with their assumption and made believe I was a salesman. One girl stayed and talked to me while the other two went off to look at the other attractions. Her name was Linda, and she said she was from Staten Island, New York. When I told her I was from New Haven, CT she said she had never heard of it.

Jimmy comes by and sees I was having a conversation with this girl and motions to me that he will see me later. After some time I told Linda I was bullshitting her. She just laughed and said, "You did have me fooled there for a while, but your sunburn gave you away." I asked her to take a walk with me around the boardwalk and maybe get a hot dog or something. She said, "I cannot leave my girlfriends. My mother told me not to leave them." I said we are only going for a walk, and we will be in the vicinity of the pier. I suggested they could walk behind us, "like they do in Italy". She got into a fit of laughter, "Oh, so you know."

Linda explained to me how her mother was "old world Italian" and I knew what she meant. I said, "My sisters had to be home by nine o'clock or else she would beat the hell out of them." We spent the rest of the evening talking about our families, and she showed me pictures of her house, which was a one family structure, and a very neat one at that. She wanted to see if I had any pictures of my home. Even if I did, I would not show them to her. My home was a shack compared to hers.

At about ten o'clock I took her back to her friends and asked her if she would spend the next day with me at the beach. She was hesitating, so I asked her if there was something wrong. She says, "What am I going to tell my friends?" I said, "We are only going to the beach, along with a thousand other people." She laughs and says, "How silly of me. Of course I will."

I picked up Linda at her hotel, and in front of her friends, told Linda, "The beach near the steel pier is nice," kind of letting her friends know where we will be. I know they checked up on us because Linda told me. After spending the whole day with her at the beach, I asked her to go out with me that evening. I gave her the place I wanted to take her and she said okay. It was a dinner show on the board walk and not far from her hotel.

Now at the end of the evening she became more comfortable with me and wanted to spend the next day with me. I said we were scheduled to go home in about another day. She then wanted to maybe correspond with me, but I said you are in New York on an Island, and this would be almost impossible for us. She kept pressing me for my address to maybe just write to me and keep in touch. I must say it was hard for me to make that conclusion, but I stopped going with girls only about ten miles from my home, and here she was about one hundred miles. I told Linda the distance is too great and how sorry I was not to see her again. We did have so much in common with our families being from the same part of Italy. On the way back to her hotel she kept pestering me for my address, so to console her I told her she will make somebody a good wife. We embraced, and I started to walk away. She just kept standing there watching me walk away. When I got to the corner I waved to her and she blew me a kiss.

As is the custom of Jimmy, he could not wait for me to give him the details of my date with this girl. I told him I had a nice time and we talked quite a bit and how she wanted to see me. "That's it?" Jimmy says, "You had a nice time and that's all?" "Jimmy," I say, "She was a nice girl and I respected her. What the hell, Jimmy, it was better than looking at your ugly face all night." Jimmy responds, "Leo, here you are out of town, you meet a girl and you spend the night talking to her, you should be ashamed of yourself. I am going to give you a few lessons on how to romance a girl." I laughed, "Jimmy, I had a great time. What the hell did you do?" Jimmy loved to tease me about my approach to girls. I thought his way was to be very aggressive.

When we would wrap up our vacation in Atlantic City, on the way home we would spend the weekend at Ted Hiltons in Moodus, CT. It was a resort where a lot of locals would spend a week's vacation. At this resort we also would sometimes spend a Sunday because they would put out a buffet table and you could have all the food you wanted. It was at one of our weekends at Ted Hiltons that Jimmy went ballistic. We met a lot of girls, but because of Jimmy's verbal and straight forward approach in asking girls to dance with him, they would politely decline because word quickly spread around that we were a bunch of roughnecks. Nevertheless, we were having a good time in watching Jimmy get shut down.

Now Jimmy always felt he was a man who knew his way around and could not understand why he was having such a hard time in securing a date for the day. As the day progressed, we got involved in some of the activities and were enjoying ourselves. Jimmy calls us and wants to know were Ralph is. We have not seen Ralph since right after breakfast when he was having a conversation with a girl. Jimmy did not think much of this girl calling her "a dog" so Jimmy said, "Let's go and look for Ralph." We scoured the resort and there was no sign of Ralph. Tony said, "Let's check our cabin. Maybe he is up there." This resort had a lot of cabins tucked away in the side of the hill, and that's what we rented because of the seclusion of the cabins.

Our cabin was stuck right on the side of the hill and to access the cabin there was a little winding path leading up to the cabin. All our minds were all on the same page, feeling Ralph sneaked up to the cabin to take a nap, so Jimmy says, "Let's go around the back and look in the window, and if Ralph is sleeping, we will all let out a great yell." At this time we had no idea if Ralph would be there. Now five of us crawl up to the window, and instead of finding Ralph asleep, there he was in bed with a girl, the same one Jimmy called a dog. Quietly we slipped down the path away from the cabin and waited for Ralph to return. Upon seeing Ralph, Jimmy lets out a barrage of expletives at Ralph, saying, "Of all the guys here this big nose bastard winds up with a girl!" Jimmy felt really insulted— the master of all women gets shot down and Ralph showed him up. We cracked up from laughing at Jimmy's antics.

1950 PNEUMONIA

In September of 1950, I contracted pneumonia. It was diagnosed as walking pneumonia, since the week I came down with it I kept feeling tired all week and could not understand why. I was not doing anything out of the ordinary, except just working and hanging out with my friends. At this time I was employed at Armstrong Rubber, and I had just gone through a very hot summer working at the rubber shop.

We used to take salt pills to replace what we expired and I thought working in all that heat was the reason I was so tired.

After about a week of feeling sluggish, I told my friend Tony that I did not feel good. Tony suggested to go home and go to bed, which I did. The very next day I came down with a fever. I felt like my head was on fire. My mother called the doctor, who came right over and diagnosed it has pneumonia. The ambulance was called, and two men brought up a stretcher and had to tie me down because I lived on the second floor, and it was a winding staircase. For them to bring me down, they had to lift me over a railing to get me down the stairs. By this time, a large crowd had gathered outside my house. It seemed like the whole neighborhood was there, wishing me well. My mother's friend was saying prayers for me has they put me in the ambulance.

In those days portable oxygen was not available, so all they did was wrap me in a lot of blankets and apply a head pack to help me with the fever. The ambulance had to drive up on the sidewalk to get as close to the house as possible. The sidewalk was just wide enough for the ambulance to squeeze through. The cars that were parked in front of the house were all moved so that the ambulance could get off the sidewalk without turning around. As I have mentioned early on, I lived in a very dense and heavily populated area, which was why there was such a large crowd assembled. I was told a lot of people were crying and praying for me. It was that kind of a neighborhood—people felt a kinship toward one another. Sometimes I wished you could have a little more privacy, but with living so close to one another it was hard to have that.

I stayed in the hospital for seven days and was administered an injection twice daily. The first few days were terrible with all the sweating and the cold shakes. The nurse that was taking care of me lived only three blocks from me. I knew of the family, but not on a social level. With the injections twice daily, I got to know her personally as she attended to me for the whole week. I can still see her coming in with the injection box, and I knew what she was going to say: "Roll over, my boy."

The doctor who took care of me had his office two blocks from my house. Mary called him because our other doctor could not make it.

He visited me for about a few days in the hospital. When I was discharged from the hospital, I went to his office for a checkup, and after his exam, I asked him how much I owed him for his services. He said, "25 dollars for everything. That includes the house visit and the hospital visits." I had to stay out of work for two more weeks to rest up, the doctor gave me a note to give to the company, saying I was to be put on light duty for another two weeks after I returned to work.

The hospital bill came to one hundred ten dollars. My father came to the hospital office with me to pay the bill. In those days you were supposed to clear your bill up before being discharged, but since my father was at work, they let me go home and return the next day to pay the bill. I drove Pop up to the hospital and as we entered the office, I was worried Pop would create a scene and argue about the bill. Surprisingly, Pop slapped down one hundred ten dollars all in small bills.

On the way home I could not stop thinking about the time I had to walk home after my operation when I was a little kid, just to save a dime for the trolley car. I wanted to get a dig at my father and remind him about that time, but since he paid for the bill I felt to leave it alone. In a nice way I asked Pop, "How do you like the car, Pop, nice ride don't you think? Better than walking." He agreed but did not notice the reference.

JERRY

I had a friend named Jerry that I would chum around with. We would sometimes go to the beach and hang out for the day. I knew Jerry since I was ten years old. We had a paper route together and formed a roller hockey team and got into a league. But Jerry was a boyhood friend of mine who had an ego and felt superior to others. We would break his stones about his acting like a pompous ass. We called him Glenn Ford because he did have a resemblance to the actor, and we would humor the shit out of him.

Jerry was quite fastidious about his clothes, and his choice of wardrobe had to be in style with wherever he was going. I remember the time I picked Jerry up for a night out on the town. His mother had just pressed a shirt for him, and Jerry picked up the shirt, looked it over and said to his mother, "This shirt is not pressed correctly." Jerry crumbles the shirt in his hands and tells his mother, "Press this shirt again, and do a better job the next time."

After we left his apartment I tell Jerry, "What the shit are you doing making your mother go crazy like that? The shirt was perfect." Jerry's response was typical, "You, my boy, have no class. Look at your collar. It is not pressed correctly. You should not accept poor workmanship." I roared back at him, "Jerry, I am lucky my sisters even press my shirts. I am not going to break their stones over some stupid collars."

On one our excursions to the beach one Sunday afternoon, we spent a nice afternoon with two girls who were student nurses at St. Raphael's Hospital. They were from out of state and were living at the dorm provided by the hospital. The girl that Jerry was interested in came from New York and mine was from New Jersey. I must say we had such a nice time just comparing lifestyles, but we all had the same common background from living in the city. We asked them for a date that evening, maybe go out to Savin Rock and get some food, and just hang out. They agreed, and I was looking forward to the evening and having a date with a nice girl.

Well the unthinkable happened: knowing Jerry was a fuss pot about his clothes, I would never even think in my wildest dreams that Jerry would even consider saying what he was about to say. The dorm rules were that no men were allowed in the building. We could only go up to the front desk and give our names and who we wanted to see.

The girls were called and we waited outside the door for them. As we were waiting at the bottom of the stairs, the girls arrived at the top, looking nice in their pretty dresses. I was envisioning a great evening, but Jerry tells his date, "Are you wearing that dress? It does not look good on you. It is the wrong color, and the style does not fit you." The girls were at first amused, then seeing that Jerry was serious, turned around and went back into the building.

To say I was furious would be putting it mildly. I was shrieking mad at this son of a bitch for screwing me out of a nice evening. I tell Jerry, "Where do you get the balls or give a shit what kind of a dress the girl had on? You and your bullshit about having the right clothes on or what is in style or not in style." Jerry states, "I have standards and you of all people should know that." I was furious, "Yeah, like I give a shit about you and your ideas of fashion. All I know is that I spent a day with that girl and you messed it all up." Jerry was great at putting on airs and trying to look classy, I have to give him that. He was a nice dresser and made a nice presentation of himself. While not being a college graduate, he had a good command of speaking, but he sometimes forgot to look around and see who he was talking to.

Another bad day that I encountered with Jerry, was when we had to go someplace on a Sunday. Jerry tells me to pick him up at about noon time. As I entered his apartment, his mother was near the stove and making sauce for the day's meal, which they were going to eat later on. Jerry's father had passed away years earlier, and Jerry and his mother lived alone. He had a sister and brother who were married.

Jerry goes over to the stove and tastes the tomato sauce. He looks at his mother and says, "This sauce is no good," and with that he picks up the pan and throws the sauce into the garbage pail. "Now start the sauce all over again and do it right this time." His mother was just standing there dumbfounded with tears streaming down her face, frozen like a statue at what just occurred. I left the kitchen because it was embarrassing for me to watch this. We left for our appointment and I never said a word about the incident the rest of the day.

Jerry had his way of living and he was not about to change. Although he took good care of his mother and supported her for the rest of her life, Jerry never got married. Maybe that was a good thing. He had his way of living and he was not going to change.

Although Jerry caused me some trouble, I did learn how to present myself to others from Jerry. Jerry had a long career with a utility company, which was a job he got because he knew how to represent himself. I remember going with him when he got interviewed for the job. He was dressed up with a brand new suit and looked like an executive. He was hired right on the spot, so he was correct in making a nice appearance. I thought he was overdressed for the job. He even carried a leather case into the interview with him although it was empty.

One day I met Jerry's brother Sal and I asked about Jerry. Sal told me how Jerry was taking care of his mother by being her full time care giver. He attended to her daily needs, including his mother's bodily functions like bathing, dressing, etc. Sal told me Jerry did not want to put his mother in a nursing home. To know that Jerry was doing all that for his mother was, "commendable". I told this to Sal and he agreed and said he does not know how he does it.

While I got more involved with my life, I sort of moved on and did not see Jerry as much, but once in a while I would stop in where he was working and chat with him. To see Jerry at work you would never know that this was a guy who acted altogether different with people. He was so professional in his work place. He was very jovial with customers and his fellow workers, but he still had that air about him, which I would remind him of from time to time. I'd say, "I will never forgive you for screwing me out of that date with the nurse. I could have had a nurse taken care of me." Jerry always got a kick out of that every time I mentioned it.

CAROL

In the same time period a new family moved in on my street. It was quite a large family, about eight in all. My friends and I got friendly with one of the boys who was our age, and he told us all about his family. He always mentioned his sister Carol, who we had never seen and how she was going out to California with her boyfriend to start a business, which we though was rather odd since she was not married to him. Naturally we asked about the sleeping arrangements, and Pat, the brother, explains that she will sleep in different rooms. Tony said, "How the hell did Pat think we believed this shit?" We really laughed that up, but about one year later Pat's sister returns from her trip. Pat said that the business they started did not go well and she returned home, so we finally got to meet his sister.

To see Carol for the first time was a shocker. We could not believe what a resemblance she had to the actress Rita Hayworth. Her hair was the same color, auburn, and it was long and curly just like Rita's. Carol was a little shorter and had a little more weight on, but in all the right places. At first glance you could see she was high maintenance. Her wardrobe alone was a standout. She presented herself differently from the neighborhood girls, and it was not hard to figure out she traveled in different circles. Carol was about six years older than us, but she seemed like she was a lot older, just the way she dressed and the sophistication about her. But like all queens, they sometimes come down to earth. The day Pat introduced us to Carol, she instantly took a liking to us, like we were something to deviate her mind from where she always was. It was a way for her to sort of just kick up her heels and have a few laughs with us, and also tease us with the notion that maybe we could get lucky with her.

The men that came to take her out all had nice cars and also were dressed to the hilt. They were mostly bookies, gamblers, and businessmen, and they lavished Carol with anything she wanted. It did not take a brain to figure that out. Pat, I think, was naïve about his sister and her friends. He was always bragging to us how all the men worshiped her. Again, no contest on that; Carol walked around like she had some royalty in her what with all the attention she was getting. Carol was ahead of her time, and I always say if Carol had someone with connections, she could have a great career in anything she wanted. She had that presence of greatness about her. At that time Carol was out of our price range. Her clothes alone would set you back a week's pay. She was nice, but not to go in debt for. We said let the assholes with the money have her, but Carol did have a quality about her that was nice. She always had money on her and would offer to buy beer for us and hang out with us, which she enjoyed immensely. We were a distraction and she knew she did not have to please us, like her boyfriends.

One day Carol calls me and asks me what I had planned for the day. I said, "Ray and I are going to the beach for the day and maybe get some food later on." "Oh," says Carol, "Mind if I come along? I have nothing to do today." So I call Ray and tell him I am bringing Carol along to the beach. Ray had never met Carol, so at first Ray is reluctant, saying, "I think maybe you should go alone with her." I tell Ray we will all go together and if you want to cut out later and go on your own that will be fine. Ray agrees and I picked him up on the way.

When I stopped in front of Ray's house, Ray was sitting on the front porch. When he comes over to the car door and sees Carol, his eyes just dropped. Carol tells Ray, "Ray, I will slide over and we could all sit in the front seat." My friend Ray was a tall, good-looking guy. Six feet in height, blond hair, but now Ray is sitting almost motionless; he was instantly mesmerized by Carol. I break the silence by saying to Carol, "I only take Ray along for a buffer to meet the girls, and then I discard him." Carol had good laugh at that and says, "Leo, you do not do so bad. Look, I called you remember?"

We spent the entire afternoon at the beach just the three of us, with Carol telling us about all her adventures and the people she had met, some famous and some of her shady characters. As it was getting late in the afternoon, Carol offered to take us to a nice bar and have some drinks and some food. We sat down at about seven o'clock in the evening, and Carol was ordering pitchers of beer, with her doing most of the drinking. Ray was like myself not a great drinker. I would say Carol consumed about two pitchers of beer herself, and never had to go to the bathroom, which I thought was strange, not like Ray and me.

By the time we finished, it was now about eleven o'clock, and I said we should be going. We left the bar, and Carol was a little tipsy but with all she had consumed you would think she would be fall down drunk. This was a girl who could really hold her drinks. She, I believe, could drink anybody under the table. We get to Ray's house and finally Carol says she has to relieve herself. Ray offered to take her up to his house, but Carol could not hold it any longer so she runs in the front yard of the house next door. She gets behind the fence, with us standing with our backs to her protecting her from view, and she relieves herself.

I told Carol that I was going to call it a night and go home, but she wanted to continue on. By this time I was dog tired and in no mood to keep on partying. Carol was clinging to Ray, enticing him to go along with her. I said, "Ray, she is all yours." Ray really did not want me to leave because of the state of inebriation Carol was in, but I was not about to stand there trying to convince Carol to leave, so I left Carol at Ray's house, telling Carol, "Ray will take good care of you."

Late in the afternoon of the next day, Carol calls me and said she wants to see me and talk about last evening. I agree to see her, and we set a time for seven o'clock. This was my big mistake. At that time, the streets would be teeming with people. This was an exceptionally hot evening, and people loved to sit on their front stoops and get out of their apartments to get some fresh air. My mother among them was sitting on our front porch with her friends.

Carol comes strolling out of her apartment, dressed in a pair of white shorts and with a halter top, bare midriff. She's wiggling down the street toward my car, which was parked across the street from my house. It seemed like everyone watching us meet at the car, and the noise on the street almost came to a halt. As I got into the car with Carol I glanced over to my house and could see the daggers in my mother's eyes.

My neighbor Bobby, who lived across the street from my house, was on the front stoop with his wife and family. For some reason Bobby thought how lucky I was to be going out with Carol and would always chide me about her, no matter how many times I told him we were just friends. Bobby would say, "You trying to shit me by saying Carol is just your friend. I already bought the Brooklyn bridge."

Upon entering the car, Carol starts off the conversation asking if I had spoken to Ray. I had, but I told her I did not. She said, "Please let's get out of here. Everyone is looking at us." So I drive down the street to the park where we would have a little more privacy since right across the street was the convent.

Carol, with a look of guilt of on her face, tells me her version of what happened after I left, saying, "I did not do anything that I am ashamed of, and if Ray tells you a different story, please believe me," I said, "Carol, why are you telling me this? I am not a priest, and you are a big girl. It sounds like I am your boyfriend, and you were cheating on me. She said, "I value your friendship and that's why I am telling you this." I thought this was a good opportunity to say how I really felt: "Well, since you feel that way then I could tell you what I think. In the time that I have known you, watching you the way you live your life, I think you are throwing it away. Right now your biggest asset is you, and in a matter of maybe ten years, age will decide your future, and you will have nothing."

Our conversation went on in this vein for an hour or so, and Carol then asks me to have dinner with her at her apartment. Her family had left town and just her and her sister are now home. Her sister had a boyfriend and would be coming home later that evening, I agreed but I went through the next yard and had to jump a fence so my mother would not see me. My mom was always sitting on the front porch and I knew she'd have something to say about my going over there. The people living in this six family building were all friends of our family. I went up the back staircase, but I still had to go by their doors. They had a screen door on, and they could hear anyone approaching, so I had to be very quiet. The kitchen of their apartment was at the back door, and that's where they were all sitting. I had to quietly pass five apartments to get to Carol's. I felt like a burglar creeping up the stairs, but because of who Carol was and her reputation, I had to be careful not to be recognized, especially since it was at night. When I got to Carol's apartment, she had the door opened for me, and closed it promptly.

Carol had the table all set, and was in the process of preparing the meal, which consisted of veal, peppers, and sausage, swimming in a nice tomato sauce. I brought a bottle of wine, while Carol was as usual drinking beer. We sat down and had a most delicious dinner. After the dinner I helped Carol clean up the kitchen. Looking at her I said to myself, "If only early on somebody put her on the right path, she would have the makings of having a great life. She was very domesticated, kept a clean house, and was also a very fine cook."

Carol had made a cake for dessert, and after we had our cake she said, "Let's go and sit in the front room and have an after dinner drink." I could not have asked for a better evening. Looking at Carol sitting next to me, I wondered how she could be so wrong with her life. While I was embracing Carol, her sister comes home with her boyfriend. The first thing I said was, "You could not have a picked a worse time to come home." He then says, "I like to be a spoiler."

Carol sees me to the door, embracing me and saying, "I can see you will be getting married before I do. You will make someone a good husband and have a nice family." Turning back to Carol as I got to the top of the stairs, I wondered what a waste that this girl who has so much to offer is coming up short by not taking advantage of what she has. I never told Carol that Ray called me that next morning and told me how he took her home because she was so drunk and did not take advantage of the situation.

Now the mistake I made was in going out the front door of her apartment. It was around two o'clock in the morning, so I felt being this late of an hour nobody would see me. How wrong I was. My mother was sitting on the front porch, waiting for me. Mom started calling me every name under the sun, calling Carol a name in Italian which means whore, plus some other expletives. I told my mother all I had was a dinner, but being associated with anyone with a bad reputation could rub off on you. It was hard to convince her otherwise. My mother is just like Bobby across the street—they assume you are doing something and all the talk in the world is not going to change their mind. I always wondered how my mother knew I was at Carol's place. Today in talking to my brother Frank, and relating the story to him, it came to me: our friends in the building must have seen me. All this and I was innocent of any actions they had envisioned, not that my mind was innocent. I was planning on having a fruitful evening (but not this time).

Carol was a girl who was looking for instant gratification and looking for stuff in all the wrong places. What she wanted was to be a homemaker, but she could not give up her quest for material things that she believed were denied to her has a young child. As a result, she turned to the sugar daddies for that, but these guys already had their own commitments.

I would see Carol frequently at the places that I hung around, such as the bar on Church St., talking with men that had the resources she was looking for. She would always come over to our table and make conversation. She wanted somehow to keep in touch with me and the rest of the guys since she felt comfortable with us. But as time went on I did not see much of Carol. I was in the process of getting to know someone that I could have a meaningful relationship with, so we lost touch. The news of Carol getting married surfaced about the same time. Much to my surprise, she married a blue collar type of guy, not someone you would think Carol would settle for (how the worm turns).

With Carol's track record, we were all surprised she found someone who had no knowledge of her, but history shows that you cannot hide from your past. After she got married, Carol ran afoul of the law by being involved in the running of a house of ill repute. When the house was raided by the police, Carol and the rest of the girls were arrested, and her story hit the newspapers. The story came out that the customers were all men of high incomes. Carol was always a high roller.

Many years later I saw Carol shopping in a supermarket. She was coming down the aisle heading straight toward me but she did not notice me. Her eyes were glazed over and she had a look of utter disgust on her face. She still had touches of her auburn hair, but it was duller and turning colors. She was a shell of her former self. Once a girl so vibrant and so full of promise, and like the prediction I gave her, but it came to pass that the only thing she had going for her, was her attraction. The old saying about only being young once was true for Carol. She threw away all of her opportunities to live in the moment. Everybody that knew Carol all came to the same conclusion: Carol had the beauty to go to Hollywood, but she did not have the mentality to be successful. If she had a met someone in that field, yes, no doubt she could have made it. In her later years, we were told she had a lot of health problems, and with her lifestyle I wondered how she lasted so long. In the end, she died a very sickly death.

RAY

Ray had a nice girl that he was seeing for a few years, but he was not serious about committing to her. He would see her every so often, and she was crazy about him but was getting disgusted because Ray was not being serious with her. I found this out one night at the dance when I met his girl, who was also named Rae. She came from my neighborhood, and we knew each other, but not on a social level.

Rae had come alone to the dance that night in hopes of maybe seeing Ray there. I also went alone to dance because nobody wanted to go. My friends went to another dance hall that I was not interested in. When I ran into her, Rae inquired about Ray since she did not seeing him. I said he went somewhere else, so Rae and I danced all night. During one of the dance numbers, Rae's heel comes off her shoe so we had to sit down for a while. I offered to take her home since she lived about two blocks from my house. She agreed then took off the other shoe and walked barefoot to my car.

On the drive home all Rae talked about was how Ray was not serious in giving her a commitment. She said she spent all this time with him and wanted to give up on him, but I knew what Rae was really doing was giving me the pass to ask her out, which I would never do. In those days it was not nice to infringe on your friend's girl, even though I would have liked to ask her out. I left off by saying if things were different, then I would talk to her.

The very next day, Ray comes looking for me. He says, "Leo, you took Rae home last night." I was surprised: "My, how fast the news travels. Yes, Ray straight home and no necking; I did not leave any marks." Ray then goes on to explain how he really thought it was nice of me and wanted to know what we talked about. I said, "It was about you and me, Ray, but mostly you. Ray, this girl is in love with you." Ray knew what I was talking about. He said, "Yes, but I am not ready for her." I said, "She will not be there forever, Ray. Make up your mind or she will be gone."

In the end, Ray never married. He lived alone in a trailer park and his weight ballooned up to about two hundred fifty pounds. I never saw Ray much after I got married, and yet I found out he only lived about two miles from me. Ray died as he lived— all alone.

MIKE DEFELICE

One of the nicest guys I knew in my youth was a man named Mike De Felice. He came from a family of ten children; five boys and five girls.

Their apartment consisted of four rooms, the five boys slept in one room, and five girls slept in another room. The mother and father had one room, and then there was a kitchen. Talk about living in cramped quarters. I thought my house was tight, but we had eight people in four and a half rooms.

I went up to the sixth grade with Mike, then we were sent to different schools to finish our seventh and eighth grade, but since we lived one block from each other, we kept in contact by going to the boys club together. We were then separated by going to different high schools and sort of drifted apart from there.

Mike, like the rest of us, would share what little we had with each other, it was that kind of friendship, and even more so when we got into our teen years. To prove this point, Mike always bet on the daily numbers, and this one day Mike hit the numbers for the amount of eleven hundred dollars, which in 1948 was quite a huge sum. Mike bought himself a car, and gave his mother some money. One day Mike comes by the corner, stops his car and said to all the guys, "Get in. We are all going out to Savin Rock for some food." Indeed, he lavished us with all we wanted to eat. He was that kind of guy, as was the rest of his family.

I had the worst luck with meeting girls who were already dating people I knew. This happened quite frequently, as I have already explained earlier. At a dance at the Settronale club, I met this nice girl, and we had a nice time that evening. When I took her home from the dance, and we agreed to meet at the next dance.

As it would happen quite often in my life, Mike comes up to me and says, in a nice joking way, that he was dating the girl I was dancing with and said he had several dates with her. He said he did not go to the club that night because he had to work. The girl never told me about him and I never asked who she was dating. I told him I would back off. The next week I met Mike and his girl, and I explained to her that since he and I are friends, I do not want to infringe. She makes a joke out of the situation by saying, "You are not going to fight over me?" I laughed, "No. Mike will get the better of me." This was a situation that happened so often. Once when I was at a bar with my friends from work, and told them of my situations, they laughed, saying, "Maybe the girls should wear name tags. This would save a lot of time."

Mike's mother had to raise the children alone for the most part of her life, as her husband had a stroke and could not work. He was a barber by trade, but every day I would see Mike's father sitting on the front stoop. Mike's mother was truly a saint. She raised ten children with little or no help from the city, and they all turned out to be model citizens; not one of them got into any trouble. When I sometimes see people be bestowed by the honor of mother of the year or today's Kennedy Center awards, I know Mike's mother should be right up there. I do not know of any mother who had to overcome the hardships she had to endure, including my own mother and all other mothers on our street, who all had hard existences. No one even come close to Mike's mother. Just putting food on the table for her family must have been a nightmare. During the bad years of the depression when we had so little, my mother always felt sorry for Mike's mother. When Mike came over to walk with me to school, mom would give Mike a little something for himself. His mother provided for the family without getting any of the welfare or food stamps they have today. The expression of living in a cold water flat does not accurately portray the true meaning of the phrase. Just think of not having hot water to bathe in and having to heat water on the stove just to have water to cook with. The families living in these flats had to go to a public bath house. The boys had the pleasure of being able to go the boys club to take a shower. How Mike's mother held that family together is something short of miracle. Whatever assistance she got from people was minimal, but she made good use of it. All of the children had little jobs to help her out. When I hear people being stressed out today, I think what the hell would they do in Mike's mother's situation? She had a sick husband and ten children.

When I would go and pick Mike up to go the boys club at night, his mother would always put on a happy face and tell us to be home by nine o'clock. She did not want her children hanging around with the wrong crowd. It was not until I got married and had children of my own that I truly understood what she had to endure. When I thought about the little problems I had with my children, like worrying about providing for their welfare, I often reflected on her massive load that she had to carry every day.

Mike got interested when I told him that there are no Italian bread products in that area. I went and secured a distributor who had a small baked goods route and was willing to take on Mike's products. The distributor lived in East Haven, not far from Mike's bakery in New Haven. The union between Mike and the distributor proved to be very successful for both of them due to the fact that there was no competition. All the Italian bakeries kept their sales in the city. They had the village mentality of the Italians who didn't venture too far from their point of distribution. All of them fighting for the same customer base, when this area was wide open, but they did not want to travel. Mike's distributor started to get many calls from other bakeries to handle their product, but he turned them all down. A large bakery made an offer to Mike's distributor which would give him a larger percentage than Mike could offer. This additional business that I brought to Mike was a boom to him and lasted about a year. This business came at a time when he was having reservations about staying in business. Mike's competition became aware of Mike's additional business due to the increase in flour that he was buying. When Mike informed me of the offer his distributor had been given, I went and searched out the scoundrel. Upon seeing me he tried to avoid me as he knew the rage I had for him. Bad news travels fast- the distributor knew exactly what I was going to say, and indeed he became very defensive, explaining to me all the extra amount of income he was going to receive. "Stop," I said, "did you not hear of loyalty? You were struggling along, I gave you a present, and this is how you repay me?" I got back at the distributor by informing other Italian bakers that I knew and sent them into his territory, but the damage was done. Mike could not sustain himself any longer and sold his bakery. He later went to work for Yale University.

His decision was good for me because it gave me an excuse to stop delivering the bread. I turned the business over to a local bakery, and they made a mess of it. Actually, it was the "village mentality" of the Italians that caused the mess of the business. They didn't want to continue traveling and I said told the fool, "You are killing yourself fighting with all the other bakeries and out there you have no one to go up against you. Plus you have all your other products that you can add on and make a very profitable route out of it." But that little venture was closed down.

50's NIGHTCLUBS

In the early 1950s, some of my friends and I would frequent the many nightclubs in the area. The night clubs had it all. You would see a comedian, and a singer, and they would have a small orchestra. The atmosphere was elegant, and they also demanded that you come well-dressed or they would not let you in. Men had to have a jacket and tie on, and some places would even furnish you with a tie and even a jacket if you did not have one. Of course the damn jacket was kind of oversized and made you look foolish, but they had a dress code and you had to adhere to it. It would be very seldom that a person would not be dressed properly. People took great pride in their choice of apparel since it was a time to present yourself to others. Donat's was a great night club because of the size of the place. I went there many times. It was a club that catered to couples, and the size of the dance floor alone was huge and very impressive.

The one we liked the best was out in Baybrook, along the west shore, right across from the beach. It was there one night that we had a nice experience. Patty Paige was headlining and we sat in the bar lounge and watched the show from there. After each set, Patty Paige would come out to the lounge and sort of relax. She came up to us and struck up a conversation, not about the show, but about the area she was working in. She was a very pleasant person; usually performers did not come out to the lounge, but she did after each set. It was almost like you knew her personally. The demise of the night clubs left a hole in our society. It used to be a place where people could meet and in a nice atmosphere. You could have a conversation and not have to shout at the person you are talking to, like we have to in the bars today. We enjoyed sitting in the lounge area and listening to the relaxing music. The performers took great pains to make sure they were dressed properly. On this night, Patty Paige was wearing a nice green gown and we complimented her on the color of her dress. She appreciated the comments and gave us a nice hug at the end of the night.

It was at a night club that I gave Teresa her engagement ring. The nightclub was called Donat's, and it was located on the Boston Post Road in Milford, right across the street from where Costco is now. It later became a restaurant and changed hands many times until it finally closed its doors.

Today, to meet someone people have to go into a bar and have drinks that most don't want. The clubs years ago made it easier by having tables set aside for some singles. Even a lot of the dance halls that I went to around the state had areas set aside for that reason. You could also partake in drinking or just sit and have soda if you wanted.

The dance hall that was one our favorite was in Waterbury. It was called Hamilton Hall on Hamilton Ave. The dance hall was upstairs, and the lounge was downstairs. In that lounge you could still hear the music but very faintly. The club in Bridgeport, called the Ritz Ballroom, was the best set up. They had a large room which had tables ringed all around the dance floor. Walking in, the first thing you would see would be the orchestra since it would be facing the front door. Sitting at the tables, you could watch the dance floor and the orchestra. The club even had all male waiters dressed in tuxedos.

The Emerald Room in Milford was a destination of choice due to its wonderful floor show and dance area. They had a stage that would rise up from the center of the room in which the performers would perform. Then they would lower the stage, and that became the dance floor. The night clubs were astounding in part due to the stage show that they presented. You would see maybe three different people perform: a comedian, a singer, and sometimes a stripper, but not like the stripping you see today, no full nudity. This room catered to large parties, such as stag parties, family affairs, etc. It was located on the shorefront of the Milford beach, and this is where we had one of our greatest nights.

SEA CLIFF

One of my most memorable nights at a nightclub was one in which I had a little too much fun. I had gone to a dance at The Sea Cliff Inn alone as everyone else did not want to go; they had other plans that I was not interested in. When I got to the dance, I entered the hall, and did not see anyone I knew, so I started to leave and go up the bar area. This girl that I knew as an acquaintance met me at the door and we started a conversation. I told her I was going up to the bar and invited her to join me and she agreed.

Her name was Mary, and she asked if she could bring her friends along with us. I agreed. Mary had three other girls with her, so I say to Mary, "I came here looking for one girl, now I have four." "See," Mary shoots back, "And now you thought you were going to strike out tonight!" We proceeded to the lounge area and secured a table.

This night I tried drinking a bourbon called Old Grand Dad, and it was the smoothest drink I had ever had. I found later why it was so smooth: it was one hundred proof, quite lethal for a person like myself who was not much of a drinker. Mary and her friends were having a real good time, letting me in on all the jokes they were telling.

Mary and her friends mostly came from my area. We knew of each other, but not on a personal level. As the night wore on, the girls were having such a good time and did not want to leave. They had a nice time teasing me about me being with four women. One girl said jokingly, "Leo, do you feel like Tarzan tonight?" I tell Mary, "You better shut off her booze. She is getting wild." Throughout the whole night, I was sitting and did not get up once. I did not realize that the drinks I was consuming were going to be so lethal. I had about six drinks in all, more than I usually have, but these were very potent ones. I look at Mary, tell her I was leaving, and would meet her the following week.

As I got off the stool, and it was like the all the lights went out, talk about a blackout, this was it. I was now groping the furniture, and that was all I could remember. Mary and her friends called a couple of the guys at the bar and they placed me in my car. I found out later that all of this happened. Mary took charge and told her friends she was going to drive me home, and to have them follow her. Mary knew where I lived, and she found a parking space across the street from my house. She went up to my house and told my family about me. My brother-in-law came out to the car and carried me into the house. As I said, I do not remember any of this, that's how intoxicated I was. I spent the rest of that night and all through the next day in the bathroom, heaving what to me, was all my guts out. At one time I thought my eyeballs were coming out of my socket. The shame of it all was that my mother was cleaning up after me, changing my clothes twice during the evening. A horrible night it was, to be sure.

It took me about two days to recover from that evening, and that was the last time I drank Old Grand Dad. It was a lesson well learned the hard way. I went searching for Mary to thank her and also apologize for being such a pain in the ass. When I did see her on the street one day shopping with her friend, I told her that was the first and last time I would get that drunk and that it was not me. I told her, "To me, you were the Virgin Mary. What you did for me I will always remember, and also the rest of the girls, I cannot thank you enough, and may I have the next dance when we meet?" "Leo, I will be looking forward to it," Mary says. The next week I met a girl at the beach and started dating her so I didn't go back to the dance hall for a while. I met Mary about six months later on a Thursday night while she was shopping, and she told me she was going steady with this fella she met about five months ago. "Leo," Mary says, "My dance card still has your name on it." and with smile and a hug we part. Two years later I see Mary's name in the paper— she got married.

The custom of the dance halls in those days was for the men and the ladies to stand on opposite sides of the room. The men had to go across the room and ask the lady of his choice for a dance. It could be quite embarrassing for a guy if he got refused in front of the other ladies, with that meaning no other girl in that group would dance with you if one refused. To make it worse, the guys would laugh at you for getting "shot down". The girls would offer all kinds of excuses, like they are tired, or that they had a headache. Some of the girls would look you up and down for approval. This was their right to do since some guys presented themselves so poorly. One such instance that happened at one dance Jimmy and I attended. It turned out to be quite hilarious. I asked this one girl to dance, and she refused. I turned and looked at the rest of the girls and knew they would do the same. So back I went to Jimmy and he says let me try. He went to the same group of girls and asked the first girl, "May I have this dance?" very politely. She said she has a headache. He goes to the next girl and she also says the same thing. He then goes to the third girl in line and immediately says, "I have some aspirins for you." She looked at Jimmy, like who the hell is this clown, so he says, "I want to have the next dance with you, so maybe these will help you out."

In my conversations with women about the way girls and boys view the custom of approaching each other to socialize, I realized it was just as awkward for the girls. They said it was difficult to stand there and wait to be asked for a dance. Sometimes they had to endure insults because of their refusal. One girl didn't even want to go to the dances because she said she felt like she was in a meat market being viewed. She considered most of the boys a bunch of jerks. Now I had an understanding of how they the women felt, so in my later encounters I took that into consideration.

At one dance there was a very attractive but snobbish blonde girl, what we call a bitch, today, and she was rejecting many requests for dancing. She was with a small group of girls standing along the wall. Not to get shot down, I approached the girl next to her, and she was not interested. I went out of my way to say thank you and maybe next time. She smiled, and I went to the next group and asked the girl I was interested in. She obliged and we danced for a few numbers. When I brought her back to her group, she asked if I could dance with her friend. I danced a few numbers with her and did the same thing. The blond girl was standing a few feet away watching me dance with the girls.

I was given a challenge by the guys I was with to go and ask the blond girl to dance. They were betting I would get shot down. I was a little nervous walking across the room toward her, but remembering what my friend Jay taught me by being aggressive: "That's the only way. You got to have a set of peppers." I went right up to the blond girl and asked her to dance in front of her friends. She looked me in right in the eyes and readily accepted.

Of course I was gloating a little, so I had to dance her in front of my friends and kind of linger there rubbing it in. This was a girl that refused more guys than all the other girls she was with. Her name was Sophie, and she was of polish decent. Once I broke down all the barriers that she had in mind, such as being a stuck up brat, she explained she was tired, "of boys acting like little boys, and that they needed to grow up."

I spent the rest of the evening dancing with her, and Sophie started to loosen up and not be so uptight. I asked why she consented to dance with me, and Sophie says she liked "the way I acted like a gentleman when being refused a dance, and not being a boar about it." At the end of the evening I asked Sophie for her phone number, and she readily agreed to have me call her.

When I went back to the guys and told them about Sophie giving me her phone number, they said, "Leo, the number must be the number of the graveyard." I say, "You asses, eat your words. I got a date with the big blond."

When I called Sophie for a date, she requested I take her to a dance at the polish hall in Wallingford. It was for her church, and she would appreciate it. It was okay with me. The price was only two dollars a person which was a cheap night for me. Sophie says she will be standing at the bottom of the hallway of her apartment, which I thought was kind of strange since I would not have to go and meet her parents. Usually the parents wanted to see who their daughter was going out with.

Sophie lived above some stores, and the building was not in great shape. I believe she was ashamed for me to see her apartment. Before that date and the ones that would follow, it was always the same: meeting me downstairs. I told her my house was no better than hers, and she said, "Please try and understand why." I realized then it was because of my nationality.

When we got to the dance I noticed she was a different person. She seemed to be more sociable and very loose. Maybe it was because of being with most of her own people. The polish people are all a group of hard working and fun loving people, but like the Italians, they still maintain a lot of the old world values. I should've known; I have been down this road before.

I dated Sophie about seven times, and knew from our dates that this was not going to go anywhere. First of all, she was seeing someone before me, and quite steady at that, and he was polish, so while I enjoyed her company and thought she was an easy person to please, I did not want to extend my time with her. We had a lot of fun dates, but I didn't want to be in a holding pattern while she figured out what she wanted in life. First of all, she had the family problem to contend with. Then, the guy she was dating before me was a tall, good looking guy and of the same nationality which was a hard nut for me to crack. I stopped seeing Sophie because I knew what my limitations were. She went back to her guy, and years later after I got married while I was out Christmas shopping, I bumped into Sophie. It seemed the glow of youth was missing from her face. It had been about eight years since I had last seen her. She was a changed person for sure and when we spoke, I realized why. She told me she had to get a divorce because her the Polish boyfriend, now husband, turned out to be a drunk.

SUMMER CRUISE

One of summer pleasures was going on a weekend cruise aboard a ship that was named the Richard Peck. The ship had a long history of being a ferry boat around the long island sound, but it was converted to being a sightseeing boat. This boat would be docked at the bridge on Water Street, and on weekends they would take people out to the Long Island area and back. The boat provided music and dancing, and it lent itself for a great place for singles to meet without any restrictions.

The ship would leave early in the morning and return late at night which gave people plenty of time to socialize. It made for a great atmosphere, and a relaxing way for everyone to be at ease. The dress was smart casual. The guys and I would enjoy the trip. I mean, what was there not to like? One of my friends even had a shipboard romance and wound up marrying the girl he met, as did a lot of people. These excursions out on the water made for such a nice way for people to introduce themselves to one another. People tended to be more sociable and be able to hold a conversation. While I did not have a shipboard romance, I did meet a lot of the fairer sex.

This and other venues of pleasure is what is missing today. Today they should have something like that. Instead of going on a computer and meeting a faceless person, or standing in a bar or "club" as they call it, listening to some of the worst music ever written, people should be comfortably talking to each other in a relaxing atmosphere. Today's bars and clubs are dangerously overcrowded and you cannot hear the person standing next to you. If you even wanted to meet someone, you'd have to use a sort of sign language to communicate that.

LORIE AND LUCY

I attended a show at the Oakdale in Wallingford featuring the Italian singer, Connie Francis, and during the middle of the show she stopped and talked about her life. She lived with a father, who by her description of him, was nothing but a tyrant. Connie made a statement that would pertain to the next two girls I was to meet. In describing about how she would get to leave her house, she said, "Two ways: either in a box or a white dress."

So at a bowling alley one night, I met this girl named Lorie. We were on different teams, but not competing against each other. Our leagues were different, but I started to strike up a conversation with her, due to us being next to one another in the same alley. The guys started to make comments about what the hell was I doing talking to this girl, who by their definition, was not pretty, I said, "Not pretty my ass, she consented to have a date with me, and by the way John, who are you going out with Saturday night?"

On our first date she tells me she is living alone with her father. Her mother had passed away a short while ago, but stepping into her house, I found it to be very clean house, much better than my own home. I was impressed, what with her having a full time job and having to help out members of her family, I wonder how she got the time.

Lorie and I had dates that covered mostly movies, concerts, etc. She was agreeable to any suggestion I made, unlike some of my other dates, who would almost demand their preference. Lorie was a very passionate girl, to a point. Remember, this was the 1950s, but to me it was not an issue. We had a lot of fun, and I was satisfied, but the true character of Lorie came one Saturday night. We were planning to go to a show. I called Lorie and told her I could not go due to my having to spend a lot of money to get my car repaired. I told Lorie I was broke and was really ashamed to mention it to her. Lorie yells at me, "Hell, I will cook dinner for you. After dinner my father is going to his club, and we could go for a walk down to the water." Lorie fit the description laid out by Connie Francis. She was tired of being a maid to her father who was very old school, and since she was the last one of her brothers and sisters, her father felt she had to take care of him. It was a very unpleasant situation for Lorie, but this was something I did not want to get involved in.

So I had to rethink my future with Lorie. Having to get involved with her father was not the best of situations for me. We discussed about having a long term relationship, but that was not what Lorie had in mind. Knowing how bad she wanted out of her predicament, she could not abandon her father. Although she discussed this scenario with me, what she had in mind was to broach the subject with her brothers and sisters, to maybe work a co-parenting plan.

Lorie had had a lot of difficult dates in her quest to get out of the house. She explained to me how some of her dates turned out to be nothing but a wrestling match. One in particular was a date with a boy from my neighborhood who I went to school with. She said she became a little more liberal with her affection, and it turned out to be disastrous for her. I told Lorie, "You have to consider yourself a store. No merchandise until you pay for it." That comment broke her up into a fit of laughter, so much so that she wanted to excuse herself to go into the house. She said, "Leo, please. I have to go in and change." Still laughing uncontrollably, she said, "It almost sounds like I am a hooker." "Well," I said, "You could take it up that way but what it also means is do not sell yourself short."

I decided to tell Lorie that I was not the answer to her problems, since I could not deal with her father. Lorie told me how she had a meeting with her siblings and it did not go well. They said that they had enough to take care of with their own families, and the fact that she was single proved she should have to take care of her father. Lorie said, "I had the bad luck of being the last in line and having to bear the burden of being a daughter and a house maid to my father." We parted on very good terms, and she was understanding of my reluctance to take on this burden. Lorie knew of my situation in my family, what with an uncle and a sister who drove us all crazy, and that I did not want to repeat or get into the same predicament.

As the years went by, and I had gotten married, our paths would cross again, but through our children. I never met her, but it was one day when my daughter Gail came home and told me about this lady who came to pick up her daughter who Gail was going to school with. They were in the same room so Lorie lived in the same neighborhood but for some reason we never met.

About ten years ago reading the obituaries, I seen her picture in the paper, and read how she had passed away from a long illness. The piece described the many charitable works she was involved in. I was very impressed, knowing firsthand the challenges she was dealt by her family, and that she took it all and went on with her life. But also the same page, there was an accompanying story about Lorie, listing the many people she had helped in her life, along with bringing up her own children, who went on to become prosperous business people. As I kept reading the article, my emotions got the best of me. I knew Lorie and what she had to endure, and yet she came through it and never faltered. She truly did not let the past define her life.

LUCY

This last girl I was to meet before I got married, was a girl named Lucy. My friends and I were at the beach one day, and in our area was a bunch of girls having a beach party. They had a lot of food and invited us to join them. After eating with the girls, they put some music on, and we started dancing. We were having such a good time until the lifeguard came over and said, "You guys are causing a lot of disturbance to other people. You are going to have to tone it down or leave the beach." So we picked up all our belongings and moved to the end of the beach. It was an area that people did not like due to the rough sand and many rocks. We spent the rest of the afternoon there with the girls, singing and making a lot of noise with nobody to bother us. Everybody mingled with one other, and we did not pair off, but one girl named Marie started to talk to me, and I found out she only lived three blocks from my house. I had never met her, but we talked about the movies, and Marie said she would like to go to the movies with me, so we made a date.

To me it was just a date and my interest in her was not that strong. After the movie, we went for some food, and Marie told me she did not have much luck with the boys asking her out. I said, "You do not seem to be so shy. I met you on the beach and here we are." She responded, "Yes but the ones I want do not ask me out." I blurted out, "So why did you ask me out?" Marie's face was now getting red and admitted she was ashamed that she said that. I let her down nicely by saying, "It is all right. I did not have anything to do anyway."

The girls in the group were planning a picnic, and they asked us guys if we would join them. We agreed, and we went shopping with them for the supplies for the picnic. It was at the picnic that I got acquainted with Lucy. Now the girl that I dated was in the group, and she did not approve of my spending much time with Lucy, her friend.

At the end of the picnic I asked Lucy if she would let me take her home, and she agreed. At her house I asked her for her phone number. Lucy gives me her number with a twinkle in her eye, "Leo, I hope you will call me." I said, "You can take that to the bank." To Lucy's surprise, I called her the next night to chat with her about going out to a show. Lucy yells out, "Leo, do you know who called me?" I had no idea. She said, "It was Marie." Marie gave Lucy a hard time on the phone for moving in on her territory. I told Lucy I only had one date with her, and it did not turn out well. I answer back, "Lucy, Marie gave me the impression she was doing me a favor, so the hell with her!" Lucy responded, "Leo, I am glad that you called, and I hope this did not disturb you in any way." I answered back, "No problem. When can I see you again?"

After the dust up with Marie, Lucy calmed down, and I felt kind of bad that they got into such a heated argument over something that I thought could have been prevented by me explaining to Marie that I was the one who chose to go out with Lucy.

With that episode out of the way, Lucy and I started to see a lot of each other. Lucy's family welcomed me into their home and made me feel very comfortable. I also got to know her family, especially her father, Steve, who I started to click with really well. He had a good job with a major corporation and he treated me with a lot of respect. He never talked down to me, but instead acted like I was on his level. He and I would discuss world affairs, sports, and politics, and mostly we were on the same page. After dating Lucy for a couple of months, Steve told me he was glad to have me in his home, and hoped the best for my relationship with Lucy.

I was figuring that Lucy and I would date long term, and maybe think about marriage later on, but I did not know Lucy had other ideas, and started to make the conversation turn to marriage on a steady basis. This topic was staring to get on both our nerves. Many times she would hint about getting more involved with me. I know what she meant, and I realized that for some ungodly reason Lucy was in a hurry to get out of the house. She had, as far I could see, no pressing problems, such as Lorie had. Lucy gave me plenty of leeway with her, but this was not the way to go.

Lucy was determined to step up her quest to pressure me into some hasty decision. With my small bank account, at this time it would be next to impossible to consider marriage, especially with what she had in mind. Also, it would break her father's heart and ruin his view of me. I had too much respect for him to do anything to disgrace his family.

After Lucy and I dated for about ten months, she phoned me and said she wanted to see me the next night. When we met, she quickly got to the point, which was marriage. It was then I told Lucy I was not ready and maybe she would do better if she found someone else. She did not take my suggestion with any sense of saneness, she went into a tantrum, after I calmed her down, Lucy said she would not bring up the subject again, but I held firmly, and ended the relationship that night.

It was kind of hard for me as her mother and father were so kind to me; they were almost like my big brother and sister. They were very modern thinking, generous and thoughtful, but I know Lucy and I would have had a hard time living together. Lucy had this bad habit of not listening to reason. In those days girls could not go and get an apartment, so the only way out was in a white dress. Connie Francis was right, but Lucy did not fit the description of some of the other girls I met, who had some valid reason to hurry up the situation.

About three years after I got married, I ran into Lucy and she told me she had gotten married and was going to live in upstate N.Y.

CHAPTER FIVE

Starting New Life

MEETING TERESA

One Saturday night in June of 1953, I went to the Sea Cliff Inn. As I arrived there, I decided to not go into the dance hall, instead opting for the bar area. At this point I was getting disgusted with the dances, as you would meet the same people; I was looking for something different.

I figured I would just maybe have a few drinks and some food later on and go home. I ended up talking with some girls in the lounge area and they too had the same concerns about dating. The girls said they did not like standing along the wall and wait for the jerks to come and ask them to dance, so it was the same for the boys, who got tired of being turned down. We had a lot of laughs.

But as I left the bar, which was now about eleven o'clock, I decided to venture into the dance hall and see what was going on, maybe meet someone. This was a square dance which I attended many times, but after having several drinks, I really was not in the best of shape to start twirling around the floor since square dancing is very physical.

I got into this set of people, and the first girl I meet was Teresa. We teamed together for the next several numbers and as the dance was coming to an end, with my head spinning, a little dizzy really, I offered to take Teresa home and she accepted. Teresa was at the dance with her two girlfriends and she told them she was coming home with me. As I was driving her home, she asked me about where I lived and she said, "Gee maybe you could have taken my friends home. They lived in the same neighborhood as you."

By the time I reached Teresa's house, the drinks were kicking in and I could not wait to get home. But because of a natural reflex of mine, of always asking for a phone number, Teresa gave me her number even though I did not have any pencil or paper, so I had to remember the number. Being in a state of intoxication, I kept repeating the number to myself on the way home. I still remember the number, HO-70854, and about two weeks later I called Teresa for a date.

When I met her parents, John and Ann De-Angelo, I went through the same interview, as with all the other parents I met. Questions such as where my father worked, and what part of Italy they came from, but in this instance, it was not a problem. Teresa's aunt and uncle came from my neighborhood and they knew of my family, so there was a comfort level that her parents felt good about.

After several dates I asked Teresa if she wanted to spend a day with me. I wanted to take her to New York City for the day, which was not an easy task, being in the times of strict supervision. First of all, I was taking a girl across state lines and we were not married. Teresa said she has to get permission from her parents, which she did, and they gave her their blessing, (I wonder what the generation of today would think about that!)

We spent the day in Central Park, going to the zoo, and taking a row boat out into the lake. After several hours, we decided to go home but on the way home we stopped off for some food. I still got her home by seven o'clock in the evening with her smiling parents to greet us.

Courtship in those days consisted of "state your intentions quickly or move on". I must say, Teresa's parents, for being old world, were pretty liberal, for their time. Just by giving me permission to take Teresa to N.Y.C. for the day was something. I do not know if my mother would have done the same for her daughters. After three months of dating I asked Teresa for her hand in marriage. She accepted, but with one caveat: we had to save up some money together as I did not have enough to get married. She agreed and about one year later we got married.

The wedding took place in East Haven and we had our wedding dinner down the street from where we met. The price of the chicken dinners were three dollars and fifty cents. It was the custom then to invite family to the dinners and friends to the reception later on, so the restaurant allowed us to bring our own liquor and beer in, and the family would make sandwiches.

Since the families would split the bill evenly and at the end of the dinner I went into the kitchen with my father and father in law to settle the bill. My father's half came to about one hundred ten dollars. As my father was taking his money out, I was getting nervous about how slow he was reaching for his money, and then my father started to count out his share, ten dollars at a time. To me it was an anti –climatic Moment, sheer torture, one hundred dollars to my father was a lot of money, but he came through with it and for a wedding present he gave me fifty dollars.

I picked up the tab for supplying all the liquor and beer, plus paying for the three-piece band, which was one hundred dollars. My brother Frank supplied the wedding cake, since he worked for Libby's, an Italian bakery, plus the owner of the bakery donated all the gifts we gave out to the people at the wedding, which were little china figurines filled with candy.

Our honeymoon was spent in, you guessed it: N.Y.C. and the Pocono mountains. At the Poconos it was a resort and seven days cost us about two hundred dollars, which included room and board, with three meals a day. We stopped off in N.Y. on the way to the Pocono mountains, and again on the way home. While we were there, we went to the Latin Quarter night club and saw a wonderful floor show. After that, whenever I went to the city, always walked by where the Latin Quarter was.

After our honeymoon, we settled in our apartment on Hamilton St. The place was a mess, due to the previous tenants being a very dirty family. It was a third floor walkup and we had spent the entire summer prior to our wedding painting and putting new wallpaper on the walls. My friend, Tony, helped me a lot with all the work. Our rent was eighteen dollars a month, our electric bill was one dollar a month, due, I believe, to a faulty meter.

An elderly couple lived on the same floor as us. The woman's name was Pimpenel and the husband's name was Nicola. I called her Pimpie for short, a very nice woman, extremely helpful, always wanting to do things for us. She was a lot taller than him, sort of like Mutt and Jeff.

As nice as she was, Nicola was the opposite and had the habit of always being drunk. He would tend to get nasty when he did, but being so short, I was able to keep him in line, and help her out with him. One night in particular, we had come home from a movie, the hallway leading up to our apartment, was lit by a small bulb, and even in the daytime it tended to be dark. I was leading Teresa up the stairs, groping the walls in the dark, when suddenly I stumbled on what I thought was a very lumpy object. I looked down and it was Nicola, who had passed out at the top of the stairs, dead drunk. Teresa lets out a scream and Pimpie runs out of her apartment upon hearing the screams. Pimpie was so used to Nicola coming home late and drunk that she never seemed to worry about where he was. She knew he always went to his club, which was just around the corner from her apartment. After I calmed down Teresa and Pimpie, who was apologizing for her husband, I picked up Nicola, and carried him in to his apartment. Nicola was like a limp rag doll, I believe he weighed no more than ninety pounds, Pimpie speaking in Italian, "this son of a bitch, I do not know what to do with him, some day he will kill himself. Grazia Leo, for being so understanding to us, I thank you and Teresa, for your compassion towards me."

After about two years, we were faced with the problem of having to relocate due to the high way coming through our neighborhood. All the old timers, who had spent their lives living in the neighborhood, were on the street, complaining about where they going to live. Again, this was the "village mentality" of the Italians; they did not like change. Although we tried to find a home, nothing seemed to fit our budget so we had to look for another apartment. I did not have a lifeline to grab.

OUR LIFE TOGETHER

Teresa and I agreed that I was going to be the bread winner, and she wanted to be a homemaker. Teresa enjoyed the task of keeping house, and the rearing of the children, to which my long hours away from home did not leave me much time. I believe I made the most of it, making sure to cut out time for them, and hopefully, it was recognized, by my children. Teresa's culinary work, I believe left a lasting impression on Janet and Gail, who also became wonderful cooks in their own right.

In 1968, while attending a movie at the Whitney Theatre on Whitney Ave, we saw a travel short about the island of Bermuda. We were so impressed with the presentation of the subject matter and about maybe being able to go there someday. We felt that maybe when the children got older we would have a chance to go. In a discussion with my brother-in-law, Bill and his wife Virginia, they said, "go and leave the children with us for the week." And so we went.

After that, we visited Bermuda several times over the years. One time in particular in our later years, we had a hilarious departure from the island. I was summoned to the airline office and was told that we were going to be put on a flight a day later and they would pay for our lodging. Upon arriving at the airport, we did not see any other passengers. As we boarded the plane, I asked the flight crew, "where is everybody?" They said, "A mix up had occurred," which was an understatement for sure. We sat in first class, the only two passengers on a four engine plane.

Our first family trip to Miami Beach, Florida was an experience we never forgot. We took a late flight and arrived by midnight. As we arrived at the hotel, we were told that there was no room for us. I called my travel agent even though it was 1:00am. She got us a room at another hotel and then we were shuffled back to our original hotel. The hotel upgraded our rooms and gave us luxury lodgings right by the pool.

We went on many other trips to the Pocono Mountains, Hershey PA, Washington D.C and New Hampshire. The trip to Hershey, PA was memorable because it was during a hurricane week. We only had one good day to visit the chocolate factory.

The trip to Washington D.C. visiting our nation's capital was a favorite. The kids especially enjoyed the tour of where they made money.

On our 25th wedding anniversary we went to Hawaii with my brother-in-law Louie and his wife Jennie. Our anniversaries were one month apart. We stopped in Las Vegas and San Francisco through the auspices of both our families.

I had to make do for our family vacations, by having to work around the time that was allotted to me due to my seniority in my work place and had to choose destinations that allowed for the weather.

When Janet became a travel agent, she secured many good deals for us. That was a plus not having to go to an agency to plan the trips.

Teresa and I both loved going to the Broadway shows in New York City. We made many excursions into the city, mostly on a monthly basis. We would have either lunch or dinner in some of the most elegant restaurants, a treat in and of itself. Our entertainment tastes were of the same. Along with going out of town, we also attended many local venues for entertainment.

We also went to Atlantic City, New Jersey, to see many of the top names in show business. Atlantic City brought back many memories of when I was single and visited many of the locations my friends and I attended. One in particular, a restaurant named De Angelo's, sounds futuristic.

LIVING WITH THE IN-LAWS

My sister-in-law Rose was going to move out of her apartment, which was on the second floor of Teresa's family home. My sister-in-law was buying a home, so the opportunity presented itself for us to take her apartment, so we moved from the third floor to a second floor apartment. The move occurred during a severe snowstorm in the month of March and our daughter, Gail, was moved earlier before the weather got out of hand.

My brother-in-law, John, hooked up the gas stove so we could have heat in the apartment. The stove I had purchased had a heater in the unit, so it was a combination, heater and stove. Although the apartment was renovated years earlier, it did not have insulation installed, so the stairs in the back of the house were not enclosed. That also made for some very cold days and nights, being on the north side of the house.

Conversely, the summers were just as bad, due to no insulation in the roofing area. All we had above us was a tarred roof that would boil over during the summer. My brother-in-law, Tony, gave me a big fan that they had used down at his club to help cool off our apartment. I never knew how hot it was living there until one day Gail got sick and I called the doctor. When he entered the house, the first thing he said was, "God, this place is like a furnace! How the hell are you living here?" I showed him the fan which was turned off because of Gail. I did not know what was wrong with her and did not want to have any drafts in the house to make her condition worse.

It did not matter. Gail had to be taken to the hospital because she had pneumonia. I believe Gail was less than two years old at the time, but as bad as I thought we had it on the second floor, my in-laws downstairs would feel the cold worse than we did. The house had a central register in the corner of the room to heat the entire first floor, and to make matters worse, it was sending heat up to my apartment through a register in the center of our rooms. After Gail came home from the hospital, I put fans in the front room and the back room to cool off the apartment.

So living upstairs from my in-laws was to me like having an extended family. I inherited six brothers-in-law, all to my benefit and they treated me as one of their own, so much so that John and I long conversations about going in business together. Some of the ventures we looked at was a package store, a moving and trucking business, and also about purchasing some real estate.

The conversations never materialized to anything concrete. I had a small family that I had to consider and make sure I could provide for them. John, on the other hand, was not married at this time, so our priorities were different. To just go off and quit my job with no income would have proven to be a hardship for me, so John eventually went with a friend of his and purchased some multi-family units in New Haven.

My father-in-law had a backyard garden which was his passion, but not everybody agreed with his desire to follow him, especially when it came time to dig and hoe the yard in the spring time. I would help him as much as I could, but having an early morning call for work only left me with sometime in the afternoon to help him. My brothers-in-law also pitched in, coming from the city to this was all new to me.

I did not know what the hell a septic system was, but that was all about to change, very quickly. One day, when I was going down to the cellar to bring some of our extra belongings, I smelled an awful odor. When I inquired about this to my father-in-law, he showed me where it was coming from: there was a trap door under the stairs covering a tank that held all the waste from the house. He explained how he would empty the tank by putting the waste into the garden. Welcome to the world of living in the suburbs! He also said for me to be careful about throwing anything but human waste into the toilet. This was a huge awakening for a city boy.

I now had two girls, Gail and Janet and we started to look for a home. We had been living there for about ten years, but we wanted to find something centralized, and not too far from where we were. At this time, Teresa did not drive, so that drove us to look in our immediate area, but to no avail. Looking for a first home could prove daunting for someone like me, who was not very handy with tools.

1960's-1970's Move to Branford

The problem that was acute for me was this crazy social experiment that the government wanted everybody to get engaged in: bussing children from one part of the city to another, and also to involve students from the outlying districts to be bussed back and forth. Gail was, I think, six years old, and Janet was three years old and they only were only two blocks from our school.

In May of the year, I was informed that Gail was going to be bussed to a school in New Haven, near the center of the city. I went to see the principal of the school, and politely told her that she can take my daughter's name off the list since we were moving to Branford. The principal said, "That is sad, because I think it would be a good experience for the child," I responded, "Fine, then you can put your daughter on the bus for me." Then I said, "They named this "Project Concern", not thinking about my daughter, who will be on the bus about two hours a day. Whose concern are they thinking about? Not mine."

My sister-in-law Rose told us about her husband's brother in law, who had a lot in Branford that he was going to build a house on, and wanted to know if we would be interested in seeing him. We agreed. His name was Charlie and he would build about three house a year, sort of a building contractor. The lot was in a centralized area and near a bus stop, but while I was negotiating with Charlie about the price of the house another problem arose.

This problem cemented my desire to push up the date with Charlie, and to start building the house. Mind you all this and with no contract, just a handshake, and the deal was this: I give him one thousand dollars for a down payment, and if I did not like the house he would give me back my deposit.

After I moved to Branford, it was such a relief to think my children only had to walk one block to school, and they would come home for the lunch hour. Some of the teachers lived in my area and it made for a nice, comfortable place to raise a child. One day I was downtown watching a parade and standing next to me was a gentleman who started a conversation with me. Of all things, he brought up the fact that he was in favor of the school bussing program.

I waited until he finished his explanation of the many opportunities that this program would give the children, then I asked him a simple question, "What school do your children go to?" "Oh", he answered, "My children go to a private school, but I think it is a good idea." At this time the government wanted to include all the suburbs because a lot of the people were fleeing the city.

This was also the man that I would encounter later on, when the town held a lot of meetings on this proposal of bussing. He was very vocal and in favor of bussing, until one man questioned him about his children's school of choice and he saved me from asking the same question.

When the meeting was finished, I met this guy outside the school, and in a nice tone of voice explained, that the government was playing with children's lives, and that was one of the reasons I moved to Branford. I did not want my children educated in another town or city.

Despite my ideas, he was adamant in his views and would not change his stance. The thing is this guy and I would cross paths many times in town and he would never speak to me again, because I used some bad language in my opposing remarks to him. I also gave him the Italian salute with my hand.

This program failed on its own due to the cost and it was nothing but a political ploy to win over voters. Amazing, later on when I was doing business in the city, I had conversations with some of the people I was doing business with, and they too had reservations about sending their children into maybe a hostile area. This program was nationwide and caused a lot of tempers to flare up and caused more harm than good. It was universal that most of the people in favor had their own children enrolled in private schools.

My wife and I saved up for ten years to purchase our house in Branford and still I had to borrow some money from my sister-in-law, Rose, to make the down payment. The price of the house was twenty two thousand dollars and with our down payment our monthly payments were one hundred seven dollars a month.

It might seem so small by today's payments, but I came from a rent paying thirty five dollars a month. I actually sat down in my new house one day and was worried about how in the hell I was going to make it. I came to my new house with only enough furniture to cover our bedrooms, a kitchen table with six chairs, and the living room and dining room were laid bare for the first year we lived there.

When we moved into our neighborhood and got friendly with some of the parents of other children, they would come over and tell us we had to wait for some time before we could furnish the rest of the rooms. Well, I did not want to wait. I took on some extra work on my route and put in longer hours to make more money and buy the necessary furniture for the house.

We went out and bought the furniture for the living room and dining room, then this one bitch came over one day, after we got everything set up, and in a jealous rage, looked around, and said, "You should have waited. Everybody else took about two years before they furnished their houses. how did you do it?," I politely opened the door, saying, "We are very busy and thank you for coming over, but please call the next time," We never seen her again.

I purchased the house in 1962, six years after my father passed away. I just wished he could have seen my house, and see what a difference it was from my home on Greene St. My home at that time covered twelve hundred square feet, about three times the size of our house on Greene St. I know he would have been so proud to think his son had such a beautiful home.

After what he went through with my sister Mary, to think that his son did this on his own, and never gave him any problems, unlike his daughter. When he came to visit me on Hamilton St., our first apartment, he had the look of a happy father seeing his son settled in with his family. I think he got more enjoyment in seeing Gail than me.

GAIL

The birth of our first born child, Gail, was on February 26, 1956. This day still resonates in my memory due to the great expectations of being a father. The pressure of being the sole supporter of a family gave me the impetus to buckle down and concentrate on creating as good as father can be. Gail's birth was not an easy time for Teresa. Teresa was in labor for the better part of 36 hours. In those days fathers were not allowed to be by the bedside of their wives except for only for periodic visits.

My family and friends were so elated when I came home with the news of the birth of Gail. I vividly recalled standing on the corner in front of St. Michael's hall after the Sunday mass with people waving greetings from across the street. It was a very uplifting time for the Marino family and the De Angelo's. After, I went home and joined my family for Sunday dinner and then went up to the hospital to see Teresa and Gail.

After Teresa and Gail were discharged from the hospital came the task of carrying Gail, along with the many items of clothing, etc. up to our apartment and then going back downstairs to help Teresa. She was in the midst of climbing the stairs and luckily for me the neighbors in the building came to assist me. Our stay at the apartment would only last for about a year as redevelopment in New Haven was starting to take hold, and we were given eviction notices. We had little time to invest in looking for a new home. Teresa's sister, Rose, was going to move out of her apartment above her mother's house and we were given the opportunity to take her flat.

My brother-in-law John, who was very playful with Gail, but a little on the rough side, liked to throw her around, and Gail enjoyed his attention, but one day it got out of hand. In the midst of rough housing with Gail, John was flipping Gail up and down, and on one flip he tossed Gail up in the air, but a little too high. Gail's head hit the overhead light and all the glass came tumbling down on her head. I heard the scream and rushed in and took Gail away from John, who turned white has a sheet. Gail's head was covered with glass but no cuts. I gently removed the glass from Gail's head but we were all concerned with maybe glass getting in her eyes.

John got his ass reamed out from his mother and father for being so rough with Gail. To John, this was the way he expressed his love for children, not to mention the light fixture, which he said he was going to pay for, but he never did. I would break his stones about it from time to time and we'd laugh about it, but it could have been a serious accident.

Gail herself was quiet the ruffian. She liked to jump around and always wanted to play. Gail had a playpen that we would put her in so that we did not have to worry about her going out the door, since the back stairs were quite steep. Well, one day coming home from work, Gail heard me coming up the back stairs, and started to jump up and down in her playpen. She would get excited every time I came home, but this time she jumped so hard that she went through the floor of the playpen and demolished it. That was the end of her playpen days.

One day while changing the diaper on Gail, I got to thinking about how dangerous it was to pin her diapers, even though we had the safety pins that locked. Always making sure the pin would not open, as I was folding the diaper over, I wondered why instead of pins, why not have some kind of tape, to secure the diaper, I even experimented with using regular tape, but it would not hold for long. I tried several different types of tape, but to no avail, but someone else was also thinking of the same thing, about a year later, they came out with a diaper that had Velcro to fasten the diaper. At least I was thinking, but not fast enough. The mistake I made was not to bring the idea to a person who could develop it. I did not know who to talk to, but then much later a better product came on the market: Huggie's.

Gail was a very photogenic child and won awards in photo contests. Her dark hair and light skin accelerated by her cheerful attitude. She attended kindergarten at Woodward Avenue school and loved it there. In first grade she attended St. Rose's School. Over the years Gail has revealed to me how badly she suffered as a student at St. Rose's School.

Going to grade school was a problem as Gail had to walk 30 minutes every morning and afternoon to get from our home on Fulton Street to St Rose's School. As a very timid and shy 7 year old child, she was abused mentally and physically everyday by the catholic school. The nuns would hit children for any little infraction, including not knowing the correct answers to their constant questions. Most of the children in the class were subjected to daily beatings with a paddle. The nuns had their little pets and those children were exempt from abuse. There was no compassion for 7 year old children who were babies really. The nuns had no patience when the student didn't have the correct answer to a question or couldn't recite verbatim the words to "the act of contrition". Since most of the class did not have the correct answer they would have to line up, bend over and get whacked with a paddle. This to a 7 year old growing child! One day a boy, Justin, who wore glasses, was told to take them off, put in his back pocket and bend over. Needless to say, Justin did not have glasses when he left school that day and all because he didn't know his math answer. This is very sad because the nuns were representing God!

One day this torment boiled over for Gail and she hatched an escape plan. Gail unlocked the gate to the school playground and ran from Blatchley Avenue all the way home as a 7 year old child. She cried and begged her mom not to go back there but her grandfather drove her back. In those days when children would tell their parents about the abuse at school, the parents sided with the authorities. Compared to today, it is quite the reverse because teachers are afraid of the kids and their parents.

The abuse would be lasting in children's' memories forever. When we moved to Branford, I put her on a waiting list for St. Mary's School, but luckily there was no room and she attended the public schools. When Gail became a mother, she made sure her three kids got the best teachers and would not fear school like she did. She wanted them to love school, enjoy it and flourish.

When Gail was in 2nd grade, she came home from school one day and said that I have to go to her school and see her teacher, along with some other parents. She had trouble learning a thing called an "abucus". It was almost like an adding machine, but this had beads, that went up and down. I had put in a long day on my route and was in no mood to start learning some crappy adding machine, plus it was a cold and icy night.

As I left the meeting and went over to my car, I was standing on some ice that was near the door. I reached for the door handle, and started to open the door, and the next thing I knew I slipped under the car, up to my waist. People leaving the meeting with me ran to help me up from under the car. Even the priest came out to see what happened and he offered to take me home, but I said I could manage.

That fall would put me out of work for three months. I was hospitalized for two weeks but after coming home, I had a relapse. My family had to call for help and some policemen came and took me back to the hospital but because my doctor was not available to admit me back to the hospital, I was sent home. I was in excruciating pain- I literally had to crawl up the stairs and I could not stand up, so I pleaded with the doctors in the emergency room to let me stay in the hospital, but they did not want to go against the rules. They did not want the responsibility of admitting me. Can anyone even think about that happening today?

The next day my doctor called and I was admitted and put in traction for another week, which were weights that they put on my legs to pull my back in line. Not a pleasant experience, and to make matters worse, after I was able to go back to work, my company gave me a hard time, so I had to go and see the company doctor to get a complete physical or they would not take me back. I was cleared by my doctor, but that was not enough, I had to fight to get my job back because then if I left with that on my record, I would not be able to get another job. Nobody would hire you if you had a physical handicap that could occur again because of the insurance.

My boss, Pete, fought like hell for me, even going so far as taking responsibility for me. Pete was putting his job on the line by doing this, and yes, there were days after I went back to work when I did not have the strength to get out of bed, but I would not call in sick. If I did, Pete's bosses would have been all over him. That fall would plague me for a great many years.

During Gail's teen years she worked at Waldbaums Supermarket as a cashier. She had to experience a dreadful incident at this job. One day a couple came through her line with a cart loaded with groceries, and as Gail finished ringing up their order, which amounted to one hundred dollars, they distracted Gail by asking her a question, to which Gail had to go to the courtesy booth for the answer and as soon has Gail went up the aisle, the couple darted out the door with the unpaid groceries. Returning to her station and not seeing the couple or their groceries, Gail let out a cry for help. The manager ran out of the store to try and locate the couple, but they were gone. Gail, now in a grave situation is responsible for the loss and her job, according to company rules, instant dismissal. The next day I went to the store to see the manager who I knew personally from having served him when he was a manager of another store. I offered to reimburse the store for the full amount, recalling his words, "Leo, just you coming here, is good enough for me. Tell Gail to come back and forget about the money." I thanked him, with the words, "now I have to do all my shopping here," he laughed at that one.

I was very proud of Gail for attending Quinnipiac College and Stone Business School. She got a job at Presidential Reality and worked at the Towers in New Haven and then a law firm.

JANET

Our second daughter, Janet, was born on February 19, 1959 and at that time I was employed has a milkman for Sealtest Dairy. To get time off was just as bad as asking for the moon. I had to wait until my regular day off to try and help my wife with the new baby. Janet was a model baby. She was for me a shot in the arm being that she slept pretty much all night and did not make any disturbances. Once she got her bottle she was off to sleep, a milkman's dream.

My hours were brutal as it was, arising at around three in the morning, so getting to sleep by nine o'clock, and not having any interruptions, meant a lot to me. The dairy had a policy of giving a present to all the new arrivals in the family. Gail and Janet both received a large blanket when they were born and a month's supply of free milk.

My mother could not pronounce Janet's name correctly, she would call her Jan-nit, and Gail was pronounced Jail. My parents had a hard time accepting these new names. They would have wanted me to name them old world names, yet they never made an issue out of it, like some other Italian families did. The custom was to name them after the man's father or mother. The year 1959 saw me changing jobs. In June of that year, I went to work for Wonder Bread. The bakery would have contests for different products to spur sales. In my first contest, which was a new box of donuts that they were putting on the market, each route has base to surpass. Well, it so happened, the donut contest was around Halloween. On my route was a Catholic High School, so I went to the head Nun and sold her on the idea of a donut and cider week. She agreed, and that week my sales tripled my base, so I won the contest.

The prize was a twenty five dollar savings bond, which because it was in the year of Janet's birth, I saved it for her, and I gave it to her many years later, although it did not grow that much.

On Fulton Street, Gail and Janet made friends with the family next door who had daughters. They would leave the house and play with them all day. Like so many families on the street, they also had a small garden with a stationary table for them to eat on.

One day while they were playing at friend's house, Janet climbed on the table and fell off hitting her head. I took her to the doctor up the street. He diagnosed it as a concussion and told us to let her lie still for a day. That was the end of her adventurous climbing days.

We moved to Branford and she continued her ways and made friends with all the children in the neighborhood. Janet wanted me to get her a dog, but that was not on my agenda, so I convinced her into getting a doll house, which I built in the backyard. Janet and her friends had a nice time playing in the house.

When I first started to lay the ground work for the floor of the doll-house, I went out and bought some lumber for the foundation of the house. Keep in mind, I am a klutz with a hammer and saw, I did not even have a level, I started to put some two by fours together, and was in the process of laying down the floor, on the two by fours, when Mr. Carillo, who lived across the street came over, he said, "Marino what the hell are you doing? This thing is all out of whack. It is going to be all out of shape when you get through with it." Carillo goes home and comes back with his tool box.

Carillo was a craftsman. He built his house himself. He was also a mason and his job in the factory was the head maintenance man. He had built a beautiful brick house so when he came over, the first thing he does is tear up the floor I had just put down, saying, "You have to start with a good foundation," Carillo says to me. "Carillo, I have to get this up in a hurry, or else I will have to get my daughter a dog!"

So Carillo got the floor all laid out and told me to start getting the lumber for the walls and advised me how to structure it. After I was in the process of finishing the walls, Carillo comes over and said, "Marino, you will never be a carpenter, you make too many rough cuts,"

"The house is finished, Carillo, that's all I give a shit about. Now my daughter will forget about the dog," I told Cosmo, "Next time you need some work done, call me," He responds in Italian: "fon ghoul" translated means "up your rear end".

Janet also was in the Girl Scouts, which meant I had to buy a lot of Girl Scout cookies, and go out and sell them for her. The Girl Scouts were always having some kind of drive for some cause so Janet was always busy with them. During the Memorial Day parade, I took a classic picture of Janet when she was marching. She has this look of having a frown on her face, almost in the style of being mad, very serious.

One day, when I was working for Hostess Cake, I took the family to show them the area I was working. The furthest part of my route was the Goodspeed Opera House in Haddam. It was a nice day for a ride, but on the way to the opera house is an old swing bridge. When a boat has to go under the bridge, it could take up to about one half hour to swing back and forth.

On this day we got caught in the middle of the bridge opening and had to wait. All the while Janet and Gail are taking all this in and looking nervous about going over the bridge. As soon as we got home, they wanted to know how many times a week I had to cross the bridge, "Twice a week, Tuesdays and Thursdays".

After that they remembered when it was those days and told me to be careful about the bridge. They had this fear of the bridge falling down. Especially in the winter, they would ask me if I had to cross the bridge that day, being so young and worrying about their dad, always gave me some cause to try and relieve their fears, by telling them even if I did have to go that way, I would say no. I reassured them it was a very safe bridge even though it was old and well kept, but still they would remind me on those days.

At a young age Janet had a problem with her legs. They were turning inward and to correct this, an orthopedic doctor recommended that Janet be fitted with some leg braces. It was a contraption that came down from her hip and she also had to put her feet into a set of shoes and even had to sleep with them on. The doctor felt this was the correct way to help her legs to form correctly. The doctor said it was because her hips were not aligned properly. Janet tolerated this and never complained about having to do this. I knew that she had to be in a lot of discomfort but I was so proud of her, and still am.

Janet had to endure this procedure for several months and when we took her back to the doctor for some X-rays, the doctor said, "All looks good to me. The worst of the problem is over. If she has any recurrence from this when she gets older, she might have to have surgery on her hips," but Janet never had to face that decision- the brace and shoe contraption worked.

I was very proud of Janet attending the University of New Haven. Initially, she was interested in travel and tourism since she was working as a travel agent. She received an AS degree in Travel, Tourism and Hotel Management. After the two years she decided to continue on and received a BS in Business Administration all the while holding down two part time jobs. This was at a time when the thinking in most families was that girls did not have to have a college diploma. This is how I was brought up but how wrong it was. Today it would be unthinkable to not send your daughters to college. Although, even with a college diploma nowadays, it does not mean instant success, but I guess you have to give them the opportunity to do so, such is society today. The training to become a person in the hotel and travel business paid off for Janet, as she is very capable of arranging and securing the necessary arrangements for whatever arrangement is needed.

DAVID

On July 16, 1962, I went to work, hoping that Teresa, who was pregnant at the time with our third child, would not go into labor until the weekend. Getting time off from the company was a nightmare and short of bleeding to death, you had to come to work.

But, as luck would have it, Teresa started having frequent labor pains at about mid-morning. Luckily, my brother-in-law Billy was home at the time and was able to take care of her. He rushes Teresa to the hospital, and very quickly, our son David was born. Billy then calls the bakery and asks them to contact me on the route with the good news. When they finally track me down it was about eleven o'clock in the morning, and I was on State St, in the middle of my route. I call the hospital and speak to Billy, who exclaimed, "You have a baby Boy!" With that news, I unloaded the rest of my order and got to the hospital as quick as I could.

Even with this news, again, the company was all business, first asking me about the sales on my route, and then as an afterthought, "oh, by the way, we hear you had a baby boy," not missing a beat. The supervisor, Sal, goes into a lengthy lecture on the amount of sales for the next week that he expects of me. How nice.

As a young boy David was into sports, especially baseball, staying out late during the summer months to play with his friends. It was a grind for me to take him to practice and to the games with my job and that was bad enough, but having to sit in a field that had a swamp in the vicinity made it really miserable, even with the spray on.

The coach was a likeable fella. He treated the kids as if they were his own, so I along with the rest of the parents, asking maybe next year, "Get us the hell out of this swamp." The coach exclaims, "Me too, this will be our last year here, you can take that to the bank."

When David got a few years older, I took him with me in the summer time on my route. It was always on a Friday when I had my biggest order. I would pick up my order then pick him up from home. He got to know the product line so well, that he was like a regular route man. I believe this experience served him well, well enough that he later on in his teen years he worked part time in the supermarket, when he was attending high school, and even during his college years. After college, David went to work for Blue Cross, working in an office, but when I started my business, he would say, "Dad, hurry up and get me out of here!"

As a very young boy, David would sometimes wake up with me when I went off to work, and watch me through the window as I drove away. I remember because he was so small he had to stand on the ledge of the radiator, waving to me, and also because of his habit of not sleeping well: David would sometimes get up and walk around the house.

One particular evening, I was awoken by a loud noise coming from the kitchen. I turned on the lights and saw the back door open and heard footsteps outside the back door coming closer to the screen door. At that time I did not have a light for the outside so I grabbed a knife from the drawer and was ready to thrust it through the door, when I heard a voice, "Dad, it's me." My body went has limp as a rag doll and the knife fell to the floor. I staggered to the nearest chair sat down.

Seeing David walk through the door, I was overcome with emotion. Just the thought of what might have occurred shook the hell out of me. I was hugging and cursing him at the same time.

David's habit of waking up and walking around was one thing, but now this sleep walking was leading him to go outdoors. The next morning I went to the hardware store and purchased locks to be placed at the top of the doors, well out of reach for his height, and luckily he grew out of that habit.

On one of David's early walks, he came into my bedroom and said. "Dad, there is a big bird in the living room," "David, what the hell is it now, you dreaming this shit, I have to get up and go to work in alittle while." I get up and viola, there was a large bird withering on the floor of the room, with its wings still flapping a little. It had flown right through the bow window. I went and got a large old blanket to pick up the bird. When I returned, the bird was completely motionless. I picked up the bird with the blanket and brought it outside. The next day I called my next door neighbor and explained what had happened. He said, "because of the moonlight, which was bright last night, the bird mistook the window for an opening," I said, "Maybe I have to put up a sign for the birds to read, not a fly through," Mr. Holmes said, "Welcome to the paradise of suburbia."

David, gave me another great scare one time. Coming home from work one day I see Janet standing on the front steps with blood on her clothes, "Daddy, David fell off the bike he has a large cut on his head," I covered David with a blanket and rushed him to the doctor's office in town. The cut was repaired with some sutures and the doctor said to bring him home and let him rest. But to me David was not responding. I instead drove him to the hospital where he was diagnosed with a concussion. They were going to keep him there for observation. After a day or so David was discharged with the instructions given to me for what to watch for, any effects, such has vomiting, etc. Janet's version of the accident was that they were descending down a steep roadway when David lost control of his bike and went head first over the handle bars tumbling down the hill. It was to me a very scary time to come home and seeing

Janet on the steps calling me. In those few seconds, all crazy thoughts going through my mind. Did something happen in the house and who else is hurt? Once I saw David, I was out the door with him.

David always wanted to help me with the yard work. But being so young, I gave him chores not of the mechanical nature. He wanted to help with the lawn cutting and using electric devices. I would tell him maybe next year until finally the next year did come and one day I relented and showed him how I use the hedge cutters with the explicit instructions to never put his hands near the blades. After about a half hour David was getting comfortable with the machine. As he tried to turn the cutter over, to cut the other side of the hedge, David, let his fingers get to close to the blades and cut the inside of his fingers. I was standing so close to him and I still could not stop him in time. I grabbed his hands and squeezed his fingers together thinking they were severed at the inside of his palm. I rushed him to the emergency room, the cuts were deep but not sever enough to do any damage. This was just a stupid dad, who learned his lesson the hard way.

David graduated with honors from high school and went on to graduate from the University of New Haven.

FAMILY PARTIES

One of my fondest memories was and is the tradition of my family giving me a special birthday party due to my Christmas birthday. They took note of me never really having a day for myself. They would set aside the first week in December and plan all sorts of activities. This is when my playroom was put to good use. There was plenty of room for the children to romp around in. Sitting at the dinner table, watching the children interact with one another, was and is still priceless.

Especially during the holidays, we would have many parties at our home. I would put out a huge ping pong table and a folding table strung out the length of the room. The room would be full of family enjoying themselves and socializing. These are my memories that time cannot erase.

PETITION FOR SIDEWALKS

One of the biggest selling points for me in purchasing our home was the fact of the school being just one block away from our home. It was an elementary school up to the eighth grade, I believe. From there, it was on to the high school, and that then became a problem for us.

The town informed me that Gail could not have bus service due to the fact we were less than a mile away from the high school. She would have to walk to the high school, along with the other children in our area. I couldn't believe it so I went and measured the distance with my car and sure enough, it was exactly one tenth of a mile short.

This was all well and good, until one day as I got home from work early, Gail came running down the street, crying to me that a man tried to get her into his pick-up truck. The area in question did not have a sidewalk. It is located on the hill where the railroad station is now.

I got into my car, went to the police station and reported the incident. I did not have a description of the truck, but the police said they would monitor the area more closely. This response did not please me, so I then went to the town hall and asked to see the first selectman, John Sliney. I found him to be very respectful of my concerns. Mr. Sliney asks me, "Mr. Marino, lets you and I take a ride and see what can be done about this," Mr. Sliney puts on his straw hat and takes me for a tour of the area in question. At that time the factory known as the M.I.F. was in operation. He explained most of the employees lived in the area and he never had any complaints about the sidewalk, or lack of one.

"Mr. Sliney," I say, "This is my teenage daughter we are talking about. The people you are referring to are all workers who use this path and nobody would ever bother them. There is no distance between the road and the path; it is all one road. Does something have to happen before any action is taken? I had an aunt who was killed on a road similar to this. To add insult to injury, I now have to worry about someone snatching my daughter."

After standing on the path for a while talking, a car comes speeding down the hill, breezing right by us, almost blowing Mr. Sliney's straw hat off his head. We both looked at each other, and after a few Moments of quiet staring, Mr. Sliney speaks: "Mr. Marino, I believe you have made a good argument. I think this surely has to be addressed, and quickly. This property we are standing on belongs to the railroad, and to get them to fix this, you will need to get all your neighbors to sign a petition regarding this problem." I said, "Damn it Mr. Sliney, so much bullshit we have to go through when everyone could see, you need a sidewalk here," Mr. Sliney understood my concerns and said, "Mr. Marino this what is called red tape crap."

So now I am on mission. It was me against the town to try and remedy this horrible situation. The selectman said it was not going to be easy. The owners of the property would argue against it, but I told Mr. Sliney, "They are going to have one crazy Italian to deal with."

So I got in touch with one of my daughter's school mate's mother. She and I worked out a plan to scour the neighborhood. She would take one section and I would take my end of town. We purchased some legal pads and went out every night signing people up. Not surprisingly, I met no resistance from anybody. On one of my first nights, I went to one of my neighbors' homes and really lucked out. This man was an accountant for the state of CT. He looked at the petition and said, "You have the right idea, but the wrong paper. I will get you the correct forms for people to sign. The town will take it more seriously since it will be more professional."

I called the girl's mother and told her of my meeting this man and how he was going to help us. She was thrilled. We then got the legal forms and set about getting signatures. Everybody signed the new forms. I went out every night for one week. After we got all the forms signed, we then marched into Sliney's office and slapped the petitions on his desk. He had a startled look, "God, you people work fast," I was pleased he was impressed, "I told you, you are dealing with a crazy Italian, and also an Irish lady, who is just as determined, as I am."

He then says, "By the way, Mr. Marino, did you have anything to do with that car coming down the hill?" laughing, reminding me about what it took for him to agree with us. One month later, after all the petitions were approved, the sidewalks were put in on both sides of the hill, but our children still had to walk to school.

I believe it wasn't until the next year that all the high school children were put on the bus. But again, the town waited for a horrible accident to happen before they decided to take action.

A little boy was walking on the side of the road, got hit by a car and died as a result. There were no sidewalks and this happened about a year after I had the dust up with the town officials about the same problem. This is exactly what I told Mr. Sliney. I understood the problem the first selectman had with so much horseshit to go through, just to get something done. His heart was in the right place, but his hands were tied. In the time I spent with him, I found him to be a very caring man who did whatever he could for people.

It was shortly after that they put sidewalks in on both sides of the street. The area in question was the property of the state. They maintained the roads, which is why I understood why the town did not have the responsibility of having sidewalks placed there and also why it is so difficult to cut through all the red tape needed. There are so many people involved in the process, as Mr. Sliney explained the situation of my problem that it took such a long time to try and get someone to remedy a problem on their property.

NEIGHBOR MIKE

One of my neighbors who lived a few houses away from me turned out to be a very good neighbor for me. His name was Mike and he was of German decent. When I moved to Branford, he was the first one to welcome me and my family and offered me assistance in anything that I needed. When I met him he was sixty five years old and retired from the same factory where my father-in-law worked, but he had the look of a forty year old. I thought he was pulling my leg about his age. He had a mop of white hair, but other than that, he had the body of a young man. Over the years he helped me out alot. Mike especially came to my rescue one day when this neighbor across the street was giving me a hard time about my children running around the yard and making noise. Although their voices were no louder than the cars on the street, Mike said, "Do not mind her. She does not like the fact that you came from the city and have three small children. Plus in your case, you're Italian," Mike said, then continued, "I will go over and talk to the old bitch and straighten her ass out," I do not know what Mike said to her, but she never bothered me again, but only gave me dirty looks every time she would see me.

When Mike had to have some surgery at the age of ninety, I thought he was all through. He was walking very slowly with a walker and he wasn't his usual self. Normally, Mike would walk every day around the neighborhood, and very fast, and to see him with the walker was a shock. About six months later, I was cutting down a stump with a saw. The stump was of a brush I wanted to uproot and about two inches in diameter. Mike came over and saw me and said, "Wait one minute," Mike says, "I will be right back."

Mike came over with large clipper and commenced to wrap this clipper around the limb and cut the limb right in half. I looked at him and was amazed. Here he was after just having major surgery, and he cut the limb right in half with one stroke. Mike was over ninety years old at the time and I told Mike, "You sure know how to hurt a guy." I was forty years old at that time, He was laughing about how I should eat more spinach. Mike was of small frame, but he had the strength of a bull.

At the age of one hundred, Mike contracted a thyroid problem. He said the doctors wanted to operate, but he rejected it. He said he lived long enough and wanted to go. The last time I seen Mike was a week before he passed on. To see Mike that day nobody would have thought he had anything wrong with him, he had the picture of health, very robust.

I stopped by his porch and we had this long conversation about life. Mike said he had no regrets and that he lived a pretty healthy life. He said it was his time. In talking with Mike that day, I marveled at his acceptance of death. Mike told me when he feels the time is near he will call hospice and tell them he is ready. He got up and we shook hands and hugged one another. I thanked him for his friendship and wished him a safe journey to heaven.

Every time I look at the back of Mike's house, I think of him. At the wake for Mike, I met quite a few of our neighbors and they all said we will surely miss him. Mike gave me a lot of advice about taking care of my house, especially during the time I was having trouble with water in my basement and as he helped me, he did the same for others.

COURT REPORTING

During this time period between the 1960s and the1970s, I worked with a man who introduced me to a friend of his who presented me with an opportunity to broaden myself and to advance to another occupation. One day, Ray, my friend from work, asked me if I wanted to stop and have a drink with some of his friends. I agreed and I told Ray, "How can I refuse? It would not look good for me to say no to an African American," I could joke with Ray about race since we had that kind of rapport. He would always kid me about Mussolini, riding on the white horse, and going to war with a small country who he could not beat.

Well, at the bar I was introduced to his friend Larry. Larry was a very well dressed man who spoke with authority. His command of the English language was astounding and he was very articulate in his description of his work. As he was explaining to me his daily routine, I had to stop him, and not being ashamed of asking, about his title of being a Court Reporter. I thought he worked for a newspaper. Larry laughed at that one, "No," he said, "I take down all the proceedings in the court."

Then Larry set about explaining what a Court Reporter does. It sounded so interesting, since I always loved to work with words and spelling was one of my best subjects in school. Larry took me out to his car and showed me the machine that he takes dictation on. It was such a little piece of equipment. Larry explained how you only have about fifteen keys, and you are working mostly with symbols, sometimes two keys for a sentence.

Larry noticed my interest and asked if I wanted to come to his school, where he taught one night a week, and spend some time there to get some more information. At this time I was earning about thirty thousand dollars a year and Larry said that starting out with forty thousand would not be difficult.

Now I was really interested. The thought of not having to get up early and not having to drive a truck in all kinds of weather was enticing. Also, having a position instead of just a job clinched it for me. Larry was also an African American, and he related how he had to really buckle down and study for this profession; working in a factory was not in his mindset.

I looked at Larry and was impressed on how one can better themselves and not bitch about the short comings of life. Inspired, I then enrolled in the next year's class. It was a small group of people, mostly students, who wanted a career that the public schools were not offering. With all the energy I could muster up, I went at it full force, but what was against me was having to work from four in the morning until about four in the afternoon and then go to class at night. It was not easy for me; there was no place for me to study in my house with three small children running around and the television turned on all the time. Usually, I would stay upstairs in the kitchen, while everyone was in the playroom downstairs.

While class was one night a week, I still had to practice for my next week's lesson. Larry would dictate and we would have to tape record the lesson. At home, I would have to transcribe the lesson and hand it in the following week. The process was me typing out the transcription of the subject matter.

This job of being a Court Reporter had three different phases to go through. First, you had to type out the words, then you had to relay them to a tape recorder, and last, give them to a typist to type out. Now the process is all done by a computer: the reporter types the words into the computer then the computer now spells out the words with all the corrections. All done in one operation, the words come out on the screen and can be relayed back.

In the old system if someone wanted to know what was just said, the reporter had to unroll the tape and read back the requested material. Now all the words are already transcribed.

Larry brought the class to the Yale Law School to listen in on the mock trials, we had permission to record the proceedings. I went three times to the Law school and I was able to take the conversations of three people speaking simultaneously. To me this was the most interesting position anyone could have. You had to have a clear, focused mind and listen to every word then type it correctly.

After my year was up at the school, Larry gave us a test to prepare us for the city finals. I passed one test, but failed on the state test, which was the one that gave you the license to work in that field. Larry felt bad about me not passing the test, but I did not feel so bad since only one girl in the class passed the test and I was twice the age of everybody else in the class. The following week Larry invited us all up to the school and he had some sandwiches and soft drinks brought up from the restaurant down stairs to celebrate the end of the class.

Knowing how bad my desire was to obtain that position, Larry offered me the opportunity to continue to study for it on a basis of not having to attend classes, but he would tutor me privately, being that I was friend of Ray. Larry wanted to help me in any way he could, such as inviting me over to his home, where he had a private study. I declined solely because of my job. The hours I was putting in at work did not leave much time for studying. I did not want to take up Larry's offer and have us both disappointed. It was extremely gracious of Larry to extend me the courtesy to continue on. He said he had faith in me and would do whatever he could to help me, realizing what I was up against, the time restraint and all.

What was truly amazing about Larry is that race did not factor in his desire to help me, in fact he only brought it up once, when we were having a discussion about race. This was the time of all the Civil Rights era in the country and it was a time of great turmoil. Larry turned to me and said, "Leo the only thing I feel bad about is that my son has restrictions, such as not being able to go into any barber shop and get a haircut, but as I prospered, I expect him to do the same."

The term of "gentleman" is a fitting description of Larry. He taught me about tolerance just by being in his presence. After our chat, we shook hands, and as we parted, Larry looks at me and says, "Leo you have my phone number, my offer will always stand with you, bless you and your family."

A few years later, Larry had a massive heart attack and passed away. I was away on vacation at the time and my regret is that I should have reached out to his family.

REAL ESTATE INVEESTMENTS

As I was getting on in age, I started to think about my future, as I thought of many times. Not only mine but my children. They were now all approaching their teenage years and higher education was in their future, so I started thinking about some kind of investment to carry me through. Real estate intrigued me, especially income producing real estate. I thought of my friend Bill, the pie man, who delivered his product alongside me and of his real estate holdings. He had purchased three houses in Norwich, which totaled nine units. By his estimation, that would give him enough income after he finished with the pie company along with his social security and his union pension.

Bill put all his resources into the properties, so that when he retired, he would have clear sailing and no heavy expenses for the properties. In detailing to me what I should do, I saw that Bill had what you'd call a life well prepared, so now I had to educate myself into getting as much information as I could.

I started to look at all different kinds of real estate. It for me was quite a problem due to my hours on the job, but after some two years I decided to purchase a three family unit in the vicinity of Yale University. It needed some work, but with advice from a friend, was told it was manageable.

All the tenants were either students or employed by Yale. After some initial major repairs, such as two new furnaces, having the cellar ceiling covered with sheet rock, installing a fire escape for the back of the house, the city of New Haven told me that the house was not an official three family unit. I immediately took them to court and produced the document that stated that it was, and then they left me alone.

I purchased the house in 1972 and I paid forty thousand dollars, taking out a thirty thousand dollar loan on the property. After some time, I started to look for more units since having just three units would not produce enough income. One day I ran into this Italian man, Nick, who was looking at same piece of property that I was interested in. He was a painting contractor and had extensive holdings in real estate.

He invited me to a restaurant for coffee and although he spoke broken English, I learned a lot from him. He took me around to some of the apartment houses that he owned and one thing he stressed was that owning multiple houses was not the way to go. He said, "too many roofs" and for me to think about purchasing large units like he had. His units were at least twenty or more in one unit, but my concern was in taking care of them. Nick had the resources- he had men working for him, so if a problem arose, he could send one of them to address it.

Nick told me when he started he had purchased a four unit building and moved up from there. It was quite remarkable, I thought. He arrived in this country twenty years earlier and was already so accomplished. But some of his property I was not impressed with; the tenants he had in those units were mostly low income people and he had to go and physically collect the rent or they would not pay.

On the day I went with Nick, he was showing me how he has to collect the rents. Although he did have some good property, where the tenants sent in their checks, most had to be collected by hand. We started at about nine in the morning. He rings the bell and the tenant knew exactly who it was. He had the money ready, but the next one was a woman who comes to the door in her night gown and tells Nick she has a problem with paying the month's rent. She then tells Nick to come into the house and maybe we can discuss this and work something out. Nick looks at the woman and tells her, "Lady, all I want is the rent money. I do not want your ass. Now go and get the damn money or I will throw you out into the street," She goes into the bedroom and gets Nick the money. I knew that this was not the type of people I wanted to deal with.

When I was with him he did educate me about looking at the

structures of buildings. I took Nick to a twenty unit apartment building I was interested in and he said he had looked at the same building a year ago. He pointed out the poor workmanship in the design of the building, especially the back where it was bulging out.

The next person I encountered in my search for real estate was a teacher who had a lot of holdings in the city. This guy was a character and I met him the same way I met Nick, both of us looking at the same property. Most of his holdings were rented to Yale students and he said he constantly had to check the properties because he would rent the apartment on the basis of how many people were going to live there and that would determine the rent.

His name was Marvin, and from him I learned the meaning of having a thick skin. When he would enter the apartment and the tenant would complain about a problem, Marvin would look at the problem and say it will be all right. Once the tenant showed Marvin a hole in the ceiling and said when it rained the water would come in. Marvin looks at the hole, saying, "Let's wait and see if it gets any worse." Now the guy tees off on Marvin, "How the hell would you like to live here and every time it rained you had to fill up a bucket full of water?" Marvin calms the guy down saying, "Maybe next week we will look at it." It was the same everywhere I went with Marvin; he never took any complaints seriously.

One day Marvin called me and asked me if I was interested in purchasing some property in the same section of the city that he had property. I said sure and met him on a Sunday morning at about nine a.m., rather early I thought. He said he had to be in the area to check one of his apartments, which was naturally rented to students. It was what he had told me earlier, he had suspicions that students were piling up in one of his apartments. Marvin told me to come along and see. I asked Marvin, "Is it okay with the renters for you to come on Sunday morning or did you have to call them?" "Leo, as a landlord you do not have to call anybody. You can visit your property any time you want," Marvin explains. Marvin had the keys to the apartment, and when we walked in, there had to be about a dozen bodies lying around the place.

The stink of foul tobacco smoke was in the air. I asked what it was and he said, "That, my son, is what they call weed."

It looked like a den of inequity, a nice phrase for a "whore house". Very few of them had much clothes on. In fact we continued to step over bodies until he got the right one, the one that rented the apartment. He got the guy up and sat him on a chair. He picks up the guy's pants, and goes through his pockets and comes out with some cash and says, "This is for your friends. I will give you until tomorrow to get the hell out of here. You violated your contract with me."

"Marvin?" I ask, "How can you just barge in people's apartments without notice? I thought you have to give them the courtesy of a phone call before you entered," "You do not," Marvin explains. "Just tap on the door and walk in. With some characters, like these pigs, just use your key, and let yourself in." This was not the kind of renters I would be looking for. I know Marvin said he was getting good rents from them, but to me it was not worthwhile.

Marvin showed me around the neighborhood, and I was impressed with the area, especially being near Yale University. But my part of the city had more of a classier neighborhood since more faculty members lived in my area. But Marvin was getting higher returns in his area. Unlike my previous mentor, Nick the painter, who leaned toward more large apartments, Marvin was more involved in student rental. It was good, but could pose more of a problem. The student market came with some good results because they did not make any demands on how the apartment looked. As long as they had a room to sleep in, they were happy.

I was renting the property I had to a nice couple with a baby on the first floor. The husband worked for Yale and the same with the lady on the second floor. I had one student on the third floor in which I gave him a reduction on his rent for taking care of any small problems. To me, it was a nice rental property; I had a nice mix of people, not so if you had all students.

But has fate would have it, my first floor tenant was given an opportunity to further his career, so he had to move to Boston. He loved working for Yale and wanted to stay in New Haven with the possibility of maybe purchasing my house. We had such long talks about having to make these decisions, but the opportunity proved to be too great to pass up.

My next tenants were three Yale students, all girls. They were recommend by my first floor tenant, Bob, who was moving out. Bob said he knew them from school and that I would not have to worry about the rent. They proved to be nice girls and did not cause any problems; my worry was if they were party people, but not so.

The only problem I had with them, if you wanted to call it a problem, was their housekeeping. They were kind of sloppy, but not in a damaging way. They gave the neighbors an eyeful by sitting in the backyard with their bikinis on; they would think nothing of coming to the door with a skimpy outfit. The day I sent my friend Fred the plumber over there, to fix a bathroom problem, one of the girls comes to the door with the top part of her pajamas on and nothing on for the bottom. Fred looks at the girl and he did not want to enter the apartment, for fear of being accused of molestation. He tells her, "Lady, I will be right back. I forgot to bring the right tools." Fred goes back to the warehouse and gets one of his helpers to come along. He was not going in there alone.

Fred calls me on the phone, "Leo, what the hell is going on in that apartment? The girls were walking around half naked, even with us in the house!" I didn't know what to say, "Freddie, what the hell do you want? They are from Yale and they are very liberal, and extremely loose, as you can see. They need a course in housekeeping, but they are good kids, and I have no problems with them."

Fred says, "If I told my wife she would not want me to go back there." "Freddie," I say, "I had the same problem. I would always bring my son with me whenever I had to go to the house. It was my fault; I should have told you, but I never seen them, like you describe. What the hell, Fred, it was better than going to a show, you got your money's worth!" "You bastard Leo, you wanted to get me in trouble with mama," Fred and I would always remind each other of that day.

Owning income property can sometimes be a pain in the ass. After I lost my third floor student, who had graduated, the one who took care of all the small stuff, I was left to hear from the tenants' complaints, such has when one called me to say that the hall way light was not working. I went over and checked the electric in the other parts of the hall and it was working, so I took out the bulb and replaced it, and it worked. The tenant looked at me in amazement; she did not know how to change a bulb, yet she was employed by Yale. I asked a silly question, "How do you change the bulbs in your apartment?" "Oh," she said "Whenever some-one comes over, I make them do it." What an educated ass.

Another time I was called because the tenant said they did not know how to bring the storm windows down. I went over and slid the win-dows down and again, a look of surprise from the tenant. This is when I missed my third floor student; he was doing all the bullshit stuff for me.

My plan for this house was to someday live on the first floor and to give one of my children the house in Branford to live in. The first floor had two fireplaces, a sun porch, and two bedrooms, living room, din-ing room, and a large kitchen, plus a two car garage, and a nice back yard. I would have two rents coming in and I would have a beautiful area to live in.

When my daughter, Gail, got married, she and her husband, Russ, moved into a unit and it was a nice arrangement for me. She had a nice start up rent, and I had the peace of mind of not having to go over there for all the bullshit crap. At this time my mind was still on obtaining real estate and I wanted to have at least twenty apartments. It was part of my real estate portfolio, with my pension and social security, and it would give me a good income. Real estate was my love but forces beyond my control would change that.

I had checked out some apartments in Branford that were up for sale. One involved fifteen units in two buildings, and my cost at that time to purchase these units was one hundred fifty thousand dollars. A friend of the family, who owned some units in Branford, advised me against purchasing them, as he said the cost was too high. He knew how much the owner had paid for them, and it would not be advisable to buy them. Since he was pretty savvy about the history of property in Branford, I declined to buy them. Unfortunately, the units I am talking about are now grossing one hundred eighty thousand dollars a year. Every time I pass those units I want to choke him and myself.

The years of 1972 through 1978 were years I spent researching the real estate market. As I met different men who had extensive holdings of real estate, my education on this subject was improving. The three family I purchased gave me some experience as to what to look for, along with the advice of the people I met. Some good, some bad, but the main lesson I learned was to go with your instinct.

Purchasing large units could be fraught with very many issues, including the structure, and the market you are addressing. Everybody is looking for the same tenant: upscale professional people, and as I have mentioned earlier, my working hours did not give me the time to devote to real estate. I did have an agent, but he was not very effective, but he did give me a lead once. He called me up at work and said there was going to be a five unit for sale on Whitney Ave. and to go right to the property, as the owner was on the premises. This home was an old Victorian mansion, divided up into five large units, all rented to Yale employees. I got held up at work because the sales manager wanted to hold a meeting. The meeting lasted one and half hours, and after the meeting I rushed down to the home but I was too late. The owner had already took a deposit and said the house was sold. He would not take a counter offer.

My life at this time was consumed with my children growing up and, having to make provisions for their future, coupled with me trying to advance my own career, such as schooling for the position of court reporter, real estate, etc. all the while always looking for a way to put this altogether. The load was tremendous on me and it would have an adverse effect on my health, later on.

GAIL AND RUSS'S WEDDING

In the year 1975, Gail met her future husband, Russ. After going steady for three years, Gail and Russ got engaged. We started to plan for a marriage. During their courtship, Gail and Russ had a bad experience. After we all had dinner together one evening, we sat and talked about the upcoming nuptials. It was getting quite late, so we all got ready for bed and left Russ and Gail in the living room. After some time Russ decides to go home, but when he opens the door to the house, and looks out, his car was gone.

Somebody had stolen his car while he and Gail were sitting in the living room. Russ said he did not hear any noise and the timeline was quite short; I had seen the car outside just before going to bed. Russ's car was an old Rambler, quite beat up in fact, even the police could not figure it out. Who the hell would rob such an old car? Maybe it was for the parts, but nobody came up with any plausible answer. Here was Russ, coming from living in the city, and nobody steals his car, and now he is out in the suburbs and gets his car stolen.

As we started preparing for the upcoming marriage, Russ's parents, Rachael and Russ, came over to our home. We made the plans for the wedding. Russ's parents knew of a caterer, who was a family friend, and we then went out to rent a hall. Russ's father suggested we take a ride up to New Hampshire to purchase all the liquor and beer. We spent a nice day together Russ and his father, me and my son, David. It was so nice to plan a wedding with everybody agreeing on all the preparations. The weddings then were mostly held in various halls. You had to rent the hall before you went to the caterer, and sometimes the caterer would not agree with the management of the hall.

This being our first wedding, I did not realize how much it would take to put it all together. It seemed like every week brought a new challenge. The movie, *Father of the Bride*, while I thought it was a little over reached, was not far from our experience. It seemingly involved all members of the family. Gail and her sister, Janet, did a lot of the heavy lifting. Mom went along to help to decide many of the details of the wedding such as the proper cards, clothes, invitations, shower gifts, etc.

After the wedding, Gail did not have the problem with her living quarters. I offered Gail and Russ the first floor apartment in my three family home. I had a doctor from Yale who was living there at the time and gave him sufficient notice to move out, so that Gail could have the apartment.

As we started to clean the apartment, I did not realize how much it would take to get the place suitable for Gail and Russ. The doctor of Indian descent and his family left the place in an awful, dirty condition. "How," I said, "Could they live here like this? I thought doctors would be clean!" I only went there a few times, usually just to chat then leave so I never noticed anything amiss. On the first day we began to clean the place, we smelled an odor of decaying garbage. We checked every room and the odor was everywhere. I went over to the radiators, which were the old kind, the ones that were standing alone with no baseboard. I looked behind the radiator and had to back away because the stench was so putrid. The area behind the radiators was full of garbage and all of the rooms' radiators were the same. In fact, when we went in, we found left over food on the kitchen floor.

I had to get a plumber and have all the radiators pulled away from the wall so we could clean the areas. We filled up three barrels of trash. We then commenced to repair the apartment and spent the better part of three months renovating the place. I thought that was the extent of our problems there, but I would be wrong.

One day, as I was sanding one of the doors out on the back porch, I noticed a car driving by very slowly. Later, I saw the same car come by a second time. I thought maybe they were looking for a house number. How wrong I was! This was another experience in being careful. Not placing much stock in the car, I never even mentioned it to anybody. It was just some nosy people, I thought.

A few months after Gail and Russ moved into the apartment, Gail and Mom left to go shopping for furnishings for the apartment. Upon returning, they seen the kitchen door ajar, and carefully entered the house. They no sooner opened the door when two guys came running right by them, pushing them aside, almost leveling them flat out.

These two guys took the time to go through the whole three floors of the house. The second and third floors only had some minor stuff stolen. The second floor tenant had some change in a tray, and they took that. Gail had some of her jewelry taken, and what we found in the yard after they left was a large screw driver, almost like a crow bar. I still have it as a souvenir. A reminder of a lesson learned was always be skeptical and to definitely not to enter your house if you see the front door opened.

I realized these men were driving the car that was surveying us that day. We then went about making the premises more secure. We boarded up all the cellar windows and installed some security locks on the doors.

Another scary moment came when a squirrel came sliding down the chimney. We went and opened all the doors and windows so he could get out, but he was running all around the house, tearing up all the furniture. I called an exterminator, and he came in with a long pole to poke the squirrel into one of the windows. He then shut the window, and the animal was trapped between the screen and the glass. The man gave me a long pole with a blade on it and told me to gently cut the screen and stand on the side. In the meantime, he was squirting some liquid under the window to force the animal to go for the screen. I cut the screen and the son of a bitch flew right by my head. The mess the squirrel made was quite extensive. We had to replace some of the furniture and the drapes.

My next project was to seal up the chimneys. I went and put some screen and even had the tops coated with cement. Normally, the animals would come from all the trees around the house. I even had them cut back along with a large tree in the driveway.

Our first granddaughter Kara was born in this house, and after I seen Kara in this house, I felt all the problems were well worth it. That my daughter, Gail, and Russ had a nice home to begin their life together, this was something my father wanted to do for me, but because of my uncle Leo, it came with too many strings attached. I did not want to be a custodian, and they wanted to put me into an old house owned by my aunt, who was a bitch on wheels. For me it would have been rent free, I heard my aunt was pissed (Good!).

This, as I said, was a good arrangement for the both of us. Gail and family had a nice place, and I had the comfort of not having to run over there for the crappy calls. Russ took care of the property, just like it was his own, and I appreciated it, but as good as it was, Gail and Russ were looking for a place of their own, which was understandable.

So after about five years they informed me that they wanted to purchase a new house. Now I had to make a decision, because the picture was changing for me, too. In the ensuing years Gail and Russ gave Teresa and I three wonderful grandchildren: Kara, Alexa and Andrew.

THE YEAR'S 1982-1986 Selling the House

In 1981, I heard the rumors of the company wanting to downsize their operations and move me to the Montville area. They were consolidating their routes, which was no good for me, so I started to prepare for my future without Hostess Cake. My plans were to put in my twenty five years and to possibly have enough rental units to sustain me.

Due to this news, all of my plans had to be moved up a notch. Not having all my plans in place, I had to either secure other employment or to start a business, so I got the idea of starting a cookie route. From being on the route for so many years, I knew what the market was missing and set about procuring the product needed to make it on my own. I went to the library and researched all the top bakeries. When I came home with all the information, I had Gail and Janet write letters to the people in charge of sales.

The amount of letters were tremendous. I think it was somewhere around one hundred, and it took us quite some time to complete. The girls had a table set up down in the playroom, with papers strewn all over the room, plus a board set up to track the letters.

The responses were mostly rejections, but very cordial, informing me of what I needed to do to secure their product. One major flaw was that I did not have a business address. The one rejection letter I treasured the most was from an ex-president's son, who was the president of the company, named Franklin Roosevelt Jr. It was a hand written note, and he thanked me for the opportunity to someday do business with me but his rejection was due to the same reason as above. He also commended me for my new venture, and wished me well. Sadly I misplaced and lost all of the letters, especially his.

Now the process of trying to sell my home would prove to be a formidable one, due to the high interest rates at the time which were hovering around fifteen percent. I had a real estate company that I signed on with, but they were only successful in bringing very few buyers. After six months with them, I dropped them and started to place ads in all the papers myself, even the New York Times. Surprisingly, I received three inquires, due to its proximity to Yale university.

I believe that if I knew how to make a better presentation on the phone, I would have sold the house myself to the people from New York. I did have a serious buyer who was a doctor from Yale that saw my ad and came over to look at the house. Since I knew hardly anything about finance, he offered me a thirty thousand dollar down payment and asked me to hold the rest of the mortgage myself. We agreed on the sale price to be one hundred and seventy thousand dollars.

Not knowing, and not asking anyone for advice, cost me big time. The doctor was the one who came up with sale price of the house which shows just how interested he was in the house. Just writing this makes me sick. I never went and sought the advice of anyone, which cost me the deal of a lifetime, since the deal never came to fruition. The doctor was from a pretty influential family, which I found out after, when it was too late.

I finally secured the services of another real estate agent. I do not remember her name, but she was recommended to me by my lawyer, Shelly. She was a woman from across town who looked at the house and informed me of what I needed to do to sell the house. She, like all real estate agents, was very optimistic. Being skeptical, I signed on for six months, but as I found out, she was not like the rest of the agents. She would bring people over on an almost weekly basis and was relentless in trying to sell my house. The tenants did not appreciate her because of that and eventually I gave her the tenants' numbers so she could make the arrangements to view the apartments. She proved to be a powerhouse of a sales person.

I felt if she could not sell this house nobody could. Of course, then, it was to be inevitable that an incident would come out of this, a most embarrassing one to be sure. This was right up there with anything you would see in a movie where a door opens and people are surprised. This one was shocker.

She calls me one day and said she has two hot prospects, two women, who wanted to move into the area, but she had no response from the third floor tenant, and asked me if I would come along so that she could show them the place? When I got there, she informed me that I did not need permission from the tenant to enter her apartment.

I asked her if it was correct to do this and not break any laws. She said as the owner, you have the right to enter any apartment, in your building, without permission. So we went and viewed the first and second floors and eventually moved up to the third. Now, the staircase going up to the third floor was a winding wooden staircase, very creaky, and the women had on high heels which made quite some noise. When we reached the door, I was shouting out the tenant's name, "Lois!" I am shouting. I started to tap on the door, calling "Lois, Lois!" and still no response.

I found that the front door was unlocked, so we entered the front room then the kitchen. Now off the kitchen was an alcove that Lois used for a makeshift bedroom, with mirrors in the ceiling on both sides of the walls. Now the four of us enter the kitchen alcove area and on the mattress on the floor was Lois with her legs spread eagle and her boyfriend of the Moment on top of her. The screams from all the woman accompanying me could be heard down the street.

The two women started running down the stairs, still in a state of shock, similar to Lois. The agent and I went into the front room and waited until Lois got dressed. I started to apologize immediately. I explained I made every effort to notify them of my presence. Lois's boyfriend was understanding about it all, but not Lois, who was in a tirade. Calming her down was fruitless, and her boyfriend told me to forget about it, and go home.

I then tore into the agent when we got downstairs, informing her that we did a stupid thing. She was adamant about her right to enter any apartment and would show me the rules regarding the subject. About two days later I received a letter from Lois berating me for this most unfortunate incident. Lois did not hold me responsible, and she understood it was the agent who pressured me into entering the apartment, but she was still disappointed with me for going along with the agent, who she said had no decency. Lois said that I should be ashamed of myself with the words, "Leo, I am truly shocked at you, and I know you are a very respectful man, but this really hurt me."

What a day that was. Never in my life would I ever contemplate barging in on someone, and I would not want that done to me. But to this day I do not know how the hell those two people did not hear us coming up the stairs with me shouting and the woman clanging up the stairs in high heels. I guess the height of passion knows no boundaries. In speaking with the young man later on, he said that Lois is in another world when she is in the heat of the Moment.

My agent finally secured a buyer for the house, which was good, but bad timing, as Gail's house was still in the planning stage. I did not think I could sell the house before their house was completed, as it was selling very slowly. The agent brought many people to view the house, but it was always the same: the interest rates were a deterrent, and the buyers wanted me to reduce the price of the house, which I did not want to do.

The buyers that eventually bought the house were friends of the agent who were looking for this type of home so close to the university. They felt they could get some high rents, and I tried to talk them into allowing Gail and Russ to stay in the house until their home was completed, which would only be about a few months, but they wanted such a huge amount for the rent that it would not be feasible for them to stay there.

When I purchased the house, I gave the previous owner, who had the same situation, the courtesy that I felt should have been extended to us. He had his mother in law living on the third floor and I gave her ample time to move out. The buyers were, in my mind, heartless business people who refused me the same arrangement.

So Gail, Russ and granddaughter Kara, came to live with us until their house was built, which was a period of about six months. Kara was one and half years old at the time, and I must say, I enjoyed having them live with us. Yes, it was a little cramped at times, but Kara made up for any and all inconvenience that we all experienced, especially when I was having some back problems and had to remain in bed. Kara would come and visit me to talk and give me her words of wisdom. She kept us all amused with her antics.

Selling the house at a nice profit gave us cause for a celebration by going out to a beautiful restaurant for dinner, which I believe was in Westport. I really did not think the house was ever going to sell since this was the worst times for people trying to sell their homes. After paying off whatever obligations I had, I cleared about seventy thousand dollars, money that would later go to help all my children in purchasing their homes.

STARTING THE NEW BUSINESS

My time was now being taken up on a full time basis with the start-up of the new business. This was one of the main reasons for selling the property, along with not having Russ and Gail living there. Making long range plans do not always work out the way you want them to. My dream of retiring to that property was changed by the forces beyond my control.

I was going through a lot of changes. Having to start a business at the age of fifty- two was not something that was on my radar. Here I was with three teenagers at home and thinking about their long range plans such as higher education, and I really did not have the resources to finance the future of my business, along with keeping up with my children's futures.

Being in business with my brother, Frank, and his friend, Tommy, was helpful, since they had to shoulder most of the sales end. It was a tough first three years in the business. Yes, there were times that got me very depressed about succeeding, but with the three of us there was no turning back. We had a nice team.

Since I was the one with the route experience, I had to lead the way in the promotion of our products. I went out and secured as many drivers as we needed to advance our business. Some good, and some terrible.

As I was the one leading the way, as far as advancing the promotion of our business route distribution wise, the most important number was the amount of sales that I was able to generate on our first route. I was bringing in about three thousand dollars a week in sales, which was enough to keep us afloat. Still, with that amount it was not enough for the three of us to draw a salary. Luckily, Tommy was still engaged in real estate, and deriving some income; Frank had his hands in an electronic business with another partner, but minute as it was, he was able to keep himself in some kind of monetary independence.

A distributor who had a similar product line, and was in competition with us, expressed a desire to sell us his business, which included ten drivers, who had their own routes. This presented an opportunity for us to advance quite quickly. Now we would have the tonnage to purchase large blocks of products and get a better price and make a greater profit.

It also gave us some bargaining room with larger groups of stores. We would now be able to cover a great part of the state, a plus when you are dealing with the chain stores. As our retail business was growing, we now felt that we could divest ourselves and to go into another part of route sales, which was the wholesale business. It would include serving restaurants, and mass feeders, which was a lot of volume and a lot of headaches.

This part of the business was more demanding because of the timeline. The hours were brutal- all early morning routes, whereas retail sales did not demand that kind of commitment.

We were all working, putting in long hours, trying to get established, and I for one did not pay attention to my health. I did not have the proper rest and didn't really pay attention to my diet. These are the things you do not think about, but what I learned was that your body is like a rubber band- you could only pull it so far.

And so it happened to me: I was out working in my yard one day, trying to keep up with the yardwork along with the business but I always felt like I didn't have much time. I felt a sharp pain in my chest.

I ignored it and went on with my work. David was coming out of the house and said he was going to work at the supermarket. He asked me if I was all right, and I said yes, but really I was not feeling good. I just shrugged it off has being tired.

David had no sooner left, then I said, this is not good, I went into the house and informed Teresa that I was going to the clinic to get checked out since it was a Saturday and my doctor did not have office hours. So off to the clinic I went, which was just a ten minute drive from my home. The doctor that checked me looked at me and said, "How long have you had this discomfort in your chest?" I answered, "About some time, but today it was kind of severe. I was working in the yard and started to feel quite crappy. I felt it was because I was doing too much work, cleaning the yard and such."

The doctor told me he detected an abnormal sound and that I should go to the hospital right away. He called an ambulance, and I informed Teresa that I was going to the hospital, and she can come later on. I no sooner got to the emergency room when they informed me that I had to have a procedure as soon as possible.

My family contacted my brother-in-law Joe, who called his cardiologist and had him take my case. He kept me in the hospital for a few days and then discharged me without having to have a procedure, such as angioplasty. This was a big mistake and I would eventually have to have this procedure later on.

Because of the nature of the wholesale business, every account that you secured had to be visited quite often, so that any problems could be addressed promptly. On this day I was visiting a very profitably account that I had just signed up. I had to meet some people from Springfield, MA so I told them to meet me at this account in Hartford, and we would have lunch together. How I would regret this day! I ordered a crab salad sandwich and it tasted so good. I went into the office of the restaurant and told the buyer that I brought some people to the restaurant and that they had an enjoyable meal.

That evening I started to have pains in my stomach area, and diarrhea. It got so bad that I could not get up the next day because my body was so stiff I could hardly walk. Thinking it had to do with my heart, I called my cardiologist, and he had me come into the office. When I saw him he said, "I think you should see an orthopedic surgeon, you might need an operation."

I dismissed his advice out of hand and went home instead. I knew it was not my back, because I had experience with back trouble and knew the pains were different. I called my brother, Frank, and he got me in to see Dr. Fasano, who at that time was not accepting any new patients.

At this time I was walking with a pair of crutches since I could not stand up. Upon seeing me walking down his hallway, Dr. Fasano told me that I had a case of food poisoning. He did not even examine me. All he did was look at my eyes, told me to sit down, and ran some tests to confirm his diagnosis. I then had to give him a stool sample that he would send out.

Dr. Fasano, said to me words that I still remember, "I will have you walking in three days," He gave me some medication, and in three days I was walking. Tests came back and confirmed what the doctor said- I had contacted food poisoning. The East Shore Clinics called me and wanted to know where I had eaten. I was reluctant to tell them, but it was foolish on my part since I did not want to lose the account.

Interestingly enough, the restaurant was closed that same week due to a lot of people getting sick there, and some of the people had to be hospitalized, they were so bad. I should have brought a judgment against them, but again, I hesitated. I needed every piece of business and did not want to lose them. I look back and know that was a stupid mistake. I suffered for the next six months; it left me very weak.

While I was seeing Dr. Fasano, he said he would like to perform some extensive tests on me, starting with a complete physical. I agreed with him and shortly thereafter we set up an appointment. When Dr. Fasano examined me, he literally put me through the ringer, starting from the top of my head to my toes, and it was during this exam that he detected an irregular sound from my heart. He suggested that I go to a cardiologist for a complete make up. He also ordered me to take a stress test, and when he went over the test results on my next visit, from the look in his eyes, I could see he was not in agreement with results. Dr. Fasano was shaking his head in disbelief.

The stress test results were positive for me, and yet the doctor that gave me the test said I had performed well, but not well enough for Fasano. How soon I would learn how good a Dr. Fasano is and how perceptive he was in his diagnosis.

Three weeks later I was rushed to the hospital with a lot of discomfort in my chest. Dr. Fasano was called along with my cardiologist and I was admitted that evening. I was told that either they will perform an angioplasty or have an open heart operation. They then prepared me for surgery. I was told that all my arteries were blocked, and they would try to give me the balloon test first, and if that does not work, open heart would be performed.

That next day they performed the angioplasty and were able to open my two main arteries. The third was ninety percent blocked, and they felt it would more damaging for them to try to open it up, and so I was to spend the next four days in the hospital.

During this time, I had to endure a patch on my arm which transmitted medicine to my heart. This gave me head splitting headaches, and along with that I was to lie still and not move because they had a plug in my artery, and any movement would cause it to rupture.

The evening before I was to undergo this procedure was one that will last in my memory forever. A lay man from the Catholic Church came to visit me. He pulled up a chair and started to talk to me about what I was about to endure. In a reassuring voice he explained that no matter what was to come out of this, that I would be in good hands and not to worry.

He spent an hour with me, and we talked about my life and my family. It was like an experience that would never leave me. He took me on a journey of why we are put on this earth. To me, it seemed I was talking to somebody from heaven; it was so surreal to me. While he was there with me, my pain seemed to subside, and all the discomfort I was enduring seemed so small. Although he was not preaching to me, just listening to him and his very presence calmed me immensely.

During our conversation he placed a rosary bead in my hands. To be honest, I never learned how to say the rosary, and not to try and fake it, I asked him to go along with me. He laughed and said he understood. While he was talking to me, he made a joke out of it saying, "You do not want to lie on your last night." We covered a lot of ground in that short hour. He said he wanted to pray for me, and would I join him. So we said some prayers, and he blessed me. As he was leaving the room, he stopped at the door, turned to me, and said we will meet again.

When he did come back, it was a few days later. Lennie, who was the catholic lay man, was standing by my bed with all the vestments of the church wrapped around him. He was saying some prayers, and in walks my wife and sister-in-law. They see what they thought was a priest giving me the last rites. They both let out a huge gasp. Lennie calms them down, and explains the situation to them. I told Lennie, "You have to excuse them. They are just being Italian."

To think that this man would take time out of his life to go and comfort others is remarkable. In our conversation Lennie explained why he does this work. He was administered to by a complete stranger when he was having a bad time in his life and in some little way he wanted to repay that goodness. We shook hands, and I am very sorry that I did not take the time to further our friendship.

When my time was up for discharge from the hospital, I had to wait for a doctor to come and take out the plug. She was from the group of doctors that were taking care of me. The nurse said, "Leo you are in luck to have her do this procedure of taking out the plug. She is noted for being very gentle and very quick to stop up the artery with a suture." After the doctor removed the plug, I let out such a sigh of relief. After lying there for four days and not being able to move, it was a complete exhilaration.

The expression of selling yourself first, came back to me in reverse. I recall the day I went on a sales call to a restaurant in Avon, CT. The owner, John, was interested in a special type of bread, to which I could secure for him. Upon entering the kitchen, I was amazed at the cleanliness of it and also of him, who had on a crisp, clean white shirt. After introductions I placed my box of samples on the table in the kitchen, knowing not to place them on his cooking counter. As I started to unravel my box of samples and my price lists, the owner said to me, "Mr. Marino, leave everything here." John calls his wife Lucy. "Lucy, please bring Mr. Marino a bowl of soup." This was at 10 in the morning. John, Lucy and I sat down at the table. Being Italian, John and Lucy started the conversation about the origins of my birthplace in Italy. I thought to myself, here are these two people who have a large restaurant to operate, but they are taking time away from their duties to talk to me, not about business, but my personal life. After some time, John then got up and said, "Okay Mr. Marino, let me see what you have." His wife Lucy excused herself. After viewing my product and price list, John looked at them favorably, but the size of the product had to be adjusted. As we parted, John and I shook hands with admonition and said, "Leo, family first, then business." This was a lesson learned in reverse.

This episode was a game changer for me. I started to educate myself, and read everything I could get my hands on to further understand why I got into this condition of poor health. I realized I had to change my diet, and pay attention to my cholesterol reading if I wanted to maintain good health.

Returning to work, I now had to adjust to not being so aggressive and to slow down my pace. It was not easy for me, spending the better part of my life, arising up at three or four in the morning, and not having a good breakfast, eating a fast lunch, or maybe none at all, and rushing to meet deadlines. This I knew had to come to an end or else I'd wind up back in the hospital. So with Dr. Fasano helping me to get on a healthy program, my health started to improve, and for me it never stopped, with a regimen of diet and exercise I was feeling better than I ever felt.

The part of the business that was most taxing for me was the wholesale end of it. The retail part of the business was something that I did for the last twenty five years, and I was comfortable with it, I could handle it. But as the wholesale part of the business was also a drag on all of us, we decided to sell that end of the company and return to our original plans and remain a retail company.

We started to put out feelers to sell the wholesale end of our business, after quite some time someone called up and was a serious candidate who was interested in purchasing the wholesale end of the business, but this would also create some additional problems. The one that loomed the largest was that we would no longer need the warehouse that housed our business. The buyer wanted to have his own warehouse and not be vested with us, so while the negotiations were going on with the buyer, I came up with the idea of opening up a store to sell our product to generate a good cash flow.

About one year after we started the company, David, my son, expressed a desire to enter the business. He had graduated from college and was working at Blue Cross Medical, an office position, which he was not pleased with. I had put David in charge of the store, in addition to serving a club store as part of his duties. So between the store and the club store, he would be able to earn a decent weeks pay. This was also the year David and Lisa were planning their wedding, so it was a very busy year for me, with the wedding and selling off half the business.

So Dave was experienced, more so than some of the drivers I had. All I had to do was tell him who to serve and did not have to explain what to do with the products. He was a great help to me, as I was all alone in my department who had route experience. We even had Gail working in the office part time, much to the dismay of her daughter, Kara, who was not too pleased with having to go and spend time with her grandmother.

Not that Kara had any discourse with her grandmother; she just wanted to have Gail home with her, so much so, that whenever Gail had to come to the office, Kara would always say to her mother: "You are not going to go to Del-Mar today?" That was Kara's famous saying. She was kind of like a little general. Kara would pout, but she would never give her grandmother any problems. A little milk and cookies would fix that.

The wholesale business was a nightmare, the hours were brutal. The routes serving the restaurants had to leave early which meant that the products had to be received before eight P.M. every night and most, if not all, the products came from New York City. The one night that stands out in my memory, was a rainy and icy night when the products would not be delivered. I wanted to call off the entire next day's business, but the drivers would all be hurt by not having any product. It pained me to have to send David off to New York to secure the products. The streets were all very slippery, and the highways were just as bad, but David said to me, "Dad, do not worry. I will be all right." As he left the garage that afternoon, heading for New York, I got emotional, thinking what the hell am I doing, putting my son in peril. I had driven through these kinds of icy storms for years and knew of the danger it entailed.

I went out into the driveway of the garage, and spent the rest of the afternoon, laying down salt and sand. Our driveway was slopping down at a forty five degree angle which was quite steep. I stayed at it until about six in the evening and then went home. I was exhausted from the weather, but during the evening all I kept thinking about was how David was doing. Listening to the weather reports only made me more nervous.

Finally, David came through with the products and arrived safely. I had to go down to the warehouse extra early that next morning, and David had just left to go home, if my memory serves me right. On that morning, we had a driver whose job it was to go and pick up the product, but the ass seeing it was a bad storm decided not to come in. That is when we decided to have the bakeries we were buying from deliver the baked goods.

This segment of the business had its good features. The baked goods that we were selling, mostly to restaurants, and on order only, meant that we did not have to take back any returns, which was a great selling point for us. The part I did not like was that most of the restaurants were very bad payers; they wanted us to extend them credit for a two week period, unlike the stores where they paid you on a daily basis.

A driver expressed a desire to only have quality accounts, and he was willing to wait to build up the route. We wanted to help him so I told the driver it would take us about a year to put it all together. He was adamant about not doing small accounts; he said he had experience with another bakery and that the little guys were all a pain in the ass.

So we worked along those lines and started to secure the accounts he wanted. The account that he prized the most was the Hartford Hospital, so I went after the account. It took me the better part of two months to set it up, what with meeting with all the people involved and all different department heads. The baked goods were going to be distributed to all sections of the hospital. After I received an approval from them to give me all the sales of baked goods for the hospital, the administrator said, "Mr. Marino, we would like to see your warehouse and office before we commit and give you final approval." "No problem," I said. We set up a date, shook hands, and as I started down the stairs, running actually, I could not believe I had secured the account!

When I got back to the office and told my partners the good news, they could not believe it. So now I had to prepare for the visit by informing the office staff of who I had invited and to have everyone looking good on that day. I made sure that the warehouse was spick and span and I told the shipper not to have any trash laying around.

On the day of the meeting, I went to work and had all the price lists and whatever other information they would need all printed up. I had the conference room all spruced up with the table all set up with all the paper work. Each chair had in front of them the required paper work. It was all very professional. I even had a table set up with all baked goods that they were interested in purchasing.

When the parties arrived, I took them first into the warehouse and showed them how the orders were processed. The warehouse was old and was a problem to keep clean, but the efforts by me and the shipper paid off, as they were really impressed with the cleanliness of the work space. I then took them up to the office, and on cue, everybody was busy; the girls all were dressed up and looking real good. Then I introduced them to Tommy and Frank, and showed them around the office, which is what they wanted to see because they had reservations about dealing with an individual, and instead wanted to see a company. We then sat down in the conference room, and discussed our future business together.

After our conference with the hospital officials, we adjourned and took them out for lunch, and had a very productive afternoon with them. They now decided they were going to increase their orders with us after seeing our operation. To start with, the account was going to start off with sales around six thousand dollars a week, quite a huge sum in those days.

I informed Eddie, the driver who was going to service the account, of our negotiations, and asked when he could start serving them. He was, to say the least, a very happy man, and so were we. All that effort that I put into securing the account, which at times I thought would never be. The thing is that I never gave up, in spite of all the obstacles that I had to overcome, such as convincing the buyers that I could offer them better service and fresher products. In other words, I had to out sell the company that was presently serving the account.

JOE THE DISTRIBUTOR

I would be remiss if I did not tell this story of one great person that I was associated with in my business. Joe was a distributor for me. He needed to have a route that he could do in the evening, because he had a wife who had M.S. and he needed to attend to her in the daytime. It was at this point when his wife needed his care the most. Joe took her to doctor visits and made sure she took the right medication. He had someone who came in at night so he would be free to work for us.

At the time, I had a route available which served restaurants. This would be an ideal situation for Joe; he did not want to serve stores since that would conflict with his daily routine. Joe purchased the route from us on the sales we agreed upon. So the first week Joe takes over, we lost one of our major accounts, the U.S Coastguard. Now we had to either refund some portion of the sale, or to give him some accounts to make up the difference.

I set out and let all my other work slip by in order to make Joe whole again. I then picked up some real grade A accounts to even out the sales agreement we had with Joe. Believe me, it was a busy month. Frank made contact with a national hotel chain, and I was able to visit the locations to secure them for Joe. I was so happy to be successful in obtaining these accounts. In fact, we more than made up for the lost sales and after Joe starting serving his route, I went out to his customers and tried to upsell them, in order to give Joe more strength with his accounts.

What I found on these visits was that all of his accounts thought of Joe as the best thing since sliced bread. They were so elated, saying they had never seen a route man who was so ultra-neat in his work. Joe would deliver the product during the night and have his orders so perfect, with the invoice on top of the order, and in rotation, so it could be checked easily.

One funny story that was told to me by one of Joe's accounts was from a customer he had. Eddie, his customer, told me how in doing business with Joe, if Joe was owed some small change, he would want it. Eddie said, "Leo, I purchased some extra product for my home, and I owed Joe a quarter. He stood there waiting for me to give it to him. I mean, a lousy quarter. He waited for me until I got it for him." I said, "Eddie, did you not tell me how grateful you are for having such an honest man serving you, and you did not have to worry about any shortages, and how the orders were always perfect? See, Eddie? Joe might want his lousy quarter, but he will never take anything from you. I call that a good exchange." Eddie replied, "Leo, forget I even mentioned it. I feel embarrassed about it, and you are right." At this point, Eddie's face was a little flushed.

Since Joe was working nights, and attending to his wife during the day, it did not leave him much free time. On visiting his home many times, I found the house to be in immaculate condition. Joe had nursing experience from being in the service, so that was a plus for him. Even being in a fragile condition, his wife still managed to help out as much as she could- a remarkable feat, due to the onset of M.S.

Another gem of a story was one Joe experienced while on his route. Joe was on very friendly terms with the wait staff of a particular account, due to dealing with them on a daily basis. They knew about Joe's wife and were very concerned for Joe, realizing the pressure he was under to provide for his family.

Joe then told me the story of this waitress who genuinely felt sorry for Joe and really was very much in touch with Joe's plight, that being his wife was not able to satisfy him and to please Joe sexually. She then offered to service Joe, with no strings attached, but Joe declined the offer. He did not want to hurt her feelings, and make her think she was not appealing enough. This was the mark a true gentleman, which Joe was in spades.

On the few times that I met Joe's wife, I found her never to be downcast in spite of her health. She was such a strong person and very appreciate of having Joe has a husband. Joe never let her get down on herself; he was that upbeat.

As time wore on, M.S. was taking its toll on his wife. Her health was affected to the point that she had very little movement, and I surmise she was in a lot of pain. It was no surprise that the news came one day that Joe's wife had passed away. She put up such a valiant struggle with this horrible affliction of her body just wasting away.

After the death of Joe's wife, Joe felt he did not want to work nights anymore. There was no need for him to remain in this type of work, so he sold his route and decided to follow his dream of being a nurse. He left our company and is now working with a national health care corporation, nursing. In the business of food distribution, Joe was what anyone would want working for him. He had the loyalty, and above all, the honesty and trustworthiness you would want. I always said if I had ten distributors like Joe, I would give them the key to the warehouse and go to sleep; he was the epitome of what a route man should be.

After Joe left I still kept in touch with him and I would meet with him periodically. Joe knew of the birth of my granddaughter Jaclyn, and offered to sell me the van that he used to transport his wife around with. He wanted to sell it to me for a reduced price, but Janet felt it would not be needed, and that eventually Jaclyn would be capable of entering and exiting a car on her own, which she does.

As an owner of a company, to have one of your associates leave, and especially a good one, it leaves a void in you. I missed Joe more than my partners, Frank and Tommy. Not that they were not also affected by his leaving, but I was the one who worked with the distributors on a daily basis. I was the gate keeper. They came to me first, since I was the one who understood a route man's problems, and I could relate to them.

BAD BUSINESS ASSOCIATES

On the opposite end of the spectrum is another person who shall remain nameless but is the complete opposite of Joe. I had a long association working with him while in the employ of another company. My best description of him would be rude and crude. He took great delight in mocking and insulting people, most of the time for their physical appearance.

He was married to a wonderful woman, and her family started them both off with a nice home, and I might add very little debt. Any man would have been happy to be in his position, but not him; his life was all about him, and him alone. For his repayment to her, he gave her a lifetime of untold stress. When they were in front of a group of people, he would go into his performance of being a boor, but it did backfire on him one day. He burned one bridge too many, and in short, like an elastic band, it will only go so far before it snaps.

The ass had been harassing this one guy for quite some time, and the poor fellow did not know how to respond, but his three friends knew what to do. They started the big asshole on a fervor, and then beat the shit out of him. They left him on the sidewalk moaning and groaning, and he was crying out for help. We were in the vicinity, and we just walked away. He never even mentioned this to us since he knew how we felt about him. It was a long time coming, but this would not be the last time he would encounter a similar incident like this, and that's why I call him a big asshole. This kind of person will never learn, and he still continues to insult people. As they say in Italian, "Tu Fai Appost" trans: "on purpose," words of insult are one thing, but as he always took liberty with everyone, it finally caught up to him, feeling he was somehow invincible, or immune, especially with women, one time he went too far.

In one of his accounts, there worked a young girl, who for the life of me, I will never understand how she was taken in by his bullshit, but she started a relationship with him. It was precarious at best, but she did not know that, due to the fact that the ass showered her with all kinds of gifts, and the relationship into a long gated affair.

He was such a cocky bastard that he had the damn nerve to take this girl on a vacation, telling his wife he was going on a golfing trip with his friends. Only the lie unraveled when his wife was surprised to run into one of his buddies, the one who was supposed to be on vacation with him.

His wife had the information of the time of arrival of his plane and was waiting at the airport for him to return. In those days there was no cell phone to alert him, and also no hand held cameras, that his wife could have used, but it did not matter, ass was a dead duck. She watched him get off the plane with the girl and was finally was going to make him pay big time for this affair. The rubber band that I described, finally broke. He was handed his divorce papers soon after.

I did do some business with him later on, because to me his personal life was his own, and since it did conflict with my business, we formed a business relationship. He was a distributor, and I was his supplier, and that was it. But as time went on, he reverted to some of his old cocky ways. The ass always wanted to get something from you, and he did, sadly to say through a third party, of which I was very fond of, it pains me to this day when I think about it, the ass had a way of corrupting anybody.

After several episodes of mismanagement, we terminated his purchases, and reduced his income to a pittance, he was forced to start another line of product, as I stated in my story about Joe, the differences were immense, in these two individuals, human nature being what it is, has a way of manifesting itself, In my business I had the fortune or misfortune of associating with some pretty wonderful people, the crap I just mentioned, was to be sure a minority.

KARA

Along with starting the business, we also welcomed our first grand-child, Kara, on May 6th, 1982. From the time Kara was born, Gail already had the notion to put Kara into the modeling business. About the time Kara was five or six years old, Gail was making inquiries with an agent about placing Kara into modeling jobs, mostly print ads, which was what Kara was offered, with the promise of maybe eventu-ally securing a slot for a T.V. commercial.

At home, Kara had the personality of being very open in expressing herself to anybody, or anything. But she was a little on the shy side in front of strangers, which later on would prove to be disastrous in securing a very lucrative slot for a commercial. Kara was getting a lot of experience being in front of cameras and was posing for ads in mag-azines, store promotions, etc. I was able to help Gail drive Kara down to New York for her many jobs since I had the flexibility of being able to leave my business when I needed to.

Doing this type of modeling work did not pay enough, but it was a great place to start, since we were able to meet many people who maybe can help you later on. To the photographers, Kara was a natural because of her curly red hair and her little round face. They were all looking for something different, and they were able to pair Kara with a diverse group of children.

One of the many disappointments I encountered in that business was the feeling of being rejected for a slot, which happened to a lot of people in this type of work. For me being rejected was something I had experienced many times in life, such as not securing employment, but I did not like the wholesale rejection of people, picking one person, and telling everyone else to go home. Kind of cruel, I thought.

One of the worst rejections came for a commercial that Kara was one of the top three persons to be selected. The photographer pulled me aside and said that he wanted Kara and that she was the best fit for the job. I was so elated and excited for Kara. This would be her first commercial! Only a few minutes later, the owner of the studio came out and very rudely pushed Kara aside and told the photographer she wanted this other child. At that moment, my heart dropped; I felt so bad for Kara. Being this close and having to endure that rejection, as I said, was the worst part. The people in that business did not do things in a mannerly way. You would think they would have the decency to not make a scene in front of a child. What I found out from the photographer was that the child that was picked was the same nationality as the owner. He apologized and told me not to be discouraged since this would happen quite often, so be prepared.

I have to insert this little gem, Kara forgive me. The opportunity finally came when Kara was selected for a commercial for McDonald's. Driving down to the city, I already had visions of seeing my grand-daughter on television. Getting to the studio was a hassle, due to the heavy volume of traffic, but on this day nothing would upset me. This was to be our moment.

As we walked into the studio, everybody was busy getting prepared for the shoot, as they called it. They lined up Kara in front of the cameras to get a position on her, and after all the preparations were done, Kara was then led into the room for a walk through.

The subject of the commercial was for Kara to bite into this huge hamburger and exclaim how wonderful it tasted. Kara picks up the burger she was supposed to eat and looks at what was on the inside the burger. Apparently, she did not like what was inside and would not take a bite out of the damn burger. After several attempts, they called off the shoot and had to get someone else.

On the way down stairs, I said, "You little shit! All you had to do was take a damn bite out of the burger!" "Grandpa," Kara explains, "I did not like the burger," "Kara!" I yell back to her, "All you had to do was bite into the burger, one lousy bite is all you had to do. I do not care if it was crap in there." Under my breath, I let out some expletives that I cannot print, and with that went my dream of being an agent for Kara and finally getting away from the lousy hours of my business.

Kara redeemed herself to me for being a great granddaughter and made me proud when I attended her graduations, which included two Masters, but to Kara my old saying still is, "All you had to do was take one lousy bite." Unlike then, Kara now understands the value of a dollar, as she works as a high school English teacher in Enfield, CT. She was married in 2015 to Dan Barrett on the beach in Florida and the whole family was able to attend. They now live in East Granby, CT.

WORK ISSUES

Recently Frank and I have been reminiscing about some of the crazy shit that happened to us as I have been writing this book. During our conversations, we remembered that there was mainly one person who was forever giving us agita and always trying to see if he could get away without paying for his product. Since this man was at that time purchasing a great amount of product from us for a new business, we welcomed it, but we always had to be forever cautious. Whenever he was in the building, it was sort of like a cat and mouse thing. We were keeping him under wraps and not letting him get any ideas as to how he can carry out his plans of taking product without paying. We thought we had succeeded, until one dark day when Frank discovered a lot of unpaid accounts. These were accounts that normally paid us on a regular payment plan, so Frank started calling them and was informed the checks were sent and they have the cancelled checks to prove it.

So Frank goes down to their place of business, and gets copies of the checks. The amount came to well over three thousand dollars, which for our business at that time was quite a huge sum. The checks were cashed and credited to this driver's account. Now we had to figure out what to do with this information. Frank calls the driver and has him come down to the office. He lays out the paperwork, and the driver disputed the amount. The asshole thereby admitting his thievery, and the driver settles for the prescribed amount given to him by Frank.

But the discussion did not end there. Our partner, Tom Basti, wanted to have him arrested, but after much soul searching and adding up the amount of business that this worm was buying from us, they decided to accept his offer to reimburse our company. How the driver got his hands on the checks in the first place was a mystery for a while until we found out he knew how to unlock the office door. He got in there by way of saying he had to use the toilet. From that day on he was not allowed to even enter the warehouse, unless accompanied by one of us. His order was placed on the platform, which prevented him from entering the building.

Even so, this same worm, still tried to rip us off. We had moved to a larger warehouse, which at that time, we were doing wholesale and retail. The man we had in charge of the warehouse was a man named Domingo. He was a no nonsense person who was an extremely reliable man, honest and hard-working, so this next incident got right to the core of his bones.

One night as Domingo was serving the drivers their orders and also collecting their payments, he placed the money he had collected inside a paper bag, one that he used on a regular basis, and left the bag on his desk. As all the drivers departed, he discovered the bag missing, so he starts to panic. He calls Frank even though the time is now about two a.m. Almost hysterically, Domingo did not remember where he placed the bag and he checked his whole area. Frank asked who was down there this night, and Domingo gives Frank the names. One name stands out, the worm, so Frank wakes up our nephew Gary, who was staying with him in his apartment at the time.

Frank and Gary drive over to the street, where the worm is serving his customers. The worm sees Frank and Gary coming, so he locks the doors. They bang on his truck, shouting, "Where the shit is the money?" The worm responds, "Frank, I was just holding it for you." After some time, the door opens, ever so slightly. Fear was now griping him, and he hands over the bag of money to Frank, all the while still lying his ass off, saying that the bag was on the desk and he took it for safe keeping. When Domingo heard that yarn, it made him real furious.

Now the die was cast, and Frank gave permission to Domingo to have the worm drive into the warehouse, but not be allowed to get out of his truck. Someone would bring him his order. Domingo would really lay the worm by getting his order last, making him be late for his accounts. Now the worm was squirming, complaining to Frank on a regular basis, even with him in the truck, Domingo had keep his eye on him. To Domingo this was a great insult, this ass stealing from him.

Domingo treated the company's money as if it were his own. He had great respect for Frank, Tom and myself, and in turn we regarded him as part of our family. He was paid well, and he appreciated it, and as an aside to this man's character, Frank approached Domingo and offered him a raise, telling Domingo, "You never asked us for a raise, so we are giving you one. Why did you not ask us?" Domingo responds, "I will let my work speak for me; if I do not do well, I do not deserve one."

ALEXA

During this time period in 1986, we also had another granddaughter born, a sister to Kara, Alexa. One day we took Kara up to the hospital to see her sister. On the way there, Kara looks up at the hospital and bemoans the fact that she does not look like her parents, due to the fact that Kara had red hair and her sister had the same hair color as her parents. Now Kara felt she was an outcast. Kara states that, "She looks just like them." Alexa had the cutest little face, and she had a little turned up nose. I always admired the way Alexa would smile every time she would see you. She was a very pleasant baby.

The birth of Alexa came with more excitement. I now started to feel more like a grandfather, and I would get a lot of teasing at work since I did not have a grandson, but my answer was, "until next time." Alexa having dark hair and dark eyes, was the personification of a little Italian girl. I only wished that my mother could have seen these two little girls, Kara and Alexa, and all my future grandchildren.

Alexa, being the second born, is right up front in her grandparents' hearts, a most cheerful child and a grade A student. She loved to dance (ballet, jazz and hip hop) and received a 10 year award. Alexa, also a very industrious person, took on a part time job at Neil Roberts School Uniforms in Milford when she was only fifteen, and was still was able to keep up her grades at school. In fact she never stopped working, even when she was at college at Eastern Connecticut State University. She graduated with a degree in communications in

2008 and all this determination paid off, as she is now employed in communications for Verizon.

NEW BUSINESS WITH BILL

As my business was starting to grow, we were expanding our area of operations, branching out into different markets, and with that came the problem of obtaining good route men to service all the new accounts. One day this man, Bill, came into my office. I knew of him only through other route men. Bill was working for Wonder Bread when he heard about our expansion and said he wanted to make a change. Bill came with a good resume, and he had the experience I was looking for.

So the area that I was now opening up was for the most part abused by other vendors, and the potential for growth was overwhelming, so Bill came over to us, and I gave him quite a bit of territory with which to work. It was a pleasure to have Bill, since I did not have to teach him how to display his products. He was a natural who had a disarming personality and was very sociable with the grocers.

A plus in the retail business, Bill was the same no matter who he talked to; he treated every customer with respect. I was able to secure a huge supermarket for him, one that would give him a huge boost in sales. I was now riding with Bill, helping him with all the new business that I had given him since we were having a tough time trying to set the route so that we would not be late in our deliveries.

This super market that I had obtained for Bill was giving him a hard time. They were very demanding about time and placement of product. Although I was given ample room to display our product, it seemed every day we got to the store the manager would have something to complain about. He was very abusive to us and would actually belittle us as if we were his employees. I was with Bill for two weeks during this time, and it was the same every delivery, especially talking down to us about displaying our product, but Bill always made him look foolish, pointing out the amount of sales he was getting from the space we were allocated.

After about two weeks, I left Bill and had to attend to my other routes. About two weeks later, I had to go in the same area and secure another account, which would also be a supermarket about the same size. To make this appointment, I had to dress up with a jacket and tie since it was with a buyer who controlled several more supermarkets. So after I made my sales call, I decided to stop in and see how Bill was doing in his store. I put down my briefcase, and started to arrange the display of Bill's cake on the shelf to make it more presentable.

Now the manager comes walking by and introduced himself to me and addressed me with a much different tone of voice. I went on about fixing up the display and talking to him. He then commends me for displaying the product so neatly. As I am now standing in front of him, and looking him in the eye, I told him who I was and that I was the same guy he had cursed out with Bill just two weeks ago. He backs away and could not believe I was the same person. His face was now turning red as a beet, then he apologized and walked away.

Funny how a different set of clothes would make all the difference in the world. I guess I was human to him in a suit. After that, Bill said he never bothered him again, and in fact, he gave Bill more even space. I encountered that same problem many times over the years. Some managers felt superior to the vendors, but this guy was the exception

The same problem arose when I had to go and visit a new chain store to set up for my driver and secure space for him. This chain of stores was new to our area, and the person I made the appointment with was not in his office. His assistant called him on his phone and directed me to the rear of the store. When I got there, I saw he was busy speaking with another person, but I was standing in the vicinity of his conversation, and being polite to let him know of my presence.

The jerk stops talking and comes over to me. I hand him my card, he acknowledges my appointment, and I told him I will wait until he is finished with the person he is talking to. In front of all the people in this room, he takes my card, throws it on the floor, and tells me to go and stand in the corner until he is ready for me.

I left the card on the floor, and kept standing where I was. Now he purposely kept speaking to this salesman, waiting for me to just leave, but since this chain of stores would represent quite a boost for us I remained waiting for him. The reason for his animosity, I was told by one of the floor managers, was that he did not want to take our product. He felt it would not be a good fit, but I knew his office had wanted our product in all their stores, so he was trying to provoke me into not seeing him.

When he finally comes over, I do not extend my hand, but instead I just hand him all the paper work, which included our pricing. He directed me to his grocery manager, and not saying another word, I turned and left him standing there. Not a nice way to start a business friendship, but such is the human frailty. Six months later, the ass was fired.

1986-1990 Janet and Anthony's Wedding

1986 was a busy year for us, with the advent of the marriage of Anthony and Janet on October 4th. They had been courting for two years. Anthony's grandparents came from the same neighborhood where I grew up and they owned a music store on St. John Street. Who knew the many times I passed that music store, that this guys grandson would someday be my son in law. The music store was right next to the old bath house, were I would go and take my showers and swim in the pool. Anthony's mother, Christine, and I came from the same neighborhood and would regale each other with stories about the bath houses, even though she was not too fond of it since there really was no privacy, and everything was out in the open. There were only stalls with no doors to undress, and dress up. This was also a time that did not include the wearing of bathing suits.

And so just like her sister, Gail, I left it up to Janet as to what kind of wedding she wanted. We also had to consider Anthony's family in making the arrangements. Anthony's mom was very agreeable to whatever Janet and Anthony wanted, so the decision to have the wedding dinner held at the Aqua Turf restaurant was a good one, but also a burden for some of the people I wanted to invite, mainly my relatives, who were really old school. This was the village mentality again.

When they heard it was in Southington, (about a half hour away) they thought it was maybe on the moon, so they declined.

All the pre-wedding went well, but unlike Gail's wedding, this time we did not have to search out the products ourselves, the restaurant did all that.

But as well as the wedding was planned, there had to be a slight hitch somewhere, which came on the day of the wedding. The morning was chaotic at our house, what with all the bridesmaids coming over and meeting at our house, waiting for the cars to take us all to church. In some confusion, Teresa was cleaning her diamond ring in the bathroom and somehow it got wrapped in a tissue and tossed in the pail. As everyone was dressed and ready to leave, Teresa can't find her ring and Janet starts to panic.

All bedlam broke loose. Now everybody was looking for the ring. Every inch of the kitchen was combed over to no avail. After what seemed an eternity, especially with the hour of the wedding approaching, Janet's friend, Annie (AnnMarie Craven), took the garbage pails outside, dumped them on the picnic table and went through it. Lo and behold, Annie holds up the ring screaming "I found it"! Teresa's ring was wrapped in a tissue. Janet was so excited and thankful that her friend found the ring, she hugged Annie and said "thank you, now let's get to the church". Just something to make one's hair turn white, mine mostly, and just as the ring was located, the cars arrived.

Janet and Anthony had a nice courtship, followed by a gorgeous wedding, and settled down in Branford, and in the ensuing years gave Teresa and I two wonderful granddaughters: Jaclyn and Jessica.

1986 GROWING BUSINESS

1986 also was the year when my business was starting to grow. We had to find a larger warehouse to conduct our business. Tom and Frank had found a large space right in the center of the city, which made it easy accessible for all our drivers, although not in the best of neighborhoods; we had a halfway house right around the corner and across the street from us was a building that housed the homeless who would sleep there.

One day while I was cleaning up the driveway, this young girl comes running down the ramp, screaming and crying and was shaking all over. I offered to call 911 for her, but she refused; she wanted me to give her money. Now, she had dope addict written all over her. I never seen anyone in such a state before. I offered her food, but she refused, and she kept looking all around her, probably seeing if there were any policemen around. To get rid of her, I called down to the door to see if my warehouse man could call someone to help her, but with that, she took off like a rabbit.

Another time I was sweeping the sidewalk in front of my office, I ran into another joker. I had an appointment with a client that day and we were sprucing up the entranceway. This guy comes out of where the homeless people were housed, and he was carrying what looked like a brief case, trying to look professional. He comes up to me and asked if I could give him five dollars, because he said he was on his way to search for employment.

I told this ass, "Here, I will give you the five dollars, if you will sweep the whole sidewalk, down the whole block." He then goes into a monologue how why he cannot sweep the sidewalk due to his health problems. While he was talking to me he was wobbling back and forth, a nervous kind of shaking. He then tells me he will be late for his appointment if he sweeps the sidewalk. At this time, I was really toying with him; he also had dope addict written all over him. He gave me more excuses in ten minutes than I would get from all my drivers when they did something wrong on the route. I should have fixed him up with that queen who was also shaking to beat the band.

All the people that were housed across the street would come over and try to get some food, but as soon has you mentioned work, they took off and never came back. One day my warehouse man was going to throw out some moldy pies. He had assembled them out in front of the driveway to get them ready to take them to the dump. A guy comes by and said he wanted to eat them. He is then told they are not edible due to the mold problem. So my man says, "They are not for humans." The homeless man exclaims, "Who said that I am human?"

He then swipes a pie from out of the pile and bites into it.

I guess he was not human after all. The bastard did not even get sick, but after that we had to find another way to dispose of our waste. I was worried about what if someone gets sick eating our products. They could sue us even if we did not give them the product.

Our big time of the year was around Thanksgiving. At that time the pies were a big attraction, and I had to start going around taking orders about two months before the holiday. Every year there was always a problem getting enough pies to fill our order.

The worst year and what turned out to be our last year with the promotion of pies was one of the biggest flops of my career in the bakery business even though we did everything humanly possible to ensure this program would succeed. This particular year we went and took orders from all our customers and placed them with the bakery a full two weeks ahead of schedule. The amount of the orders from all our drivers came to fifty thousand pies, enough to fill two trailers. I alone had five thousand pies ordered for my route, which at this time included the New London area. One of my customers was the commissary store located in the sub base. Their order came to one thousand pies. I had to go out and rent a twenty foot truck to handle this amount of product.

Even our drivers went out and hired extra help, with two men on each truck, to help them for the two days of deliveries. This was going to be our biggest week ever. The morning of our first delivery everybody was on time to receive their orders, but the trailer that came in did not bring enough product to satisfy one man's order.

Out of five thousand pies that I had ordered, I only received one thousand units, so what we had to do was to parcel out and try to fill each order as fairly as possible. We only received one third of the pies that we ordered. Then the fun began when I had to try to fill each order on my route. I knew I was going to be cursed at by all my customers because they had gone out and promised their customers that they would have the pies for the holiday. With the sub base as my first customer for the day, the manager was waiting for me to show up. He had secured three tables for me to place my pies on.

I did not have enough to fill even one table. I told him of my problem, and I was going to make up a story as to why I did not have the amount of pies, but I was honest with him and told him how the bakery slipped up and did not deliver what we had ordered. I even took him out to the truck and showed him this huge truck with the small amount I had. His name was Lenny, and he was going to be the most understanding this day of all my customers.

Lenny says, "Leo, you are just lucky that I like you, or else I would just throw you out on your ass, but you are going to get enough of that today from your other customers, I will have to bullshit my commanding officer and tell him there was an accident at the plant." Lenny then puts his arm around me and tells me how he feels sorry for me, and that I would not lose my account with the store. Lenny said he was in tight with the commanding officer and for me not to worry.

Now on to rest of the route. My helper and I went into every store, with not even one third of their orders. It was a miserable day to say the least. One of my customers got real nasty with us. He had orders for three hundred pies, and he had every right to be angry. He explained he now had to face all his customers, with some not getting any at all, and how he might even lose some of his customers because of this screw up.

Because of my relationship with the grocers, I did not lose any customers over this, but the sour taste of this would linger, and the trust barrier was gone as far as giving me anymore orders for pies in the future. Actually this turned out one of our last years to take this many orders. We found out that the pie company filled out the orders of one of the biggest chain stores and cut our orders. After the holiday, the pie company had the balls to call us up and asked us how many pies that we wanted. We told them to place them where the sun does not shine.

The loss to us in potential income was the profit of one dollar a pie. On my route, that would come to five thousand dollars. My helper was going to be paid two hundred dollars for his day's work, and with the rental of the truck deducted, it would still give me a profit of about forty five hundred dollars for the day.

Now not only did I take orders for the pies on my route, but I also went and helped drivers on their routes. This one small supermarket up in the Hartford area, which was a family run affair, was a great account that I had secured for my driver, one in which he did extremely well. The owner gave me a wide latitude in placing our products for sale, and this store had a reputation for delivery of quality food, and the service to go along with it. Whenever I was in the area, I would stop in and chat with the owner. He would always have me sample his latest brand of provolone.

He had given me an order for one hundred fifty pies that my driver, Ronnie, was going to deliver. I instructed Ronnie to fill his order and to cut the chain store on his route. This was a no brainer. Ronnie has this store that gave him some great sales, with the owner pushing our product, but the bastard, with the limited amount of pies he had that day, he then dumps them all into the chain stores, and tells all his customers the pies did not come in. What Ronnie did want to do was to have to argue with all his customers by giving them less than they ordered, like I had to do.

So about a week before Christmas, being up in the Hartford Area, I stopped in to see my friend, the owner of this nice market. What a mistake this was. Frank, the owner, was cutting some beef, he looks up at me, and with the knife still in his hand says, "Leo, you son of a bitch. You got a lot of nerve coming here. I gave you a nice order for the pies and I did not get a single one. I had to listen to all my customers, trying to explain to them the bakery had a fire," This is what Ronnie had told him.

When Frank had found out the Waldbaum's market down the street had some pies, Ronnie told Frank they were from the first order, and that the bakery had the problem later. Now Frank still talking to me, waving the knife in his hand. This guy was on fire, and remember, this store was built on service, and this is what set them apart from the chains. This ass Ronnie never told me what he did, especially telling his customers different stories.

Why Ronnie chose to tell Frank the story about a fire, was crazy. All the stores keep in touch with each other. That day was our last day in this account. I wondered why Frank waited for me to come in, instead of just throwing Ronnie out. I now realize Frank had to tell me himself. Although, a year later I stopped in, I go over to the meat counter, with a piece of cardboard in front of my face, and my hands up. Frank, as usual, was cutting meat. He looks up and puts down the knife, and goes into a fit of laughter.

"Leo, you asshole. Come back here and sit down. Have a nice slice of cheese." We discussed family. I told Frank about my grandchildren, and he did the same. We compared notes about the pleasures and misery of owning your own business. I did not go to see Frank about resuming business together, which was not my intent. I understood his anger and did not want to bring up the subject, I respected him too much for that.

As I started to leave Frank looks at me saying, "figlio me" translation: my son, "When you could get a different driver for me have, him stop in, "Frank," I say, "This was a social call, not a business call," Frank then tells me in Italian, " What do you think we are, "forestiere," translation: "outsiders".

Another venture we tried was opening a retail bakery in the mall in the sub base. This is where the service people and their families shopped. A lot of retail stores selling products to the service men and families, mostly at discount prices, so the thinking was we had a captive crowd. It was a good idea; the navy brass were very excited about having a fresh bakery on the premises, as there was none in the area. I got the idea from serving the commissary store. These people were kind of isolated from the rest of the community, but the products we were selling were all baked goods from New York.

The manager put us in a good location right next to an ice cream outlet. I then became friendly with the baker who worked in the mess hall, who gave me the idea of hooking up a fan, and tying a little bag of cinnamon over the fan with perforations in it. This way the smell of fresh cinnamon could be inhaled as soon as you entered the building.

The bakery was selling eighty dozen bagels a day, plus all the other pastries. It was just starting to take off when a jealous distributor, who was also purchasing the same products from the same bakery, began to sabotage our product. His area was about twenty miles from us, and the truck from New York stopped at his place before it came to my warehouse. This resulted in me being shorted every day. Frank and Tommy tracked down the culprit, and they complained to the owner of the bakery. All the time we were being charged for product we did not receive.

I could not sustain the pretense of making excuses, and we could not get the product the mall wanted, so after about a year, we had to shut the operation down. Frank and Tommy then had their hands full trying to settle the account with the bakery. They wanted to still charge us for the product, but eventually it was settled. A lesson was learned from this: you have to have control over everything, you cannot depend on the whims of others.

The work that I alone put into this thing, going out and purchasing the showcases needed for the bakery, scales, cash register, were purchased mostly from a store that was going out of business. The thing that we needed to control was the flow of product, which was something we never figured on, and it came back to bite us in the ass.

We tried this operation one more time, but this time it was a dairy store in Milford, which was being set up to sell space to vendors. Now, I was busy with other programs and could not devote the time to spend at the store. We had a lot of people working, but nobody really in charge. I would set up the store in the morning, and then have Gail, Janet, and other people manning the store. In the end, this venture would be a money loser for us. The concept was a good one since we did not have to spend a lot of money setting up the store, but it was not feasible in the midst of our other demands.

Before we closed out of the store, I had the idea of enclosing our bakery in so that other people could not have access to it. All the departments were accessed easily, but since our goods were left out in the open when we closed at night, it invited the part time workers working in other parts of the store to enter our area and take what they wanted.

In those days we did not have any cameras in the sales area.

After we pulled out, another bakery took our space, but due to the mismanagement of the owners, the place closed down about a year later. What this taught me was to stay at what I knew best, and that was servicing the market. I always loved the retail market, and the give and take of meeting customers. Yes, it was good, but you cannot mix the two. Either you service or you sell.

DAVID AND LISA'S WEDDING

The year of 1988 was a busy year for us, with another grandchild on the way and a wedding between David and Lisa.

David, while employed by our company, was introduced to a wonderful girl, Lisa Piersanti. The introduction of David and Lisa was by our son in law, Russ's mother, Rachel, who was a neighbor and close friend of the Piersanti family. Lisa's father worked in the same factory as my sister, Betty, so the lineage was there. In the Italian lingo it was called, "mmasciata," translation for "introduction". They met in 1986 and were married on October 1, 1988. They had a wonderful wedding.

Just like our other two weddings, Lisa's family and we agreed to let David and Lisa make the arrangements for the wedding. They decided on a catering hall in Wallingford. David told me, "Dad, you do not have to do anything," "Yes, I know. Just show up with the check," I told him.

The stag party for David was an eye opener for me. We had a wonderful comedian who kept all the guys in stitches. After the dinner and the jokes, they came and got David and put him in the center of the room. Then the lights were dimmed, and the music started. In comes a belly dancer, who starts to dance all around David, by now whose face was turning beet red. At the end of the dance, the lady ended up on his lap. Unknown to me, it was Lisa who had hired the dancer, my future daughter-in-law. It was a nice gesture on Lisa's part, and it made for a beautiful evening.

As with Gail and Janet's in-laws, Lisa's parents proved to be some of our great friends. Sometimes making plans of this nature requires the partnership of two families agreeing on money matters. Some weddings caused a lot of discourse between families, but luckily, we were spared that. The families my children married into had the same concerns.

David and Lisa, gave Teresa and I three wonderful granddaughters: Krista, Alyssa and Gina.

JACLYN

On October 18, 1988, after the wedding, we had the birth of a baby, born to Anthony and Janet. I was notified of the birth by David, who sounded very nervous and said the baby had some complications, but what it was he did not know. Teresa and I went to hospital that evening and was told the baby had been born with a condition called Spina Bifida.

Janet had a c-section and when she was released, Anthony and Janet came to live with us for about a week. After the birth, the baby had to remain in the hospital for 3 weeks and had three surgeries. They named the baby Jaclyn. She had the sweetest smile I had ever seen on a baby; her whole face would light up.

About some time later after Janet and Anthony moved back to their home, I had the misfortune of contracting food poisoning, and what I was experiencing was a great loss of movement. I was feeling very weak, but I finally got to see a good doctor, Dr. Fasano, who diagnosed it correctly. The first doctor said that I need to have back surgery, that even I knew was crazy, so I called my brother and he got me to see Dr. Fasano.

One night Anthony, Janet and Jaclyn came to pay me a visit, one I never forgot. I was sitting in the sofa chair in the living room, and due to my condition I was not able to walk. I had to use crutches. Jaclyn comes by the chair, and she puts her hand on my shoulders, saying, "Don't worry Grandpa, you are going to be all right." At that moment I wanted to pick her up and just hug the shit out of her, but I did not have the strength to do so.

One of the things that Janet did for Jaclyn was to put her in the modeling business. It was such a great motivation for Jaclyn. She was excited about posing in front of the cameras, hoping someday to maybe get a good contract from some of her jobs. This required a lot of trips down to New York City and sometimes New Jersey.

The one shoot that I never forgot was the one in Central Park. It was in the middle of July, a very hot and humid day. Jaclyn, I believe, was modeling winter clothes. This location was in the middle of the park, by the large water fountain. Unknown to me, they had put a wristwatch on Jaclyn for the shoot. So after the shoot, I put Jaclyn in the stroller, and started to head out, when this woman comes up to us and takes the watch off of Jaclyn. I protested, but she said it is the property of the shoot. I admonished her for being so rude to the child, but she just looks at me and walks away. "City people," I say.

Being such a hot day, Janet asks where we could go and get some ice cream. We had some time to kill before we headed down to the Lower East Side for another call. Coming out of the park, I see the Essex house, which is a four star hotel that I once stayed at. I suggested we go there, Janet says, "We are not exactly dressed for that place." I had shorts on, and the stroller Jaclyn was in looked a little worn.

This was going to be one of my best moments. Upon entering the hotel, we got the stares of the staff of the hotel, like what the hell are you people doing here. We were not exactly dressed the way the other guests were. I go over to the hostess and tell her we wanted to go inside and have some ice cream. I explain I need something for Jaclyn who was perspiring badly, and we need to cool off.

The snooty bitch looks at us and says, "This is not an ice cream place." She wanted to deny us admittance, but just then a waiter comes by and said he would seat us at his station. He felt sorry for Jaclyn, so we went in and he said he would fix us up with some nice ice cream. He said the hotel makes their own, and he came out with three huge dishes. It was the best ice cream I had ever tasted.

We sat there and rested, and cooled off at the same time. It was an enjoyable hour, especially with the waiter's attention to us. Later on he came over with the check, and it was about ten dollars, but I gave him a twenty dollar bill and told him to keep the change. On the way out we went by the hostess station and heard the waiter telling the hostess about the nice tip I gave him. She had a look of amazement. As I went by I say with a smirk, "You have a nice day," I wanted to tell the bitch, watch out how you judge people, but Janet said, "Dad, let's go."

After another early morning shoot in the same area, I decided to take them to the Plaza hotel for lunch. We ate in the Palm court, and this time they did not have anything to say about our dress code. We were seated at a nice table, and it was there we were introduced to the new style of pasta called penne. They brought it out for Jaclyn, and I think Jessica was there. The check for the five of us was about thirty dollars, not bad for a fancy hotel. This was the same room Teresa and I would go after the shows to have coffee and dessert. They featured a piano player, a violin player, and person playing the harp. They would come by the table and play any song you wanted to hear, all for the sum of thirty dollars. The dessert was tremendous. They had big round table in the middle of the room, and you went with the waiter and picked out any dessert you wanted. Along with the choice you made, they would give you a big helping of whipped cream and your choice of fruit.

On the way home from one of our shoots in the city, something hilarious happened. We were leaving the city at about the time of the evening rush hour. The traffic was heavy, and I was debating about what highway I was going to take home. Ultimately, we decided to go home by the West Side Highway, the way we came. I was in the middle of a conversation with Janet, oblivious to my exit to the parkway leading to Connecticut. I mistakenly take the wrong exit which was the one before the exit leading to the parkway. Just as I was making the turn, Jaclyn who was sitting in the back and slouched down in her car seat, says, "Grandpa, you are making the wrong turn." Jaclyn knew the route better than I did! How she was able to see the exit sign I do not know; Jaclyn really amazed me.

Jaclyn's sense of direction would serve her well later on as she travelled alone on her way to the University of Arizona after graduating college. After some time in Arizona, Jaclyn returned home to finish her education at Gateway Community College, were she received an Associate's degree.

Although Jaclyn was born with a disability, it did not in any way deflect her purpose in life. She was game for everything and her resume included, amongst other things, track and field, road racing, swimming (excelling best in breast stroke), skiing and scuba diving, of which she went to the Cayman Islands. Jaclyn took part in the swim program at school and set some good record times, which made me very proud. In the midst of all of this activity, she somehow found the time to work at Walgreens pharmacy part-time.

After receiving several job opportunities, Jaclyn accepted a position as an office assistant for East River Energy in Guilford, CT. She loves the job and the people she works for. I am so happy because it is such a nice fit for her, especially since she does not have to travel a great distance from her home. Jaclyn has also followed in the family tradition of being a sports fan of the New York Giants and the New York Yankees.

1990-1995 ANDREW

On the fifteenth of February in 1990, we were blessed with our first grandson, Andrew. I believe he weighed around nine pounds, with a mop of black hair, and a ruddy smile. When I had first seen him, he had his fists clenched, as if he was looking for a fight, menacing, scrappy looking, but a bundle of joy. I thought to myself, "poor Andrew", as he will be outflanked by having all female cousins. The one saving grace was that he will be treated like a king on a throne due to the distinction of being the only grandson. But he will soon learn that although he is top dog, he is still younger than his sisters, which meant he will have to miss out on a trip to Bermuda because of his age.

Gail and Janet came to Teresa and I with a program that Bermuda was hosting: a free week for the children. They decided that we could take Kara and Alexa, not knowing that would be a big problem for Andrew. The preparations were made, and the trip was booked for the four of us: Kara, Alexa, Teresa and I. We stayed at the Southampton Princess, a beautiful hotel overlooking the bay.

On the morning that we went to pick up Kara and Alexa, Gail had her hands full trying to placate Andrew, as he was jumping up and down crying why he was not selected to go along. Kara and Alexa were having some fun with this moment, giggling that the little big man has to stay home. He had to see his sisters go off on a trip, and he was not going. It was quite a sight to see Andrew at the door being restrained by Gail, as the driver was backing out of the driveway. I was looking at Andrew, saying to myself, "I hope the little shit will not hate his grandparents."

Another memorable experience with Andrew happened one day when he was attending pre-school, called I believe, Mandana. I was asked to pick him up, as Gail was at that time employed by my company and could not make it in time. So off I went to the school, getting there promptly at the appointed time. Upon entering the school, I seen Andrew, and I motion for him to come to me. He runs to me. As I started to gather his belongings, the teacher stops me at the door asking, "Who may I ask are you?" I respond, "I am Andrew's grandfather, Leo Marino." The teacher looks at Andrew and says, "Andrew, what is your grandfather's name?" Andrew is hesitating, and I am now looking at him, thinking, hurry and answer you little shit. He says, "Oh my grandfather's name is," again hesitating, "oh my grandfather's name is Leo." Phew- a bullet dodged. The teacher smiles and hands Andrew over to me, "I hope you understand Sir, it is our policy." I exclaim, "No problem! I am glad to see that you take the precautions. Andrew had me worried for a minute."

On a trip to Disney World in Florida, on which we accompanied Andrew and his family, one moment is burned in my mind. His father, Russ, buys Andrew a pirate gun, and all week he was playing with it. As we were departing for the airport, Andrew had his prized gun on his person, but going through the security line, the TSA agent confiscates the gun, taking it out of Andrew's hand. This set Andrew on a rampage, screaming and crying. I felt so sorry for him, but they have rules, and it was such a real looking gun. Russ and Gail begin calming him down, saying, "Andrew, we will get you another one." "No," Andrew answers. "I want that one," stomping around. The little guy now knows the feeling of rejection.

Another memory that reminds me of Andrew was on a trip to New York City. I secured tickets for the very popular Broadway show, Beauty and the Beast. I got us seats on the first floor, tenth row, to the right of the stage. It was a section that was raised slightly so all the kids had a good view of the stage. The show was as great as people had said and for lunch we went to Sardi's Restaurant. When I made the reservations, I asked for us to be seated on the first floor, and they followed my instructions and placed us right in the middle of the room.

When Andrew sat down and saw all the food, he announced that he was ready to "start stuffing his mouth", so much so, that toward the end of the meal, he stood up on his chair and upchucked right on the table. The waiter came over and changed everything and he was so courteous about it, telling us not to worry and that this is "all in a day's work." I left a nice tip, even though I believe all the help has to share it, but on the way out I slipped him a twenty dollar bill for himself. He thanked me all the way out the door.

Andrew was a 4 year varsity letter winner at Branford High School. He helped the baseball team win the 2006 State Championship. He accomplished 2 time all-SCC conference and all State selection. He was awarded most outstanding hitter, MVP and team captain. He was recruited by a majority of northeast universities as a pitcher and pitched at Eastern CT helping the team reach NCAA regional final in 2011 as a late inning reliever.

KRISTA

Also in 1990 we ushered in a new arrival, a baby girl born to David and Lisa, named Krista. Krista was born on April 21st and we now had four granddaughters. At the time, David and his family were living about a few minutes away from my home. They bought a large raised ranch in a new development but David had to finish off the basement to have more living space. It was a nice area with a lot of children for Krista to play with.

Krista, to her grandparents is the quiet one, as she had a dedication for knowledge and loves to read. As a young child, Krista was involved in school programs, such has playing softball and dancing, which was at about the age of five years old and lasted about ten years. One of Krista's passions is her desire for reading. I might say a voracious one at that, much like her cousin Kara. In fact she has read so many books that she has a Kindle so she can download them, and every year she goes to the Branford book fair and fills up a bag of books. Krista, loves both fiction and non-fiction, but as a child she loved the Harry Potter series. We would often compare notes with each other and discuss what she was reading. I found Krista and I shared the same passion and taste for our selections of reading.

One day, was the surprise of all, Krista called and asked me for my copy of *Gone With The Wind*, a 1939 classic, both the book and the movie, being surprised because I did not even think anybody from my grandchildren's generation would have an interest in it, and sadly, I loaned or misplaced the book, but I had other illustrations that went with the book, plus the video. Eventually Krista did obtain a copy of the book and was enthralled by the story. She read the whole book in a short period of time. After that Krista and I continued to compare books from time to time.

Knowing that Krista was so studious, it was surprising to me when she wanted to go to The Fashion Institute of Technology in NYC for college. I was thinking more of a traditional educational experience, being as studious as she is, but she was determined to succeed, striving toward a job in fashion, another area of interest for her. Upon graduating from college, Krista obtained employment in the fashion industry based in Manhattan, New York. Currently Krista is living in Queens, N.Y.

SELLING THE WAREHOUSE

It was around the early 1990s when we decided to sell off half of our business. We had two different business going: one was a wholesale, and one was a retail. It was hard to concentrate on both at the same time, so after about a year of trying to locate a buyer, we finally had an interested person who wanted the wholesale end of our business. It was actually easier to operate due to the fact that mostly all the product was pretty much all ordered in advance, and the business was all established, so the new owner did not have to do any sales work, just manage what he was buying. We had taken all headaches out, as far as the receiving of the goods from New York, and we sold the business at a pretty good profit.

But then we were faced with another problem, as the new buyer did not want to stay and operate the business in our warehouse. He wanted to have his own place, so he decided to move. Now we had a large warehouse that we did not need. So we put the warehouse up for sale, but being in the inner city, it was not going to an easy sell. We also had a problem with the city of New Haven. They gave us a letter of intent, saying they were interested in the property, so we had to put the sale on hold and could not sell until the date of the letter expired. At the time we did have some offers, but we could not sell because of this letter.

Well, the shit hit the fan as they say. The city notified us saying after such a length of time that they were not going to adhere to the letter of intent. They decided they were not interested, and now we were up the stump after all this time. We had to put the warehouse up for sale again. We did seek out counsel to see about suing the city over the agreement, but as they say, "you cannot sue city hall."

Now after such an agonizing time trying to find a buyer, even with the help of a real estate agent, we did not have any success trying to secure a buyer. Since I was reading the real estate pages every day to see who was purchasing property, I came upon this small article one Sunday that was about the state looking to purchase a large building in the city.

I put down the paper and called my brother Frank and told him about the article. The very next day he gets in touch with Cornell Scott, the person who was in charge of purchasing for the state. Frank then gets Tommy and sets up a meeting with Scott. Now, here we have a real estate agent and a signed contract with the real estate agency, so we had to notify the agent about the interested buyer, meaning we still had to pay the agency even though we secured the customer ourselves.

Tommy did a good job of presenting our property to the state, and we made a nice profit on the sale, but the thing that bothered me the most was paying the agency their commission when we did all the sales work. They showed up at the closing and got their check, plus that year the state came out with the state income tax, so they also got their share- a nice profit for them. After we sell the warehouse, we then broke up the remaining business and moved into smaller quarters, with Tommy taking the retail part of the business, which included the route drivers, while Frank Jr., myself, and David took the sales end of it, which included serving vendors and supermarkets with a line of bread for the delis. It was a rough going because we then had to build up the business all over again, start from scratch really. The part of the business that we took was also under fire from other people who wanted to cut us out of business, and were going after our vendors and offering a cheaper price.

But, as they say, when one door closes and another one opens up. We were given a product to deliver to the club stores, which was a fore runner for us to get other products into the stores. The product that we had obtained was an item that a distributor did not want to handle anymore, so with my brother Frank making contacts with a salesperson that was able to introduce us to the person in charge of buying for the club stores, we were able to secure more products in more club stores.

At about this time our new business was taking hold but with a great amount of work, and a lot of hours put in by Frank Jr., myself, and David. This bread business had to be administered seven days a week. Serving the supermarkets with this product meant we had to make sure all the stores were being served, which meant having to out on Sundays to fix up the displays and make sure the stores did not run out of product.

After some time Tommy did not want to continue on with his part of the business that he had, and we wound up with the drivers again. I, for one, wanted to reduce my hours of labor, and set about having Frank Jr. and David take over the business, with me still working, and following up on our retail program with the supermarkets. We also had a snack cake program and had to secure more drivers to serve them, so now the business was on track but still had a long ways to go before the dust cleared. The markets we had were strung out all over the state, which meant a lot of traveling for me to supervise the program. We had tables in the stores, and I had to make sure they were being served properly.

While this was going on, a cookie distributor came up to me with a proposal to handle his product. He had about ten supermarkets at the time, and they were not being taking care of properly. The problem was that the product was being shipped to the stores, but it was not being displayed properly. This was where I came in. I told him I would visit the stores and come back with a price for the labor of handling his business. I went and visited all of their stores, which were spread out all over the state. I calculated the hours involved, including traveling time, and when we met I gave him my offer. I would need one thousand dollars a week, plus he would have to furnish the car and expenses for the week. He comes back with a counter offer of four hundred dollars a week, plus I would have to use my car, and he would furnish the money for the gas. I told him in a nice way to keep his offer and not let the door hit him on the way out.

The amount of business in profit to him was about twelve thousand dollars, what I was asking was a mere pittance. On his side of the deal, he then gets a man to do the program for him, but he failed in three months the program collapsed. This would have been a good income for us in the new business, and I could have taken care of this along with my regular markets. What he did not know was that I knew just how much profit he was making on the program because I was purchasing the same product.

Soon he came back with another offer, and it put us on a more solid footing. The cookie distributor was a savvy business man, and he was just trying to save as much as possible, but he did not look at the whole picture. He had quite a large cookie business and this was small potatoes to him. I guess he felt that he did not have to pay the amount I had requested, as he did not think it required the labor involved.

With the new business that was being added on, in addition to our club stores and the retail end, the warehouse now was getting to be too small, so the purchase of a new warehouse was being discussed. With me now in a semi- retired state, Frank Jr., David, and Frank Sr.

together purchased a large warehouse to house Frank Sr.'s business, which was the marketing arm of our company.

Another one of my great disappointments was the time we had sold the warehouse after breaking up the business. Tommy came up with the idea of investing the profit we had made on the warehouse and purchase some property for the long term. To me, it was a good idea, as I had always wanted to be more secure financially, especially with my age and to have some extra added income for life so Tommy and Frank found what they determined to be a great opportunity. They presented it to me, and we went and looked at the property. I thought it was a no brainer, due to the national corporation who was leasing the property and with a long term lease to go with the deal.

So Tommy went about setting the wheels in motion to secure the property. Tommy spent a lot of time researching the deal. This was a company that was a large trucking firm, and they used the property to house and maintain the vehicles. The location was great for us since the property was located right in the middle of the state. Our investment in the property was not a huge one due to the creative financing that was involved.

Our profit from this arrangement would give each one of us about three thousand dollars a month in income for the rest of our lives. I was also intrigued by the fact that my children would benefit from this due to inheritance. The lease was for ninety years, I believe, a nice sum to leave our families.

After what seemed to be forever, Tommy had secured a bank that was going to finance the deal, and with all the inspections complete, they had set a closing for the sale of the property. We had to travel to Hartford for the closing, and going along with us was our great friend and attorney Shelly, who had been such a great help to us for a very long time. He was not only our attorney but part of our family.

On the way up to Hartford, I kept thinking that this was what I had always wanted, a secure income, over and above any other income. The deal was a little complicated to me, but Shelly took plenty of time breaking down the details. He had a nice way of explaining the process to me so that it did not seem that he was patronizing me.

As we all settled down into the conference room where the papers were going to be signed, I felt a sense of freedom about my future. This was to me, one of the benefits of all the hard work that I had put into the business, and now I felt all we had to do was finalize the deal, sign the papers, and go home and celebrate.

At the last minute, a phone call came in that was to shatter that dream. The bank that was financing the deal said that there was a problem with the property being contaminated, and that they were backing out of the deal. I was shocked. They had already given us the green light, and yet they were closing out of the deal. Well, this was one time that Tommy, who a had short fuse from time to time, let out some of the expletives that could be heard throughout the building. All of a sudden, the doors to the room were closed to drown out Tommy's rebuttal. We could not understand how after all this time, that they or some one of their lawyers, did not touch base to speak with the parties involved. I sat there thinking, how the hell could this be happening?

Tommy, by now, was not to be calmed down. He had put so much time into this, and to see it coming apart, his anger was well justified. In fact, Shelly, Frank and I were just as taken aback by this letdown. Shelly tried his best in speaking with the closing attorneys about the events unfolding, trying to salvage the deal.

In a conference call with the representatives of the bank, Tommy let out all his anger on them, and it was not pretty. Shelly was seated next to Tommy and tried to get some answers from the lenders as to why this was sabotaged at the last minute. All Shelly got was lawyer speak, in other words all bullshit.

On the way home in the car, the four letter words were plentiful for all the persons involved. I sat there thinking this nightmare could not be happening. Less than an hour ago I was on dream street, and now I was going home empty, my lifelong dream of financial security was going down the toilet, along with the prospect of leaving my children a great opportunity for income for them in their life time.

Maybe it was just a coincidence, but the property was eventually approved to someone else. I believe some of the people down at the bank allowed one of their friends to move in on us, a conspiracy, if you will. Our fault was that we should have investigated and looked for another bank. Tommy and Shelly did reach out to an attorney who was more versed in this matter to see if we could not get some redress in court.

It just goes to prove that all the aspirations and dreams you have, if left up to other people, over which you have no control, will never come to fruition. As the saying goes, you can have all the dots covered, but if you do not oversee the dots yourself, it will never get done. A sad chapter in my life, one I often think about, but not to the point of dwelling on it forever.

JESSICA

Janet and Anthony welcomed another daughter on February 2nd, 1992. Being born on Groundhog Day will turn out to be an omen for Jessica. From the earliest moments in her life, you could see how connected she felt to animals. She would light up at just the sight of a dog, One day I was in the park with Jessica and I saw her fawn over a dog. So I started teasing her, "Jessica, it is only a dog." Jessica gave me a stern look, and said, "Grandpa, all dogs are beautiful." I tried to explain to Jessica that I have allergies and dogs are one of them. You should have seen the disappointed expression on her face. "Gee, Grandpa that is not fair for you." I replied, "Well, that is just one of my allergies, so you see Jessica, you have to make adjustments in life."

From an early age, Jessica would constantly badger her mom and dad every year for a puppy. She always talked about dogs, wore shirts with dogs on them, and even hid notes for her parents in places around the house, just begging for a dog. Her wish was finally granted when she reached the age of ten years and she was blessed with a puppy. They named her Elle and they became inseparable.

Looking back to when Janet was about Jessica's age, I remember Janet begging for me to get her a dog. To appease her, I built her a little house in the backyard and the con worked. She was happy with the change, which was good since my life at that time did not include the care of a dog.

Being the restless child that Jessica was, and very adventuresome I might add, she partook in many activities, such as dance classes, softball, soccer, and swimming, which she continued on throughout high school. She excelled at the breast stroke. All this activity and she still had time to be employed as a cashier at the Big Y in Guilford. There was no moss gathering under her feet!

Upon graduating from high school, she went to Keene State College in Keene, New Hampshire. She graduated with a B.A. in communications. While in college, she joined a sorority and spent one spring break painting houses in New Orleans for the hurricane victims. During her junior year, Jessica studied abroad in Florence, Italy from August to December and had the opportunity to tour many countries in Europe. She worked part time at La Luna in Branford in order to save money for this trip. In May of 2014, Jessica graduated.

After college, she returned home and secured a position as a hostess at Eli's on the Hill and also took a part time job in New York City, working in sales at a Macaron Café. When she was not offered a full time job, she severed her employment.

Jessica eventually did find a full time job but it required her to move to Denver, Colorado. She was to leave for Denver in January 2016 so that December Jessica and Krista took me to New York City to visit the Museum of Natural History, one in which they knew I had a great desire to visit. They planned the whole day and what a great day it was to spend with my granddaughters.

After viewing the museum, Krista wanted to take us to a nice bakery. As we were walking down the street towards the bakery, I seen this long line of people, so I asked Krista, "What are they waiting for?" She was discouraged, "Oh, that is the bakery." As we approached, the girls got in line, and I went up to the front to see what the bakery looked like. It was down in the basement, a little shithole, so I returned to the girls and said, "Ladies, I do not do lines, especially one half block long." They laughed, and we agreed to move on to our restaurant for dinner, one in which they have eaten at several times before.

Upon reaching the restaurant on Ninth Ave. we were disappointed because the restaurant was closed. So we went across the street to a nice Italian restaurant and learned from the waiter that the other restaurant had no choice but to close due to increasing rents.

A humorous thing happened after we settled down and placed our orders with the waiter. I needed to use the restroom, and standing in the back of the restaurant were the two waiters assigned to our table. I made some comment how hectic things were in the city. One responded, "What are you complaining about? You have two nice chicks with you!" I laughed, "Yes, I do. They are also my granddaughters!" They both smirked, as they are so used to seeing eighties and twenties together. It made an old man feel good.

On January 2, 2016, Jessica moved to Denver, Colorado and found an apartment with some friends. She was determined to make a success, and she obtained a position working at a dispensary. This position required quite a bit of education for Jessica, but one in which she excelled at.

In December 2016 Jessica left Denver and took a position at the Vail Ski Resort, working in the reservation department and living in the employees housing. Since this was a seasonal position, she figured the benefits of a very low rent will give her the opportunity increase her savings account and has the extra attraction of unlimited free skiing. After the season, she will go back to Denver and the dispensary.

ALYSSA

1993 saw the birth of my granddaughter, Alyssa, on April 13th. I always considered her the quiet one, but she was anything but. Alyssa, following in the footsteps of Krista's, she also took up dancing and softball, starting at the age of five and lasting for about ten years. She was a very athletic child with softball being her favorite sport. She was so involved and dedicated to the game that she broke her arm twice but she was still not fazed. She plowed on until one day the pitcher on her team got hit in the face with a line drive, and after that season she gave up her desire for baseball.

When Alyssa entered high school, she took up cheerleading, which seemed not as dangerous, but still very physical, as she would soon find out. Cheerleading was not just about standing around; dancing up and down with pom-poms and being tossed up into the air was all part of the routine.

Well Alyssa's dedication paid off. By the time of her senior year, she was named captain of her co-ed team, and to cap it all off in her senior year her team won the state title. Those were four years well spent with her four grandparents filled with pride.

After graduating high school, Alyssa chose to go to Springfield College, but after spending one year there, she decided this was a bad choice for her and switched over to Quinnipiac University, and there she continued her passion for cheerleading. Again, by her senior year in college she was again named captain of her team.

After college, Alyssa went on to get her Master's in Education and graduated in 2016. To say I am so proud of all my grandchildren would be an understatement. They are all college graduates and with no burden of having loans hanging over their heads, thanks in large part to their parents, who have worked hard and made many sacrifices to see this happen. Along with Alyssa's many accomplishments, is her booming personality, which will help her achieve whatever goals she has set for herself; she is a very disciplined girl. One thing Alyssa will have no problem with is her chosen profession: teaching. She has a booming voice and she projects well. I am sure all of her students will have no problem understanding her. She reminds of a teacher I had in grade school, a Miss Horowitz. She was tiny, but when she spoke, everybody paid attention. Right now she is a paraprofessional in the Madison school system, and she is working on passing her state tests so she can get certified to teach full time. Then her lifelong dream will be fulfilled, a life well planned.

50TH WEDDING ANNIVERSARY

As our 50th wedding anniversary year was approaching in 2004, our children, Gail, Janet and David suggested we all go to Disney World for Thanksgiving. The emphasis was on spending the Thanksgiving holiday in Disney which was something different. Unbeknownst to Teresa and I, this was going to be a surprise 50th wedding anniversary for us. What was shocking to me is that nobody gave any clue as to what they had in store for us even though all the family members knew about it (especially the grandchildren).

We were booked at the Disney Yacht Club. Janet took charge of all the travel arrangements (a superb job) for 16 people, which was quite an undertaking. Gail and David assisted in the planning of the itinerary. The only request I thought was strange was when Teresa and I were told we had to bring some formal clothes because we were going to a nice restaurant and the whole family was going to be dressed up. Also they said a family portrait would be taken. For two days it was mostly casual, in fact the children even invited their Uncle Bill and his friend Sandy who live in Florida to join us for one of the dinners. It was a nice to have my brother in law Bill and Sandy spend the day with us. We shared some good memories.

On the day of our family dinner Gail and Janet had a hair dresser come to our room and do Teresa's hair and still I did not think much of it. They did say it was for a family portrait, but this really surprised the hell out of us later when we found out what all the fuss was for. Janet came into our room and said the three of us were going together because the others were already there. As we were going down in the elevator, Janet had this twitch about her, but still I did not know. She escorted us off the elevator through the hotel and said, "We have to walk down this walkway to the restaurant". As we got to the end of the walkway, turned the corner and headed up another walkway into a courtyard, lo and behold we see our entire family standing near a gazebo altar waiting for us.

We walked down the aisle and renewed our vows for fifty years of marriage. Standing in the gazebo was a minister, a witness, and a photographer. People at the resort were coming out of their rooms onto the balcony to view the ceremony, which was very impressive. We took our family pictures there. After our ceremony, we went to the restaurant and had a wonderful dinner.

The next day Teresa and I were told to dress up for a special dinner for just the two of us. A limo picked us up and took us to a first class restaurant. Teresa and I were treated like royalty. This was a trip well planned with lasting memories.

CHAPTER SIX

Reflections on Life

1995-2000 NEW BUSINESS

Restarting the business, I ventured into a whole different aspect of sales. I was now having to deal with buyers of the chain stores to secure the stores for the drivers we now had and to give them exposure into a greater market, other than the "Mom and Pop" stores most of them relied on. This would also give us some greater tonnage in the market. This was not an easy task; I now was having to deal with some great egos, since I mostly had to deal with the managers of stores, who were very accessible to speak to, but the buyers on the other hand, you had to make an appointment with.

Some of these guys had the feeling that they were the owners of the stores, and the purchasing of products was left up to them by the owners of the stores, with one guy actually telling me that the product I was presenting was not a good fit for his stores, saying his customers were above grade and would not approve of my product. I would shut them up by advancing the idea of giving him some free product and to tryout in his stores. By me pointing out different products that he had already in his stores on the same level as mine, that always got them to get off that bullshit.

In this quest, I was successful in obtaining small groups of chain stores for my drivers. The new concept was gas stations turned into food stores, sometimes owned by a large corporation, and other times by a small group of people, mostly of Indian decent. They proved to be a very tough sell. To them, there was no bottom line, but when you struck a deal with them, and convinced them of a steady flow of product, they would go out of their way and call up their friends for additional business. They did this to make sure of them getting them a steady flow of the product. By them making you stronger, they would have a better flow.

For me, it was much better dealing with the owners rather than going through a third party, as I have stated above. Buyers could be very sadistic in the way they treated vendors sometimes. I guess the power of denial is overpowering to some.

Another time of gross misconduct by a buyer was when I was approached by a chain store manager who expressed a strong desire for my product to be sold in his store. Since he did not have authorization to purchase my product, he gave me the name of the buyer.

As the week of my appointment drew near, I was confronted with some problems in distribution and had to devote my time to solving it so I could not make the appointment. I asked my brother Frank to fill in for me and bring the needed samples up to the buyer. It should have been a slam dunk sale since we knew the managers wanted this product. So Frank brings up all the necessary price lists and samples of some of our other products to see if they could be authorized. Well, Frank meets with the son of the owner and makes a wonderful presentation; he had all of the samples laid out on the table.

The arrogant son of the owner takes one look at all our products and dismisses them immediately. He then takes all the products off the table and throws them on the floor, saying, "These products are all a bunch of crap." Now that the products are on the floor, Frank, instead of picking them up, proceeds to stomp all over them, making a shit house of the office. All the while, the owner's son watched with the look of amazement on his face.

This is an example of what I mentioned earlier about some of the abuse sales people had to endure at the hands of incompetent and spoiled family members who were put in charge of purchasing. This particular chain of stores was notorious in its treatment of vendors. A few years later when this chain had a serious financial problem, and the news was spreading around the world of distribution, it was as if whatever problems they were having was well deserved. Cheers went up all around the area.

I appreciated working with the drivers in the new phase of our business. In the world of retail selling, we had a new line of snack cakes that were selling for a very reasonable price, and we now had the opportunity to make a serious dent in the snack cake market, namely going after the major bakeries' sales. The time was ripe for us due to the fact that the market was looking for new products. We were now giving the stores a better profit margin and a more diverse product.

I was able to secure groups of stores with this program and to give the drivers some much needed additional sales. One of my drivers, Chris, whom I had a great respect for due to his excellent reputation on the job. Chris ran the neatest route. He was very attentive in serving his customers and keeping the stores in good condition, all the products were well displayed, and he was on excellent terms with all the customers. Yet, the one area where Chris and I disagreed was on the volume of inventory in his stores. I would always preach to Chris about not leaving any room for anybody to move in on his space in the stores. When I tried to explain to Chris, this was the way I started my business, by keeping your back door closed, as the saying goes, so the other vendors can not have any opportunity to move in on you.

But since none of his customers had any serious complaints, I continued to secure a nice set of stores for Chris. Chris had experience as a vendor for the vending machines, so I could see why he served his route the way he did. In his previous business, he would replace what was sold, and not have any back up inventory. So the task at hand for me was to try an educate Chris to the world of retailing. Retailing was far different than vending machines, because in retailing space was a premium. If you did not leave enough product to cover your space, other vendors would take over.

I found Chris to be a very dependable route man. In visiting his accounts, all his customers always had a kind word about him, especially one heavy volume gas station that I had secured for him. The owner and I agreed to have us bring in a large table to display our products on, which was unusual for a store this size, but our sales tripled after we brought the table in, and Chris was elated.

I would meet Chris on the route from time to time and we would stop and have some coffee. We had the same likes; Chris and I had the same appreciation for the Broadway shows in New York. At that time I tried to get down to the city at least once a month to see the shows. Every time we saw each other, Chris and I would compare the merits of one show compared to the other. Chris was a smoker, heavy I thought, but I never mentioned it to him. We only had a conversation about smoking once, and I told Chris about me having asthma as a child, and that I never had the urge to smoke.

One day, we were having coffee, and Chris disclosed that he was having some health problems. He said the doctor wanted him to take more blood tests to find out what the problem was. I did not ask him about the extent of the issues; he did not explain in detail, and I did not want to pry.

So it really came as a shock to me the day I came back to the warehouse to hand in my day's findings to see Chris empting his truck, which was very unusual. I asked him why, and Chris told me he had been diagnosed with stage four cancer. I just stood there not knowing has to what to say, but I put down my briefcase and started to help him. He immediately declined my offer. We just for a moment stared at one another. After the truck was cleared, he extended his hand and thanked me for my friendship and said he was now going on a new journey. I wished him well and said I would be in touch with him.

The guys and I were in the process of putting together something for Chris, such as a visit from all of us, but sadly, by the time we agreed on what to do, I was notified that Chris had passed away. It seemed the time had gone so quickly. I now believed his cancer was pretty well advanced, more than I realized. It seemed like just a short time ago I was standing on the platform talking to Chris and now he was gone. The death of Chris which was attributed to smoking, just like so many of my dear friends, but no matter, the problem still has you left with deep feelings.

PRISON ACCOUNTS

Another phase of my business that I was really interested in was trying to secure the prison accounts, which were very lucrative. But after spending some time securing accounts in the prison system, I was able to get a foothold in some of the larger institutions. I was successful in obtaining an account in Somers, one that I would have to visit on a weekly basis to write their order for the following week. This meant me having to go up to the prison, and the manager would come down and walk me to the store so that we would go over the next week's menu.

The manager and I became friendly to the point that he was thinking about turning over all his outside purchases to me. Needless to say, I was overjoyed at the prospect of obtaining the business. I served the account myself personally to make sure we got off on the right foot. It was quite a task making deliveries to the prisons. They would check your truck, both inside and underneath the vehicle.

We then hired a driver to start making deliveries for us, my brother Frank hired this fellow Ronnie, who was a friend of my niece Cindy, but with one little problem: he had just got out of prison. Ronnie spent seven years in prison for shooting a guy during a card game, and in fact, Ronnie was an inmate at Somers prison. After a little while, he told us that he was not allowed to serve the prison, since the rules stated that an ex-con cannot serve the prison, and Ronnie was spotted by one of the guards. We then had to make some changes in our route distribution.

I found Ronnie to be a very affable person, yet in discussing the reason for his incarceration, Ronnie said he had no regrets about shooting the guy. He even told me the story about that day. It was during the game when he began to feel the guy was cheating, so Ronnie excuses himself and goes home and gets his gun. He come back, and without any reservation, shoots the guy right at the table. He then said he lays down the gun and waits for the police to come. All of the men present, Ronnie said, just stood there. He said they were frozen by fear, but not at Ronnie. I believe Ronnie's situation was one of a long simmering dispute between the man he killed and himself.

Ronnie had a good attorney, but an expensive one. He told me it cost him thirty thousand dollars for the lawyer, but at trial Ronnie was sentenced to seven to twenty years. He took a plea agreement. Rather than going through a full blown trial, where he would have gotten a much harsher sentence, he accepted the plea.

I asked him how the hell he felt about getting sentenced, with the likelihood of spending the better part of maybe twenty years in prison. In short I said, "Ronnie, was it worth it?" Ronnie explains, "I had no remorse about shooting the son of a bitch. He was a no good bastard." This was almost like my friend Jimmy, who was sentenced for going A.W.O.L. in the army. To hear you were going to be locked up for that length of time would blow my mind.

Ronnie also told me about his experiences in prison. He was assigned to the prison bake shop, and his job every day was to make sheet cakes for the prison dining room. Ronnie said he took great pride in his baking. I said, "Ronnie, why the hell don't you open a bakery?" He said he did not like the early hours of the bake shop business.

One of Ronnie's complaints during his stay was having to live in a two man cell, especially if you do not like the person. Unfortunately in Ronnie's case, he did not. The guy they assigned to his cell was a very dirty and very obese man. In short, he smelled. So Ronnie pleads with the captain of the guards to let him have his own cell. Finally, they found Ronnie a cell of his own that was kind of isolated, but Ronnie had to accept where he was located, or else go back to his old situation, which he dreaded.

On one of my sales call to the prison, Vinnie the manager, decided to have some fun with me. Getting to the store required you to walk down the same hallway as the inmates. While they had to adhere to a line in the hall on both sides of the hall, we had to walk in the middle. Normally Vinnie would escort me to the store and back out to the waiting room. This one time Vinnie leaves the office and said he will be right back. After some twenty minutes, I ask his assistant, "Where is Vinnie? It is getting late, and I do not want to be stuck in traffic." His assistant then tells me that I could go, and he directs me on which hall to take out of the office. I look down the hall and see all these rough looking inmates. I said I am not going anywhere; I will stay right here. At this time I did not know Vinnie was hiding in the stock room laughing his ass off. Seeing how scared I was, he comes out and said he was testing to see how brave I was, "Vinnie, you ass, I will tell you, you had me shitting my pants. I was prepared to spend the night in this office and not move."

Ronnie had the same problem as Chris; he also was a heavy smoker. Riding with him on many occasions, I made sure to keep the window open, much to his displeasure, especially on a cold day. The truck was a van and did not have much room for the smoke to disappear. Ronnie was also a gambler; not a large bettor, but nonetheless a steady one. One of his routes took him by the casino. After he would finish his deliveries, he would stop off and spend some time there.

Meeting Ronnie one day on the way home from his route, we stopped and had some food, I asked him why he was so late in finishing his route, he explains saying, "Leo, I was losing quite a bit, so I stayed and tried to recoup my losses." So I asked the foolish question, "Ronnie, then how did you do?" I lost more money, Ronnie says. He then goes into a recitation to explain to me the fine art of gambling. Ronnie says, "When you are losing, you should double up, and bet more to recover." I say, "It looks like your system is a failure, you ass," I laugh at him saying, "The Indians must love you and your system.

Ronnie also told me the story about how he would go and play cards with the dope dealers down in the city. He described how they did not care how much money they would lose, because they had no other place to put it. He bragged about how stupid they were about all sorts of gambling. He said they loved playing cards with him, and he never felt any fear for his safety. Thinking about it now, Ronnie was just like them. He never showed any fear to me about anything. Along with this same story, Ronnie told about the day he won five thousand dollars. During one of the card games, they ran out of money, and one of the guys told him, "Stay here. I will be right back." Indeed he comes back with another bag full of money. At the end of the night, Ronnie wins another two thousand dollars, and the dealers say they have to end the game because they have to go out into the street. Ronnie goes home a happy man.

But not all his nights were this profitable. He said they got lucky from time to time, but for the most part, he was ahead of them. When Ronnie gave me the location of the card games, I told him, "I would not even go down there with a police presence." It did not bother Ronnie one bit. I believe being stupid and brave go hand in hand.

It was during this period with Ronnie that I had a store set up for a massive display, but I had to put it on hold due to me having to a colonoscopy. I had to have removal of some polyps, and I was not to do any heavy lifting for the following week after the procedure. I reset the date of putting up the display. Ronnie was going to do the work of displaying the product, and I went along for the ride to make sure everything was all set up.

After we finished the store, we went and had some breakfast. While I was sitting there waiting for our food, I felt something wet in my pants. I got up and went to the bathroom, and all I could see was blood in the back of my pants. I then felt a lot of abdominal pain. Ronnie rushed me back to the warehouse, but by then the pain was worse and an ambulance was called. During this time Ronnie was very calm and tried to soothe my fears.

At the hospital, it was discovered that the polyps had to be redone to be more secure. After they redid the procedure, they sent me up to a room to spend the next two days to recover. That night a nurse came in and took one look at me and said, "I am going to have to clean you up. The people downstairs did not do a good job of cleaning you." She was right. She took two large towels and wiped off all the blood on my lower body then changed all the sheets. By this time I was so weak, but I extended my hands to thank her, very feebly. She returned the gesture by caressing my forehead and then left the room. She was the night nurse, and I never got to say goodbye to her and express my appreciation for what she did.

Sometimes Ronnie would use the van we assigned him for his private use, which was alright with us. But sometimes he would take the van also at night to go over to the tele track to bet on the horses. One night after a session at the track, he went over to the diner and was having some food with some of his friends. He parked the truck outside the restaurant and stayed in the diner for a length of time.

When he came out to get his van, he discovered it was missing. He did have some product in the truck that he was to deliver the next day. The robbers must have seen the product in the van and stolen the van and all. What hurt us was that the van was one of our best vans. We did have some others, but they were mostly junk. I believed Ronnie's story, but others did not, and I will have to leave it at that. When my sister Mary passed away, Ronnie was very generous in helping with the finances, so to me it was a wash.

One day a man named John comes into my office, and said he was looking to obtain a route. His family business was sold by his family, which included his two other brothers. The business was located in very influential area of his town, and they catered to a wealthy class of people. He said his brothers wanted to retire, and he did not want to take over the business by himself.

John did not have any route experience, but he had worked in retail since he was very young, so to me at least he was trainable. I took him on and together we went out and started a route, with me giving him some supermarkets to help him get started. John was a fun guy to work with. He seemed to have a casual outlook on life. I was impressed by him: being less than forty and having a nice home all paid for with some money in the bank, due to his share of the sale of the business.

John did have a bad habit, but one in which I thought he had a handle on. He told me of his association with a bunch of guys who would get together and play cards on a weekly basis. Nothing unusual about that, I thought. John did say they played for high stakes, but he said his wins and losses were about even, so he was happy. Gambling never really interested me, as I looked at gambling as a fool's way of trying to beat the odds, but it could also be good therapy for some, like the idea of social gambling.

Maybe there is no such thing as social gambling, but most people that I put in that group were people that would take a set amount to gamble with, and when they reached that level, they would call it quits. These people say they had some fun with it, and it did not take away from the family. To them I always say, "Bless you, for having the resolve to keep your promise."

John, on the other hand, was not in that class, as I would find out later. He was into some deep trouble by having huge losses that he could not sustain. The people he was gambling with were well financed and had the means to cover all their bets, but not John. He was into the games for quite a huge sum of money. He was offered a deal to wipe out his debt. He had to deliver a package to an address in town, and he would have his debt erased. This package had to have some stink to it to erase a debt, but John had no other options. Either pay up, or deliver the package. John takes the deal.

The day of the delivery he drives over to the address, and with the package in hand, goes up to the house. Unknown to him, the feds were at the house. They swarm all over John, and have him arrested on a drug charge. The package contained a few pounds of cocaine. This obviously had to be a set up. He was being sacrificed; in short, the feds wanted to nab someone, and John was fed to them to get them off their trail. John was offered a deal by the feds. They asked him to give him the name of the person who gave him the package, and they would give consideration when it came to being sentenced. John tells the feds, "If I give you the name I will be dead in a very short while." So John goes to trial and is sentenced to seven years in prison.

When John was out on bail, he came in and emptied out his truck and gave me all the information on his accounts. That day on the platform John had the look of a man who in his eyes made a mistake but did not appear to be bothered by it in the least, but underneath, the strain was there. Here was a guy that had a nice start in life; a home all paid for, money in the bank, and yet he throws it all away for the pleasure of gambling. To me, I never met an easier going guy; he was such a pleasure to associate with. After John served his time of seven years, he came up to me, and wanted to restart a route. At the time I did not have an area for him to work in, so he hooks up with the driver that took his area, and arranged to work with him. He also had some other employment to go along with working with the driver. I was disappointed for him but happy to see him have some employment.

One of my ideas to start a whole new business within a business was to have a single vendor serve all the prison commissary stores, just like the stores I was presently serving. Only I would take it a step further by including everything, except the sale of cigarettes, and along with my program of baked goods, would be the inclusion of the many dry items they were purchasing from different vendors.

In discussing this with all of the store managers in the prison system, I found many of them in agreement. I wanted to set up a computer program, whereas they would call in to our computer and place their orders, and we would then deliver all the orders intact with the inmates' numbers on it. All they would have to do is serve it to them. This would clear up all the confusion in their stores with no labor involved from them. I also envisioned setting up the warehouse with tables to fill their orders and to have about two delivery trucks serving all the locations. All of the managers agreed that it would clear up a lot of space for them because they wouldn't have to carry all that inventory.

There already was a national company serving the prisons throughout the country that would supply the locations with all the hard goods, but my selling point was that we would be able to serve them on a day's notice while their major supplier could only make weekly visits. My friend Vinnie and I discussed this many times and he was even more interested in this than I was. He was all for the program, saying he was going to retire in a short while, and said, "Leo, I will come and work for you." This program would be able to involve all of our families, and it would be their business to run. I had all these ideas, but to put them in place meant to get to the right people in charge. This is where Vinnie came in. He gave me the name of the person to contact up in Hartford.

Frank and I made an appointment with this person, who wanted to know our proposal. Frank made a wonderful presentation, laying out the specifics. I gave him the logistics, the mechanical part of it, since I was on the ground floor, and in detail, spelled out the savings the state would benefit from our program. He said that he would forward our proposal to the next level of management. In government speak, this translated to: "a lot of bullshit people to go through." Now, since I first advanced this program, other people were also thinking about something similar. But with Vinnie monitoring our progress by giving me the best information he could, our program was succeeding.

In the meantime, Frank had a friend who worked up in Hartford for the state, but in a different department. He told Frank for us to hang on and wait until the next administration who would come in after the next election. Then we would have a more friendly reception for our program. I alone put in an entire year to chasing this idea of mine. I spoke to many people who could help us in our endeavor, but there were so many layers of government to go through, it was mind numbing.

Unfortunately the new administration that was voted into office, the one that was supposed to help us, turned out to not be so good. We were informed by Vinnie that another company that already had ties to the state was going to be awarded the contract. Vinnie felt very bad for me, and in one of my last meetings with Vinnie about this subject, he really expressed a great sorrow for us being rejected. While I was feeling awful about this failure, I knew in my heart that sometimes, forces beyond your control can cause things to be taken away from you in an instant. I felt that this loss was almost the same has the snack cake rack proposal I made to a major company, and it too went into the shitter.

GINA

On August 15th, 1996 our last granddaughter was born to David and Lisa. She was a baby girl named Gina. I still remember seeing her for the first time, as I do for all of my grandchildren. It seemed she had a smile on her little, round face. To me it seems rather curious how some memories of certain dates never escape you, especially with my three children, and now with my grandchildren. Such wonderful memories.

David would bring Gina over quite frequently. We played with her in my living room and down in the playroom, where she had more room to roam. I would put her on the rug near the television, and we would watch the T.V. together. What Gina liked most was the stroller. I would take her out in the driveway and give her a little ride around the house. She was always up to being pushed around for a ride, but I did notice one day she seemed kind of listless, and not her usual self. At the time, it seemed normal; I thought she was just tired, and wanted to sleep.

One day, David came over with Gina, and I was holding her sitting in my rocking chair. On this day, Gina's head was slumping over. I thought it was my rocking her too much, but she had this smile on her face, which indicated to me she was not that ready to fall asleep. She was just kind of falling in and out of sleep, but still with that smile on her face.

It was maybe a few days later David informed us that Gina would have to be taken to the hospital. It was a problem with her heart; she was born with a tear in her heart that needed repair. When we got to the hospital, we were informed by David that the surgery was not going well, and they were having some difficulty. This was a bad moment for our family. David had the feeling of maybe he might lose Gina. Lisa's family, Gail, Janet, and the rest of us rallied around David to give him support. It was a very emotional day for all of us, but especially for David and Lisa. I went into the corner of the room and tried to control my emotions but it was no use. I felt angry that the doctors at the time of Gina's birth didn't notice this problem. It is times like this when you feel so helpless and out of the loop. I also had the same feeling when Jaclyn was born. Again, I cursed the doctors, and whoever was in attendance at their births. I felt abandoned by God.

As the hours dragged on, everybody was waiting for some word from the medical staff. Finally, David came out and said Gina was out of surgery and in the recovery room. He said we should all go home and he and Lisa would stay at the hospital and will keep us informed. On the way home, I for one, could not believe that this was happening so fast. One minute you are holding a child and the next moment, you hear she is in the hospital.

Two days later, Gina was placed in a room to recover and we were allowed to see her. On entering the room, the first thing I noticed was that nice big smile. It was the same as Jaclyn's when I visited her the first day. I felt my, these two little girls are two tough little chicks.

After Gina was discharged from the hospital, she was closely watched and monitored by her physician. I kept thinking that maybe her life would be limited. I had a boyhood friend, who had a heart problem and was not allowed to take part in any sports. He would just come out to watch us play, but with me also having an asthma problem, I was also confined most days to being a spectator.

But Gina was not to be denied. She amazed me by her endurance, taking part in a lot of school sports and activities. Gina, following in her sisters footsteps, also played softball and danced. She excelled at dancing and spent three years on the intermediate school team, going on to numerous dance competitions, even going to Disney World for the national championships.

Upon entering high school, Gina applied for the cheerleading squad, and was approved. She was in the same squad as Alyssa, who was then a senior, so they spent a year together on the same team. After her freshman year she switched over to the dance team, where she had great success. When she graduated from Branford High School, she did so with high honors, and as a member of the National Honor Society. After high school, she enrolled at Quinnipiac University where she is currently majoring in communications. No bar is too high for Gina.

To me, Jaclyn and Gina were inspiring with their tenacity to succeed at all costs.

2000—2005 Loyalty and Greed

In the same time frame, but a little bit earlier, I was soon to learn that loyalty was a word some people refused to adhere to. This next story is a story of how mixed loyalty and greed go together. In the midst of building our business, we had some great experiences dealing with distributors who were grateful for the opportunity we were giving them, such as providing them a route, and all they had to supply was a vehicle to suit their business. On the other hand, we had those few bad apples who made life miserable for us. This is one of those stories.

Frank was enthusiastic about securing the services of this person, Pat, who had a lot of route experience, and since we were on a new piece of business, Pat would be the right fit, even with no training at all. At the time Pat had a small route, and he was excited about us wanting to give him some rather large corporate accounts. It would be the opportunity of a lifetime for him, so we set about making the route for Pat.

Pat would be working on a great percentage, and the orders from these accounts were tremendous. These were our accounts since they were secured by us, and by billing them that way they would remain in our possession (Pat would soon learn about that). To serve these accounts, the distributors had to adhere to our pricing of the products. This is the way corporate accounts want to do business; they did not want to be surprised by different pricing.

With the understanding between our company and the distributor, they had to agree to purchase all the products from us, which was more than fair because in the past some customers would complain of a different product than the one we sold them. We gave them some room to purchase outside of our warehouse only in the case that we could not supply the product that day, as it rarely happened, due to us being shorted by our bakeries.

Pat was a very dependable distributor. He was always on time to pick up his order, and his purchases from us were always about the same amount, until one day Frank brought to my attention something strange about Pat's purchases. They were declining, but his billing from the customers was the same (red flag). Frank was getting some complaints about the quality of the rolls from the customers on Pat's route. I went to check out the complaints, and I found that the product that was shown to me was not ours. The bread Pat was giving them didn't have the same texture as the New York bakeries we usually work with.

Unbeknownst to us, Pat was purchasing the bread from some small bakery on his route. Frank made Pat aware of our concerns, and he said he needed some extra product and had to find a way to satisfy his accounts. But we knew he was caught in a lie because what I discovered was that he was serving them for quite some time with this other shit. Frank went to his customers and he saw that not only were they not getting the correct product, but they were also not being charged the correct price. At that moment we knew that was it. A person we had put a lot of stock in was now going to be quickly terminated.

Frank and I knew that we had to quickly end our business relationship with Pat, so we set up our plan to have someone else serve these accounts. So Frank and I split up Pat's accounts: I took one half of his accounts and Frank took the rest. In one day we put this ungrateful piece of shit out of business. We left him with just about no customers to serve, even the ones he had himself. All gone in one day.

He was totally shocked when he called his customers for the next day's orders, and was told that he was replaced. What got Pat was the way we put him out. He did not realize, nor think, we could react so fast. On meeting Pat when he came in the last time to adjust what he owed us, I spoke to him and reminded him of the "Golden Rule", which as the saying goes, "He who has the gold makes the rules."

2005-2016

We started our business with a small shed in the backyard of my brother Frank's yard, and we went on to have no less than five warehouses that we rented. After being in business for about twenty-five years, we finally purchased our own. At that time, I was in a state of semi- retirement, so the warehouse was purchased by Frank Sr., Frank Jr., and David.

During these years the business evolved from retail and wholesale, back to retail, and serving the club store market, getting back into the supermarket business, and having a new program to offer them was in and of itself, an expensive proposition. It involved either supplying the markets with expensive display units or purchasing space in their stores.

Frank Sr. and Frank Jr. secured some major chains, of which we had to supply large display units, which were very costly. The program that was to be displayed was mostly a snack cake program, such as snacks selling for either two for a dollar or three for a dollar; a very high volume product due to the price points.

As usual, a program of this magnitude is met by some pushback from the chain store managers. Most were excited about the program, but you also had the usual suspects who no matter the amount of sales derived from the program, they did not want to give up the space that was needed for the display. They always found fault, bitching about any little infraction the distributor would make.

One such individual down in the Fairfield section, was always complaining about my distributor. I spent a lot of time having to go and see this piece of dirt. The infractions he presented to me were of such a small nature, I really did not know how to answer him. I think he was going through a change of life, and I told the distributor, Scotty, to avoid this asshole as much as you can, and he did.

After some time, when it seemed there was nothing I could do, I had a meeting with his supervisor, and explained our problem to him, and asked him to visit the store and see for himself. The supervisor and I had a nice productive meeting and he told me he would monitor the situation, which he did, and never found any problems with Scotty's service. He also told me to be patient, and he would work it out. Scotty came in to see me one day, and I asked him how everything was going, he said, "Happy days are here, the asshole got fired." I said, "This is the best news I've had in a long time!" The both of us started jumping up and down on the platform, like two little kids, in a school yard, sort of like the scene in *The Wizard of Oz* when the wicked witch is dead.

In this era of managing, there now came the advent of having to deal with female managers. This was all new ground for me, being in the business the better part of fifty years, and only having male managers, who had their own agenda, as far as personalities and favorites. I have to say it was refreshing; the female managers addressed you has a person, and for the most part did not use curse words while addressing you. I had a great rapport with the buyer at a high volume independent chain store that we were serving. He was happy with the service and called me one day for a meeting. The owner of the store wanted to offer us the best spot in the front of the store for a large display unit.

At this time we were doing quite well at this store even with just having a huge table in the back of the store. The buyer said our sales would double, and maybe triple, with having more exposure at the front end of the store. The devil is in the details, and for my part of the deal, I was to supply the store with a large endcap that would wrap around the front aisle. This was a very tempting offer, and my mind was already adding up the potential profits.

The other shoe dropped when the buyer gave me the cost of the offer. The deal was for me to supply the display unit and have to pay for the space it was allocated, which was twenty five hundred dollars a year. After digesting the offer for about two minutes, I said, "I thought Jesse and Frank were dead, and they would be the only ones who would make this deal. With no disrespect, give this offer to Hostess Cake. They are the ones with deep pockets." The buyer said, "They do not have the price points that you have." I shoot back at him, "All the more, you know how much we are working with. The only one who would profit from this deal is your store." Although my mouth was watering just thinking about the amount of sales we could get from that location, I gently declined the offer. Years ago I had served that store, and I knew of its potential, but the numbers did not add up.

Another person who had about five supermarkets, and who recommended me to the owner of the stores, was a family member of a store I was doing business with. Dominick, the owner of the store, said, "Go and see him. He is my brother in law, and he will set you up." This was only too good to be true, and it was, with me signing up five stores all in one day.

The owner of the five stores was expecting my call, as Dominick already made the approach for me. On the way over to his office, all I could think of was which one of my distributors I could give these accounts to. At the meeting with the owner and some of his managers, I laid out all the paperwork, with some of my samples displayed on a rack so they could view them.

Everybody seemed pleased. It was the same program of two for a dollar and three for a dollar. They all said it would be a good fit for their customers, many of whom would embrace this program. After all the managers left the meeting, the owner and I sat down to work out the logistics. I presented him with my plans of distribution. Then the bombshell went off. He said, "I figure the sales in each store should be about five hundred dollars a week. What I want is to give each store the amount of product of one week's sales. My payment plan is that I pay my vendors on a monthly basis." I got up from the table and shook his hand, telling him the offer is great, and I would call him to inform him of our starting date. He was all smiles, and he even walked me down the stairs, telling me, "Hopefully, we can get started soon," patting me on the back, "I will be waiting for your call," he said. I walked to the car, thinking, "This shithead. Figures, either me or everyone he deals with is stupid." That is why I led him on thinking he just reeled in a big dummy. You should have seen his face when I told him how I was enamored and grateful for this offer. He must have got off, licking his chops. I always remember, and still picture him, standing at the bottom of the staircase with me, reminding me to call him. Meanwhile, I could not wait to see Dominick.

The very next day, I went to see Dominick, and I said, "Dom, you will have to sit down for this one." Dom said, "You got the stores?" I responded, "Not in this life, Dom, or in anyone's lifetime. Your brother in law had me confused with some major corporation, and that I had very deep pockets." I explained what transcribed at the meeting. Dom could not believe what I told him. I gave Dom my best wishes and thanked him for his effort. Dom owned one market, and I did business with him for quite some time. His father was just has nice; they went out of their way to please any vendor. It was one way of a small guy helping another small business man. But I could not leave without telling Dom my true feelings and give him all of my respect. Dom did not even think about his brother-in-law even making such a weird offer. I said, "Dom, I am leaving you with these words. I just met the biggest asshole and piece of shit in this business. He is in a class by himself." Dom agreed, and we both laughed our asses off. Dom then tells me, "When I see him, I am going to say how happy you are with the deal, and how you are going to call him, I want to see him squirm with delight with something that is never going to happen. The guy called me several times, and I never returned his calls. I had the office tell him I was busy setting up that program with other stores, and he would have to wait his turn. What a dirt bag.

A mistake we made, and a big one, was giving a member of our family a job helping around the warehouse after he got out of jail. He was a dope addict and in and out of rehab, and now he claimed to be cured and off any substances.

This kid had good marks in school, and to me, he was a very bright student. His parents divorced when he was a young lad, and by his theory, that was one of the reasons he went into drugs. "A bunch of shit," I told him. "Other people had the same problem, or more, and they became very productive with their life. Spare me," I told him.

As a recovering addict, the trust is not automatically there, but my brother Frank felt he was redeemable. To this day, I still do know how the hell we were so stupid, in having shit head work for us. Well it did not take long for nameless to show his appreciation. He started stealing from us. Little things, but still, they added up, and it did not take long before he went on another bender. To catch him in the act, Ronnie, who was working for us at the time, hated him and wanted to catch him, so he spent a whole night in the warehouse, waiting for shithead to come in. He wasn't able to catch him that night, but we did get him soon enough.

We changed the locks on the doors and couldn't wait to see what happened. Well, eventually we did. Since he could not enter with a key, he decided to take his mother's car and use it for a battering ram to break down the door. He used the back of the car to ram down the door, and the rear end of the car was badly damaged and there was paint from the door on the side of the car. After he broke through, he stole the copy machine and other products in the office. It did not take much police work to find out who did it. It was too bad Ronnie was not in the warehouse that night. He had been at the stakeout the night before. Ronnie would have busted him up badly, and I might add, he would have taken great pleasure in doing so.

It is said some people have nine lives, and this guy is one of them. He OD'd twice and recovered. This guy once had an accident with a small plane that he was the pilot of at the time. He crashed it into a house and managed to survive. He had so much promise: a great student, and he wasted it all, by going down the wrong path in life. By his own admission, he told me he had used every kind of drug he could get his hands on, as dope addicts usually do.

Throughout his time as an addict, he knew how to play the system by taking advantage of all the different monetary programs offered by the country. While he was in prison he was still collecting all his checks due him. He certainly knew all the loop holes provided by the government. Substance abuse people will go to any lengths in the pursuit of cash to feed their habit, even stealing from their own families. They lose all sense of decency, become morally corrupt, and bankrupt of any social fear.

Getting on with our business, I was now involved in trying to rebuild what we had after selling out half our business. I, along with David, Frank Jr. and my brother Frank, decided to try and secure the Commissary store on the Sub Base in New London back for us. The manager, Lenny that I knew when I was serving there, was placed in another store. He and I had a good rapport, so when I went back to the store and introduced myself to the new manager, I told him of my prior service to the store and my sales at the time with Lenny. The new manager, whose name was Bill, said he was going to attend a meeting in the next week, and he would be seeing Lenny.

Two weeks later I went back to the store and met with Bill. As it had always been said in this business, you have to have a lot of friends. Lenny told Bill of the great service he received from our company, and Bill was elated to hear that. Now I am sitting there, talking to Bill, and we were discussing what part of the store he could fit us in. As we walked around the store, I pointed out the space I had before, and said my product sold exceptionally well there. The product I had, Bill said, "This product is what my customers want. It is the same as what they bought back home, mostly from down south."

Actually Bill was more excited about our program than I counted on. We now went back to his office, and he gave me the phone number of the head buyer for the store. She had her office in Washington D.C. This would be a new procedure since we were authorized the first time. Then Frank only had to travel a few miles up the road to secure the account.

Now the fun would begin for me: trying to get this person on the phone to talk to me. After several days of calling with no luck, I went back to the store to see Bill. He then tries himself, and no luck. He then calls one of his friends in the same department and explains our problem. The person then puts Bill on hold, and after some time they resumed the conversation, with his friend saying to have me call in the next few days, and she would talk to me.

When I finally got to talk with the buyer, she told me of the store's desire to purchase our product and gave me instructions in which she wanted to see our product and our pricing. So I went and made up a large box to ship the samples in. My friend Dave in the office, who was in charge of all billing, helped me put together a nice package, and Dave printed out all the price lists, making it very professional looking.

After a week went by, and I did not hear from the buyer, so I started to call her. I received the same thing: she was away from her desk and would get back to me. I went back to the store to see Bill and explained my progress. Bill then gives me another number of a person who was her associate. Bill told me to call her early in the morning, which I did. This person gave me the time to call the head buyer, as she was in and out of the office all day. Still no luck, back to the store, this time I met a vendor who was in the same predicament, trying to connect with the buyer, and he told me of a bad scene with her, the buyer.

He told me how she made an appointment with him, and he had to travel all the way to Washington to meet her, which I knew I would have to do. So he travels all the way down there, gets a room at a hotel, which is not the cheaper one he wanted since they were booked.

The next morning, he arises early, so as not to be late for the appointment. He had to bring a suitcase full of his products, and he wheels them all through the early morning traffic, plus carrying a briefcase full of papers. He finally gets to her office building, and now has to find her office. His appointment was for nine o clock, and when he finally finds her office, it was eight thirty.

When she comes to the office shortly after nine, he said he did not like the look on her face. He greets her at the door and waits until she calls him in. All the while, he is getting a little nervous. Her secretary was now going in and out of her office, and then the secretary informs him the buyer will not be able to see him today. She says, "Come back next week, and she will see you at the same time. He was incredulous, "Lady, I come all the way from Connecticut. I am a small business man, this is a hardship for me."

The secretary goes back into the office, comes out and tells the man, "Then the meeting will be canceled, if you do not comply with her wishes." He accepts, and then when he gets home, he gets a call from the buyer's office, stating that the buyer will be out of town and they will call him to reschedule the meeting.

When he told me that story, I went over to Bill and wanted to know what to do. I did not want to travel all that way and come back empty. Bill then tells me, "The buyer is one big son of bitch. She has all this power, and it went to her head. I am ashamed to say it because she is a sister." Meaning that the buyer and Bill are both African American.

Bill was one sweet man, and he spent quite some time on this deal, and now because of, his words, "Nothing worse than giving a big fat bitch a little power," it was miserable for people to get authorized for the store. I told Bill the last time my brother went to the local office, we made our presentation, and we were authorized. Now all this horseshit. Bill said, "It was politics. They brought a lot of the management decisions down to Washington to give jobs to the favorites of the party, and this is what we have to put up with." Bill then walked me to the door, gave me the look of disappointment, and apologized for not being able to help me. We shook hands, and I looked into his eyes, and said, "Bill, I met a lot of nice people in my business, but you are at the top of the list" "Leo," Bill says, "I thank you for the generous comments, and wish you well. Maybe the big one will someday get canned, and I will call you." We exchanged a hearty laugh, and I left.

So while I did not get the store, I continued on to my next target: the Coast Guard Academy, which I also served at one time. I went in on a cold call and introduced myself to the head chef and buyer. I gave him the particulars of our program, and he was very interested since he was having a problem with his present supplier. I made an appointment to make a formal call, and he said he would have the chief buyer at the meeting. I presented all my products and price lists, and they had everyone in the kitchen come over and taste the bread and cakes. The head chef was so elated, he asked me for a startup time, even though we still had to get the paper work through, so I could get paid. He said it was just a formality.

Not trusting him would be my big mistake. I told him that I wanted to make sure I would have everything ready, such as my distributor, and most of all, the products. He then gave me the forms for us to fill out and return them to him, but the chef wanted the products delivered to him in the meantime. So instead of me starting to serve the account out of my car, I opt to put him off for a few days. What a mistake that would be.

As this was happening so fast, the chef said could I come back and see another person, who made all the purchases for the kitchen. The sales person wanted a special grain bread that they could not obtain from their supplier. The day I go back to see them, they were having a cookout for the trainees. I was invited to sit down with them. The spread was fantastic; all top shelf food. I told the chef that I was in the Navy, and I did not eat like this. Jokingly, I said, "Sign me up for twenty!" After we ate, we went into the office, and the bread in question that they had wanted was approved, but our price was not what they wanted to pay. This was a contractor who supplied the food for the mess hall, and the price difference to them was out of line.

Previously when I served the Coast Guard, the purchases were made by the personnel of the Coast Guard, and with them price was no object. That's how the government works.

So if I had put some products in my car and started serving them the very next day, at least I would have gotten my foot in the door. We could have been serving them with limited items, but then I could have worked my way up to eventually securing all the bread products. I should have listened to the head chef, but I thought the account was secured and wanted to make sure everything would be in place, so I played it too cool. Score one for the dummy.

At the time we had starting serving the Wal-Mart stores, which was a difficult account to serve. While you get approval from the main office, you then had to go through the store manager to see if he wanted your program. The store managers could make or break you, and they had the final say. A very good friend of mine was serving the store I was distributing with a bread program and doing one thousand dollars a week; it was good store for him.

He comes in one day and finds that his space was cut in half. He goes to the manager and complains. The manager told him he wanted to put some other product there. My friend Pat, who was by nature not given to any outbursts, started yelling at the manager. I pull him away, and told him to call the office. He wanted to choke the guy, and I should have let him. The manager was a no good bastard, but Pat finally got his space back.

I had a friend of mine, Artie, who had owned a small store, one in which was matter of fact, one of my first accounts when I went in business. He gave me a lot of space in his store to display my cakes. While he was not associated with the bakery section in the Wal-Mart store, he nevertheless helped me obtain a great position for my table, and even on my off days he would fix up the display for me. Artie went out of his way to help me.

Artie had a quite personality, but he was also firm. When I was serving his little store, he and I would spend some time talking, mostly about family and business. He was also interested in how I had started my business at the age of fifty-two, since he too had to make that decision before he bought the store. He realized the difficulty in starting a business, so when I approached Artie to sell my cakes, he was enthusiastic for me to succeed.

As my business started to grow, I turned the distribution over to other people, but I still kept in touch with Artie, stopping in whenever I was in the neighborhood of his store. I enjoyed his company, and Artie always interested in my progress. He was happy for me and my success, and conversely, dejected for any failures.

After some years went by Artie decided to sell the store, and went to work for Wal-Mart, which is where we continued our friendship. That's when it was a nice reminder to not burn any bridges in life because there were a lot of people I was not fond of, but business is business.

After some time I got on with other programs and did not get to see Artie much. He stayed with Wal-Mart for a while until one day in another supermarket, I ran into Artie. He told me how he left Wal-Mart and was now working for a soda company. He was actually working for another friend of mine, Mike, with whose father I worked with at Seal Test Dairy. (It really is a small world.) Mike and Artie had a close relationship; they were more like friends, both great guys, and not at all like boss and worker. Mike also came from a career in grocery retailing, being manager of a supermarket, and they made a great team.

In the warm months, mostly on a Sunday morning, I would run into Artie sitting on a park bench waiting for Mike when they would go out for breakfast together. At this time Artie was not married since his wife had passed away, and Mike was not married, so they would get together for breakfast. Artie and I would cross paths from time to time on the road, but as we got older our conversations were about health. I was going through some problems with my prostate, which Artie was also experiencing, but on a lesser scale. We'd also talk about other health related problems that we might have, and although he was living in town with me, I could never get together and spend some time with Artie. He was a pleasure to talk to.

As the problem worsened with my prostate, I continued to update

Artie. He was now interested, but he did not like the details of having to go through any tests. The tests are very uncomfortable, even painful, and I had them done twice. To me, it was something out of the middle ages. It felt like the urologist who administered my two tests must have forgotten the damn anesthesia. Artie was not a big fan of having any intrusive tests, similar to most of us, but he actually was adamant about not going through any of the tests that I mentioned.

When I finally had no recourse but to have the surgery due to insufficient empting of my bladder, it was quite some time before I saw Artie again. I believe maybe three months had passed since my surgery before I met Artie on a Sunday morning while he was waiting for his friend Mike for breakfast. I sat down on the bench with him, and at first we just talked a little about business, then he asked me how I was doing. I related to Artie my experience of having surgery. Now he was really interested. He wanted some details, knowing his fright of this surgery, and he knew of mine, I explained to Artie that everything went well with the surgery. I told Artie what the operation consisted of, and how they place a catheter in you and leave it there for a day or so, and then on the day of discharge, they get you up and have you urinate on your own. My problem was that due to an enlarged bladder, I was not able to urinate properly. The hospital will not discharge you if you cannot urinate on your own, so with me they went and reinserted the lousy catheter in me so I could get home. That was the only part that was painful, along with the usual discomfort of any surgery. When the nurse placed the catheter back, it felt like a knife being place inside of me. They furnished me with catheters so I can manually remove my urine. That next morning as I was getting set to place the catheters inside me, it was an act of god, and I urinated on my own. Now as I was telling Artie this story, he was getting all jumpy, and he was adamant more than ever about not having that surgery, or any other intrusive surgery.

I told Artie I had no choice but to have the surgery. Yes, the after effects were painful because of my bladder problem, but other than that, I would have nothing to complain about. But with Artie, anything that had to do with the prostate was off limits. Artie never told me the extent of his problem with the prostate, but he must have been told that he was a good candidate for surgery. Also, he did not say if he had any tests for prostate cancer, which I did, and mine were negative. That test was tolerable, if a little uncomfortable, but worth it, for having peace of mind. He must not have had it because of his reluctance to experience anything with the prostate. About some time later I was wondering why I was not seen Artie on a Sunday morning. I felt maybe I was just missing him, and they changed their routine. Not so. As I was one day reading the obituaries, I saw Artie's name, and it was quite a shock.

Artie passed away from cancer of the prostate.

BACHMANN'S POTATO CHIPS

As the business was changing, Frank and David took on a whole new business: they purchased a distributorship of Bachmann's potato chips. To me was a good move but also, a challenging one. The business came with the addition of fifteen new drivers, and could add to our sales of baked products. I now had to educate myself in something altogether different.

My job was now a little more interesting. I had to mix potato chips and snack cakes. What bothered me the most about the chip business, was that the product being placed on shelves, for the most part, were out of my reach. This program and the product was totally different from what I did for so many years. Working with baked products were easy because they were always placed on a low level. Potato chips, on the other hand, are quite large, and they are placed on a higher level. For me to address fixing up the shelf, I had to go in the back room of stores and get a milk crate to stand on.

With the new business, came a person who was hired to administer the sales of the chips business. I worked well with him, since I worked alongside of him when he was running a potato chip route. He was very astute as a sales person, and it was a pleasure interacting with him on all the programs. I now had a new line to sell, which gave me some added power in making a presentation to a new customer, since I was able to supply them with a great variety.

Although the area of distribution of the chips was confined, since there were other distributors in the state, there was still enough room to sell to. The downside of the chip business is the elephant in the room, namely, Frito Lay, who commanded the greatest space in all the stores.

In going out trying to secure new business for the chips, there was not much I could do in the way of securing supermarket's space since that had to be done from the office of Bachmann's. I did have some success with the smaller stores, in which the major suppliers did not want to serve. Some were excellent, and one in particular gave me one half of the space allocated for potato chips because I told them you can also have a different snack cake line, so it was a nice package for them.

With the addition of the chips, we were now able to add these to our regular drivers' sales if they wanted them. Some of our drivers took on the chip line and are doing quite well with them. I did have an experience with a rather large account, something on the level of the Coast Guard, another goose chase. I got a tip that the UConn Campus store up in Hartford was going to make a change. I visited the store and saw the potential of some great sales between the cake program, and the chip program. I secured the name of the buyer and made an appointment. As the day of the appointment drew near, I received bad news: a call from the secretary said we would have to postpone my sales call until a later date.

When we did get around to resuming our discussion, it was with a new person, one who did not know shit about what the hell I was talking about. He was the head of some department, a real yo-yo. I brought all my samples of the chips and cakes, and I placed them all nicely on a table along with my price list. When he saw them, he wanted to know what they were, so I murmured to myself, "Oh shit, why me?" After some time I saw nothing was getting through to him and he then tells me to leave everything and he will look at it and call me soon. In other words, thanks, but no thanks. Nothing worse than to have to speak to someone who has no knowledge of a presentation.

After Frank Jr. and David had this business for some two years, another company buys out the distributorship of Bachman's chips. Frank told me that they did not really make much profit by having the chip business and so another venture came and went. We did put a lot into to make it work, but one thing came out of it: Frank and David kept on as an employee, the wife of the man that they bought the chip business from, Debbie, who is a wonderful addition to our company.

REFLECTIONS ON MY MOTHER AND FATHER

MOM Taking Care of Mom

This is of my mother of whom I am forever grateful.

The many times that I came home either from school, or later on from work, somehow never thinking, that Mom had a bad day, even though she did indeed have them but she never ever complained. I guess her thoughts were that all her problems were minute to yours. If it was after school, a little snack was available, and after work, it was a nice meal, as best she could prepare it.

My mother felt her problems were hers and not yours so she didn't feel the need to express them to anyone. She was being badgered on both sides with a difficult brother-in-law, and some of his sisters, my aunts. I say some of them, not all of them, since she did have a great rapport with a few of them.

Many times I came home from school to see her sitting in her rocking chair at the window, looking out at the street below, people walking, and the factory across the street, and actually identifying the workers coming and going from the factory.

As soon I entered the room, Mom would arise, and if I had some place to go after school, Mom would admonish me to be sure to be home by five o'clock for dinner. It would be the same for the rest of my siblings. We never asked what we were going to eat since the menu was the same every day, but sometimes she would mix it up a bit. After my brother Frank entered grade school, she was now left to herself. It was a great part of the day since it was the little time of solace she truly enjoyed after bearing seven children. To think about it now, the respite must have been welcomed. After she did her house cleaning, which took her well into the noon hour, some of us would come home for lunch, and then she'd have time to rest a while until we came home from school. After we came and went, Mom would get ready to start the evening meal.

During Mom's transition from our home on Greene St. to a rent on upper State St., I was employed as a milk man. At the time I was living on Fulton St. where I had an apartment in my in-laws home. Teresa's mother and father gave us that opportunity since we had to be relocated due to the redevelopment program in New Haven, which also caused my mother to have to do the same thing.

Living with my mother at this time was my sister, Betty, and my brothers, Frank and Ralph. My sister, Vera, had married earlier and had her own apartment in the city. I would visit my mother as often as possible, yet my hours on my milk route did not leave me much opportunity to do so, but as I often thought about what my mother did for me, I made every effort to visit her. Knowing that my brothers and sister were away at work, and Mom would be home alone, I would stop off on my way home from the dairy to spend some time and chat about any problems she was having.

Mom would always ask me to bring my daughter Gail; she so adored her. Once when I had some errands to do in the neighborhood, I left Gail with Mom for a little while, and as grandmothers are wanton to do, smother them with food and love. When I returned, Gail and Mom were sitting on the porch with the neighbor next door. Gail had spotted my car coming down the street and started to jump up and down on the porch. Mom said, "Leo, you were only gone for a short while. Leave her here, and come back later."

I believe you do not fully understand this love of a grandparent until you are one yourself. Living in a rent did not sit well with Mom since she was so used to having the freedom of doing what she wanted. She now had to adapt to being a renter and of being confined until her siblings came home, so my visits played a great role in filling in that void. She and I would revisit our lives on Greene St., but I always steered away from any bad memories she had encountered, and I knew, and Mom knew, some subjects we kept away from.

During this time Mom was starting to have some health problems. Nothing serious, but enough to give her thought about her mortality. My sister, Vera, attended to her doctor appointments and took care of that aspect of her life, which in and of itself was a blessing for the rest of us, as Frank, Betty, Ralph and I had commitments to our jobs.

One of the funniest moments for me, came when Mom had to visit a dentist. She was in need for some serious dental work due to neglect and/or ignorance of paying attention to her teeth. Vera and I took Mom to a specialist, who dealt with patients that were difficult, since Mom was deathly afraid of even hearing about a dentist. It came from her generation, out of fear and ignorance.

The day of Mom's visit I had to bring Gail with me because my wife had something to do with her mother, so the four of us went to the dentist's office. I parked the car right in front of the office just so that we could get easily in and out. Gail was very young at the time and she, like a lot of children, wanted to roam around, so we decided that Gail and I would stay outside, and sit in the car. Vera and Mom entered the office, but as they were entering the office, Vera turned around to me and made the sign of the cross. How that was going to play out, we quickly found out.

After about one half hour, I seen Mom come running out of the office with the cover sheet attached to her neck. Running after her, came the dentist and the nurse, then following Mom was Vera, all of them trying to stop her. Gail was in the car, laughing hysterically, at the sight unfolding in front of us. I could not give chase and leave Gail alone, so Mom ran free from the dentist. Later Vera explained to me that the dentist gave Mom an injection and left the room for a few seconds. He turned around, and Mom was already out of the office. It was certainly a sight to see- Mom with the sheet strapped to her and three people chasing after her.

Here was woman who gave birth to seven children, all born at home, and some delivered by a mid-wife, with no medication to alleviate any pain, and yet she was reluctant to go to a dentist. How many times I reminded her of that fact. I brought up the experience to Mom when she was giving birth to my brother Frank, and reminded her how she sat up in a rocking chair that evening, having labor pains, and the next morning, Frank was born. Vera and I had to sit outside while Doctor Conte was administering the birth.

Mom scoffed at the comparison, saying, "O' dentista bruta," and yet she encouraged me to have to go the dentist in school whenever they had the dental program, which was offered to families at that time who did not have the means to afford dental care.

As Mom expressed her desire to see if we could find her better living arrangements, I had to tell her that maybe something would come up. She still wanted to move even though her sister-in-law was moving next door and would have my cousins as neighbors. She was always telling me, "Addo mie portat," translation, "Where did you bring me?" Mom had Betty and Ralph home with her; Frank was in the army at this time.

At the time Vera was living in a third floor cold water flat, and she considered the idea of maybe buying a two family house to have Mom on one floor and her on another. Vera talked it over with her husband, and they said they wanted to do this. We had the money from the house on Greene St. and thought it would be a good investment. We found a house in the Fair Haven Heights; it was ideal. Mom would be located in the front of the house and Vera in the back part, but both of the floors would be on a first floor level.

Before we moved, we had to have a wedding, as Ralph decided to get married. It seemed everything was happening at once. For me purchasing this home would be a blessing, as at this time Vera was a stay-at-home Mom and was in the process of starting a family. To have this house, with a lot attached to it, would be good for the children. All of this meant that I would not have to worry about Mom, as Vera would be home during the day and Betty would be home at night. The physicality of taking care of Mom's needs would be met. She would be in good hands as far as her finances were concerned since us boys could take care of that end and make sure she has the means to take care of herself.

Mom was having her little health problems and had to be in the hospital from time to time. At one time we had to put her in a convalescent home, which every time I would visit, the first thing she would say, "e wio a casa," translation: "I want to go home." The problems Mom was having caused her to be put on some medication that reduced the fluids in her body, which caused her to lose a lot of weight, making her almost skeletal in appearance.

At the time of Mom's problems, I was going to a fine doctor, Dr. Barile. He had a way of speaking to the elderly Italian people and conversing with them in their dialect that even Mom felt at ease with Dr. Barile. It was he who had detected that Mom had a mini-stroke when she was a young child which caused Mom's left eye to always droop slightly. The whole time we had thought it was normal. Also, her skin color was on the yellowish side, which was a sign of kidney problems to come, and they did.

At one time Mom's kidneys were really causing a problem, and she had to be taken to a hospital to have them flushed out. In the ensuing procedure, she lapsed into a coma, which was to last several days. Mom recovered and was sent to a convalescent home, where she was to spend the next four weeks.

Over the next year or so, Mom was battling all these ailments which made it tough for my sisters, Vera and Betty, with Vera having to take care of her young family, and transporting Mom to her doctor appointments. Vera did not have a car, so whenever I could I would take them. At this time Mom was becoming quite a burden to take care of.

At this period of time, my bakery route was located in the vicinity of Mom's house, so I was able to stop there and offer whatever help I could, which mostly meant I tried to keep up her spirits. I would stop in and see Mom at least twice a week, and to bring my children, Gail, Janet and David as often as possible. That always picked up her spirits. Mom was not a demanding person; she accepted whatever time we could give her. With Betty at work and Vera tending to her own family, Mom would be alone a lot, but she always had Vera in the next apartment, just in case she was in need of anything.

On my visits with Mom, I would check around the house to make sure everything was in working order, and we would sit and talk, mostly about her past life, and how happy she was in spite of her health problems. Mom also had a hearing problem, sometimes she would not hear me knocking on the door, so I obtained a key from Vera and would let myself into the house.

It was on one of my visits that I came into the house, and Mom was sitting by the window and not by the T.V. set. Quite strange, I thought to myself, Mom was in a very pensive stare, just sitting and looking out the window. There was a slight breeze coming through, and the lace curtains were flapping around her hair, almost angelic-like. That she did not rise when I came into the room, surprised me.

Mom looked at me and not saying a word, motioned me with her arms outstretched to come and sit down near her. I pulled up a chair, and did not speak to her, I wanted to let Mom have her Moment. I knew she was in a reflective mood, and I did not want to intrude on her thoughts. We sat there for some time.

As we sat there, my thoughts were floating back to Greene St. and in almost the same situation, it was Mom who was sitting next to me, when I was a young boy and very sick, it was mother and son bonding together, with no words spoken, and yet we were saying quite a bit to each other.

As Mom turned around to me, she now had the sun shining on her white hair, her face slightly covered by the lace curtain, but I could see the strain her health problems put on her. A face that used to be so round, now was just a hollowed out shell, and when she did speak, it always was about Gail, Janet and David; her face would light up at any news of their well-being.

Despite going against Italian traditions, my Mom never made an issue with my children's names. It was the custom in the Italian families to name the children after the family members, but Mom accepted my selection of naming my children whatever names I wanted. Yet,

Mom could never get Gail's and Janet's names correctly. She had a hard time pronouncing them; Gail was always "Gailie", and Janet, was always "Jan-nit".

As I was getting ready to leave, Mom did not get up, but she held out her arms, and we embraced. As she slowly let our arms slip away from each other, Mom gave her blessing to my wife and children, as she did every time we met. It was Mom's motto to take care of your family. As I stood near the door, looking at Mom, I thought of how brave she was in not mentioning her health problems.

On the way home, I had Mom on my mind. I thought about Mom going through her various health problems, and how my sisters had the responsibility of taking care of her physical needs. Vera made sure Mom was keeping up with her meds, which was a tough thing to do. She had to battle the old world habits of a person who was suspicious of anything and everything, especially when it came to adhering to the advice of doctors. Betty had the task of keeping Mom has comfortable as possible.

One day which was a very memorable day for me, I had brought my daughter Janet with me to visit Mom, as Gail was in school, and David was only about one or two years of age. I told Teresa that I was taking Janet with me, so it would give Teresa some time to do what she wanted. On arrival at Mom's house, Mom was standing near the window, and upon seeing Janet, Mom opened the door and started to embrace Janet as if she was a visiting queen.

Janet had a startled look on her face because at this time Mom's facial features had the mask of sickness, but what made me proud of Janet was that she never backed away from Mom, but instead embraced her. Vera came from her apartment and said she was going to make some coffee to go with the cake she had made.

Janet takes off her coat, and to the surprise of Mom and Vera, goes over to the table, and starts to help set the table without being asked. We were standing and looking at Janet, the look of amazement on the faces of Vera and Mom was priceless, not to mention her father's.

Mom was now being admitted more often to the hospital. She was now having kidney failure, along with liver problems, which would eventually take its toll on what strength she had left. Her last admittance in the hospital was one in which she would not recover from. Mom would have an extended stay, this one last time.

To visit Mom, I would have to go straight from work about three times a week and also go on weekends. I went from work so that my family did not have to wait for me to have dinner, and I would grab a fast meal on the road then head to the hospital. My visits would last about one hour, some times more, depending on who was also coming to see Mom. Previous to being admitted this last time, Mom had a bad attack at home. Vera called me and said, "Leo, come on over. Mom is in some state of shock, and she is calling for an ambulance."

I arrived at the house just has the ambulance pulled in. Vera and Betty were also very upset and as I started to go upstairs to Mom's bedroom, all I could see was a lot of blood on the walls in the hallway leading to the bathroom. I knew this had to be a very serious situation. Mom was passing blood, and Vera and Betty tried to get Mom to the bathroom, but were not successful.

This time Mom's internal problems could not be repaired, even by any surgical intervention, and so on my visits I could see Mom's condition deteriorating. Sometimes the end of life is not pretty. Mom was having a hard time and it showed, in spite of her courage to stay strong. As much as I always steered the conversation towards my children, of which Mom was always interested, I sometimes made up a story, being as I ran out of things that we had already talked about.

On my last visit with Mom, one that is imbedded in my mind and soul, Mom asked me to sit closer to her bed. She then told me to hold her hand. We sat there holding hands for a while, and then Mom made me promise her that I would always be good to my family. I joked to Mom, "I promise to not go home and beat them."

Mom and I reminisced about some of the good times, and some of our problems that were not so good. The subject that I wanted to broach, which was I guess on both of our minds, but one that was left unsaid, due to the severity of it. Mom knew that I knew, and we appreciated and respected each other's feelings on it. I could see that on this night Mom wanted to stay away from any hurt feelings that she had to endure. For me to come right out and really let out all my anger to Mom for not confiding in me at the moment of injustice, this I could plainly see, would be wrong of me.

Holding Mom's hands I thought to myself, these are the hands that consoled me in my hours of greatest pains, and also the hands that saved my life. In discussing that sorrowful night of my asthma attack, Mom put it back on me, saying, "ha fatto buon," translation, "You did good." I had Mom laughing reminding her of the nicknames for Ralph and I, that I was referred to as, "O piccerillo, Ralph as O gruosso, translation, " little one-big one," and one of Mom's sayings, "Jiame Chine," translation "Let's go," which she would say whenever she wanted to change the subject. When I used to say the words in Italian, "Chi Da Morte," translation "the dead one" she would go off on me and chastise me for cursing. I never understood the full meaning of the words, and Mom felt we should not be talking of the dead.

Looking at Mom in bed, she was so frail, and her grip on me was starting to loosen, but that determination in her eyes was as strong as ever, Mom patted my head, and drew me closer to her face and cupped my face in her hands. She again thanked me for me a good son to her. Mom cherished all her children, much to my dismay, due to the ongoing problems I had with my sister, Mary, and I sometimes would get frustrated with Mom for not being able to rein Mary in. I finally knew what Mom meant when she said all her children were equal by an Italian story on the subject. In the story, when a boy asked his mother the same question, regarding the boys problems with his siblings, the mother held up her hand and said look at my hand, "I have five fingers, all of them are different, and yet they all work together."

As Mom was embracing me, I felt she did not want to let go. She had tears streaming down her face, but the tears were not of pain but of sheer joy of just holding me. It was now time for me to depart. I told Mom I will try to get to the hospital a little early the next day and spend more time with her, but Mom did not answer. I stood at the edge of the bed, and we just exchanged eye contact. Mom put her hand up to her lips, and in a feeble way blew me a kiss.

Early the next morning I got a phone call, one that I somehow knew was coming. It was from the hospital, telling me that Mom had passed away. They wanted some members of the family to come and identify the body. I believe I went with my brothers, but I do not remember which of us went. When we got there, Mom was in another room all by herself, very barren I thought, it was really just a holding room. The orderly lifted up the sheet, and there was Mom, her eyes were closed, but her mouth was open. We were looking at the mask of death.

The cause of death was listed as, "cirrhosis of the liver". The doctor asked us about how much my mother drank since her liver was that deteriorated. We all looked at one another, explaining she never even had a glass of wine. It was later brought out that she was sick when she was a little girl and had the fever and a mini-stroke, which gave her the droopy eye look.

Mom was seventy three years of age, and the year of her death was October 28th, 1970. Now my family and I had to prepare for Mom's funeral. It was held at the same funeral home where my father was laid to rest. The director of the home was a family friend who treated us extremely well.

At the wake, I was very surprised that all the drivers that I worked with, even the people who worked in the bakery, attended. The bakery people gave a nice card, along with a nice donation from all the workers. I was overwhelmed by the generosity of everyone, even the office staff and all the top officials of the company.

AFTER MOM'S PASSING

After the funeral, a bunch of the guys I worked with came over to my house, to pay their respects. Naturally with the drinks I offered, it did not take long for the talk to turn to all the good times we had. The one story that always got everyone's attention was of Bernice the waitress. She had a vendetta against the owner of the restaurant she worked for. She wanted more pay, and he would not give it to her.

So about six or eight of us would stop in every morning and have some breakfast. The guys would order everything under the sun, such as ham and eggs, steak and eggs, etc. Bernice would charge us only two dollars for the whole bill, while the owner of the restaurant would be slaving on the stove. This place was a very busy restaurant, and very popular, since it was on a one-way street and had easy parking.

On this day that I was referencing, a man came up to the owner while he was cooking, and said he only had a fifty dollar bill, and could he accept it. On this day, every seat in the restaurant was taken, a real busy day, so the owner takes the fifty dollar bill up to the cash register and continues talking to the customer. At the same time he is reaching into the cash drawer to look for the money to cash the fifty, he puts his hand into the drawer and does not find any money; the drawer is wiped clean.

The owner looks at Bernice, "Where the shit is all the money?" Bernice yells back at the owner, "I put the money in the drawer. I do not know what the hell happened to it!" The owner yells back to Bernice, "You fat son of a bitch, I want my money!" Bernice answers, "Are you calling me a crook, you Greek bastard?" Now the owner picks up a knife and waves it at Bernice, yelling, "Give me my money, you slob!" Bernice did not even flinch saying, "How dare you accuse me of stealing, I will have you arrested for slander."

Bernice, we all agreed, was the coolest thief we ever saw. Here she is getting caught red handed, and turns around and calls out the owner for calling her a thief. I mean she did not even leave dust in the register, she took everything. The day Bernice cleaned out the register was her last day. The owner was still waving the knife and chasing Bernice out the door.

When WWII ended, and the factories turning to peace time goods, my sister Mary, came up with the suggestion of getting Mom, a semi-automatic washing machine, which consisted of a rotating tub with a wringer placed on top of it. Mary felt that by getting this type of machine instead of a completely automatic one, it would be an easier transition for Mom. The procedure was after the clothes were washed in the machine, Mom had then to take the clothes from the tub of the machine and run them through the wringer. The washer had some dials on it for operational use, as when the machine changed cycles, the machine would stop and then Mom had to go to the position, and when the wash was done, she would pick up the clothes from the machine, and run them through the wringer. No more washing all the clothes by hand. It was simple, but yet for Mom, change came hard.

To Mom, it was like asking her to learn how to fly an airplane. Every wash day it was the same story. Mom would look at the machine, baffled by the numbers in front of her, and call out to one of us for help. She was fine with turning on the machine, but having to change the settings gave her agita. Time took care of that problem. Finally, when the family had to move into new quarters, a new washer was purchased, and Vera and Betty took over the duties of doing the laundry.

As I am writing this story, I am looking at myself, using a computer keyboard hooked up to a screen for the explicit purpose of writing and not venturing into any computer programs, and not even retrieving my e-mails. So Mom, if you are watching, change is also hard for me. The apple does not fall far from the tree.

I think back often of how my mother felt about seeing her grandchildren. I know Mom, along with my mother-in-law Anna, would devour them, judging from the way Mom embraced Gail when she was a baby. No matter how many times I visited Mom with Gail, the expression on her face belied the loneness in her heart. Later on with Janet and David it was the same, and the thought of seeing her grandchildren, it would surely be happiness unsurpassed.

POP

How does one begin to sum up the life of a loved one from my memories of a great family man and a wonderful husband to his wife? The devotion to his family and his children's welfare drove his need to provide for them under some of the most excruciating times in our history. In doing so, he instilled in his children the core values of a strong family life. What was imposed on me by my father was to have a strong character in spite of any obstacles that life throws at you. I especially learned that lesson from him by the way he conducted his life in the face of adversity. There were almost three years where he did not have a job and yet he was always doing whatever he had to do to keep his family intact, which was no small feat without a life line from the government.

Much to his dismay, he succumbed to accepting whatever help his single older brother supplied, but with a price, one that plagued him for the rest of his life. His brother never letting him forget the tribute. What my father imparted on me was that lesson, "prepare yourself for life, whatever you receive you will owe" and as he once told me, "some bills never seem to get paid," in reference to his brother.

And eventually I found myself in the same situation when I had to borrow some money from a family member to make the down payment on my house. The loan came with the caveat that along with repaying the loan, they expected servitude. Although it was not expressed that way verbally, I could feel it through requests for service. From the moment I received the money, my first priority was to repay the loan quickly.

How I remember going with my father on Saturdays to the farmer's market to see what he could bargain for. We mainly accepted produce that had a short expiration date, but was very edible. Also on the weekends we went to the back of the furniture stores to collect the wood crates that we used for fire wood.

The great depression left an indelible scar on my father. Being out of work for three years and being forced to scavenge for the necessities of life allowed for him to harbor a penchant for frugality. When he was finally able to return to work, saving money was his bible. This led to many disagreements between Mom and Pop. In my teen years, I knew what my father went through, but I still did not comprehend his frugality, as young people soon forget. At the time I did not have the responsibility of family, and could not completely understand how going through a tough time, and how the bitterness of the great depression never left him.

The outstanding thing I remember about my father, is how he assimilated into the English language while still keeping his roots in the Italian language. In our house that was a necessity, as Mom spoke no English. The many compliments I received from my friends and associates upon meeting my father was that his English was flawless, and he could hold a conversation on any subject; he had such a clear understanding of the times we were in.

In my father's generation, and continuing into my generation, the man was supposed to be the sole provider for his family. When this cycle was disturbed during the depression, it left a devastating effect on most men of not being able to provide. It was not easy for them, and certainly my father. As a young boy sitting with him on the porch for many hours, he had a look of hopelessness on his face, but he still would give me the impression when he would wrap his arms around me that everything would be all right. Those moments with my father never left me, and they carried me through life with the knowledge that you cannot depend on other people to define your life for you.

Mom, I fervently hope you and Pop will look at the story of our family and my recollections of our lives with approval.

LAST MEMORIES OF POP

One of my last memories of my father was before we moved from Hamilton St. I saw him walking home from work, down my street, like a man bent over from the labor of working all day in the factory. How I had seen him so many times coming home on Greene St. but this time a lot more slowly, as if his steps were measured, and they were.

This passage on my father was started on 12-2-16 and completed on 12-4-16, exactly sixty years after the death of my father. I wanted to finish this piece on the fourth of December as it holds a lot of significance. He was a man of character and a father who helped shape the lives of his children. My brother Frank, Ralph and I reminisce about him often, so much so that Frank, had a picture of my father, which was encased in an oval frame, reproduced and gave us all a copy of it. The picture was taken of my father when he was in his late twenties. The reproductions were so great that they all look like the original.

Leading up to my father's death, I was living in an apartment on the second floor of my in-laws house. Pop called me and asked me to come over. Upon arriving, Pop asked me to go up into the attic and get something for him. He said his legs were hurting and climbing stairs were painful for him. That I knew, from the slow gait he had, but I attributed it to his advancing years.

My conversation with him at that day was about him being overly tired. Climbing stairs was now a drudgery for him. We discussed for him to see a doctor, but as usual, his answer was, "What the hell can they do for me? It's my legs and old age." Typical of my father's generation, who had a great distrust for the medical profession. I knew this from watching him go to the drugstore and have the druggist mix him something for whatever ailment he had.

On the night of December 4, 1956, we had just finished eating our evening meal, and I was holding Gail and keeping her amused while Teresa was doing the dishes. The phone rings, not in our apartment, but in a hallway leading to the downstairs apartment. My in-laws granted us the use of their phone so that we can save money on a separate phone.

The call came in about seven in the evening from my family, informing me that Pop had passed away. It was a shocker, but under the circumstances, with all the knowledge of his impending health problems, no action was taken due to resistance from him. Pop's ailments today would be red flagged, as they were classic symptoms of heart problems.

Pop died doing what he usually did every evening after work: stopping at his friend's bakery to pick up the Italian bread for the evening meal. They would sit down and discuss the day's events and also maybe have a glass of wine.

On this evening, the owner of the bakery tells my father to stay a while. The owner had to go upstairs and said he would be right down. He had living quarters right over the store. When the owner came down, he found my father slightly slumped over the table, as if resting his head. He walks right by him, talking to my father, with my father not responding. The baker turns around, goes over to my father and shakes him but no response. He immediately calls the police and an ambulance. My father was dead from a massive heart attack, something that was brewing for a while, as all his arteries were blocked.

I was informed of my father's passing by my uncle Leo. It was a very cold call, with no lead in to the cause of death, just, "Your father is dead," then a moment of silence. Then my response, "Where is my father now?" Uncle Leo, exclaiming, "He is at St. Raphael's hospital. Come by the house and pick me up so we can go together."

Entering the E.R. we were directed to a holding room, and my uncle went in first, and then motioned to me to come and view my father. I looked into the room, and seen a body with a white sheet covering it, so I did not advance any further.

The hospital gave me all his clothes and personal stuff. That he was carrying seven hundred dollars in cash, quite a sum, and that no one took advantage of the money and kept it, was amazing. Then I realized why he did not come up to my apartment that day. I lived on the third floor and Pop was having heart trouble so he could not walk up a flight of stairs. If he ever went to a doctor to find out why he was so tired, he would have known his arteries were totally blocked.

Walking to my car with my uncle talking to me, I was in a state of disbelief, and I did not hear a word he was saying. I looked at the son of a bitch, thinking it should have been him, the brother who gave him so much grief is alive and here I am walking with him.

I am grateful pop got to see my daughter, his granddaughter, before he passed away. I could still remember the huge smile on his face, the last time he held Gail in his arms, how proud he was. It was a moment that should have been recorded.

The Amity Club

As a young Italian American growing up in New Haven, CT during the 1940' and 1950's, there were many clubs available to me that dealt with the various regions of Italy. These clubs were set up to help their "paesani's". These were people from the same towns or areas in Italy. In the 1930's membership to clubs with national affiliations were composed of native born Americans. These clubs made it difficult for Italian

Americans to join.

Italian professionals had access to these clubs but acceptance was minimal. A leading architect in New Haven, CT, Mr. Frank Rubino, arranged for a group of civic minded Italian American professional people to form their own service club. The Amity Club was founded in 1936 to promote charitable, intellectual and civic pursuits. In 1991 I joined the Amity Club of New Haven. My brother Frank was a member and introduced me to the club. As a proud member I have witnessed many philanthropic awards to education, scholarships and worthy projects. Attending the meetings and social events gives me great pleasure and a feeling of brotherhood amongst the members.

ACKNOWLEDGEMENTS

First and foremost, I'd like to thank my brother Frank for the many hours that he spent helping me with this project. We researched our family history, going back to the origins of our family in Italy and spent countless hours at the city hall of records in the towns of our parents' birth, actually going back three centuries. It gave us a true insight into the lives of our parents, grandparents, great grandparents and beyond. This helped me tremendously in my preparations for this book, to give my family a history of their parents and grandparents, a bible on which to share with their siblings.

To my wife Teresa for her understanding of my many absences from home and patience of accepting the many hours I devoted to this project.

To my granddaughter, Kara Barrett, who injected me with the passion to complete this work after I had stalled out due to some personal complications that I encountered early on. Kara, in her wisdom, helped me to bypass my stumbling block. Sometimes unlocking life's doors brings one to areas they are not prepared to address. Kara gave me some suggestions as to the format of the story and led me back to a place where I could write without any repercussions from my memory.

When I had written for quite some time and was nearing completion, I contacted Kara, asking if she could help me put the book together and start the machinations of editing this book. Kara said, "No problem,

Grandpa. I have Dan here, and he is also interested in writing." So a collaboration was born and the work was emailed to Dan and Kara. I might add they helped during a very busy period in their lives with the purchase of a new home and a myriad of chores to complete. Kara would read the transcripts and give me her input on the storyline and gave me great guidance to which I am profoundly appreciative of.

This project for me was a great under taking but with the stewardship of Kara and Dan, putting together this assemblage of writing softened the pain. Seeing all my work come back from Kara in print made me so proud of my granddaughter, Kara, that she would put aside her life to help her grandfather.

And to a most valuable person, Mr. Dan Barrett, my granddaughter Kara's husband, who so graciously granted me his time in helping to undertake this project by being my co-writer. With Dan being an English teacher and a writer in his own right, we were able to co-mingle with Dan taking my words and putting them in a book form. Also to Dan for his ever generous praise for me, saying that he had only to do some minor adjustments in my story. True or not, but they were words of encouragement, to which I am deeply humbled.

Kara and Dan who were with me from the beginning. The countless hours of meetings, which I know was a stretch for them due to the distance between our homes. All the electronics in the world does not replace a face to face meeting. A debt of gratitude to Kara and Dan.

As Kara and Dan are preparing for the birth of their first child in November, Janet and Gina stepped in to help out. I am very grateful to have so much support!

To Janet, who in the midst of a full time job and busy life, wanted to get involved and help see the book to completion. Janet and I spent untold amount of hours together revising and moving parts of the book around. These revisions would be emailed to Kara for a final review. Janet asked Gina to give her a hand. I greatly appreciate this group effort in supporting my book. Thank you Janet.

To Gina who gave me as much time as she could spare which added up to quite some time while holding down a job and getting ready for her last year at college. Sitting next to Gina as she was typing, I was so proud just being her grandfather at the way she went about revising most of my work and giving me input. She had fresh ideas on how to re work the story. Thank you, Gina.

To the gang down at K&G Graphics, led by, Romi Kaminskas Jr. & Roger Guay, who gave freely of their time and expertise in how to present my photos for the book and to take time away from their work to attend to me was and is greatly appreciated. Thank you to this great company.

To my children, Gail, Janet, and David. Their dedication to my life is the catalyst of this great desire of mine to leave something for them, a written history of my life, with all the good and bad deeds of my life.

To also include the offspring of my children, my grandchildren. It was with them in mind that I started this journey to give them a pictorial history of their grandparents, great grandparents, and great-great grandparents. It was with the blessing of my grandchildren, and the enthusiasm and encouragement they bestowed upon me, to complete this project, thank you, Kara, Alexa, Andrew, Jaclyn, Jessica, Krista, Alyssa and Gina.

My brother Ralph, for the many donations of pictorial history and of helping me with the dates of the stories on which I have written and of his memory of precise moments in many of the stories of my youth. Although many of Ralph's possessions were lost, some of which would have added immensely to this book Ralph had a treasure trove of films, dating back many years in our lives.

To my sister Vera, who gave me the encouragement to start this project, and for her uncanny memory to help fill in the dates. She supplied me with a great many photos of our family, along with documents depicting our family history. Vera, whom I relied on heavily to obtain, and in some cases, refresh my memory of tales of our family life, some of which, have left me with a huge burden of some bad memories. But thankfully, Vera helped me work through them and for that I am grateful.

My sister Betty, for her precise knowledge of many aspects of our family. For helping me clarify some events in my life, and in helping me to understand the true nature of the unfolding saga to which I am forever grateful. This book would not have been written without Betty, who in her infinite wisdom, set me on a path of helping me to disassemble fact from fiction. Betty provided me with the courage to foster on, and not let the past engulf me. Betty's memory helped me to restore confidence in myself and gave me the impetus, and also the invaluable information that came at a most crucial time for the direction of this book.

To my brother in law, and great friend, Joe Cappiello, who assisted me in assembling a host of material, such as books, photos, information about the location of many of my stories. He also introduced me to some very influential people, who gave me access to their files, and gave me a treasure trove of information, that until that time in my project, was unobtainable. Joe was a life saver, with one caveat from Joe: "Make sure you say something nice about me." Joe's stewardship provided the motivation that I needed at that time in my project. Joe not only gave me inspiration through words, but by giving me his time, which amounted to quite a lot.

To Robert Esposito, owner of the Branford Book and Card shop, who supplied me with some very interesting photos of our neighborhood. They were photos of importance as to the relation of my story of a time in my life when I had a newspaper route which took me to that section of the city. This coincided with some of my memories of a time when I realized that other people had a worse living situation than I had.

To Sal Defelice, a character boyhood friend of mine, who was running through life and did not know why. From Sal came some of my best and worst stories, of which Sal supplied, gleefully I must add. Sal took delight in every aspect of his life. His memories of events was astounding. Sal provided me with tales that for publication had to be sanitized. I relied on Sal for some of the most interesting tales of our neighborhood, and his acts of showmanship and bravado, appear in quite a few of my remembrances.

A close neighbor of mine, and lifelong friend, Mr. Sal Pisani, helped me with a story in this project about a fire with a great loss of life in a factory right in my backyard. He was a great witness and supplied his knowledge of what actually happened. Sal recounted to me in detail the series of events that unfolded that tragic night.

To my cousin Anthony Esposito, for giving me many photos of his family and mine and sharing the many memories that went with them.

And to my cousins, the Santacroce Family—Jean, Rosemary, Nicholas, and Fred—for supplying me with a great range of photos. Uncle Steve and my mother were brother and sister, so it was with great pleasure that they helped me to piece together the story of our family.

My in-laws, the De Angelo's, allowed me great access into their lives and supplied me with a wealth of information which gave me the fortitude just by their very presence in my life.

To Ralph and Jeanette Barrie for encouraging me to put together this project and for their interest in my writing this book. They supported me by giving me great reviews for the portions that they had seen, and to Ralph, for helping me to remember our working days when we were both associated as route salesmen for Wonder Bread.

To the De Angelo children, my brothers-in-law, Joe, Nicholas, Anthony, John, Louis, and Mario. My sisters in law, Julia, and Rose. From them came the great memories that I cherished and helped me in this endeavor.

It is also with sadness that some of my storytellers did not live to see their stories in print, or of the many photos they supplied me. The interest in my project from them was astounding, and to the people to whom I missed, due to their passing on, they had so much to offer, but time was not on our side.

To my niece, Susan Campagna, (Vera's daughter) for researching her mother's archives to produce some of my family's history, which helped to shape and mold my story. This helped to put together the missing pieces of my earlier life, the years of growing up with my brothers and sisters, and long lost photos from my memory of events. Susan took time from her busy life to extend herself to me, I am grateful beyond words.

To my friend and family attorney, Sheldon Hosen: On discussing this book with him, Shelly said, "You cannot leave a greater gift than that, one that your grandchildren, and great grandchildren will cherish."

Shelly was more than a family attorney; he was a friend first and our conversations about family are something that I have instilled in the works of this book. He was a friend of more than thirty-five years, but it seems like yesterday when I first met him. He was wearing a sport jacket with a rumpled up vest in which he kept his pipe. Never one to seek out the niceties of life, he was at his ease being in our company, and he gave me a sense of accepting whatever you can reach for and to be happy for it. I have many stories to tell about Shelly, including his guidance in the matters of business and finance that could fill a book.

Allow me this one story that encapsulates the life of a man not preoccupied with his image. David and Lisa were getting ready to purchase of their first home. I turned it over to Shelly and he made all the arrangements. The closing was set for a location in Milford, and the seller and his attorney were already seated in this conference room. The attorney was all dressed up in a three piece suit with all of his papers neatly stacked and at the ready. Shelly, running late, comes bursting into the room with a bunch of papers all loosely put together, excusing himself for being late. The other attorney not too pleased.

As the closing was unfolding, the attorney asked for a copy of a statement. Shelly, ruffling through his bundle of papers, turns to me, "Leo, did you bring the copy of the statement?" I responded, "What paper are you talking about?" Shelly then pulls out the requested copy from his pile with a smile. It was Shelly's dry sense of humor of which he entertained me with, for a long time.

Sheldon Hosen passed away December 17, 2016 at 77 years of age.

Boy's Club - 31 Jefferson Street, courtesy of the New Haven Museum

Top row left: Leo 4th-person, 8th grade graduation at Columbus School 1943

2nd row: Leo 1st person on right1, Eaton School, 6th grade 1943

Left to right: Mom and Dad, Ralph, Betty, Mary, and Leo

Left to right: Ralph, Leo, and Mary

Left in boat: Leo Kindergarten Columbus School

Dad

Left to right: top row: Mary and Leo 1st row: Vera, Frank, and Mom

Mom

Mom and Dad's wedding 1922

204 Greene Street

Stanleys Department Store, courtesy of the New Haven Museum

1939

Looking east on Green St. from the corner of Chestnut St. In 1939

Corner store courtesy of the New Haven Museum

Mickey Rooney - Judy Garland (1941) Loew's Poli, courtesy of the New Haven Museum

New Haven Arena, courtesy of the New Haven Museum

Mom, Leo at age 16

Leo and Connie

The House on Greene Street **409**

Hotel Taft courtesy of the New Haven Museum

Uncle Leo

My sister Mary on far right (background factory)

Far left: Leo 1st person, Stage Show in San Juan, Puerto Rico

Leo Greene Street 1946

2nd row: Leo 1st person on left

Leo 1949

1st row: Leo, 1st person on far left, Squadron Picnic, San Juan, Puerto Rico,

Leo on ship 1946

Leo (left) and Chief 1947

Left and right: A.J. Schifiano, Al Limoncelli, G. Telisio, Leo, and Al Loper

San Juan, Puerto Rico, Leo and Marianna

Teresa A. C.Gilbert Company, top left of photo 1950

1st person on left: Teresa A.C. Gilbert, Teresa

Left to right:
1st row, Al Spadoro
2nd row, Frank Defelice,
al raccio, Jim Spadoro
3rd row, Joe Mana, Ray
Stopka, Leo, and Ralph
(brother)

Leo 1949

Leo

Lowes Poli College, courtesy of the New Haven Museum

Columbus School

Left to right: Chickee De Felice, Mamie De Felice, Carolyn Marino, Josephine Anastastio, Dolly, Frank Marino, Libby Della Muro, (Libby's 3 daughters), Anthony Ciarlone, (kneeling) Mayor Dick Lee and Frank Marino Jr.

Columbus School 1908

Prindle Alley 1910 Robert Esposito, courtesy of the New Haven Museum

Mrs. Leo Marino, the former Miss Theresa DeAngelo, was married on Sept. 25 in St. Vincent de Paul's R. C. Church, East Haven. (Barrie)

Teresa Marino, 9-25-54

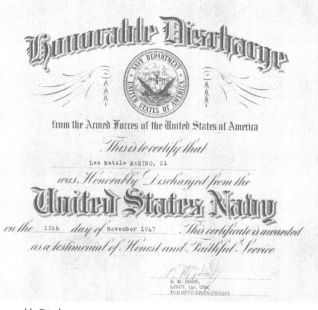

Honorable Discharge

THE UNITED STATES OF AMERICA

TO BE GIVEN TO
THE PERSON NATURALIZED

CERTIFICATE OF CITIZENSHIP

No. 4537369

Petition No 18986

Personal description of holder as of date of naturalization: Age 46 *years; sex* Male *color* White *complexion* Dark *color of eyes* Brown *color of hair* Brown *height* 5 *feet* - - - *inches; weight* 140 *pounds; visible distinctive marks* None
Marital status MARRIED *former nationality* ITALIAN
I certify that the description above given is true, and that the photograph affixed hereto is a likeness of me.

ORIGINAL

Francesco Marino (*Complete and true signature of holder*)

DISTRICT OF CONNECTICUT } *ss.*
NEW HAVEN

Be it known, that FRANCESCO MARINO *then residing at* 204 Greene Street, New Haven, Conn. *having petitioned to be admitted a citizen of the United States of America, and at a term of the* U.S. DISTRICT *Court of* DISTRICT OF CONNECTICUT *held pursuant to law at* NEW HAVEN CONNECTICUT *on* September 23rd, 19 38 *the court having found that the petitioner intends to reside permanently in the United States, had in all respects complied with the Naturalization Laws of the United States in such case applicable, and was entitled to be so admitted, the court thereupon ordered that the petitioner be admitted as a citizen of the United States of America. In testimony whereof the seal of the court is hereunto affixed this* 23rd *day of* September *in the year of our Lord nineteen hundred and* Thirty-Eight *and of our Independence the one hundred and* Sixty-Third.

C. E. Picket

Clerk of the U.S. District *Court.*
By _____ *Deputy Clerk*

Seal

DEPARTMENT OF LABOR

Fathers citizenship paper 1938

UNITED STATES NAVY
Identification Card

MARINO, Leo
• Name

Leo N. Marino
Signature

Color Hair Brown Eyes Brown
Weight 121 Birth 12/25/

Void after _____

Nav. Pers. 546 Validating Officer

Leo's I.D. Navy

Leo's I.D. Navy

State of Connecticut Bureau of Vital Statistics

Marriage License
Town of New Haven

1. Groom's Name Francesco Marino 1a. Bride's Name Letitia Santacroce
2. Age 30 yrs 2a. Age 24
3. Color white 3. Color white
4. Occupation Mechanic 4. Occupation
5. Birthplace Italy 5. Birthplace Italy
6. His Residence 204 Gold 6. Her Residence New Haven
7. Single 7. Single
8. Name of Father Raffaele 8. Name of Father Nicolo
9. Maiden name of Mother Maria Aruzzo 9. Maiden name of Mother Maria Rosa
   Francesco Marino one of the persons named in this Marriage

License, do solemnly swear that the statements therein are true.
Sworn to before me this 14 day
of Sept 1922 Signed Joseph Chapman
John J. Buckley

This Certifies, that the above-named parties have complied with the laws of Connecticut relating to marriage license, and any person authorized to celebrate marriage may join the above-named in marriage within the town of
Dated Sept 14 1922 John J. Buckley Registrar

Marriage Certificate

I hereby Certify that Mr. Francesco Marino *and* Letizia Santacroce *the above-named parties, were legally joined in marriage by me at* St. Anthony's Church *this* 29th
day of October 1922 Signed Rev. Lino Merlo
Address 25 Gold St. Official Capacity priest

THIS CERTIFICATE RECEIVED FOR RECORD ON
November 6, 1922

certify that this is a true transcript of the information as recorded in this office.

Michael V. Lynch, Registrar
Carol L. Lion, Deputy Registrar
Victoria R. Longo, Ass't Registrar

Mom and Dad's marriage license 1922

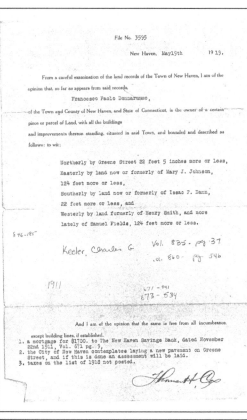

File No. 3595

New Haven, May 19th 1919.

From a careful examination of the land records of the Town of New Haven, I am of the opinion that, so far as appears from said records,

Francesco Paolo Donnarumno,

of the Town and County of New Haven, and State of Connecticut, is the owner of a certain piece or parcel of Land, with all the buildings and improvements thereon standing, situated in said Town, and bounded and described as follows: to wit:

Northerly by Greene Street 22 feet 5 inches more or less,

Easterly by land now or formerly of Mary J. Johnson, 124 feet more or less,

Southerly by land now or formerly of Isaac F. Dann, 22 feet more or less, and

Westerly by land formerly of Henry Smith, and more lately of Samuel Fields, 124 feet more or less.

846-185

Keeler, Charles G. Vol. 835- pg. 37
.ol. 860- pg. 546

1911

671 - 941
673 - 534

And I am of the opinion that the same is free from all incumbrance,

except building lines, if established.

1. a mortgage for $1700. to The New Haven Savings Bank, dated November 22nd 1911, Vol. 671 Vol. 9,
2. the City of New Haven contemplates laying a new pavement on Greene Street, and if this is done an assessment will be laid.
3. taxes on the list of 1918 not posted.

Deed for 204 Greene Street 1919

Francesco Marino (DiMarino) 8/27/1892

Father: Raffaele   Married 5.12.1874
Mother: Maria Apuzza or Del Pozzo
Raffaela

Family members:
Alfonso Marino - 2.25.1875   age 3
                 6.2.1878
Maria Rosaria Marino   10.1. 1876
Beltina Marino   10.27. 1881
Leopoldo Marino   2.23. 1884
Raffale Marino   12.14. 1886
                  Died 1890

Elvira Marino   7.1. 1889
Francesco Marino   8.27. 1892
Concetta Marino   10.20. 1895

Giovanni Battista } parents of papa's father
Maria Paolillo   } Great grand parents

Father's family origianl name DiMarino

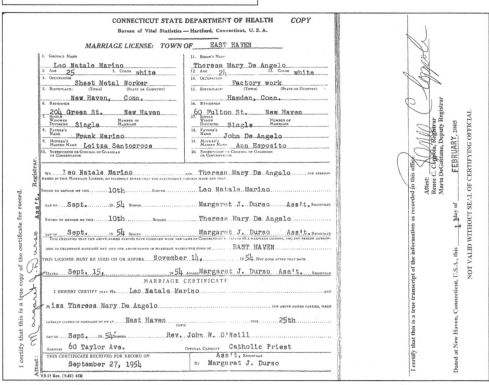

CONNECTICUT STATE DEPARTMENT OF HEALTH   COPY
Bureau of Vital Statistics — Hartford, Connecticut, U.S.A.

MARRIAGE LICENSE: TOWN OF   EAST HAVEN

1. Groom's Name   Leo Natale Marino
2. Age 25   3. Color white
4. Occupation Sheet Metal Worker
5. Birthplace: (Town) New Haven, Conn. (State or Country)
6. Residence 204 Green St. New Haven
7. Single Widower Divorced Single   Number of Marriage
8. Father's Name Frank Marino
9. Mother's Maiden Name Leitza Santocroce
10. Supervision or Control of Guardian or Conservator

11. Bride's Name   Theresa Mary De Angelo
12. Age 24   13. Color white
14. Occupation Factory work
15. Birthplace: (Town) Hamden, Conn. (State or Country)
16. Residence 60 Fulton St. New Haven
17. Single Widow Divorced Single   Number of Marriage
18. Father's Name John De Angelo
19. Mother's Maiden Name Ann Esposito
20. Supervision or Control of Guardian or Conservator

We, Leo Natale Marino and Theresa Mary De Angelo, the persons named in this marriage license, do solemnly swear that the statements therein made are true.

Sworn to before me this 10th Signed Leo Natale Marino
Day of Sept. 19 54 Signed Margaret J. Durso Ass't. Registrar

Sworn to before me this 10th Signed Theresa Mary De Angelo
Day of Sept. 19 54 Signed Margaret J. Durso Ass't. Registrar

THIS CERTIFIES THAT THE ABOVE-NAMED PARTIES HAVE COMPLIED WITH THE LAWS OF CONNECTICUT RELATING TO A MARRIAGE LICENSE, AND ANY PERSON AUTHOR-IZED TO CELEBRATE MARRIAGE MAY JOIN THE ABOVE-NAMED IN MARRIAGE WITHIN THE TOWN OF EAST HAVEN.

THIS LICENSE MUST BE USED ON OR BEFORE November 14, 19 54 Not good after that date.

Dated Sept. 15, 19 54 Attest Margaret J. Durso Ass't. Registrar

MARRIAGE CERTIFICATE

I HEREBY CERTIFY THAT Mr. Leo Natale Marino and

Miss Theresa Mary De Angelo, the above named parties, were

LEGALLY JOINED IN MARRIAGE BY ME AT East Haven, this 25th

Day of Sept. 19 54 Signed Rev. John W. O'Neill

Address 60 Taylor Ave. Official Capacity Catholic Priest

THIS CERTIFICATE RECEIVED FOR RECORD ON
September 27, 1954   Ass't. Registrar
By Margaret J. Durso

VS 17 Rev. (7-62) 40M

I certify that this is a true copy of the certificate for record.   Attest: Margaret J. Durso Ass't. Registrar

I certify that this is a true transcript of the information as recorded in this office.
Attest: Renee C. Coppola, Registrar
Maria DeGaetano, Deputy Registrar

Dated at New Haven, Connecticut, U.S.A., this 4 day of FEBRUARY, 2005

NOT VALID WITHOUT SEAL OF CERTIFYING OFFICIAL

Leo and Teresa's marriage license 1954

Leo at Wooster Square meeting

Fathers home in Minori, Italy

Greene and Chestnut Cornerstore

Mothers home in Ciazzo, Italy

204 Greene Street

The House on Greene Street **417**

Left to right: 1st row: Leo, Teresa, and Jaclyn, 2nd row; Alyssa, Krista, Andrew, Alexa, Kara, Jessica, and Gina 3rd row: Lisa, David, Gail, Russ, Anthony, and Janet

Leo and Teresa's wedding, September 25th, 1954, St. Vincent DePaul Church, East Haven

Leo and Teresa, 50th Wedding Aniversary 2004, Disney Yacht Club Walt Disney World

Left to right: 1st row: Val Capobianco, Leo Marino, Joe Cappiello, and Steve Mirabella 2nd row: Tony DiNicola, Jim Ferraro, Frank Marino, Shelly Hosen, Joe Sensale, Frank Grazioso, Anthony DiLeo, and Mike Catania

Left to right: Leo and Teresa honeymoon Stricklands, Pocono Mountains 1954

Leo, Teresa, Daveid, Janet, and Gail vacation Downington Inn, PA 1970   *Teresa DeAngelo*

Teresa and Leo at Hammonasset Beach 1953

Teresa Eastover, MA 1952

John and Anna DeAngelo

Left to right: Jim Spadoro and daughter, Gail and Leo

Mia Alise Barrett born to Kara and Dan Barrett.
November 16, 2017

Left to right: Teresa, grandaughter Kara, great grand daughter Mia, and Leo